M000315873

CONVERSION AND COLONIZATION
IN ANGLO-SAXON ENGLAND

MEDIEVAL AND RENAISSANCE
TEXTS AND STUDIES
VOLUME 318

Essays in Anglo-Saxon Studies
Volume 2

CONVERSION AND COLONIZATION
IN ANGLO-SAXON ENGLAND

Edited by

Catherine E. Karkov and
†Nicholas Howe

ACMRS
(Arizona Center for Medieval and Renaissance Studies)
Tempe, Arizona
2006

Library of Congress Cataloging-in-Publication Data

Conversion and colonization in Anglo-Saxon England / edited by Catherine E. Karkov and Nicholas Howe.
   p. cm. -- (Medieval and Renaissance texts and studies ; v. 318)
   Includes bibliographical references and index.
   ISBN-13: 978-0-86698-363-1 (acid-free paper)
   ISBN-10: 0-86698-363-5 (acid-free paper)
   1. Civilization, Anglo-Saxon. 2. Anglo-Saxons--Social conditions. 3. Anglo-Saxons--Social life and customs. 4. Great Britain--History--Anglo-Saxon period, 449-1066. 5. England--Civilization--To 1066. 6. England--Social life and customs--To 1066.   I. Karkov, Catherine E., 1956- . II. Howe, Nicholas.
   DA152.C698 2006
   942.01--dc22

                                                          2006024997

∞
This book is made to last.
It is set in Adobe Caslon Pro,
smyth-sewn and printed on acid-free paper
to library specifications.
Printed in the United States of America

TABLE OF CONTENTS

Abbreviations

ASE	*Anglo-Saxon England*
ASPR	Anglo-Saxon Poetic Records
ASSAH	*Anglo-Saxon Studies in Archaeology and History*
BAR	British Archaeological Reports
BL	British Library
BN	Bibliothèque Nationale
CBA	Council for British Archaeology
CCCC	Cambridge, Corpus Christi College
DB	Domesday Book
EEMF	Early English Manuscripts in Facsimile
EETS	Early English Text Society
HBS	Henry Bradshaw Society
JEGP	*Journal of English and Germanic Philology*
MGH	Monumenta Germaniae Historica
OEN	*Old English Newsletter*
PG	*Patrologia Graeca*, ed. J. P, Migne (Paris, 1857–1887)
PL	*Patrologia Latina*, ed. J. P. Migne (Paris, 1844–65); Supplemental series ed. A. Hammon and L. Guillaumin (Paris, 1958–1974)

List of Figures

INTRODUCTION

CATHERINE E. KARKOV AND NICHOLAS HOWE

Like any familiar term, "Anglo-Saxon England" obscures as much as it illuminates. If it usefully designates a period that has customarily been dated between A.D. 600 and 1100 and that features among its familiar names Bede, Alfred, Alcuin, Beowulf, and Wulfstan, the term also elides questions about cultural diversity and identity, gender differences, and linguistic variation. Moreover, one must also ask how far can — or should — the designation "Anglo-Saxon England" be extended to the margins of the island, whether those margins be set in terms of religion, ethnicity, geography, language, or any other single factor? While "Anglo-Saxon England" or a derived form frequently appears in the titles of journals and books as well as a professional society in order to identify some shared ground of scholarly interests, that practice does not in itself mean that there is any commonly accepted definition for the term.

Indeed, one of the remarkable developments in the field over the last twenty years or so is the growing awareness that there are many different Anglo-Saxon Englands to be studied and, correspondingly, that there are no master narratives or paradigms that can account for all of them with equal success. Rather than evidence for disciplinary confusion or loss of certainty, this scholarly development should be taken as a healthy reaction against earlier models of Anglo-Saxon England that posited an unchanging or otherwise homogenous culture populated it would seem largely, if not exclusively, by males of the warrior class. Without denying necessary filiations of history, religion, language and geography, these new visions of Anglo-Saxon England are notable for their greater alertness to the presence of differences in local conditions, chronological periods, and cultural circumstances. In the process, these new approaches have also reinterpreted or reconceptualized some very familiar aspects of Anglo-Saxon England, such as conversion and colonization.

Anglo-Saxonists have, of course, long acknowledged that colonization and conversion made for profound social changes in Britain. The scholarly literature on the legacy of Roman colonization or on the missionary work of Augustine and his fellow monks on the island is valuable and well established. More recently, though, one can witness a shift among scholars to consider not simply the events and practical consequences of colonization and conversion but also the ways in which these events were understood and recorded by later generations of Anglo-Saxons. In that regard, colonization and conversion emerge as processes that also left their mark on the intellectual and hermeneutic practices of the Anglo-Saxons, that provided them with models for interpreting the nature of their experience. Colonization and conversion should not be read as identical or inseparable processes, but they do share certain features that provide a rationale for linking them closely, as do many of the studies in this volume.

Rarely developments that happen overnight or at a precisely datable moment, conversion and colonization are more typically long-term processes that move at variable rates across groups and areas of a population. While we may think of them as noteworthy because they achieve demonstrable ends — that a people acknowledges the authority of an outside power or accepts a new religion — that retrospect obscures the more necessary point that they are not to be apprehended within a single moment. That such dates as 410, for the withdrawal of Roman legions from Britain, or 597, for the arrival of Augustine in Canterbury, have deep resonances within insular history should not obscure the fact that they are chronological conveniences and not accurate measures for the duration of such events: the withdrawal of legions and the arrival of missionaries alike had both a long pre-history and an even longer post-history within British and English culture. That this should have been so clearly true of both conversion and colonization explains in no small measure their value as interpretive concepts for addressing cultural variation. Put another way, conversion and colonization in the England of the Anglo-Saxon period were often localized phenomena that registered themselves at different moments, in different places, and in different forms of cultural production. Correspondingly, the surviving evidence for these processes takes a stunningly wide range of forms, as one can see from the studies included in this volume: manuscripts, place-names, jewelry, the diseased bones of the dead, literary and historical texts in various languages, maps, metaphors, lists, and the like. This evidence also shows quite extraordinary variation across time and place: some of the visual materials, for instance, are early and found chiefly below the Humber while the textual evidence crosses generic boundaries of histories, lists, poems, sermons, and monastic rules, and the extant traces of disease are scattered among burial sites that have been dug by archaeologists often with very different purposes in mind. Taken as a group, these studies demonstrate that traces of conversion and colonization — both as processes that affected the Anglo-Saxons and in turn as the Anglo-Saxons became their agents in later centuries — can be found across the extant historical record.

There are limits, however, that come with treating colonization and conversion as identical processes or synonymous terms. Most immediately, each has its own primary sphere of activity: colonization is a political process that imposes the will of the imperial center on a newly-conquered region; conversion is the (seemingly) voluntary process by which individuals and peoples accept a new faith. These descriptive statements may be true about the primary effects of colonization and conversion in Anglo-Saxon England and elsewhere; but the historical record demonstrates as well that new political affiliations are often accompanied by changes of religion, and new religions often bring with them shifts in political allegiances, especially as elites are redefined through the choice of religious belief. And sometimes, try as one might to keep them apart, the relations between political colonization and religious conversion become blurred yet further by historical or geographical factors, as when the same center or capital city becomes the source from which emanated the impetus for both colonization and conversion. Such, over many centuries, was the role played by Rome and its attendant language, Latin, in Britain and later in England.

Still, there is reason to maintain some sense of separation between colonization and conversion if only to explore useful distinctions between the political and the religious. In that regard, one might note that the Danelaw resulted from a political settlement that allowed for the cultural and linguistic colonization of the northern regions of Anglo-Saxon England but did not entail a consequent change of religious belief in that same region. Or, to complicate matters, one can think of the Danelaw as a colonized area in which emerged possibilities of religious conversion, though paradoxically (or so it might seem at first glance) among the newly-settled Scandinavian populations rather than the long-resident Anglo-Saxon ones. Or, to cast the Danelaw as a borderland in the terms of post-colonial theory, it can be seen as a zone of cultural hybridity or mingling in which diverse populations and their related but not identical languages came into mutual play. The value of such thought-experiments lies not in some display of theoretical legerdemain but rather in reinforcing the distinctions between colonization and conversion — and yet also in acknowledging the limits of these same distinctions.

That colonization and conversion offer powerful interpretive concepts for studying Anglo-Saxon England tells us something necessary about that culture as well as our own. The growth of post-colonial studies as an academic discipline over the last generation has certainly influenced the study of medieval Europe in general as well as that of pre-Conquest England in particular.[1] The studies in this volume bear the mark of that influence in broad terms, though each in its own

---

[1] Among the many recent volumes devoted to the medieval and the post-colonial, one might cite *The Postcolonial Middle Ages*, ed. Jeffrey Jerome Cohen (New York, 2000); *Postcolonial Moves: Medieval to Modern*, ed. Patricia Clare Ingham and Michelle R. Warren (New York, 2003); and *Postcolonial Approaches to the European Middle Ages*, ed. Ananya J. Kabir and Deanne Williams (Cambridge, 2005).

way brings into question the presentist assumptions and values that often mark the more theorized versions of post-colonial studies. Most compellingly, the studies in this volume demonstrate that relations of power — religious, ideological, economic, to cite the most obvious — do not conform to any one universally applicable paradigm.

Underlying the dynamics of colonization and conversion, indeed enabling each as a practical matter, is the work of translation, both in the strict sense of converting text from one language to another (in Anglo-Saxon England most often Latin to Old English, but also between Old English and various Scandinavian languages) and also in the more expansive sense of shifting cultural knowledge, beliefs, and even objects between groups. Translation may often begin as a matter of linguistic interchange, but it rarely if ever occurs without bringing into play or conflict other forms of influence, borrowing, and commingling. So present is the work of translation in these studies that as editors we thought for a moment of adding that term to the volume's title but refrained from doing so lest we turn it into a list. It would be better, we thought, to identify translation as a mechanism or method that frequently underlay the work of conversion and colonization. As a linguistic interchange, translation enabled the spread of Latin texts — to cite the most obvious case — across the vernacular cultures of England in ways that can be traced at the level of explicit statements but also of implicit ideological concepts. Other acts of translation occurred across less marked linguistic borders, as when Old English texts circulated elsewhere in the north of Europe or Iceland.

Identifying translation as fundamental to colonization and conversion has the added benefit of suggesting that these processes were not one-way flows of cultural power and influence from external and presumably more powerful or prestigious sources but rather offered at least the possibility that the converted and colonized did sometimes speak back to those who had converted and colonized them. That process of speaking back, or of seeing translation as an act that affected the source text or culture, appears throughout these studies. Whenever one of the contributors addresses or even alludes in passing to the influence that Anglo-Saxon writers had in their turn on the Roman Church, for instance, or to the conversions accomplished by Anglo-Saxon missionaries on the peoples of northwest Europe, then we can witness the workings of this larger form of translation. Tracing this kind of translation, especially in our current state of knowledge, does not always yield as satisfying a case as tracing an Old English work to its Latin original can provide; sometimes it means relying on possible allusions, distant echoes, stylistic resonances. But in doing so, it also holds out the opportunity of allowing one to adduce a wide range of evidence and interpretive paradigms. If the process of cultural translation is often less susceptible of proof or even of vivid demonstration than is that of textual translation, its effects are often more widespread and diffused. That is to say, they can be more culturally central. Reading Anglo-Saxon texts and artifacts as responses to the work of colonization and conversion also adds, we would suggest, a kind of deep history to the ways in which these processes are theorized in our contemporary discourse. Those accustomed to thinking of English as the language of colonial agents or Protestant missionaries in Asia and Africa over the last several centuries, for example, might find it startling to learn that it was not always the language of the dominant population. There are, in other words, forms of historical understanding that can help us to translate between the medieval and the modern in ways that will enlarge and complicate the theoretical paradigms of post-colonialism.

Reading through the studies in this volume, as they move chronologically from the early conversions of the British and English through the late period of Anglo-Saxon and Scandinavian cross-influence, one sees a healthy mistrust of any master narrative or grand interpretive generalization about Anglo-Saxon England. Whether explicitly or implicitly, these studies argue against any evocation of cultural homogeneity, however convenient, to explain early and late, northern and southern, male and female, clerical or secular — or any other binary one might offer. Instead, these chapters show a careful attention to the contingencies of time and place, which is another way of saying that each works within the particular limits of evidence about Anglo-Saxon England available to us in the early twenty-first century. Throughout this volume one encounters references to damaged or incomplete manuscripts, yet-to-be excavated archaeological sites, contested chronologies, broken or blocked channels of cultural influence and transmission. A conscious understanding of the limits of our evidence, such as the authors of these chapters reveal, is not simply the sign of good scholarship. It is also a means to articulate possible directions for future study, for testing those limits to identify ways of overcoming them.

The papers that follow are organized so that they move from the conversion of the Anglo-Saxons and written accounts of it, to the use of Anglo-Saxon texts and ideologies in the conversion of other peoples. Rather than the movement of armies and nations, conversion and colonization become in this schema the work of texts, objects, and the social practices of everyday life. Artistic style, textual translation, the treatment of disease, the compilation and recording of a list, have just as much to tell us as the written accounts of migrations, battles, invasions, and royal or ecclesiastical synods. They also help to fill in some of the silences of the written record, and to remind us that there are no master narratives aside from those which later scholarship has, often unwittingly, constructed. It is the small picture — the surviving British place-name, the non-princely burial, the manuscript marginalia — that time and again provides a necessary counterpoint to the narratives constructed around Bede, Sutton Hoo, or the *Regularis Concordia*.

In his "From British to English Christianity: Deconstructing Bede's Interpretation of the Conversion," Nicholas Brooks reminds us that Christianity had arrived in Britain four centuries before the arrival of St. Augustine in 597, the date traditionally seen by many scholars as the beginning of a Christian England. Brooks goes on to ask a series of questions about our interpretation of both this date and the sources: "Have we been too ready to accept Bede's concept of a separate English ethnic identity and his reluctance to recognize the contribution of British Christians to English Christianity?" Can we rethink the "apparently unbridgeable hiatus between British and Anglo-Saxon Christianity?" Brooks emphasizes that Bede's account of the conversion is both politically motivated and based on a limited set of sources, primarily those originating in the east of England. Evidence from material culture, place-names, and British inscriptions suggests that the picture was far more complicated than the written sources reveal, and that at least in some places British Christianity did contribute significantly to the development of English Christianity. He looks specifically at the evidence provided by *Eccles* place-names, the location of British and Anglo-Saxon episcopal churches, and the archaeology associated with each. He concludes that "if we are to avoid approaching the conversion of the Anglo-Saxons with unduly Bedan spectacles," we must allow for and identify the regional differences underlying the territories that eventually came to be known as "English."

Carol Neuman de Vegvar also asks us to reexamine some received monolithic scenarios of the conversion period, this time from an art historical and archaeological perspective which focuses on the conversion of artistic techniques as deliberate cultural statements. In "High Style and Borrowed Finery: The Strood Mount, the Long Wittenham Stoup, and the Boss Hall Brooch as Complex Responses to Continental Visual Culture," she questions our reliance on certain high-status burials such as Sutton Hoo (or now Prittlewell) for our understanding of the relationship between Frankish and Southumbrian culture during the conversion period. In particular, she questions the conflicting all-or-nothing models of either Kentish domination by Merovingian France, or Kentish resistance to a Frankish axis of power. How does consideration of a range of "converted" grave-goods from some of the less prestigious Southumbrian cemeteries alter the picture? Like Brooks, she provides evidence that a more nuanced reading which reveals shifting and variable attitudes towards continental culture is necessary, concluding that the issue is ultimately one not only of "the politics of centers or politically identifiable units but also of the self-projections, ambitions, and desires of individuals, families, and communities with their own agendas." The material record, like the written one, provides us with no one narrative framework for the processes of either conversion or colonization.

In her "Changing Faces: Leprosy in Anglo-Saxon England," Christina Lee examines the evidence of burials, the treatment of the diseased and disabled prior to death, and literature in order to ask whether the conversion to Christianity led to changes in the ways in which people with illnesses were treated. Were the diseased and disabled considered "lesser human beings" and were they excluded from society either before or after the conversion to Christianity? Did new ideologies carry with them new social ideals as well as practices? Skeletal remains, she notes, show that skilled physicians were available throughout the period, even to the pagan Anglo-Saxons, while burial evidence shows that attitudes towards the bodies of the diseased did vary over time. During the conversion period, the higher-status burials of some lepers reveal that the disease was no impediment to prestige burial — at least for some individuals. However, the establishment of a strong Christian church changed things, as becomes particularly evident in the wake of the tenth-century reform with its eschatological outlook. In later Anglo-Saxon cemeteries, the graves of lepers were often separated from those of the non-infected population, and this practice is likely to mirror changing attitudes towards the diseased in general. Lee draws on the writings of religious authors such as Ælfric to support her findings, for they saw physical disease as a sign of moral disease, and thus classed lepers among the sinful and despised.

Conversion and translation intersect in Nicole Guenther Discenza's paper, "A Map of the Universe: Geography and Cosmology in the Program of Alfred the Great," as it explores the conversion of classical texts to new texts via translation. Translation in this context also does political work by helping to further Alfred's own agenda, itself centered on the twin foci of England and Rome. As she emphasizes, this is an area in which textual culture and lived experience could be at odds with each other. For classical and early Christian authors, Rome and Jerusalem were the twin centers of the world, while England and the British Isles were confined to its edges. Some of the texts translated during the reign of Alfred — *Orosius* or some of the Psalms, for example — either marginalize or are silent about England, while others — such as the Chronicle or the Old English Bede, texts written by English authors — re-center it. Still others, such as the *Soliloquies*, map an internal geography that is free from any specificity of external time or place. The program as a whole, however, serves to convert a marginalized England into a more central place, albeit one that can never replace Rome.

As almost all the papers in this volume emphasize, texts are powerful tools in the process of colonization or conversion, be they works of translation, history, fiction, hagiography, prose, poetry, or even lists. In her "'Old Names of Kings or Shadows': Reading Documentary Lists," Jacqueline Stodnick explores the ways in which certain Anglo-Saxon lists served as a means of colonizing history and land, and of simultaneously defining English identity. Stodnick addresses questions surrounding the copying, perception, and function of documentary lists by focusing on one particular collection contained in the eleventh-century manuscript London, BL, Cotton Tiberius B.v, fols. 19v–24r. These folios contain lists of the popes, the seventy-two disciples of Christ, Roman emperors, patriarchs, Anglo-Saxon bishops, the West Saxon kings, the Anglian royal genealogies and regnal lists, the kings of Wessex, the abbots of Glastonbury, and Archbishop Sigeric's Roman itinerary. Like Alfred's translations, these texts reach out to expand the area defined as England, both within the island that bears that name and beyond it to Christian Rome. Stodnick situates this material both within its manuscript context and in relation to related lists contained in other manuscripts. She contends that the desire of the modern reader to "reconstruct" a framework of meaning for such decontextualized lists was also felt by the Anglo-Saxons, and was in fact a structural element of the list format. In reading the lists a fundamental historical sameness is created for England's once separate kingdoms, giving "England" the appearance of a politically, historically, and religiously unified entity.

Heide Estes also deals with the intersection of Anglo-Saxon historical processes in her "Colonization and Conversion in Cynewulf's *Elene.*" Many of the texts discussed in the previous two papers sought in various ways to connect contemporary Anglo-Saxon England with the world of early Christian Rome, but this work is much more explicitly a part of *Elene.* In the poem, Constantine's Rome provides a parallel to tenth-century England, a parallel which is achieved in part through Cynewulf's conversion/translation of his Latin sources, an appropriation that was made easier for the Anglo-Saxons by their belief that Constantine had been born in Britain. In this paper Estes reads the poem in the context of Anglo-Saxon relations with the Danes, both generally and through the use of very specific themes and motifs. In a close analysis of the language used to describe the people and events in the poem, she establishes that the victories of Constantine and Helen, especially over the Jews, provide the moral justification and historical precedent for the struggles of Anglo-Saxon kings and queens both in battle against the Danes and in their efforts to reclaim the lands the foreigners had settled. Gender is also an issue for the narrative world of the poem and the lived experience of its readers who witnessed the rise to power of a series of politically active queens as adept at promoting reform as Helen had been at promoting conversion.

Colonization as it relates to both gender and the religious life in tenth-century England is also at the heart of Joyce Hill's "Making Women Visible: An Adaptation of the *Regularis Concordia* in Cambridge, Corpus Christi College MS. 201." The very title of the text, *Regularis Concordia Anglicae nationis monachorum sanctimoniaiumque*, and the miniature of King Edgar seated between Saints Dunstan and Æthelwold that prefaces one of its earliest surviving exemplars, proclaim that this is a work of national importance which simultaneously strives to create a particular image of nation. It is first and foremost a text written for a male monastic community, and introduced in the London, BL, Cotton Tiberius A.iii manuscript as the product, or voice, of a united king and church. As a text written by and for a well-established male institution, it would have presented problems for women who wished to follow its provisions. For this reason, Hill focuses on the fragmentary copy preserved in the eleventh-century manuscript Cambridge, Corpus Christi College 201, part A, an Old English translation of the Latin original that provides the only surviving evidence of adjustments for women religious. While we know nothing about where or for whom the translation was made, Hill points out that we can establish some things about the translator and the probable transmission of the text. The conversion of the text for use by female readers is, however, not systematic and displays some awkwardness in grammar and syntax. Even so, it provides, she states, "striking examples" of women's "conversion" and "colonization" of an essentially male text.

Mercedes Salvador opens her paper, "Architectural Metaphors and Christological Imagery in the Advent Lyrics: Benedictine Propaganda in the Exeter Book" with the story of the conversion of the monk Eadsige as narrated in the *Translatio et miracula S. Swithuni*, a story that has at its heart one of the major concerns of the monastic reform: the unification of the church. Thematic and stylistic components of the Advent Lyrics, she argues, may have been understood by contemporary readers as reminiscent of the role of King Edgar, Saint Swithun, and the leading reformers as harbingers of unity, restoration, and peace. Salvador focuses her argument around two interrelated sets of images: architectural metaphors and Christological images of the Shepherd, the Priest, and the King. While the date of the Advent Lyrics (and the Exeter Book as a whole) remains controversial, Salvador sees their reformist motifs as evidence for their composition under the auspices of the reformers, and thus as evidence for their likely composition in the late tenth or early eleventh century.

The final paper in the volume, Richard North's "End Time and the Date of *Vǫluspá*: Two Models of Conversion," moves us beyond the territory of the Anglo-Saxons to Iceland, and traces of Anglo-Saxon and continental influence in its culture of conversion. He demonstrates that the poem, usually considered a heathen text, reveals traces of millennial Christian influence. Two competing techniques of conversion are at work here, one inclusive and synchronistic, the other exclusive and eschatological, and their combination within this single work might have as much to tell us about the larger process of Christianization in Iceland as it does about the possible date of the poem's composition.

Conversion and colonization are terms frequently applied to periods of origin, new eras brought about by the adoption, peaceful or not, of a new religion or the institution of a new order of authority. Yet, as the papers in this volume shown, they also have to do with endings and survivals, those things that survive conversion, those things that are post-colonial. We began this introduction with a brief consideration of the problem of defining "Anglo-Saxon England," and we would like to return to that problem here at its end. As Richard North's paper in particular makes clear, the culture that we identify as Anglo-Saxon was never confined to the British Isles. Originating as a product of the conversion and colonization of parts of sub-Roman Britain, it moved out to convert and colonize other geographical and cultural areas. The fact that it also lived on well beyond the usual terminal dates of 1100 or 1066 has also been the subject of numerous recent studies.[2] Even in the post-Conquest period, the borders of Anglo-Saxon England remain hard to define. There is perhaps no one scholar whose work has dealt so consistently with issues of what constituted "England" or "Anglo-Saxon England" — and the relationship between the two — as Patrick Wormald. In his many publications he taught us to question the origins of the English church and state, the constituent elements of political, religious, or ethnic identity, and the models we use to identify and define cultures of power. Above all, he showed us the ways in which the political institutions and forms of legislation created by the Anglo-Saxon kings developed into those of later medieval and modern England. They may have undergone repeated conversions, colonizations, and translations of their own, but they did live on. *Conversion and Colonization in Anglo-Saxon England* is dedicated to Patrick Wormald, not only a brilliant scholar, but also a devoted teacher and generous friend, who was to have written the preface to this volume.

There are perhaps no two scholars whose work has dealt so consistently with issues of what constituted "England" or "Anglo-Saxon England" in terms of its people and its laws, or in terms of its geography, its landscape, and its mythmaking as Patrick Wormald and Nicholas Howe. In his many publications Patrick taught us to question the origins of the English church and state, the constituent elements of political, religious, or ethnic identity, and the models we use to identify and define cultures of power; while Nick taught us to look with new eyes at Anglo-Saxon England as a physical place in landscapes both real and imagined. *Conversion and Colonization in Anglo-Saxon England* is dedicated jointly to Patrick Wormald, who was to have written the preface to this volume, and to Nicholas Howe, who did not live to see its publication. They will both be deeply missed.

---

[2] See for example, Patrick Wormald, *The Making of English Law: King Alfred to the Twelfth Century*, vol. 1, *Legislation and its Limits* (Oxford, 1999); idem, *"Engla Lond*: The Making of an Allegiance," *Journal of Historical Sociology* 7 (1994): 1–24 (repr. in idem, *Legal Culture in the Early Medieval West: Law as Text, Image and Experience* [London, 1999], 359–82); *Rewriting Old English in the Twelfth Century*, ed. Mary Swan and Elaine Treharne (Cambridge, 2000); R. R. Davies, *The First English Empire: Power and Identities in the British Isles 1093–1343* (Oxford, 2000); Lois L. Huneycutt, *Matilda of Scotland; A Study in Medieval Queenship* (Woodbridge, 2003).

From British to English Christianity: Deconstructing Bede's Interpretation of the Conversion

Nicholas Brooks

The early histories of British and of English Christianity have been seen as two separate subjects. In 1997 the 1400th anniversary of the arrival of the mission of St. Augustine in Canterbury in the year 597 to convert the pagan English was held to commemorate the beginning of English Christianity and of the English church's continuous history as an established religion. Thereby the interpretation of its early historian, Bede, was accepted. But the Christian faith had of course already reached Britain at least four centuries before that date and could indeed claim to have been an established religion for more than 280 years by that time. In interpreting 597 have we too readily accepted Bede's concept of a separate English ethnic identity and his reluctance to recognize the contribution of British Christians to English Christianity? That is the fundamental question that underlies this paper.

I. Romano-British Christianity

After more than a century of persecution, Christian fortunes throughout the Roman Empire had been transformed by Constantine's victory over Maxentius in the battle of the Milvian Bridge in 312. Constantine and Licinius's Milan rescript of the following year extended to Maximinus's former domain the general religious toleration that they had already established throughout their territories. But the rescript went on to place great emphasis on the restitution of confiscated Christian properties and buildings, both to individuals and communities.[1] Thereafter

---

[1] For the Greek text of the misnamed "Edict," see Eusebius, *Ecclesiastical History*, ed. and trans. John Ernest Leonard Oulton (London, 1927), 10.5, 2.444–52; for the Latin text, see Lactantius, *De mortibus persecutorum*, ed. and trans. John L. Creed, Oxford Early Christian Texts (Oxford, 1984), chap. 48, 70–72.

Christianity had rapidly become the "established" religion of the Roman world, and episcopal sees had been either newly set up, or else consolidated, in the *civitates* throughout the Empire.

In Britain Roman cities — somewhat artificial creations that were perhaps already in decay[2] — proved an uncertain ground for the establishment of the Christian religion. The delegations from British provinces to the Councils of Arles (314), Nicaea (325), Serdica (343), and Ariminium (359/360) were small, and some had need of conciliar or imperial financial support. Christianity in Britain, as throughout the Empire, was, however, organized on the basis of the Roman towns, and seems to have become sufficiently powerful there to bring a rapid end to urban pagan temples and, in London, to pagan offerings at London Bridge.[3] But the urban Christian communities may have been predominantly drawn from a very limited upper class, the highly Romanized British elite. The town walls, the Christian chapels and Christian mosaics in a number of British Roman villas, and the splendor of some Christian silver hoards buried in the late fourth or early fifth century point to the wealth but also to the insecurity of this British elite.[4] There is every reason to expect that metropolitan sees will have been established in the four or five provincial capitals of fourth-century Britain: London, York, Lincoln, Cirencester, and, for a brief time, possibly Carlisle (fig. 1.1).[5] Similarly we should

---

[2] The view that British Roman towns were already in decay in the fourth century derives from the numismatic record. See Richard Reece, "Town and Country: The End of Roman Britain," *World Archaeology* 12 (1980): 77–92. Nonetheless British towns received massive investment in town walls enclosing huge *enceintes* in the fourth century, whereas in Gaul only limited citadels were enclosed. See Stephen Johnson, "Late Roman Urban Defenses in Europe," in *Roman Urban Defences in the West*, ed. John Maloney and Brian Hobley, CBA Research Report 51 (London, 1983), 69–76.

[3] For the closure of urban pagan temples, see Neil Faulkner, *The Decline and Fall of Roman Britain* (Stroud, 2000), 127; for the dramatic decline of offerings at London Bridge in the second quarter of the fourth century, see Michael Rhodes, "The Roman Coinage from London Bridge," *Britannia* 22 (1991): 179–90, and the far more rounded discussion in Bruce Watson, Trevor Brigham, and Tony Dyson, *London Bridge: 2000 Years of a River Crossing* (London, 2001), 36–37.

[4] For differing interpretations of the role of Christianity in Roman Britain, see Charles Thomas, *Christianity in Roman Britain to A.D. 500* (London, 1981); Martin Henig, *Religion in Roman Britain* (London, 1984), 214–16; Faulkner, *Decline and Fall of Roman Britain*, 116–20, 127–28; David Petts, *Christianity in Roman Britain* (Stroud, 2003).

[5] John C. Mann, "The Administration of Roman Britain," *Antiquity* 35 (1961): 316–20; Mark W. C. Hassall, "Britain in the *Notitia*," in *Aspects of the Notitia Dignitatum*, ed. Roger Goodburn and Philip Bartholomew, BAR, suppl. ser. 15 (Oxford, 1976), 103–18; A. Simon Esmonde Cleary, *The Ending of Roman Britain* (London, 1989), 47–48.

presume that bishoprics will have been established in most, perhaps in all, of the *civitas*-capitals, for example at Canterbury (*Durovernum Cantiacorum*) and Winchester (*Venta Belgarum*), in the course of the fourth century.

Fig. 1.1. The Provinces and Metropolitan Cities of Fourth-Century Britain (London and York had been provincial centers since the second century. Probably from Diocletian's reign and certainly by 312–314 the two British provinces had been divided to make four. It is uncertain whether the province of Valentia was a further subdivision in the north after 367 or a renaming of an existing province. All boundaries are conjectural and schematic.)

II. The Break in Christian Memory

In no metropolitan or diocesan see can we trace a continuous episcopal history from Roman times through to the Anglo-Saxon period. Both the Romano-British and the British histories of these sees are lost to us. This hiatus in Christian tradition is explained by some as reflecting a failure of Christianity to establish itself as securely in Roman Britain as it had elsewhere in the West in the later fourth century.[6] Others would rather attribute the memory loss to Christianity's association with British military and political failures from the mid-fifth century in the face of pagan Germanic invaders who had their own war-gods and their own distinctive culture. By 597 four or five generations of pagan Anglo-Saxon rule in eastern and southern Britain may have sufficed to destroy the memory of the Christian British past there.[7] A third option might be that the British traditions of the church of Canterbury, as of other cult centers, were to be deliberately forgotten after 597 in a program of cultural and ethnic amnesia during the seventh and eighth centuries. Roman authority thenceforth might be associated, not with memories of Roman Britain, but with the assertion of a common English identity.[8] Which of these rival explanations, or what mixture of them, can account for the apparently unbridgeable hiatus between British and Anglo-Saxon Christianity? That is the question that underlies this paper's reassessment of some familiar and some not so familiar evidence. Is it possible to rethink the issues free from the constraints which our sources seek to impose or at least with a better understanding of them?

III. Bede's Interpretation

What is certainly clear is that our received account of English Christianity as the product of the Roman missions of Augustine, Mellitus, and Birinus and of the Irish mission of Aidan of Iona at Lindisfarne is an elaborate construct. It is the

---

[6] William H. C. Frend, "Pagans, Christians and the Barbarian Conspiracy of A.D. 367 in Roman Britain," *Britannia* 23 (1992): 111–23; idem, "Roman Britain: A Failed Promise?" in *The Cross Goes North*, ed. Martin Carver (Woodbridge, 2003), 79–91; Thomas, *Christianity in Roman Britain*, 265 and fig. 48; Dorothy Watts, *Religion in Late Roman Britain: Forces of Change* (London, 1998).

[7] John Noel L. Myres, *The English Settlements* (Oxford, 1986); Frank Merry Stenton, *Anglo-Saxon England*, 3rd ed. (Oxford, 1971), 18, 64.

[8] Nicholas P. Brooks, "Canterbury, Rome and the Construction of English Identity," in *Early Medieval Rome and the Christian West: Essays in Honour of Donald A. Bullough*, ed. Julia M. H. Smith (Leiden, 2000), 221–46; idem, "Canterbury and Rome: The Limits and Myth of *romanitas*," *Settimane di studi ... sull'alto medievo* 49 (2002): 797–832. See also Brian Ward-Perkins, "Why Did the Anglo-Saxons Not Become More British?" *English Historical Review* 15 (2000): 513–32.

work of one of the greatest teachers of the early Middle Ages, namely the Northumbrian monk Bede, who was writing in the monastery of Jarrow. He completed the *Ecclesiastical History of the English People* in or around the year 731, and one of its essential themes is that there had been no British involvement in the conversion of the Anglo-Saxons.[9] Bede had drawn extensively upon the rhetorical denunciation of British sinfulness in the *De Excidio et Conquestu Britanniae* of the sixth-century British (i.e. Welsh) monk Gildas.[10] Bede utilized Gildas's warnings to his countrymen to conclude that the conquest of most of Britain by pagan *Saxones* had indeed been divine retribution for the Britons' sins. For Bede, the failure of the Britons to preach the word of God to the Anglo-Saxons "who inhabited Britain with them" (*HE* 1.22) was one further indication of British inadequacies. He had no intention of portraying the growth of the English diocesan and episcopal hierarchy as a peaceful development from the British past. On the contrary, English control of lowland Britain was justified precisely because the Christian Britons had shown themselves unworthy of holding the land. In addition to the denunciations of their own *historicus* (Gildas), Bede could adduce the Britons' persistence in ecclesiastical error in his own day in rejecting Catholic practice with regard to the date of Easter and to the form of the monastic tonsure.

Bede depicted the English after their conversion as, by contrast, a godly people, who cultivated their links with Rome and prided themselves on their Roman rectitude in matters of ecclesiastical controversy. Bede was, of course, not alone in the eighth century in justifying Anglo-Saxon ethnic land-taking and in insisting upon Catholic orthodoxy. Very much the same attitudes and enmities can be found, for example, in Aldhelm's letter to King Geraint of Dumnonia or in Stephen of Ripon's account of the endowment of Wilfrid's church at Ripon with the lands of British churches expropriated by Northumbrian English kings.[11] It was also for this reason that pre-Conquest English churches largely chose to remember English saints, whose relics they preserved, and also English rulers and founders, whose tombs they honored.[12] Thus Canterbury scarcely developed the

---

[9] Bede, *Historia Ecclesiastica Gentis Anglorum*, ed. and trans. Bertram Colgrave and R. A. B. Mynors (Oxford, 1969) (hereafter cited as Bede, *HE*).

[10] Gildas, *The Ruin of Britain*, ed. and trans. Michael Winterbottom (London, 1978). For recent reassessments, see *Gildas: New Approaches*, ed. David N. Dumville and Michael Lapidge (Woodbridge, 1984), and Nicholas J. Higham, *The English Conquest: Gildas and Britain in the Fifth Century* (Manchester, 1994).

[11] Aldhelm, *Opera omnia*, ed. Rudolf Ehwald, MGH, Auctores Antiquissimi 15 (Berlin, 1919), 480–86; *Aldhelm: The Prose Works*, ed. Michael Lapidge and Michael Herren (Ipswich, 1979), 140–43, 155–60; Stephanus, *Vita sancti Wilfridi*, chap.17, in *The Life of Bishop Wilfrid by Eddius Stephanus*, ed. Bertram Colgrave (Cambridge, 1927), 36.

[12] Karl Heinrich Krüger, *Königsgrabkirchen der Franken, Angelsachsen und Langobarden bis zur Mitte des 8. Jahrhunderts* (Munich, 1971); Donald A. Bullough, "Burial, Community and Belief in the Early Medieval West," in *Ideal and Reality in Frankish*

cult of Augustine, but instead honored the tombs of the early archbishops and of the kings of Kent equally, while Lindisfarne preferred its English saint, Cuthbert, to its Irish founder, Aidan. Here, and in a host of other churches, English communities were involved in preserving English memories in a common program of English ethnogenesis.

Although his subject was the ecclesiastical history of the English, Bede devoted seventeen chapters of his first book to the history of Christianity in Roman Britain (*HE* 1.4–21). Most of these chapters have, I suspect, been seldom read by modern scholars, since Bede was here conflating known written sources and is not himself a primary authority. They have certainly occasioned no scholarly debate, even though they have much to tell us of Bede's own purposes. He needed to explain to his English readers that the Britons had been Christian before the Anglo-Saxons, and his account was necessarily sensitive. It had to avoid lending credence to British claims to rule areas that had since passed to Anglo-Saxon control. For example, tales of eminent or saintly British bishops of London or of York might have risked being so utilized. Viewed as a whole, the agenda of Bede's account of British Christianity seems clear. Its emphasis is, on the one hand, on Roman imperial and papal authority as the source of legitimacy, and on the other on British sinfulness and heresy. Thus Bede begins by recounting the reception of the Christian faith into Britain by means of a supposed mission sent by Pope Eleutherius (A.D. 174–180) to the mythical British king Lucius. After Lucius's time the faith is simply said to have been preserved in peace until the times of the Emperor Diocletian (*HE* 1.4). After a chapter on the rule of the Emperor Severus (*HE* 1.5), he describes (*HE* 1.6–7) the persecutions of British Christians, in particular the martyrdom of St. Alban at Verulamium, though he also mentions those of Aaron and Julius at Caerleon. After telling of a further period of peace, he goes on to stress the British connections of Constantius and Helen, of their son, the Emperor Constantine, and of his work in spreading and defining the Christian faith, particularly through the Council of Nicaea (1.8). He next records the growth of the heresy of the Briton, Pelagius, and then the sack of Rome

---

and Anglo-Saxon Society: Studies Presented to J. M. Wallace-Hadrill, ed. Patrick Wormald (Oxford, 1983), 177–201; Alan Thacker, "In Gregory's Shadow," in *St Augustine and the Conversion of England*, ed. Richard Gameson (Stroud, 1999), 374–90; Catherine Cubitt, "Universal and Local Saints in Anglo-Saxon England," and John Blair, "A Saint for Every Minster: Local Cults in Anglo-Saxon England," in *Local Saints and Local Churches in the Early Medieval West*, ed. Alan Thacker and Richard Sharpe (Oxford, 2002), 423–53, 455–94. Church dedications, and in particular the churches and wells of St. Helen, are a separate issue. Graham Jones, "Holy Wells and the Cult of St. Helen," *Landscape History* 8 (1986): 59–74, shows some of the difficulties of distinguishing the mother of Constantine from similarly named figures of myth and folklore and of producing any distributions that are chronologically coherent.

by the Goths (1.9) and the abandonment of Britain by the Romans (1.10–12). He records a mission by Palladius sent to the Irish in A.D. 431 by Pope Celestine (1.13), but significantly he has nothing at all to say here (or indeed later in his book) of the British missionary Patrick. Then he returns to the sins of the Britons (1.14) and to the two missions to Britain of St. Germanus, bishop of Auxerre, to combat the Pelagian heresy in Britain (1.17–21). Finally he emphasizes British unworthiness as transmitters of the faith as evidenced by their failure to preach to the people of the "Saxons or English" (1.22). From Bede's presentation the reader might therefore conclude that British Christianity before the seventh century had been both devoid of any missionary agenda and in constant need of doctrinal correction from Rome.

IV. Bede's View of the English Conversion

When Bede turns to the missions to the English (*gens Anglorum*), his account is almost solely one of missionary work at the courts of Anglo-Saxon kings.[13] The presumption appears to be that what was necessary to establish Christianity was to convert the king and his English followers at court. If a bishop could be first established under royal protection in the king's household and thereafter in a convenient see, the construction of monasteries and churches, where Christian cult could be maintained, would follow in due course. This is not an account of a "bottom-up" conversion with Christian groups (whether of British or Anglo-Saxon origin) gradually converting their masters and being strengthened in their faith through the hard path of persecution and martyrdom. It is rather portrayed as a top-down process whereby a *gens*, comprising the king and his companions (*comites*), who form the army or "folk," together take the political and religious decision to accept Christianity either from the continent or from a neighboring Anglo-Saxon kingdom. The ethnic agenda of the process that Bede describes is made clear in his account of Wine (Uini), who as bishop of the West Saxons in 664–665 found himself the only consecrated English bishop to survive the plague. Wine therefore sought assistance from two British bishops in the consecration of Chad, whom King Oswiu had selected to be his Northumbrian bishop at York.[14] Sadly, we are not told where these two bishops had come from, nor whether (nor for how long) their British Christian communities may have had contact with the West Saxons. But the participation of these bishops in the consecration ceremony was itself enough to ensure that Chad's elevation was to be

---

[13] Barbara Yorke, "The Reception of Christianity by Anglo-Saxon Royal Courts," in *St Augustine and the Conversion*, ed. Gameson, 152–73.

[14] For Wine's career, see Bede, *HE* 3.7; for his consecration of Chad, 3.28.

unacceptable both at Rome and at Canterbury, when the hierarchy was eventually re-established there in May 669 with the arrival of Theodore. That result, however, was not so much the product of Roman or of Canterbury policy as of their response to the determined opposition of Chad's Deiran-sponsored rival Wilfrid, who had gone to Gaul for consecration in the absence of sufficient English bishops.

Bede's viewpoint — though he was a monk who had renounced whatever standing his own family's origins might have carried — is that of the English ruling class and of this orthodox hierarchy.[15] In the *Ecclesiastical History* he is not evidently concerned with the faith of the rural underclass. The unwritten assumption is either that peasants will follow the example of their lords, or perhaps that the beliefs of rustics are irrelevant to the ecclesiastical history of the *gens Anglorum*, of which they formed no part. Elsewhere, of course, in a famous episode in his prose *Vita sancti Cuthberti*, Bede did show awareness of the pastoral needs of a lower social group. He tells us how in the heart of Bernicia, on the Tyne estuary, the local peasants resented the monks' prohibition of their old pagan rites and failure to provide instruction in the practices of the new cult. They rejected the youthful Cuthbert's attempt to intercede on the monks' behalf, until they were shamed when his prayers calmed the river's dangerously rough waters. Early minsters evidently had difficulty in organizing regular and systematic pastoral care for the rural laity.[16]

The map of all the places recorded in Bede's *History* (fig. 1.2) brings out very clearly another feature of his interpretation, namely just how eastern is Bede's conception of the English people whose ecclesiastical history he was recounting.[17] He does describe the establishment of a see under English rule at Whithorn (*HE* 3.4),

---

[15] It is at least curious that the name Beda is already found in "Bernicia" as one of the two *Alaisiagae* (household gods or goddesses?) in an early third-century inscription forming the left-hand of two inscribed jambs of an arched doorway to a shrine from Chapel Hill, Housesteads. It is now in Chesters Museum: see Robin George Collingwood and Richard Pearson Wright, *Roman Inscriptions of Britain*, I (Oxford, 1965), no. 1593: "DEO / MARTI / THINGSO / ET DUABUS / ALAISIAGIS / BEDE ET FIMMILENE ET N(umini) AUG(usti) GER/M(ani) CIVES TU/IHANTI / V(otum) S(olverunt) L(ibentes) M(erito)." The German *cives Tuihanti* are understood to be from the district of Twenthe, in the province of Over-Yssel, Holland, and the right-hand inscription (no. 1594) identifies them as forming a detachment of Frisians ("*cuneus Frisiorum*") and dates the shrine to the reign of Severus Alexander (222–235). I owe my knowledge of these inscriptions to Dr. Richard Morris. Beda is the hypocoristic or pet form of dithematic Germanic names beginning *Bado-*, *Badu-*, *Beado-*, etc.

[16] Bede, *Vita sancti Cuthberti*, ed. Bertram Colgrave, in *Two Lives of St Cuthbert* (Cambridge, 1941), chap. 3, 160–64.

[17] David Hill, *Atlas of Anglo-Saxon England* (Oxford, 1971), 30 (no. 41).

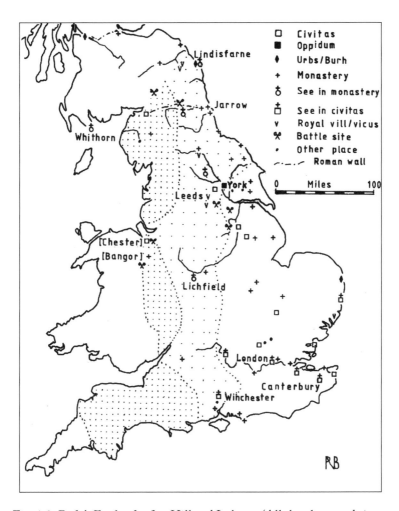

Fig. 1.2. Bede's England, after Hill and Jackson. (All the places and rivers mentioned by Bede are shown, but not the names of peoples or groups; and Caerleon (quoted from Gildas) is also excluded. The sites of major battles around the Northumbrian kingdom are shown. The shaded westerly areas are K. Jackson's areas II and III, where an increasing proportion of the river-names are Celtic [see p. 13].)

and St. Cuthbert's visit to Carlisle and the hermitage of Cuthbert's friend Hereberct in Derwentwater and he records Cuthbert's cult at the Cumberland monastery of Dacre under its English abbot Suidberct (*HE* 4.29, 32). But otherwise Bede has no English church history at all to relate west of the Pennines. In western Northumbria he therefore only knows about a narrow corridor, more or less along Hadrian's Wall from the Tyne valley to the Eden valley and to the shores of the Solway. He knows nothing of other territories on the British frontier, namely western Mercia or western Wessex. This reflects the predominantly eastern concentration not only of his contacts and sources in Bernicia and Deira, but also of most of his southern informants: Abbot Albinus of Canterbury, Nothhelm the priest of London, and Abbot Esi of East Anglia. Bishop Daniel of Winchester was as far west as his southern informants extended.[18] Whether by design or by accident, it is a fact of crucial importance that Bede's information was coming from sources that were much more eastern than the "people" whose ecclesiastical history he was writing.

V. English Settlement and Identity

We may note, however, that the churches and sites whose stories form the foundation of the *Ecclesiastical History* cover the same area of lowland Britain as the so-called "pagan Anglo-Saxon cemeteries," particularly those which may be assigned to the fifth and the first three quarters of the sixth century (fig. 1.3).[19] Of course we have been taught in the last twenty-five years not to regard those cremated or buried in such cemeteries as necessarily all comprising Germanic immigrants and their descendants.[20] Proclaimed ethnic identity is indeed unlikely to have coincided with biological descent or with burial practice. There remain wide differences between those archaeologists who consider that items or assemblages of material

---

[18] *HE*, preface (ed. Colgrave and Mynors), 2–6; David P. Kirby, "Bede's Native Sources for the *Historia Ecclesiastica*," *Bulletin of the John Rylands Library* 48 (1966): 341–71.

[19] John Hines, "Philology, Archaeology and the *aduentus Saxonum uel Anglorum* in Britain," in *Britain 400–600: Language and History*, ed. Alfred Bammesberger and Alfred Wollman (Heidelberg, 1990), 17–36 has a series of maps of fundamental value. They are updated in John Hines, "The Anglian Migration in British Historical Research," *Studien zur Sachsenforschung* 11 (1999): 155–65.

[20] *Anglo-Saxon Cemeteries*, ed. Philip Rahtz, Tania Dickinson, and Lorna Watts, BAR Brit. Ser. 82 (Oxford, 1980); Chris J. Arnold, *An Archaeology of the Early Anglo-Saxon Kingdoms* (London, 1988); *Anglo-Saxon Cemeteries: A Reappraisal*, ed. Edward Southworth (Stroud, 1990); Nicholas Higham, *Rome, Britain and the Anglo-Saxons* (London, 1992), 152–88; Martin Welch, *English Heritage Book of Anglo-Saxon England* (London, 1992), 54–107; Sam Lucy, *The Anglo-Saxon Way of Death* (Stroud, 2000), 10–15, 170–81; Howard Williams, "Remains of Pagan Saxondom? — The Study of Anglo-Saxon Cremation Rites," in *Burial in Early Medieval England and Wales*, ed. Sam Lucy and Andrew Reynolds (London, 2002), 47–71.

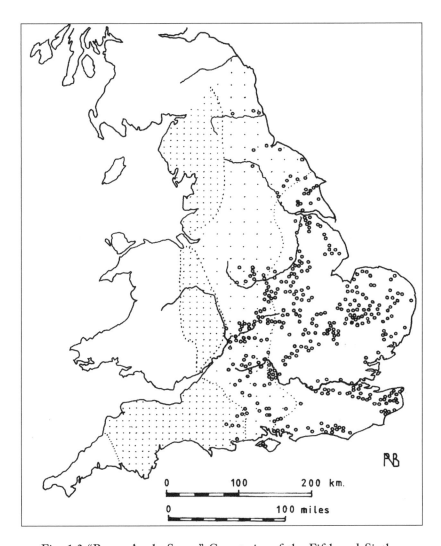

Fig. 1.3 "Pagan Anglo-Saxon" Cemeteries of the Fifth and Sixth Centuries, after Hines. (No distinction is made among cremation, in-humation, or mixed-rite cemeteries and only those in use before ca. 575 are shown. The cemetery distribution has been kindly provided by Professor J. Hines. The shading [as in fig. 2] represents Jackson's areas II and III of the survival of Celtic river-names.

culture found in the cemeteries can allow groups of migrants to be identified and those who regard such attempts as invalid from the start.[21] But these fifth- and sixth-century cemeteries were certainly new, unlike so many contemporary cemeteries on the continent.[22] They should perhaps be considered the product of a society organized along new lines, and adopting or imposing new places of burial, as well as rites and artifacts (i.e. pottery and metalwork) that are clearly broadly characteristic of the continental Germanic world. In other words the cemeteries, whether willingly or by compulsion, represent an identity statement. They are a declaration of allegiance to a Germanic rather than to a British or to a Roman culture. Of course many of the kinsfolk of those cremated or inhumed in these cemeteries may have had little choice in the matter, given the realities of local power. But it is surely still reasonable to see these cemeteries (despite the occasional penannular brooch, hanging bowl, or crouched burial) as representing one element in the "collective amnesia" concerning the British past of lowland Britain and in the adoption of an Anglo-Saxon identity. Burial and commemoration of the dead are, of course, pre-eminently occasions for reinforcing family and community identity. For this reason the obsessive concern of so much modern archaeological scholarship to show that factors other than ethnicity influence the form and the content of individual burials seems to be in danger of throwing out the baby with the bathwater.

VI. Bede's Response: Ignorance or Suppression of the British Role?

Bede, as we have seen, was profoundly ignorant of ultra-Pennine Northumbria and had no informant from Mercia or from western Wessex. He did know that Aldhelm had been abbot of Malmesbury before being consecrated as bishop in

---

[21] For recent arguments identifying groups of migrants, see Martin Welch, *Early Anglo-Saxon Sussex*, BAR Brit. Ser. 112 (Oxford, 1983); John Hines, *Clasps, Hektespenner, Agraffen: Anglo-Scandinavian Clasps of Classes A–C of the 3rd to 6th Centuries: Typology, Diffusion and Function* (Stockholm, 1993); idem, "The Becoming of the English: Identity, Material Culture and Language in Early Anglo-Saxon England," *ASSAH* 7 (1994): 50–59, here 52–54; Helen Hamerow, "Migration Theory and the Anglo-Saxon Identity Crisis," in *Migrations and Invasions in Archaeological Explanation*, ed. John Chapman and eadem, BAR Int. Ser. 664 (Oxford, 1997), 33–44. Those reluctant to identify ethnic groups include C. J. Arnold, *Roman Britain to Saxon England* (London, 1984), 120–41; Higham, *Rome, Britain and the Anglo-Saxons*, 152–88; Guy Halsall, *Early Medieval Cemeteries: An Introduction to Burial Archaeology in the Post-Roman West* (Glasgow, 1995), 56–61; Lucy, *Anglo-Saxon Way of Death*, 13–15, 155–84. For a general and highly critical interpretation of the problems of relating archaeological data to ethnicity, see Sian Jones, *The Archaeology of Ethnicity* (London, 1997).

[22] Detailed comparisons of English and continental cemeteries are still regrettably rare. But see Sally Crawford, "Britons, Anglo-Saxons and the Germanic Burial Rite," in *Migrations and Invasions*, ed. Chapman and Hamerow, 45–72.

705, but not apparently the location of Aldhelm's see at Sherborne (*HE* 5.18). He was also totally ignorant of the history of the see and territory of the Magonsæte (Hereford?) and largely ignorant of that of the Hwicce, which we can place at Worcester (*HE* 4.23, 5.23). Yet it is in exactly these west midland areas — where Bede was ignorant — that we are beginning to find evidence for continuities between the British and Anglo-Saxon churches and perhaps for British contributions to the English church.[23] In western Wessex too the evidence of the British Christian inscriptions from Wareham (Dorset) or of possible British Christian antecedents at Sherborne and elsewhere suggests that the transition from British to English Christianity took more from British Christianity than Bede's one-track account of missions to pagan Anglo-Saxon courts might suggest.[24] It is, of course, a moot point whether, if Bede had had western informants to tell of the work of British Christians, he would have suppressed that knowledge. For despite his extensive Northumbrian contacts Bede tells us nothing of claims that Britons participated in the conversion of Edwin nor that King Oswiu of Northumbria (642–671) had had a British wife, Rieinmelth.[25]

It is also noteworthy that those areas where Bede fails to tell us of the establishment of Anglo-Saxon bishoprics and monasteries are exactly those where we have evidence for the greatest survival of Brittonic speakers (fig. 2). Indeed, they coincide in part with "region 3" in Kenneth Jackson's famous map of the survival of Celtic river-names in Britain.[26] In other words, Bede tells us least about the areas where British influence was greatest and where Anglo-Saxon Christian rule took over from British Christian control with only a short — or even with no — intervening pagan period. Bede's interpretative model for the conversion is perhaps one that applies better to the areas of primary Anglo-Saxon settlement, where we may suppose that Germanic paganism had been most firmly established. There is surely an instructive contrast between, on the one hand, the

---

[23] Patrick Sims-Williams, *Religion and Literature in Western England, 600–800* (Cambridge, 1990), 54–85; Steven R. Bassett, "Church and Diocese in the West Midlands: The Transition from British to Anglo-Saxon Control," in *Pastoral Care before the Parish*, ed. John Blair and Richard Sharpe (Leicester, 1992), 13–40; idem, "Churches in Worcester Before and After the Conversion of the Anglo-Saxons," *Antiquaries Journal* 69 (1989): 225–35; idem, "How the West was Won," *ASSAH* 11 (2000): 107–18.

[24] Barbara Yorke, *Wessex in the Early Middle Ages* (Leicester, 1995), 149–80; Susan Pearce, *Devon and Cornwall in the Early Middle Ages* (London, 2004), 135–96.

[25] For Rieinmelth, daughter of Royth, son of Run, see *Historia Brittonum*, chap. 56 in *Nennius, British History and the Welsh Annals*, ed. John Morris (London, 1980); for the inclusion of Rægnmeld in the Durham *Liber Vitae*, see Nora K. Chadwick, "The Conversion of Northumbria: A Comparison of the Sources," and Kenneth H. Jackson, "On the Northern British Section in Nennius," in *Celt and Saxon*, ed. Nora K. Chadwick (Cambridge, 1971), 138–66 (here 158–59) and 1–59 (here 21, 42, 50, 56).

[26] Kenneth H. Jackson, *Language and History in Early Britain* (Edinburgh, 1953), 220.

lawcodes of King Æthelberht and of later Kentish kings and, on the other, the laws of King Ine of the West Saxons. The seventh-century Kentish kings seem to have felt no need to enact provisions for any British subjects, whereas King Ine's code makes provision for British landowners, who are assigned *wergilds* and compensations of half the value of West Saxons of equivalent status.[27] The pressures for acculturation, influencing Britons to adopt a common English identity, were therefore strong, whether we interpret them primarily as financial and legal or as military — involving the right to bear arms and to participate fully in a warrior society. What seems clear is that the process had progressed very much less far in the western areas, ignored by Bede, than it had in the south and the east.

Two topics seem to offer particularly valuable controls for testing Bede's interpretation of the relationship of British and Anglo-Saxon Christianity: the "Eccles" place-names and the sites of the episcopal churches of British and early Anglo-Saxon Christianity. Both seem to be fields where a reassessment of the current situation is needed before the opportunities for further investigations are taken up.

VII. Eccles Names

The pioneering work of Kenneth Cameron, Geoffrey Barrow, and Margaret Gelling in the late 1960s and early 1970s underlies current understanding of the Eccles place-names (fig. 1.4). They were formed from the Primitive Welsh word *eglēs* (modern Welsh *eglwys*), a loanword from Latin *ecclesia*, indicating a church of British Christians.[28] Eccles takes its place alongside other Latin loanwords

---

[27] Frederick Levi Attenborough, *Laws of the Earliest English Kings* (Cambridge, 1922). For alternative interpretations, see Louis Alexander, "The Legal Status of the Native Britons in Late Seventh-Century Wessex as Reflected in the Lawcode of Ine," *Haskins Society Journal* 7 (1995): 31–38, and Paul Barnwell, "Britons and Warriors in Post-Roman South-East England," *ASSAH* 12 (2003): 1–8, here 3–4.

[28] Kenneth Cameron, "Eccles in English Place-Names," in *Christianity in Britain 300–700*, ed. Maurice Barley and Richard Patrick Crosland Hanson (Leicester, 1968), 177–92; Geoffrey W. S. Barrow, *The Kingdom of the Scots* (Edinburgh, 1973), 7–68, here 60–64; Margaret Gelling, *Signposts to the Past* (London, 1978), 82–83, 96–99. See also Thomas, *Christianity in Roman Britain to A.D. 500*, 262–66; and for detailed local studies, see Margaret L. Faull, "Phosphate Analysis and Three Possible Dark-Age Ecclesiastical Sites in Yorkshire," *Landscape History* 2 (1980): 21–38; Denise Kenyon, *The Origins of Lancashire* (Manchester, 1991), 95–96; and Tom Williamson, *The Origins of Norfolk* (Manchester, 1995), 55, 71, 148, who however mistakenly supposes that the Norfolk Eccles-names might have derived from Icel and the Ickneild Way. A. Ward, "Church Archaeology 410–597: The Problem of Continuity," *Archaeologia Cantiana* 124 (2004): 375–95, here 376–77, hazards a bizarre case for deriving Eccles (Kent) directly from Greek.

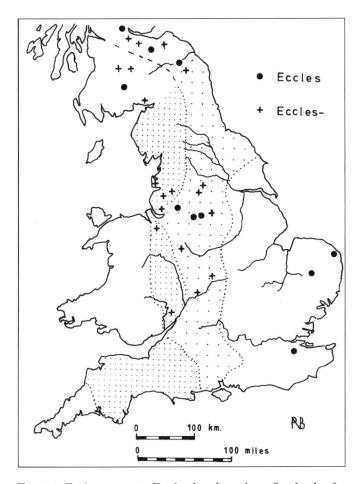

Fig. 1.4. Eccles-names in England and southern Scotland, after
Cameron and Barrow. (The shading again represents Jackson's areas II and III in the survival of Celtic river-names, but his analysis
did not extend into Scotland, so the suggested boundary between
them in Scotland is conjectural.)

found in English place-names, such as *funta*, *campus*, and *uicus* in suggesting a
degree of continuity either from the Roman or from the British and sub-Roman
landscape. Eccles-names seem to refer to a church building (or to a Christian
community) which had been distinctive in its local context. They occur either in
simplex form (Eccles) or compounded with an Old English suffix (*-tun*, *-halh*,
-feld, and *-leah*) — Eccleston, Eccleshall, Ecclesfield and Ecclesley, etc. The

distribution of Eccles-names is instructive. The single Kentish example and the two in Norfolk form a group of three uncompounded names, which are likely to be very early loans because these are areas of primary Anglo-Saxon settlement, which were in Germanic hands from the mid-fifth century. But an extensive blank area in East Yorkshire, Lincolnshire, the East Midlands, the Thames valley, and eastern Wessex separates these three from the other English Eccles-names. Here there were early pagan Anglo-Saxon cemeteries in plenty but no Eccles-names. The main concentrations of Eccles-names rather occur in areas further west, where there are in fact few or no pagan Anglo-Saxon cemeteries. They occur in Staffordshire, Lancashire, Herefordshire, and the West Riding of Yorkshire, and in southern and eastern Scotland. That is to say, the Eccles-names are found in exactly those "march" areas of western and northern Northumbria and of western Mercia where we have seen Bede's information to be thinnest and British influence to have been greatest. If these place-names denote churches or Christian communities established before the Anglo-Saxon takeover, then they must have been established in (or before) the early seventh century.

It is instructive that many of these names — such as Eccleshall in Staffordshire and most of the Lancashire examples — survived as the names of settlements with parish churches. Indeed, many of the parishes have features which suggest that they had been early medieval "minster-" or "mother-churches." Eaglesfield, near Cockermouth in Cumbria, where the church adjoins a sub-Roman (and probably Christian) cemetery, is another that clearly hints that we may be looking at British churches which maintained ecclesiastical importance subsequently through Anglo-Saxon and medieval times. Systematic topographical studies of the Eccles-names and of the local parochial and minster-church network are urgently needed to test this hypothesis.[29] On the face of it, however, the Eccles-names of northern and western England would appear to indicate churches where (*pace* Bede) Britons had indeed preached to the English, or at least to those who came to think of themselves as English, whatever their biological ancestry may have been.

The two Norfolk places named Eccles and the one Kentish example are exceptional in lying in areas of primary Anglo-Saxon settlement. Margaret Gelling has suggested that their isolation from the bulk of the Eccles-names might mean that these three place-names alone had been taken into English usage directly from Latin speakers, rather than from Primitive Welsh.[30] Just how late that borrowing (whether directly from Latin *ecclesia* or rather from Primitive

---

[29] Dr. Lloyd R. Laing has pointed out to me that the original churchyard at Eccleston (Cheshire) was oval, which strongly suggests that it was an important early British church. It had also formerly possessed a pre-Conquest cross-shaft of ninth- or tenth-century date. See Lloyd and Jennifer Laing, *The Dark Ages of West Cheshire* (Cheshire, 1986), 20–30.

[30] Gelling, *Signposts to the Past*, 82–83.

Welsh *eglēs*) could have been will depend upon how long either Latin or Brittonic speech is considered to have remained in use alongside Old English in Kent and in Norfolk. But these three names are certainly a potential challenge to the Bedan model of British-English relations, if they are held to imply the survival of Romano-British or British churches through the period of pagan Anglo-Saxon dominance. Here it is important to observe that the two Norfolk examples did become medieval parish churches, while the Kentish Eccles did not. Eccles in Kent indeed seems to have had no Anglo-Saxon or medieval church, neither a minster nor even any private church. We shall see, however, that it did have an early Christian cemetery. The possibility therefore arises that in Kent the name survived as the name of a settlement, but no longer indicated a continuing Christian community or building. The place-name may have become effectively divorced from its etymological meaning, and some support might be found for Bede's model in this area of primary English settlement. The Norfolk examples, however, might indicate the survival of two churches of Romano-British or British (?fourth- or fifth-century) origin. Otherwise we would need to conclude that they both survived as the names of significant settlements, which were coincidentally later to give birth to significant new English churches.

Each of these eastern Eccles-names therefore needs detailed local topographical and archaeological study just as much as the western examples. As an example of their potential we may consider here the Kentish Eccles, which lies in the Medway valley between Rochester and Maidstone and in the parish of Aylesford. There have been extensive excavations there which may challenge current perceptions of this place-name. In fifteen annual seasons between 1962 and 1976 the late Alan Detsicas excavated a substantial Roman villa at Eccles that had been occupied between the second and fourth centuries. When the excavations reached the villa's south-eastern corner, they encountered a substantial cemetery which post-dated the villa and contained 203 inhumation burials, predominantly aligned W-E, and mostly without grave-goods. Just twenty-four of the graves were modestly furnished; the total assemblage comprised three spearheads, seventeen knives, five buckles, two shears, two penannular brooches, one chatelaine, two modest rings of bronze and iron, and two spiral-headed pins. The site had very little stratification and few of the grave-goods are at all closely datable, let alone ethnically diagnostic. A few graves were, however, aligned N-S and these seem to have been the earliest, at least in their immediate stratigraphic location. A full report is still awaited and must now be in doubt following the excavator's recent death; but Rachel Shaw has produced an invaluable interim assessment.[31] It is particularly unfortunate, how-

---

[31] Rachel Shaw, "The Anglo-Saxon Cemetery at Eccles: A Preliminary Report," *Archaeologia Cantiana* 114 (1994): 165–88. The key finds for dating purposes were illustrated and discussed in Alan P. Detsicas and Sonia C. Hawkes, "Finds from the Anglo-Saxon

ever, that an area of pits, post-holes, and gullies adjacent to the cemetery, which was first interpreted as a wooden church, still remains unplanned and without any definitive interpretation. Two of the N-S graves (nos. L56 and K19) are stratigraphically the earliest graves in their immediate vicinity and have plausibly been identified as "founders' graves" of the whole cemetery. One (K19) is distinguished [fig. 1.5] by a fine bronze buckle decorated with simple Germanic "Style II" interlacing animals engraved upon a cross-hatched background. But the main element of the design is provided by a detachable applied band running around the edge

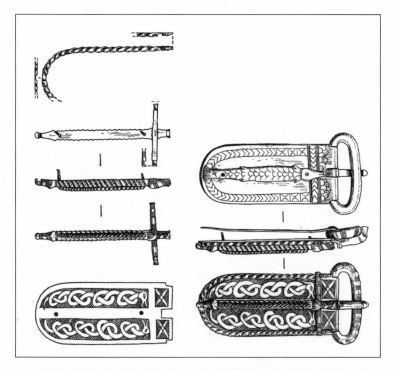

Fig. 1.5. The Eccles Buckle, from A. P. Detsicas and S. C. Hawkes. (Bronze buckle from grave K19, with (left) views of the top, side and back; and (right) of the dismembered portions of the buckle's superstructure. Drawing by Marion Cox; © Society of Antiquaries of London.)

Cemetery at Eccles, Kent," *Antiquaries Journal* 53 (1973): 281–86. Detsicas's annual interim reports on the Eccles excavations are in *Archaeologia Cantiana* from 1962, and the reports on the cemetery are found in 86 (1971): 31–35; 87 (1972): 108–10; 88 (1973): 78; 89 (1974): 44.

and dividing the body of the buckle with an elongated cross with stylised animal head terminals. Normally hidden, because on the reverse of the buckle, is a large salmon-like fish. Despite the alignment of this grave, the buckle itself may have been designed to have specific, though not too assertive, Christian symbolism.

If this grave was one of the first burials, then, as Sonia Chadwick Hawkes suggested, the Eccles cemetery should probably be regarded as a so-called "final-phase" Anglo-Saxon cemetery extending from the seventh century perhaps into the eighth or beyond.[32] Most of the graves are likely to have been those of Christians; they were dug alongside the ruins of a Roman villa that had passed out of occupation by the end of the fourth century. The cemetery lies within a quarter-mile of the medieval manor and modern hamlet of Eccles, which may itself perpetuate the dwelling-place of the villa's rural workers.[33] The archaeological record might suggest that the "founders' graves" were of Anglo-Saxon lords whose allegiance to Christianity was lukewarm at best. We may surely wonder whether the bulk of the graves were of Christians of British descent, whether or not they had come to think of themselves as English by the seventh century. Should we seek to relate the cemetery and the putative but unpublished wooden building or church to the place-name? Could the Eccles-name here have been coined in the seventh century? Or must we suppose that the location of this cemetery beside the center of Romano-British authority is accidental and irrelevant?

In the present state of knowledge, it is all too easy to let conjecture rip. Could the *eglēs* rather refer to some unexcavated corner of the ruined villa where the descendants of its British servile and peasant cultivators may have maintained some impoverished Christian worship? Could this cemetery represent a modest Anglicization of a continuing British Christian community at Eccles? These and many other questions can be asked about the survival of popular religion from Roman times. But they cannot yet be answered. What is clear is that a major research study of all the Eccles-names is an urgent desideratum. In Kent it needs to be backed by full microbiological (DNA) analysis of the Eccles skeletons and by a program to secure high-accuracy radiocarbon dates for them. Only then might we hope to know about the dates, the ethnicity, or the beliefs of those buried in the place named Eccles. Only by such methods might we determine the extent of any British contribution to Anglo-Saxon Christianity.

---

[32] Detsicas and Hawkes, "Finds from Eccles," 281–86. "Final-phase" cemeteries were the last "pagan Anglo-Saxon cemeteries," often extending beyond the conversion and containing Christian burials. For an important reassessment of the term which has led some to avoid its use, see Andy Boddington, "Modes of Burial, Settlement and Worship: The Final Phase Reviewed," in *Anglo-Saxon Cemeteries*, ed. Southworth, 177–99.

[33] In Domesday Book Eccles was a small manor held by Ralf fitz Turold from Odo of Bayeux. It was assessed at 3 yokes and had 7 villeins, 14 bordars, and 1 slave, and in 1086 was worth £4 (DB, i.7b).

Continuity of Cathedral and Church Sites?

If the Eccles place-names may be places where British churches were transferred to Anglo-Saxon use or possession, then we need to ask whether archaeological excavation and topographical research can give us any evidence of Anglo-Saxon cathedrals succeeding to major British churches. Or is the evidence rather one of a total separation between the two churches, as Bede's *History* might lead us to suppose? Before embarking on this survey, we need, however, to remember the influence that Bede has had on historical interpretation and therefore on the questions with which archaeologists have approached their investigations. In some cases it may be that the evidence has not been sought and therefore not found. Certainly we cannot point in Britain to any excavations beneath a medieval cathedral on the scale of those at Geneva, which revealed four or five earlier churches of Carolingian, Merovingian, Burgundian and late antique date.[34] Cathedral archaeology in Britain has not had the resources of the Swiss banking system at its disposal!

We may conveniently begin by listing those Roman walled settlements that became Anglo-Saxon sees: Canterbury, Rochester, London, Winchester, Dorchester upon Thames, Worcester, *Dummoc*, Leicester, and perhaps Lincoln and York. Some of these must be discarded for lack of current evidence. At York, despite the splendid example of the excavations beneath the Norman Minster and a generation of work by the York Archaeological Trust, we can identify neither the cathedral church of Alcuin's day nor any Roman or British church in any part of the city.[35] At Winchester excavation has revealed the early and tiny Anglo-Saxon cathedral church, founded in the early 660s (*not* in 648), which remained with little change until 971. But no trace has been found of the city's Roman episcopal church in that vicinity, or indeed anywhere in the town.[36] At

---

[34] Charles Bonnet, *Les fouilles de l'ancien groupe épiscopale de Genève, 1976–1993* (Geneva, 1993), 22–71.

[35] David Philips and Brenda Heywood, *Excavations at York Minster*, 1, *From Roman Fortress to Norman Cathedral* (London, 1995); Richard Morris, "Alcuin, York and the *alma sophia*," in *The Anglo-Saxon Church: Papers in Honour of H. M. Taylor*, ed. L. A. S. Butler and R. K. Morris, CBA Res. Rep. 60 (London, 1986), 80–89.

[36] Martin Biddle, "Winchester: The Development of an Early Capital," in *Vor- und Frühformen der europäischen Stadt im Mittelalter*, ed. Herbert Jankuhn, Walter Schlesinger, and Heiko Steuer (Göttingen, 1973), 229–61; idem, "Excavations at Winchester: Interim Reports," in *Antiquaries Journal* 45 (1965): 230–64; 47 (1967): 251–79; 48 (1968): 250–8; 49 (1969): 295–329; Barbara Yorke, "The Foundation of the Old Minster and the Status of Winchester in the 7th and 8th Centuries," *Proceedings of the Hampshire Field Club* 38 (1982): 75–84. The traditional date of 648 for the foundation of Winchester cathedral is an error of Anglo-Saxon Chronicle 'F', misinterpreting Bede's chronological indications.

Leicester (*Ratae Coritanorum*) neither any Romano-British church nor the cathedral of the short-lived Anglo-Saxon bishopric (737–ca. 877) has yet been located. No compelling case can be made there for the Anglo-Saxon see either at St. Nicholas's, sited in relation to the Roman bath-complex, or at St. Mary-de-Castro.[37] At Worcester the early Anglo-Saxon cathedral church of St. Peter has still not been detected, nor have we any plan of Oswald's tenth-century monastic church of St. Mary, despite the recognition of elements of pre-Conquest stonework in the fabric of the Norman cathedral and cloister. The suggestion that the town's parish church of St. Helen may preserve the site of an important British church[38] remains an exciting possibility waiting to be tested by excavation. But to my mind the claim that this was a British cathedral is endangered by the tendentious nature of the early evidence, namely the record of St. Wulfstan's supposed synod of 1092, which appears to be an elaborate mid-twelfth-century forgery. The small Roman industrial settlement of Worcester was never a Roman *civitas*-capital and is unlikely to have been the site of a Roman see, whatever developments there may have been there in the post-Roman centuries under British rule. Finally at the East Anglian see of *Dommuc*, or *Dommucae ciuitas* as it was termed in 803,[39] we can neither identify its Roman site nor locate either an Anglo-Saxon or a Romano-British cathedral. All are likely to have been lost to coastal erosion. This leaves us with four sees where there would seem to be some potential for investigating whether there was a hiatus or continuity from the Romano-British to the Anglo-Saxon cathedrals: Lincoln, London, Rochester, and Canterbury itself.

Lincoln may be considered first. As we have already seen, it would have been the site of a metropolitan see (for the province of Flavia Caesariensis) from the time of the Council of Arles in 314. If its fourth-century Roman metropolitan cathedral had been in the town's upper fortress, it has not yet been located. Some

---

[37] For St. Nicholas's and St. Mary's, see articles by John Blair in *The Blackwell Encyclopaedia of Anglo-Saxon England*, ed. Michael Lapidge et al. (Oxford, 1999), 281, 396–98.

[38] Steven R. Bassett, "Church and Diocese in the West Midlands: The Transition from British to Anglo-Saxon Control," in *Pastoral Care before the Parish*, ed. Blair and Sharpe, 13–40, here 20–6. For the 1092 forgery, see Julia S. Barrow, "How the Twelfth-century Monks of Worcester Perceived their Past," in *The Perception of the Past in Twelfth-Century Europe*, ed. Paul Magdalino (London, 1992), 53–74. For the Christian topography of Worcester, see now Nigel Baker and Richard Holt, *Urban Growth and the Medieval Church* (Aldershot, 2004), 127–37, 139–95.

[39] Walter de G. Birch, *Cartularium Saxonicum* (London, 1885–1893) [hereafter cited as BCS], no. 312. For the interpretation of the place-name, see Richard Coates, "*Domnoc/Dommoc*, Dunwich and Felixtowe," in Richard Coates and Andrew Breeze, *Celtic Voices, English Places: Studies of the Celtic Impact on Place-Names in England* (Stamford, 2000), 234–40.

portions of a remarkable fourth-century aisled building, aligned east-west with an eastern apse, have, however, been excavated in the insula beside the central crossroads of the lower *colonia*, in Flaxengate (fig. 1.6). If this were not simply a rather grand town-house, it might have been, as Charles Thomas conjectured,[40] an urban basilica: perhaps indeed the missing Roman cathedral or else a church erected in honor of a local martyr's cult in the less heavily occupied lower walled town. In the upper fortress the tiny church of St. Paul-in-the-Bail did have a central location, in the heart of the Roman forum. The earliest structure here, a prominent tomb within a rectangular stone foundation, may most plausibly be identified as a very late Roman *cella memoriae*. The first church on this site — built of timber with a simple rectangular nave and an eastern apse — is certainly witness to a concern to establish some relationship to the Roman past. The dating evidence suggests that it should be identified as a fifth- or sixth-century British church. It therefore cannot have been "the stone church of remarkable workmanship" built by Paulinus in the 620s and used for the consecration of Archbishop Honorius (ca. 630), which, after the collapse of the northern Roman mission in 633, was the base for the continued ministry of James the deacon.[41] If the Lincoln archaeologists are correct, however, it would be a crucial example of a sub-Roman British church developing into a medieval urban parish church. But at the diocesan level St. Paul's is of uncertain importance. We cannot know whether its prominent site implies that it had had sub-Roman or British episcopal functions. But when an Anglo-Saxon see was established for the sub-kingdom of Lindsey it does *not* seem to have been in the upper *colonia*, but rather at (the still unidentified Roman site of) *Syddensis ciuitas* or *Sidnacester.*[42] The location of the Anglo-Saxon cathedral of Lindsey and its relation to any Roman structures therefore necessarily remain uncertain.

---

[40] Thomas, *Christianity in Roman Britain*, 168–69 and figs. 24 and 37; subsequent excavation has not established the basilican plan or ecclesiastical function. See Michael J. Jones, "The Latter Days of Roman Lincoln," in *Pre-Viking Lindsey*, ed. Alan Vince (Lincoln, 1993), 14–28, here 16.

[41] Bede, *HE* 2.16. Michael J. Jones, "Archaeology in Lincoln," in *Medieval Art and Architecture at Lincoln Cathedral* (London, 1986), 1–8; Steven R. Bassett, "Lincoln and the Anglo-Saxon See of Lindsey," *ASE* 18 (1989): 1–32; *Pre-Viking Lindsey*, ed. Vince; Michael J. Jones, "St Paul-in-the-Bail, Lincoln," in *Churches Built in Ancient Times: Recent Studies in Early Christian Archaeology*, ed. Kenneth Painter (London, 1994), 325–47.

[42] The see is named as *Syddensis ciuitas* in BCS 312 and is rendered as *Sidnacestrensis* by William of Malmesbury, *Gesta pontificum Anglorum*, ed. Nicholas E. S. A. Hamilton, Rolls Series (London, 1870), 16. It is *Syddena* in *The Chronicle of John of Worcester*, 2, ed. Reginald R. Darlington and Patrick McGurk (Oxford, 1995), 136. For the problems of identification, see Bassett, "Lincoln and the Anglo-Saxon See of Lindsey." It is possible that *Sidnacester* was an alternative English name for Lincoln.

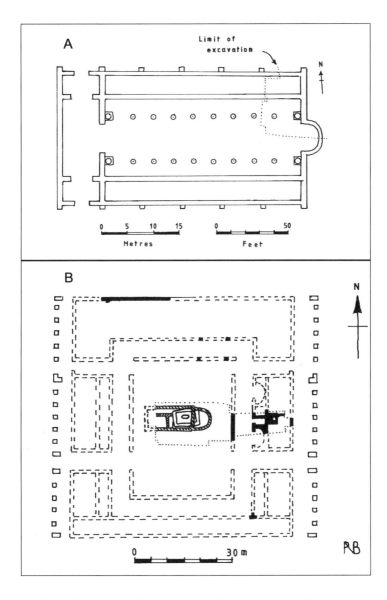

Fig. 1.6. Early Churches in Lincoln, after Morris and Jones. (A: Fragment of a basilical building in Flaxengate, at the main crossroads of the lower Roman city [after Thomas]. Note that the building could plausibly be reconstructed up to 50% shorter. B: Foundation trenches of early structures, tomb and of the [timber?] apsidal church beneath St. Paul-in-the-Bail, shown in relation to the courtyard of the Roman forum.)

London presents a not dissimilar case. The efforts of the Museum of London Archaeology Service are transforming our picture of Roman and Anglo-Saxon London. But the location of the Roman metropolitan cathedral remains uncertain since there has been no archaeological investigation beneath Wren's baroque cathedral of St. Paul's and its medieval predecessor. That prominent site near the west end of the Roman town is surely crucial for establishing whether or not there was any link between the Anglo-Saxon bishopric established by Mellitus in 604 (and re-established in the 660s) and the Romano-British Christian church. In 1992–1993, however, David Sankey excavated a site in the southeast of the city at Colchester House on Tower Hill (fig. 1.7) and revealed the northeast corner either of a great fourth-century basilica or of a great aisled granary or *horreum*. The analogy of St. Tecla's in Milan, one of a number of peripheral basilical churches with which that imperial city was ringed during the age of St. Ambrose, together with central location of a well suggests that this is indeed a fragment of a late fourth-century basilica. But the conclusion that it may therefore have been London's "Roman cathedral" is a wild *non sequitur*. If it is indeed a church, it would seem much more likely to have been, like St. Tecla's, a basilica, constructed in an area beyond the main area of urban settlement, to commemorate a local martyr. As with the possible basilica at Flaxengate, Lincoln, neither the site nor any martyr's cult survived in use through the Dark Ages there. It may therefore witness a hiatus in Christian history, but its evidence is very much less important than would be any from the main center of London's Christianity at St. Paul's.

Rochester provides some interesting parallels and contrasts.[43] Very little is yet known of Roman *Durobrivae*, except the location of its walls and of the bridge over the Medway. It was a tiny single-street town, fortified because of the strategic importance of Watling Street and the Medway estuary. But Rochester was not a *civitas*-capital and therefore is unlikely to have been the site of a Roman bishopric. The choice of Rochester as the site of a bishopric for Justus in 604 reflected the needs and priorities of the Roman mission and the availability of land at the start of the seventh century. It may not indicate any concern for continuity from British or Romano-British Christianity. Nonetheless the foundations of an early Kentish church, beneath the west end of the Norman cathedral (fig. 1.8), plausibly identified by Canon Livett and William St. John Hope as Justus's tiny cathedral of St. Andrew, have considerable interest. For beneath the south wall of the Norman nave were also recovered the footings of a wide rectangular building with an eastern apse on a different alignment to those of the probable Saxon cathedral. Despite

---

[43] For the topography of Rochester, see Tim Tatton-Brown, "The Towns of Kent," in *Anglo-Saxon Towns of Southern England*, ed. Jeremy Haslam (Chichester, 1984), 1–36, here 12–16, and Nicholas P. Brooks, "Rochester, A.D. 400–1066," in *Transactions of the British Archaeological Association Conference at Rochester, 2002* (London, 2006), 6–21.

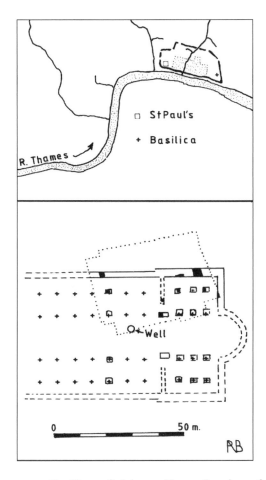

Fig. 1.7. Fourth-century Basilica at Colchester House, London, after Sankey. (The western extent of the building has not been established. The location sketch above shows the Roman walls of London. The main area of intra-mural Roman occupation is shaded and the respective locations of St. Paul's and the newly excavated basilica, to the west and east of this area and of the Walbrook, are indicated.)

(or perhaps because of) the prominence given to these fragments by the Taylors in *Anglo-Saxon Architecture*,[44] medieval archaeologists and antiquarians have, I suspect, hitherto tended to dismiss them as "Roman," without considering whether

---

[44] Harold M. and Joan Taylor, *Anglo-Saxon Architecture*, 3 vols. (Cambridge, 1965–1978), 2:518–19.

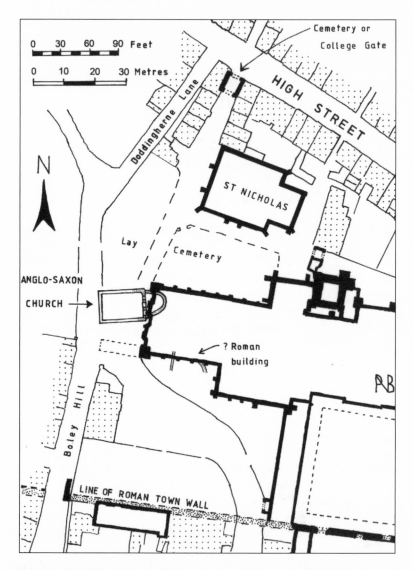

Fig. 1.8. An Early Cathedral Group in Rochester? after H. M. Taylor and
W. H. St J. Hope. (The plans of the present [Norman and medieval] cathedral and of the fifteenth-century collegiate church of St. Nicholas are shown
in relation to mid-nineteenth-century housing and streets, to the surviving
and known Roman and medieval townwalls, and to the plans of the earlier
buildings detected beneath the cathedral.)

they are likely to have belonged to a secular or to an ecclesiastical building. The possibility that we have here in close proximity a Romano-British church, an Anglo-Saxon cathedral, and the Norman cathedral of Bishop Gundulf, all on one sacred site, is surely worth considering. Sadly, the wonderful opportunity for fundraising for work in Rochester presented by the year 2004, the 1400th anniversary of the foundation of the see of Rochester, has been missed. One would have hoped that local civic and institutional pride could have funded research excavations of both these tiny and accessible sites, which are of such importance for understanding our Christian heritage. Once again, as all too often in the past, Rochester has been the impoverished neighbor of the wealthy Canterbury.

At Canterbury — as at York — we can at least benefit from superb archaeological investigations beneath the present cathedral, which have been fully and promptly published to a very high standard.[45] These revealed extensive footings of the pre-Conquest cathedral and its various Anglo-Saxon extensions, beneath the Gothic and Romanesque nave of the present cathedral. The excavators were able to identify fragments of the west end of an early Kentish church and enabled a splendid reconstruction of the pre-conquest cathedral to be essayed (fig. 1.9). But unfortunately the 1990 Cathedrals Measure (which set up the Cathedrals' Fabric Commission and the national system of cathedral archaeological consultants) also restricted excavation to the depth of any new work for a cathedral's needs that the Commission approved. At Canterbury this involved installing a new heating system and a new floor. As a result, it was impossible to pursue the crucial research questions raised by the excavations. In particular, excavations were not permitted to locate the east end of this cathedral. We desperately need to test whether the statement — recorded by Bede in the early eighth century on the basis of information provided direct from Canterbury — that Augustine "recovered" a Roman church for his cathedral of St. Saviour's is accurate. The site for such an investigation — beneath the floor of the cathedral's "Norman" crypt — is evident (fig. 1.10). We must hope that the Dean and Chapter and their Fabric Advisory Committee can devise a pressing ecclesiastical need to remove and replace the horrible nineteenth-century concrete floor of this crypt. The relative levels suggest that beneath the crypt archaeologists would immediately encounter Roman levels. There surely we might expect to find Augustine's church "built by the work of the Roman faithful" as Bede had been informed. Until that work is undertaken, it seems wisest to trust Bede's Kentish informant, Abbot Albinus of St. Peter and St. Paul, and the detailed account by the Christ Church monk Eadmer of the church that he had known as a boy novice. These witnesses of the actual building seem

---

[45] Kevin Blockley, Margaret Sparks, and Tim Tatton-Brown, *Canterbury Cathedral Nave: Archaeology, History and Architecture* (Canterbury, 1997); for a different interpretation, see Brooks, "Canterbury and Rome: The Limits and Myth of *romanitas*," 807–9 and tab.V.

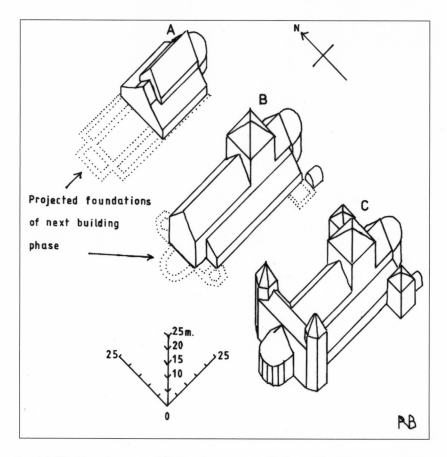

Fig. 1.9. The Development of the Pre-Conquest Cathedral at Canterbury, after Block-ley. (Isometric reconstruction of the three main phases in the cathedral's early de-velopment: A: the suggested cathedral of 597–ca. 800. B: the cathedral as rebuilt in the early 9th or mid-10th century. C: the cathedral as it existed in 1066. The recon-structions derive from the 1993 excavations in the cathedral nave and are based, by permission, on fig. 35 of Blockley, Sparks, and Tatton Brown, *Canterbury Cathedral Nave: Archaeology, History and Architecture.* © The Dean and Chapter of Canterbury Cathedral and Canterbury Archaeological Trust Ltd.)

more likely to have had accurate information than archaeologists with current interpretative models, who have been prevented from investigating the relevant parts of the building! After all, Albinus of Canterbury did inform Bede that his own church of St. Peter and St. Paul, outside the city walls, had been newly built by King Æthelberht. He had no evident motive to claim a false Roman origin for

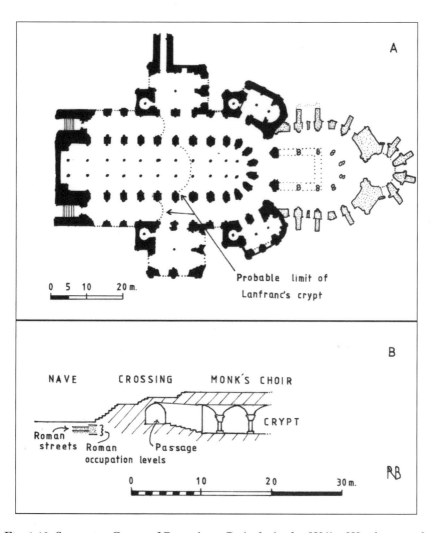

Fig. 1.10. Successive Crypts of Canterbury Cathedral, after Willis, Woodman, and Blockley. (A: Black shading represents the crypt of Archbishop Anselm and prior Ernulf [1093–1107]; the lighter shading the eastward extension beneath William the Englishman's Trinity Chapel of ca. 1180. Dotted lines represent the earlier eastward limit of Lanfranc's cathedral and the rectangular chapel at the east end of Anselm's crypt. B: Section showing the relation of the present floor levels of the cathedral's crypt, crossing, and nave to Roman occupation levels excavated beneath the nave. Note that the crypt passage shown here is the central passage into Lanfranc's crypt [rather than the aisle entrances of Anselm's crypt].)

Christ Church, if it too had been newly built. Our expectation must therefore be that Augustine did indeed recover a Roman church for his cathedral, and that at Christ Church we may one day have an example where the topography of Romano-British Christianity directly influenced that of the English church. Only excavation might be able to establish whether there had been true continuity of Christian cult there or merely the re-use of ruinous Roman buildings. There is no more important site in Britain for understanding our Christian roots and testing the validity of the interpretation of English history that Bede has left us.

Conclusion

The surveys of Eccles place-names and of urban church and cathedral sites attempted here has produced a surprisingly consistent picture, though one that could yet be radically changed by one or two major new excavations. The earliest Eccles-names in Kent and Norfolk raise the possibility of some early incorporation of communities of British Christians into the emerging settlement landscape. Likewise it is the eastern sites of Canterbury, Rochester, and perhaps Lincoln that seem to offer the best potential for continuous Christian cult from Roman times. (Sadly, coastal erosion in East Anglia has deprived us of evidence at *Dommuc*.) But in a huge tract of England from Yorkshire and the East Midlands to eastern Wessex pagan Anglo-Saxon settlement would seem to have caused an effective hiatus in Christian cult. There we find neither Eccles-names nor archaeological hints of Christian continuity. At most there was some limited Anglo-Saxon revival of Romanism among ruined sites. Only in western Northumbria, the West Midlands, and western Wessex do we encounter hints of an effective transition from British to Anglo-Saxon Christianity. Here Bede's determined silence is most unconvincing and his analysis of British neglect utterly unhelpful. We should recognize the ecclesiastical pressures that led to Bede's negative image of the Britons and the political influence in the same direction — an inheritance from the Northumbrians' bitter wars with Cadwallon of Gwynedd and from their suppression of British kingdoms in the north. If we are to avoid approaching the conversion of the Anglo-Saxons with unduly Bedan spectacles, we therefore need to allow for much greater regional differences within the territories that came to be "English." The definition and refinement of these variations should be the task of the next generation of archaeologists and historians.[46]

---

[46] See now John Blair, *The Church in Anglo-Saxon Society* (Oxford, 2005). In preparing this paper, I have been greatly assisted by guidance and critical advice from my colleagues Professor Christopher J. Wickham, Dr. Steven Bassett, and Dr. Simon Esmonde Cleary, and also from the late Patrick Wormald. They have helped me improve the argument, but are not responsible for the interpretation offered or for any mistakes committed.

High Style and Borrowed Finery: The Strood Mount, the Long Wittenham Stoup, and the Boss Hall Brooch as Complex Responses to Continental Visual Culture

Carol Neuman de Vegvar

Publications of the early 1990s on Southumbrian reception of continental visual culture required the reader to imagine a thought-world in which imitation or rejection of imported objects or art forms entailed a sort of all-or-nothing discourse of political connectivity.[1] In this context the possession and local imitation of imported objects came to be considered an index of cultural colonization, a measure of the degree to which the Anglo-Saxon elites who owned and displayed such objects felt themselves to be clients of a Frankish foreign power. Along with the richest jewelry from Kent, frequently referenced as imitating Frankish models, the mortuary assemblage in Mound 1 at Sutton Hoo loomed large in this discussion, although it has been subject to variable interpretation. In 1992 Martin

---

[1] The author thanks those who have helped her with this paper: Leslie Webster (British Museum) for her commentary at the 2003 ISAS conference on various aspects of the entire paper; Angela Evans (British Museum) for her advice on Anglo-Saxon garnet jewelry and kind assistance with obtaining an image of the Boss Hall brooch; Chris Scull (English Heritage) for access to and permission to cite a draft of his site report on the Boss Hall brooch and for sharing his insights on the brooch; Charles Little (Metropolitan Museum of Art) for his help with the Vermand material; Cynthia Cetlin and Jonathan Quick (both Ohio Wesleyan University) for their guidance on technical issues concerning cloisonné; Sally Dummer (Ipswich Museums), Richard Edgecume (Victoria and Albert Museum), Arthur MacGregor (Ashmolean Museum), and Todd Wilmot (Ryan Memorial Library, St. Charles Borromeo Seminary) for access to objects; Roger White (University of Birmingham) for permission to use the drawing of the Strood mount; and Niamh Whitfield (Morley College) for her help with museum contacts and, together with Adrian Whitfield, for their gracious hospitality. Any oversights or errors remaining are the responsibility of the author.

Carver read Mound 1 as displaying an East Anglian strategy of resistance to Frankish cultural and political influence by the adaptation of Scandinavian material culture, in opposition to Kentish capitulation to Frankish preeminence.[2] At almost the same time, in 1991, Ian Wood focused on different objects in the same assemblage, interpreting them as echoing and accepting Frankish cultural hegemony.[3] It is time to consider whether and how we should broaden and redefine these scenarios of an all-or-nothing relationship to Francia where the Kentish court is seen as a wholly owned subsidiary of the Merovingian realm, and Sutton Hoo's message as expressing acceptance of or resistance to the Kentish/Frankish axis of power. The assemblage in Mound 1 at Sutton Hoo reflects only the highest stratum of society, and in only one venue. The discussion may be enhanced by looking at examples of imported grave-goods from other sites in Southumbria, across a broader segment of the social spectrum and a wider chronological span; this paper is intended to suggest some directions for such inquiry. Taking Ian Hodder's understanding of the intentionality of artifacts as a methodological starting point, a more nuanced reading of some aspects of Anglo-Saxon visual culture may be possible, as indicating shifting and variable attitudes toward the continent over time. The evidence seems to suggest that continental connections, while of great importance in the development of Anglo-Saxon material culture, play out differently in different periods and circumstances; in other words, that receptivity is specific to more individualized contexts,[4] and that perceptions of colonialism, both by the Anglo-Saxons themselves and by modern interpreters of their age, are subjective and highly variable.

I begin with two finds from early Anglo-Saxon England that reflect connections to Francia, objects that may serve as an index of early links to mainland culture without having produced a discourse of identification through local imitation. The Long Wittenham stoup (London, British Museum) (fig. 2.1), and the Strood mount (National Museums and Galleries on Merseyside, Liverpool Museum, Mayer Collection) (fig. 2.2) started their careers in late Roman or Frankish Gaul probably as ecclesiastical vessels but were deposited in putatively secular graves in Anglo-Saxon England, where they were not otherwise locally copied or imitated.

---

[2] Martin Carver, "Ideology and Allegiance in East Anglia," in *Sutton Hoo: Fifty Years After*, ed. Robert T. Farrell and Carol Neuman de Vegvar (Oxford, OH, 1992), 173–82.

[3] Ian Wood, "The Franks and Sutton Hoo," in *People and Places in Northern Europe 500–1600: Essays in Honour of Peter Sawyer*, ed. idem and Niels Lund (Woodbridge, 1991), 1–14.

[4] Sam Lucy, *The Anglo-Saxon Way of Death: Burial Rites in Early England* (Stroud, 2000).

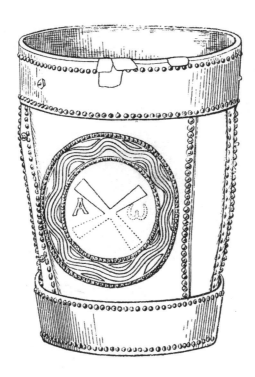

Fig. 2.1. Stoup from Grave 93, Long Wittenham (Berkshire) (British Museum). Drawing from Reginald Allender Smith, *British Museum Guide to Anglo-Saxon Antiquities* (London, 1923; repr. Ipswich, 1993), fig. 78. Above is a lateral view of the vessel; below, a planarized view of its additional three stamped plates: the Wedding at Cana; Christ Healing the Blind Man; Christ with Zaccheus in the Tree or the Agony in the Garden.

Fig. 2.2. Mount from drinking horn or cylindrical vessel, from Strood (Kent) (National Museums and Galleries on Merseyside, Liverpool Museum, Mayer Collection). Drawing from White, "Scrap or Substitute," fig. 11. The drawing shows a lateral view of the cylindrical mount (above) and a planarized view (below) showing the repeated stamped motif of enthroned individual flanked by standing figures, along with a diagram of the suspension ring and its mount. By permission.

C. Roach Smith, E. T. Leeds, and Vera Evison saw the Strood mount as ornamenting a cylindrical wooden vessel.[5] Evison saw its parallels mostly in Frankish caskets with pagan and later Christian scenes applied in metalwork to their exteriors. She cites as the closest parallel the casket with Christian scenes from the fourth-century cemetery at Vermand (Aisne).[6] Another strongly similar object is the tapered wooden vessel with Old and New Testament scenes in originally gilded copper alloy overlay, excavated in 1878 from Worms-Wiesoppenheim Grave 1 (Worms, Museum im Andreasstift), which was originally a cylindrical casket but has been restored as a beaker since excavation.[7] In contrast to Smith, Leeds, and Evison, George Baldwin Brown, T. D. Kendrick, and Roger White considered the Strood mount a drinking-horn fitting, in which case the closest structural parallels would be wide rim mounts such as that from grave H15 at Holywell Row, West Suffolk (Cambridge, Museum of Archaeology and Anthropology).[8] Christian motifs are not common on surviving horn fittings, but a cross with

[5] Charles Roach Smith, *Collectanea Antiqua,* vol. 2 (London, 1852), 159, pl. xxxvi; Edward Thurlow Leeds, *Early Anglo-Saxon Art and Archaeology* (Oxford, 1936), 14–15; Vera I. Evison, *The Fifth-Century Invasions South of the Thames* (London, 1965), 23. See also Jean M. Cook, *Early Anglo-Saxon Buckets: A Corpus of Copper Alloy- and Iron-bound, Stave-built Vessels* (Oxford, 2004), 69.

[6] On the Vermand box, see also George Baldwin Brown, *Saxon Art and Industry in the Pagan Period,* vol. 3 of *The Arts in Early England* (London, 1915), 116; Georges Chenet, "La tombe 319 et la buire chrétienne du cimetière mérovingien de Lavoye (Meuse)," *Préhistoire* 4 (1935): 34–116, here 101–4, fig. 31. The present location of this casket is unknown; Jules Pilloy, *Études sur d'anciens lieux de sépultures dans l'Aisne,* 2 (Saint-Quentin and Paris, 1895), 212, suggests that the metal plates with images that had originally covered the lost wood body of the casket remained in private hands after excavation. It was one of a cluster of seven similar small caskets with locks, probably jewel boxes, excavated from late antique cemeteries at Vermand and Abbeville.

[7] Brown, *Saxon Art,* 116; Alfried Wieczorek, "Pressblech eines Kästchens mit alt- und neutestamentlichen Szenen," in *Die Franken Wegbereiter Europas Vor 1500 Jahren: König Chlodwig und seine Erben,* ed. idem, Patrick Périn, Karin von Welck, and Wilfried Menghin (Mannheim and Mainz, 1996), 2: 930, no. 14.

[8] Brown, *Saxon Art,* 115–16; T. D. Kendrick, personal communication quoted in Chenet, "La tombe," 94; Roger H. White, "Scrap or Substitute: Roman Material in Anglo-Saxon Graves," in *Anglo-Saxon Cemeteries: A Reappraisal,* ed. Edmund Southworth (Stroud, 1990), 125–52, here 141; idem, *Roman and Celtic Objects from Anglo-Saxon Graves: A Catalogue and an Interpretation of their Use,* BAR Brit. Ser. 191 (Oxford, 1988), 121; Thomas Charles Lethbridge, *Recent Excavations in Anglo-Saxon Cemeteries in Cambridgeshire and Suffolk: A Report* (Cambridge, 1931), 12, no. 15, and fig. 141. John Yonge Akerman, "Report on Researches in an Anglo-Saxon Cemetery at Long Wittenham, Berkshire, in 1859," *Archaeologia* 38 (1860–1861): 327–52, here 350, was unsure whether the Strood mount was from a horn or from a box.

interlace design was mounted below a simple rim mount on a fragmentary drinking horn, probably from Ireland, found at Fasteraunet in Nord-Trondelag (Trondheim, Norges Teknisk-Naturvitenskapelige Universitet Vitenskapsmuseet).[9] The question of the local manufacture or importation of the vessel to which the Strood mount was attached must remain open, but if it ornamented a horn rather than a casket the parallels are entirely from Anglo-Saxon sites, as metal fittings for drinking horns have not been identified in Merovingian Francia.

The Strood mount was found in a solitary grave of Anglo-Saxon date adjacent to a Roman cemetery near the mouth of the Medway in Kent; the grave was a high-status inhumation with sword, shield boss, spear, and knife. Also found were a shield-on-tongue buckle and shoe-shaped rivets paralleling late fifth- or sixth-century Frankish types.[10] The copper alloy mount is embossed with a vine-scroll border at its base and stamped along the median of the strip with a repeated scene, probably Christian. The stamping is irregular and the clarity of the image blurred by pressure and abrasion, so that any reading of the image must be phrased in terms of possibilities rather than certainties. The image is centered on a frontally seated nimbed figure flanked by two smaller standing figures, also haloed. Above the figure at left is a cross; above the figure at right is a bird holding a ring-like object, possibly a wreath, in its beak. The central figure may be holding an infant across its lap. If so, the figure is probably an enthroned Virgin and Child paralleling those on the reliquary-coffin of St. Cuthbert (Durham, Library of the Dean and Chapter) and in the Book of Kells (Dublin, Trinity College Library MS. 58, fol. 7v).[11] If the "child" is instead to be read as a fold of drapery, then the image may represent Christ as teacher or an enthroned Christ flanked by saints.[12] This scene was evidently applied with a die, repeating eight

---

[9] Johannes Bøe, "An Ornamented Celtic Bronze Object, Found in a Norwegian Grave," *Bergens Museums Aarbok* 14 (1924–1925): 3–25 here 26, fig. 15; Jan Pedersen, *British Antiquities of the Viking Period, Found in Norway*, pt. 5 of *Viking Antiquities in Great Britain and Ireland*, ed. Haakon Shetelig (Oslo, 1940), 74, no. 103, and fig. 83; Egon Wamers, *Insularer Metallschmuck in Wikingerzeitlichen Gräbern Nordeuropas: Untersuchungen zur skandinavischen Westexpansion* (Neumünster, 1985), 116, list 4, no. 5. The mount was found in a ninth-century woman's grave.

[10] White, *Roman and Celtic Objects*, 121; Evison, *Fifth-Century Invasions*, 34. Evison suggests that some may be dated as early as 450–525.

[11] For the coffin-reliquary of St. Cuthbert, see Ernst Kitzinger, "The Coffin-Reliquary," in *The Relics of St. Cuthbert*, ed. C. F. Battiscombe (Oxford, 1956), pl. X; also J. M. Cronyn and C.V. Horie, *St. Cuthbert's Coffin: The History, Technology and Conservation* (Durham, 1985), 2, pl. 1. For the image of the Virgin and Child with Angels in the Book of Kells, see Carol Farr, *The Book of Kells, Its Function and Audience* (London and Toronto, 1997), 144–45, pl. V.

[12] Brown, *Saxon Art*, 116, identifies the figure as Christ as teacher.

times and crudely overlapping so that the lateral figure of one scene is sometimes overstamped on the opposing lateral figure of the next, and the column separating the imprints sometimes appears to be a tree supporting the bird or a staff or crozier held by the figure at right. The mount also has a suspension ring attached to it with a riveted strap loop.

Evison identified the Strood mount as from a late fourth-century production center in Northern France, earlier and closer to Roman work than the Long Wittenham stoup, while Georges Chenet dated it earlier based on parallels to Constantinian imagery.[13] However, any memories of classicizing artistic finesse the workshop tradition behind the manufacture of the die may have possessed are undercut both by the crudity with which the stamp has been applied to the metal strip and the rough workmanship of the strip's re-use: the strap mount for the suspension ring is riveted on directly over the central figure in one stamping, with one of the rivets partially through that figure's face. Whatever status the scene may have had when and wherever the die was made was not entirely preserved in the stamping process, and even less so in the re-use of this bit of copper alloy on the vessel on which it was found. This shift of attitude may result from the transition to secondary use on the Strood object which, whatever its intended function, was found in a secular grave, not in an ecclesiastical setting where the imagery would perhaps have retained more of its original iconographic *gravitas* and visual integrity, although an amuletic function for Christian imagery in this secondary and secular context cannot be ruled out. While Brown was undecided as to whether the occupant of the Strood grave was a pagan Anglo-Saxon who had acquired the object in Francia or a fallen raider from the continent, current scholarly consensus posits that grave-goods cannot be construed as indices of the religion and ethnicity of the occupants of graves.[14] However, the crudeness with which the strip is attached to the vessel suggests that this process of recycling happened in a venue where not only the meaning of the scenes was obscure but also the social value of the associations of this strip of metal was relatively low.

The Long Wittenham stoup was more clearly imported in its present form. The stoup was found in grave 93 of the Anglo-Saxon mixed-use cemetery at Long Wittenham, Berkshire, on the right bank of the Thames.[15] Grave 93 was the inhumation of a young boy, the whole grave 3 feet 8 inches long, with the body's head to the west, more strictly aligned than the other graves in the cemetery, where children are generally buried north-south. In addition to the stoup, the grave contained a copper alloy cauldron with triangular lugs, an iron knife,

[13] Evison, *Fifth-Century Invasions*, 34; Chenet, "La tombe," 92.

[14] Brown, *Saxon Art*, 116. For the issue of grave-goods and ethnicity, see Lucy, *The Anglo-Saxon Way of Death*, 173–78.

[15] Akerman, "Report," 331, 335, 345.

and a spear with its point toward the feet. Akerman considered the placement of the spear symptomatically Frankish, and Evison identified the triangular lugged cauldron as typical of those from the Namur region.[16] The stoup, a cylindrical wooden vessel about 15 centimeters in height and 10.5 centimeters in diameter, was constructed with hoops and staves as are Frankish nonfigural buckets and their Anglo-Saxon counterparts; four such buckets, probably local products, were found in other graves at Long Wittenham.[17] The stoup was covered on its exterior with four stamp-embossed copper alloy plates: three of these display respectively the Wedding at Cana, Christ Healing the Blind Man, and a scene which Georges Chenet identified as Christ with Zaccheus in the Tree but which may alternatively be read as the Agony in the Garden.[18] The fourth panel shows a christogram flanked by alpha and omega and surrounded by a nimbus or wreath. All four closely parallel the stamped bronze plates attached to the ewer from the early sixth-century Merovingian princely grave (grave 319) at Lavoye (Aisne) (fig. 2.3), a site on the Aire River near Bar-le-Duc, about a hundred miles to the south of the Namur region (Saint-Germain-en-Laye, Musée des Antiquités Nationales).[19] Even the beaded edging of scenes is similar, suggesting that both sets of plates are the product of the same workshop although not necessarily at the same moment. Evison hypothesized that the boy in grave 93 at Long Wittenham may have been "straight from the vicinity of Namur."[20] Ancestral or familial diplomatic ties to the Namur area are of course possible, although here as elsewhere the ethnicity of the deceased is indeterminable. However, the grave is not isolated but rather part of a large community cemetery of 127 graves, and the grave-goods, cauldron, bucket, spear, and knife are object types found in Anglo-Saxon prestige burials; whatever the boy's family connections, he was assimilated in death into the local social landscape. Here, as also at Strood and Lavoye, the secular assimilates the sacred, as vessels with Christian scenes are placed in secular graves. The Lavoye ewer and the Long Wittenham stoup may originally have had liturgical functions: the Lavoye ewer may have served as an aquamanile for liturgical hand-washing or a cruet for eucharistic wine, and the Long Wittenham stoup may have begun its career as a container for holy water, although I would not join Akerman in contending that it continued that role in the grave; its similarity to other Anglo-Saxon and continental buckets used as grave-goods suggests that the stoup shared the same

---

[16] Akerman, "Report," 351; Evison, *Fifth-Century Invasions*, 32.

[17] Graves 25, 26, 82, 91; Akerman, "Report," 339, 344, 345.

[18] Chenet, "La tombe," 87–89.

[19] Chenet, "La tombe," 91 and passim; René Joffroy, *Le Cimetière de Lavoye: Nécropole Mérovingienne* (Paris, 1974), 86, pl. 32; see also Alain Dierkens, "Die Taufe Chlodwigs," in *Die Franken Wegbereiter*, ed. Wieczorek, Périn, von Welck, and Menghin, 1: 189, Abb. 137.

[20] Evison, *Fifth-Century Invasions*, 32.

Fig. 2.3. Ewer from Grave 319, Lavoye (Aisne) (Saint-Germain-en-Laye, Musée des Antiquités Nationales) with stamped plates of biblical scenes. Photo: Réunion des Musées Nationaux / Art Resource, NY.

contextual function.[21] What has been imported is an object, whether individually or as part of an assemblage, but its role in burial practice merges it with regional custom, and perhaps only secondarily prestige by linkage to the original function and cultural milieu of the stoup. There is in this process of assimilation a sense that the meanings of such objects are fluid, and that an ornamented imported object may remain an index of social connections while changing its function and context. This would be even more the case for the Strood mount, particularly if it found its way to the grave as a rim mount for a drinking horn. Although the Strood mount and the Long Wittenham stoup are imports from Francia and the graves in which they are found demonstrate other affinities to the continent, there is no evidence that these isolated imports became models for local work, although northern Frankish buckets with nonfigural embossed arcade-and-dot ornament were imported and imitated in southern England in the same period as the Long Wittenham stoup.[22] The figural objects, both the stoup and the Strood mount, were placed in graves with assemblages otherwise reflecting local practice, where they may have served as markers of prestige if not necessarily religious affiliation, but their rarity indicates neither a substantial demand for imports nor any evidence of *imitatio Frankiae* in local patterns of production.

By contrast, in later Southumbrian metalwork, local smiths imitate with variable success what may have been perceived as imported techniques to create the effect of a high-prestige import in a local product. The composite disc brooches reflect a widespread and highly successful south Anglo-Saxon adaptation, initially and predominantly in Kent, of both an object type and a technique of ornamentation, garnet cloisonné, that were Frankish in immediate origin.[23] Here for the most part the garnets are inlaid on a flat surface and three-dimensional relief is achieved by layering of concentric flat levels, like a wedding cake.[24] Such planarity in design, typical of the vast majority of early medieval garnet cloisonné both on the continent and in Anglo-Saxon England, takes advantage of the tendency of some types of garnets to shear in flat planes or in shards that can be reduced to planar forms.[25] Mounting flat slivers of garnet on a domical or otherwise complexly or tightly curved surface not only is more difficult than their use in flat cloisonné

---

[21]Akerman, "Report," 336.

[22] Evison, *Fifth-Century Invasions*, 22.

[23] Helen Geake, *The Use of Grave-Goods in Conversion-Period England, c. 600–c. 850*, BAR Brit. Ser. 261 (Oxford, 1997), 120.

[24] Elizabeth Coatsworth and Michael Pinder, *The Art of the Anglo-Saxon Goldsmith: Fine Metalwork in Anglo-Saxon England: Its Practice and Practitioners* (Woodbridge, 2002), 174, fig. 27, an exploded diagram of the Kingston composite disc brooch.

[25] Mavis Bimson, "Dark-Age Garnet Cutting," *ASSAH* 4 (1985): 125–28; Birgit Arrhenius, *Merovingian Garnet Jewellery: Emergence and Social Implications* (Stockholm, 1985), 30–31; and Coatsworth and Pinder, *Art of the Anglo-Saxon Goldsmith*, 143–45.

but also requires a slightly but critically different range of techniques.[26] Among the Sutton Hoo finds, garnet cloisonné on a three-dimensional form is most easily achieved by applying the garnets to the flat surface of an inclined plane that is part of a geometric solid, as for example on the Sutton Hoo sword pyramids.[27] This process is technically identical to flat work. Sutton Hoo Mound 1, however, also contained examples of garnet cloisonné on surfaces that curve in one spatial dimension only, usually a section of a cylinder. Examples include the gently bowed plates of the Sutton Hoo shoulder clasps, the tongue-plate of the dummy buckle (fig. 2.4), and the concave lateral ridge planes of the Sutton Hoo sword pommel; these parallel continental garnetwork on curved surfaces.[28] On other objects or parts of objects from Sutton Hoo with more tightly curved cylindrical surfaces, such as on the hinge of the T-shaped mount or strap divider, the raised cylinders on the bar adjacent to the hinges of the purse lid, and the loop of the dummy buckle, tiny garnets in honeycomb cloisonné accommodate the curvature of the surface. Among Anglo-Saxon finds to date, this particularly fine honeycomb garnet cloisonné is found only on products of the Sutton Hoo workshop.[29]

---

[26] Professors Cynthia Cetlin and Jonathan Quick, Department of Fine Arts, Ohio Wesleyan University, personal communication.

[27] Rupert L. S. Bruce-Mitford, *The Sutton Hoo Ship-Burial* (London, 1978), 2: 300–2, 305–6, figs. 227–228, pls. 21a, 22e: pyramids from Mound 1; Martin Carver, *Sutton Hoo: Burial Ground of Kings?* (London, 1998), pl. VI: pyramids from Mound 17. These are paralleled on the continent both in visual aspect and in hollow construction by Frankish polyhedral earrings: example include those from the Frankish woman's grave under Cologne Cathedral (see Michael Müller-Wille, "Königtum und Adel im Spiegel der Grabfunde," in *Die Franken Wegbereiter*, ed. Wieczorek, Périn, von Welck, and Menghin, 1: 206–21, Abb. 153); from the Merovingian cemetery at Trivières (Hainaut), Tr. 290 (Morlanwelz, Musée royale de Mariemont); see also Patrick Périn, "Aspects of Late Merovingian Costume in the Morgan Collection," in *From Attila to Charlemagne; Arts of the Early Medieval Period in the Metropolitan Museum of Art*, ed. Katharine Reynolds Brown, Dafydd Kidd, and Charles T. Little (New York, 2000), 242–67, here 244. On a larger scale, the sword-belt buckle from Sutton Hoo Mound 17 (British Museum) shows garnet cloisonné on several different inclined planes: see Carver, *Burial*, pl. VI. The author thanks Angela Evans for bringing this buckle to her attention.

[28] Bruce-Mitford, *Sutton Hoo*, vol. 2: shoulder clasps: 523–35, figs. 386, 392, pl. 15; sword pommel: 288–92, 303–4, figs. 220, 433d; dummy buckle: 473–81, figs. 341–342, 346. Bruce-Mitford (304) suggests that the sword pommel garnetwork is distinct from the rest of the Sutton Hoo pieces and "compatible both with an earlier date and with origins outside East Anglia." His juxtaposition of the pommel from Hög Edsten, Bohuslän, Sweden (fig. 230) implies that he may have considered the pommel a possible import; see also fig. 95 (pommel from Vallstenarum, Gotland, now Gustavianum, Uppsala). For other continental parallels, see text below.

[29] Bruce-Mitford, *Sutton Hoo*, vol. 2: T-shaped mount (strap distributor): 468–69, fig. 335b; purse lid bar cylinders: figs. 361c, 362a.

Fig. 2.4. Dummy buckle from Mound 1, Sutton Hoo (Suffolk), detail of dummy tongue-plate and loop (British Museum) showing application of garnet cloisonné on curved surfaces. Photo: © Copyright The Trustees of The British Museum.

One technique of garnet cloisonné rarely found on a large scale in England is the application of garnets to a complexly curved surface such as a dome, that is, to a surface that curves in multiple directions simultaneously. Domical cloisonné in England is usually restricted to the tiny scale of bosses used to ornament larger objects. Perhaps the finest of these are the Sutton Hoo scabbard bosses (fig. 2.5), where step-cut garnets and their foil backings are floated in deep hollow settings which extend all the way through the thickness of the dome to the base plate; here the pressure of the cloison cell walls is sufficient to hold the garnets in place without cement.[30] The same technique was used for the large boss mounted on the Sutton Hoo dummy buckle, although the cloison design there is simpler.[31] A cloisonné boss using step-cut stones is also used as the centerpiece of the Kingston composite disc brooch (National Museums and Galleries on Merseyside, Liverpool Museum) (fig. 2.6).[32] Other disc brooches, such as the plated brooch from King's Field, Faversham (British Museum) and the Sarre II composite brooch, called the Amherst Brooch (Oxford, Ashmolean Museum), avoid this level of ambition, as does the buckle from Taplow (Bucks) (British Museum), by opting for less challenging designs for their central bosses with larger and more simply cut stones.[33] Other composite disc brooches have center bosses of carved white shell, sometimes surmounted by a single flat or cabochon garnet; in the later brooches with copper alloy cloisons the shell is held in place by a cage of reeded flat metal strips which Michael Pinder has termed "crown arches."[34]

Applying flat garnets in cloisons over any three-dimensionally curved surface raises technical issues that would be exacerbated not only by the complex curvature of a dome, as opposed to the unidirectional slope of a cylinder, but also by larger scale where these inherent problems would be more apparent to the viewer. The use of cement in the application of the stones, common in Anglo-Saxon and continental cloisonné in this period, could have filled any gaps between the

---

[30] Bruce-Mitford, *Sutton Hoo*, vol. 2, 294–97, 304–5, figs. 222–223, pl. 21c.

[31] See note 28.

[32] Cathy Haith, "32 (a–c) Grave group (selection); Kingston Down, Kent, grave 205," in *The Making of England: Anglo-Saxon Art and Culture A.D. 600–900*, ed. Leslie Webster and Janet Backhouse (London, 1991), 50–51; Ronald Jessup, *Anglo-Saxon Jewellery* (Aylesbury, 1974), 72–75, no. 20.

[33] Richard Avent, *Anglo-Saxon Garnet Inlaid Disc and Composite Brooches*, BAR Brit. Ser. 2 (Oxford, 1975), King's Field, Faversham: 37, no. 147, pl. 50; Sarre II/Amherst: 47, no. 178, pl. 67; and see also Jessup, *Anglo-Saxon Jewellery*: King's Field, Faversham: 68–69, pl. 16.2; Amherst: Jessup, *Anglo-Saxon Jewellery*, 70–72, pl. 18; Taplow buckle: 84–85, pl. 25.1

[34] Coatsworth and Pinder, *Art of the Anglo-Saxon Goldsmith*, 149; Michael Pinder, "Anglo-Saxon Garnet Cloisonné Composite Disc Brooches: Some Aspects of Their Construction," *Journal of the British Archaeological Association* 148 (1995): 6–28, here 11.

Fig. 2.5. Scabbard bosses from Mound 1, Sutton Hoo (Suffolk) (British Museum), showing an unusually elaborate variation of garnet cloisonné construction on a domical boss. Photo: © Copyright The Trustees of The British Museum.

underside of a flat stone and its bedding and helped it adhere to a curved surface. But on a domical surface, the flatness of individual slabs of garnet would have created a faceting effect which would have countered the curvature of the object itself unless the garnets were kept quite small and juxtaposed in a pattern designed to minimize the angularity of the junctions between stones. Brigit Arrhenius posited that many of the garnets applied to jewelry in early medieval western Europe were probably cut to standardized templet shapes in a few specialty workshops, and that in the sixth century some garnets were imported precut into England, most probably from Francia, in a range of shapes to suit local demand.[35] However, by the seventh century, garnetwork production had

---

[35] Arrhenius, *Merovingian Garnet Jewellery*, 98.

Fig. 2.6. Composite disc brooch from grave 205, Kingston Down (Kent) (National Museums and Galleries on Merseyside, Liverpool Museum). The garnet cloisonné here is domical only in the central boss, and planar elsewhere. Photo: National Museums Liverpool.

dropped off on the continent and high-level garnet cloisonné production centers in Kent and at the workshop that produced the personal ornaments in Sutton Hoo Mound 1 probably had in-house specialists who cut garnets to order in the requisite range of shapes.[36] In these circumstances an Anglo-Saxon goldsmith wishing to apply garnets to a complexly curved surface would have had three

---

[36] Bimson, "Dark-Age Garnet Cutting," 127; Pinder, "Anglo-Saxon Brooches," 8.

choices. If his level of proficiency at cloisonné processes was high enough and his shop included a lapidary with the necessary garnet-cutting skills he could attempt an innovative solution using specially cut stones, as did the artisans who produced the Sutton Hoo and Kingston Down bosses. Alternatively, a smith attempting a domical design, or his patron, could try to obtain garnets in small rounded shapes that might be easier to apply to a domed surface, but these might be difficult to procure in a market where most template gem cutting was probably oriented to flat cloisonné using particularly favored shapes of garnets.[37] As garnet cloisonné production gradually went out of style toward the middle of the seventh century, this market probably declined and finally disappeared, reducing and ultimately eliminating the option of using ready-cut stones. The final option would be to assemble a sufficient number of stones, possibly as provided by the patron in the form of old jewelry or available in the craftsman's own repository of scraps left over from repair jobs, and cut these down to appropriate shapes and to a small enough scale not to conflict with the curvature of the object surface.[38] Garnet cutting is a skilled craft and not intuitive, so such an attempt at on-the-job training to reshape stones would be both costly and wasteful.[39] Further, to achieve a truly smooth effect on a curved or domical surface, the surface of the finished cloisonné would require skilled grinding and polishing after the stones were placed in the cells.[40] So the transition in cloisonné from flat to domical surfaces is neither easy nor obvious from the craftsman's viewpoint, especially not if previous experience were limited to seeing a finished example of domical cloisonné, or even more so, hearing the effect described by a patron who had seen an example and wanted something similar.

One Anglo-Saxon example that makes a brave attempt at this difficult transition is the composite brooch from grave 93 at Boss Hall, on the western edge of Ipswich in Suffolk (Ipswich Co-operative Society, Ipswich Museums) (fig. 2.7).[41] The brooch was found in a high-echelon woman's grave dating at earliest

---

[37] Bimson, "Dark-Age Garnet Cutting," 127; "the spread of standard shapes such as the early heart-shaped garnets suggests central manufacture."

[38] Coatsworth and Pinder, *Art of the Anglo-Saxon Goldsmith*, 147.

[39] Bimson, "Dark-Age Garnet Cutting," 127: "At the other end of the spectrum we find the reshaping of broken garnets by the most crude chipping techniques without any attempt to straighten or repolish the edges, which can only have been carried out by craftsmen who had no knowledge of gem cutting."

[40] Coatsworth and Pinder, *Art of the Anglo-Saxon Goldsmith*, 148 note evidence of such finishing on the pendant from Old Westgate Farm, Canterbury, Kent (Canterbury City Museums) and the cross from Burton Pidsea, Holderness, Humberside (Oxford, Ashmolean Museum).

[41] Pinder, "Anglo-Saxon Brooches," 21.

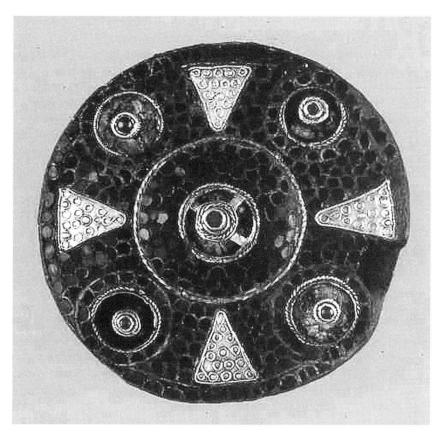

Fig. 2.7. Composite disc brooch from grave 93, Boss Hall, Ipswich (Suffolk) (Ipswich Cooperative Society, Ipswich Museums). Photo: Niamh Whitfield, by permission.

to the late seventh century, significantly later than the other graves in the cemetery.[42] The brooch was probably deposited in a leather pouch at the woman's neck, along with four circular gold pendants with central settings of garnet or red glass imitating garnet, one irregular cabochon garnet pendant, and one oval pendant of red glass, a regal solidus of Sigebert III (634–656) mounted as a pendant, a Primary Series B sceat dated ca. 690, several glass beads and silver biconical

---

[42] Christopher Scull and Alex Bayliss, "Radiocarbon Dating and Anglo-Saxon Graves," in *Völker an Nord- und Ostsee und die Franken: Akten des 48. Sachsensymposiums in Mannheim vom 7. bis 11. September 1997*, ed. Uta von Freeden, Ursula Koch, and Alfried Wieczorek (Bonn, 1999), 39–50, here 48.

spacers, and a silver cosmetic set.[43] The grave has been dated on the evidence of the sceat to the last decade of the seventh century.[44]

The Boss Hall composite brooch, seven centimeters in diameter, was clearly a high-prestige object, as indicated by the garnet cloisons applied not only to almost the entire front of the brooch but also to the pinhead on the back. Among the composite disc brooches such hidden ornamentation, for the delectation of the wearer alone, is shared only by the Kingston brooch, the most lavish brooch in the entire series.[45] The Boss Hall brooch does share with many of the other major composite brooches a typical cruciform layout of a central boss surrounded by four secondary bosses; between the secondary bosses triangular gold fields filled with filigree loops also form a bright cross against the darker field of garnets. Angela Evans has noted that the cross motif on the Boss Hall brooch is expressed with sufficient care to serve as a marker of religious identity; Leslie Webster has emphasized the subtlety with which the cross motif is integrated into the layout of the brooch as a whole and the prestige that such sophistication of design and structuring of meaning may have implied.[46]

The Boss Hall brooch was not new at burial but shows signs of wear and repair; one or more owners of this brooch wore and displayed it rather than keeping it concealed and safe in storage, despite its final burial in a leather bag. One of the secondary bosses is a replacement. The central boss was originally divided by four crown arches, of which one was lost and replaced in silver before burial. The rim consists of a coarsely-reeded strip of very thin metal; where most such reeded rims are striated on the front and flat on the back and can be up to 11 millimeters wide, the Boss Hall rim is narrower than usual and corrugated, with the back as the negative of the front, and was patched, possibly to cover a tear.[47] The extent and variety of repairs to the brooch suggests that it may be significantly earlier than the grave in which it was deposited, and that it may have been an heirloom, worn by more than one generation before deposition.

The Boss Hall composite brooch has been dated close to, if not at the end of, the sequence of Anglo-Saxon composite disc brooches. The use here of small

---

[43] Angela C. Evans, "33 (a–i): Grave group, Grave 93, Boss Hall cemetery, Ipswich, Suffolk," in *Making of England*, ed. Webster and Backhouse, 51–53, here 52. Evans notes that silver cosmetic sets are found in a number of high-end women's graves in Kent such as Kingston Down graves 7 and 142; Anglian examples are less common but do occur, as in grave 39 at Garton Station, East Yorkshire.

[44] Scull and Bayliss, "Radiocarbon Dating," 48.

[45] Haith, "32 (a–c)," 50.

[46] Evans, "33 (a–e)," 52–53; Leslie Webster, "Encrypted Visions: Style and Sense in the Anglo-Saxon Minor Arts, A.D. 400-900," in *Anglo-Saxon Styles*, ed. Catherine E. Karkov and George Hardin Brown (Albany, 2003), 11–30, here 17.

[47] Coatsworth and Pinder, *Art of the Anglo-Saxon Goldsmith*, 118, 124, 243.

garnets in copper alloy cloisons forming simple cells over broader areas of the face of the brooch is symptomatic of late date in composite brooches.[48] The other brooches usually positioned late in the series are the two from North Field, Milton, Abingdon, Oxfordshire (Oxford, Ashmolean Museum; and London, Victoria and Albert Museum); the two from Faversham, Kent (Ashmolean; and Cambridge, Fitzwilliam Museum); the brooch from Monkton, Kent (Ashmolean) (fig. 2.8);

Fig. 2.8. Composite disc brooch from Monkton (Kent) (Oxford, Ashmolean Museum of Art and Archaeology). Photo: Ashmolean Museum, Oxford.

[48] Chris Scull, *Anglo-Saxon Cemeteries at Boss Hall and Buttermarket, Ipswich*, Society for Medieval Archaeology Monograph, forthcoming.

and the lost composite brooch from Huggin's Fields, Milton Regis, Kent.[49] The layout of the Boss Hall brooch, with the arms of the cross indicated by triangular areas of filigree on gold ground between wider areas of garnetwork, echoes but inverts the layout of the Milton Regis and Monkton brooches, where the cross arms are triangles of garnetwork between areas of filigree, and the Milton North Field brooches where the cross arms are rectangular strips of garnetwork.[50] On the Boss Hall brooch as on the Milton/Ashmolean, Faversham, Milton Regis, and Monkton examples, the surrounds of the secondary bosses invade the outer garnetwork border.[51] These commonalities suggest that the maker of the Boss Hall brooch was not unfamiliar with the designs of other brooches of this type.

Christopher Scull has pointed out that the range of gold fineness in the various components of the Boss Hall brooch may reflect a late date of production, reflecting the generally declining availability of high-quality gold in England toward the middle of the seventh century.[52] Although he acknowledges that the complexities of dating ornamental metalwork on the basis of gold fineness should not be underestimated, Scull's consideration of range rather than any specific upper- or lower-end fineness as a date indicator has considerable merit.[53] To this reading might be added the sense that the presence of such a range of fineness

---

[49] Avent, *Anglo-Saxon Brooches*: 49, no. 182: Milton North Field, Abingdon (Oxford, Ashmolean Museum); 49, no. 183: Milton North Field, Abingdon (London, Victoria and Albert Museum); 44, no. 170: Faversham, Kent: (Ashmolean); 48–49, no. 181: Faversham, Kent (Cambridge, Fitzwilliam Museum); 43, no. 172: Monkton, Kent (Ashmolean); 44, no. 171: Huggin's Fields, Milton Regis, Kent, called the Vallance Brooch (formerly Dover Museum, stolen 1967). To these should be added the composite disc brooch excavated by the AOC Archaeological Group in August 2000 in Floral Street, London and now on exhibit at the Museum of London (made available by National Farmers Union Mutual, the Royal Ballet School, and Salmon Developments PLC). This brooch was found in a woman's grave, like the Boss Hall brooch enclosed in a bag or container on the chest along with other jewelry, in this case beads and rings.

[50] The Floral Street composite disc brooch likewise has triangular cross-arms of garnetwork. Tania Dickinson's observation ("Material Culture as Social Expression: The Case of Saxon Saucer Brooches with Running Spiral Decoration," *Studien zur Sachsenforschung* 7 [1991]: 39–70) that the design of saucer brooches with cast and applied spiral decoration follow "rules" that are flexible enough to encourage creativity seems to apply to these late composite disc brooches as well.

[51] Sonia Chadwick Hawkes, "The Monkton Brooch," *Antiquaries Journal* 54 (1974): 244–56, here 252–53.

[52] Scull, *Anglo-Saxon Cemeteries*.

[53] Sonia Chadwick Hawkes, J. M. Merrick, and D. M. Metcalf, "X-Ray Fluorescent Analysis of Some Dark Age Coins and Jewellery," *Archaeometry* 9 (1966): 98–138, here 120; P. D. C. Brown and F. Schweizer, "X-Ray Fluorescent Analysis of Anglo Saxon Jewellery," *Archaeometry* 15 (1973): 175–92, here 181–83; Geake, *Use of Grave-Goods*, 10.

in different parts of the brooch indicates recycling in an environment of scarcity, with fragments of metalwork either from the craftsman's collection of scraps or provided by the patron in the form of old jewelry being reused for different components of the new piece. Such frugality in the application of resources of fine metal is also seen in the Monkton brooch, where the back plate shows compass marks and rivet holes that suggest that it was cut down and reused from an earlier and significantly larger piece.[54] The recycling of materials also places the Boss Hall brooch later rather than earlier in the date range of the composite disc brooches, as gold became progressively less available for jewelry production in England from the earlier to the later seventh century.[55]

In other aspects, however, the Boss Hall brooch distinguishes itself from the rest of the brooches in this group. The rough edges of the garnets suggest that they, like the gold, have been recycled, cut down by someone unfamiliar with fine stone-cutting. They are crudely cut in very small approximately semicircular shapes; their edges are rough and chipped like glass cut with grozing shears. This is not the case for all the late composite brooches; although the stones of the Milton North Field and Monkton brooches are small, they are cleanly cut and neatly applied to the brooch surfaces as part of harmonious and restrained designs.[56] By contrast, the Boss Hall brooch lacks the finesse of design and craftsmanship of the other late disc brooches. Nonetheless, the Boss Hall brooch impresses initially by its darkly glittering opulence and by the sheer number of tiny garnets overlaying almost its entire surface. The intention seems to be to create a hybrid of two earlier traditions of metalsmithing: the Anglo-Saxon composite disc brooches, which as a series have their origin and core in Kent, and the all-over garnetwork found in the high-end jewelry from Sutton Hoo and elsewhere in East Anglia, an encounter perhaps facilitated by the possible extension outside Kent of composite disc brooch production in its last phases. The Boss Hall brooch is poised between these two traditions and participates fully in neither; it is a hybrid, and as traditions go a nonstarter. Ambitious intention is not matched here by skill, a discrepancy that Evans has attributed to a late workshop faltering in its ability to recapitulate the past.[57] However, perhaps the lack of finesse here is due not to a workshop in decline, but to a smith attempting the unfamiliar. The Boss Hall brooch attempts not only to harmonize two mutually distinct regional traditions but to combine them with an anomalous third design element: this brooch is unique among known examples of Anglo-Saxon smithcraft in its

[54] Hawkes, "Monkton," 248 and fig. 2.

[55] Hawkes, Merrick, and Metcalf, "X-Ray Analysis," 101, 117.

[56] Hawkes, "Monkton," 251: the Monkton brooch may also show some reuse of stones but without the rough reshaping seen at Boss Hall.

[57] Evans, "33 (a–e)," 53. Scull, *Anglo-Saxon Cemeteries*, suggests a date at the end of the composite brooch series, ca. 640–660, probably after 650.

application of garnet cloisonné to a domical surface larger than a decorative boss, on the comparably large scale of a composite disc brooch. What is the associative freight of this third element? Why perhaps has the patron requested that a smith undertake the attempt to incorporate it along with two regional traditions of high-status jewelry into one highly challenging and impressive piece, even at the risk of exceeding the craftsman's range of skills?

At first glance the parallelisms to the Kentish composite brooches and to the Sutton Hoo garnetwork suggest that the patron of the Boss Hall brooch sought status by displaying an object with links to the premier Anglo-Saxon centers of the early seventh century, Kent and East Anglia, although at some degree of chronological and geographical remove, where an actual piece from one of those venues was not available. In the initial site report, John Newman proposed that the grave reflects a second rank of nobility in East Anglia, outside the immediate milieu of the court that had given rise to the Sutton Hoo jewelry.[58] However, Bede and other historical sources for the period provide only the vaguest sense of the stratification of the ruling class in seventh-century East Anglia, let alone what levels of display were considered appropriate to each stratum. Since no sumptuary laws are known for this environment such as are preserved for later medieval and Renaissance contexts, it is impossible to know what would have been considered appropriate for the secondary and provincial rank of nobles Newman suggests, were it possible to be certain that such a group was clearly defined at the time. Scull more plausibly suggests a milieu of patronage by a social stratum equivalent to but later than the Sutton Hoo court, equally interested in the display of identity and prestige but separated by time rather than distance from that wellspring of innovation and inspiration in smithcraft.[59] But the decision to produce and display a brooch with garnets overlying a domical surface suggests a broader range of contacts and sources.

One possible source of inspiration is Merovingian Francia. The Boss Hall brooch is unique among the Anglo-Saxon composite disc brooches in that the garnet surround of the central boss is raised into a dome rather than lying flat as is the case for the other surviving examples.[60] The domed area supporting the central boss was made separately and let into a socket, indicating that this area required particular attention in the production process.[61] In this the Boss Hall

---

[58] John Newman, "The Anglo-Saxon Cemetery at Boss Hall, Ipswich," *Sutton Hoo Research Committee Bulletin* 8 (1993): 32–36, repr. in Martin O. H. Carver, ed., *Sutton Hoo Research Committee Bulletins 1983–1993* (Woodbridge, 1993), 35.

[59] Scull, *Anglo-Saxon Cemeteries.*

[60] The Kingston brooch has a domical surround, but it is made up of white shell rather than cloisonné.

[61] Pinder, "Anglo-Saxon Brooches," 21.

brooch parallels a category of Merovingian filigree disc brooches (Thieme Type 1.2) where the dome is ornamented with wire filigree and sometimes with individual garnets in triangular or round cloisons, but these are not tightly juxtaposed into a continuous field of garnet cloisonné as on the Boss Hall brooch.[62] In Francia, parallels can also be found for continuous-field garnet cloisonné applied to spatially curved surfaces, particularly to cylinders or other shapes curved spatially in one dimension, in the ornamentation of high-status ecclesiastical objects. The surface of the lost Eligius Chalice, made for Chelles in the early seventh century, was divided vertically into sections covered with honeycombed garnet cloisonné; as suggested by the modeling of the left side of the cup in André du Saussay's 1793 drawing (fig. 2.9), these sections were possibly hemicylinders rather than flat facets.[63] Similarly, the Theuderigus reliquary (St. Maurice d'Agaune, Valais, Treasury) has garnet cloisonné on its cylindrical ridge pole, although here the garnets are almost random in shape.[64] The Franks applied many of the same ornamental techniques to secular metalwork as to ecclesiastical objects, but garnet cloisonné on Frankish secular objects is usually applied to a flat or simply sloped or broadly curved plane.[65] So although garnets are applied

---

[62] Périn, "Aspects of Late Merovingian Costume," 246–47; figs. 21.15–21.17, 21.20–21.22; Bettina Thieme, "Filigranscheibenfibeln der Merowingerzeit aus Deutschland," *Bericht der Römisch-Germanischen Kommission* 59 (1978): 381–500, here 415–17 and pl. 3–5; Müller-Wille, "Königtum," 215, Abb. 153. A similar design is seen in the saddle mounts from Krefeld-Gellep Grave 1782 (Krefeld, Museum Burg Linn); Karin von Welck and Alfried Wieczorek, "Die Ausbreitung der fränkischen Herrschaft in den Rheinlanden," in *Die Franken Wegbereiter*, ed. Wieczorek, Périn, von Welck, and Menghin, 2: 892–902, at 900, no. 8.ii.

[63] Helmut Roth, "Kunst der Merowingerzeit," in *Die Franken Wegbereiter*, ed. Wieczorek, Périn, von Welck, and Menghin, 2: 629–39, here 631, Abb. 496. André du Saussay, *Panoplia sacerdotalis: seu de venerando sacerdotum habitu: forumque multiplici munere ac officio in ecclesia libri XIV* (Paris, 1653), plate opposite p. 200: "Calix S. Eligii." This engraving was produced before the cup was melted down along with other antiquities in the eighteenth century by order of the Revolutionary Committee's Art Commission. Eligius, to whom the cup is traditionally ascribed, was born in 586; Audoin describes his work for the courts of Chlothar II (584–629) and Dagobert I (coregent from 622–623) (Roth, "Kunst," 631). Peter Lasko, *The Kingdom of the Franks: North-West Europe Before Charlemagne* (London and New York, 1971), 93, expresses doubt that this cup served as a chalice.

[64] Roth, "Kunst," 632, Abb. 498. This silver chasse is entirely covered with garnets and other materials inlaid in gold cloisons.

[65] Roth "Kunst," 632, stresses the merger of techniques from personal ornament with an ecclesiastical material culture of Roman origin, along with the uniformity of art in the Merovingian world, with half-free craftsmen working for the courts. Examples of Frankish garnet cloisonné over a surface curved or sloped in one spatial dimension include the fifth-century scabbard mounts of the *spatha* (two-edged sword) of Childeric,

Fig. 2.9. André du Saussay, *Panoplia sacerdotalis: seu de venerando sacerdotum habitu: fo-rumque multiplici munere ac officio in ecclesia libri XIV* (Paris, 1653), plate opposite p. 200: "Calix S. Eligii." The shading of the vertical cloisonné sections indicates that they are hemicylindrical rather than planar. Photo: Vincent Massa, Kelly & Massa Photography, Lester, PA, by permission of Ryan Memorial Library, St. Charles Borromeo Seminary, Wynnewood, PA.

to cylinders in Frankish ecclesiastical metalwork, there are no extant examples of Frankish domical continuous cloisonné to parallel the Boss Hall brooch. Truly domical garnet cloisonné on a scale analogous to the Boss Hall brooch is found only much further afield, as on the eagle fibulae from the Domagnano Treasure, part of a woman's jewelry assemblage of about 500 from Ostrogothic Italy.[66] Here however the smith has artfully assembled rhomboidal, triangular, and other geometric shapes rather than rounded forms to cover domical bosses, a larger version of the solution used in the Sutton Hoo scabbard bosses. Rounded shapes in domical garnet cloisonné, as on the Boss Hall brooch, are found on the bird-shaped saddle mounts from Apahida II, a fifth-century Gepid chieftain's grave near Cluj in Rumania (Bucharest, Muzeul National de Istorie a Romaniei) (fig. 2.10).[67] Here semicircular cloisons simulate feathers on the domical torsos. Birgit Arrhenius has pointed out that such feather- or scale-like inlays are ultimately based on Egyptian and Sumerian enamelwork designs, and that when garnets

discovered at Tournai in 1653, destroyed in 1831 but known through the seventeenth-century colored drawings in Jean Jacques Chiflet, *Anastasis Childerici I. Francorum regis sive thesaurus sepulchralis Tornaci Neruiorum essossus et commentario illustratus* (Antwerp, 1655), 204; see Ursula Koch, Karin von Welck, and Alfried Wieczorek, "Das Grab des Frankenkönigs Childerich I," in *Die Franken Wegbereiter*, ed. Wieczorek, Périn, von Welck, and Menghin, 2: 879–84, here 881–83; also bow fibulae from the aristocratic woman's tomb under Cologne Cathedral (Müller-Wille, "Königtum," 217, Abb. 154). A rare example of Frankish domical garnet cloisonné is found in a pinhead .9 cm in diameter from Grave 9 at Niedenstein-Kirchberg (Schwalm-Eder-Kreis) (Kassel, Hessisches Landesmuseum): see Ursula Koch, Karin von Welck, and Alfried Wieczorek, "Die fränkische Expansion in rechtrheinische Gebiete," in *Die Franken Wegbereiter*, 2: 902–21, here 918, no. 24.b.

[66] Wilfried Menghin, "The Domagnano Treasure," in *From Attila to Charlemagne*, ed. Brown, Kidd, and Little, 132–39, figs. 12.2, 12.4. These late fifth- to early sixth-century Ostrogothic eagle fibulae, 12 cm. in length with domical central bosses, were found in 1893 at Domagnano in San Marino. One fibula has been in the Germanisches Nationalmuseum, Nuremberg, since 1898; the other is in a private collection in New York. These fibulae were part of a woman's jewelry set; although eagle brooches are widely found in Gothic graves in Italy, France, and Spain, they are rarely part of women's assemblages. Raised central bosses covered with garnet cloisonné are not uncommon among the eagle fibulae; the Domagnano examples are, however, significantly larger than most eagle fibulae and their central bosses are comparable in scale to the domical center of the Boss Hall brooch.

[67] Kurt Horedt and Dumitru Protase, "Das zweite Fürstengrab von Apahida (Siebenbürgen)," *Germania* 50 (1972): 174–220; Rodica Marghitu, "4.8 Männergrab II von Apahida, Bez. Cluj/Klausenburg, Siebenbürgen/Transylvanien, Rumänien," in *Das Gold der Barbarenfürsten: Schätze aus Prunkgräbern der 5. Jahrhunderts n. Chr. zwischen Kaukasus und Gallien*, ed. Alfried Wieczorek and Patrick Périn (Stuttgart, 2001), 147–55.

Fig. 2.10. Pair of bird-shaped saddle mounts from Apahida II (Cluj) (Bucharest, National Museum). The torsos of the birds are domical; the heads, wings and legs are flat. Photo: Muzeul National de Istorie a Romaniei (Romanian National History Museum).

are applied in this way they are generally cut by hand, rather than by wheel as are the geometric and step-cut examples.[68]

---

[68] Arrhenius, *Merovingian Garnet Jewellery*, 58. This approach is very widespread in Egyptian Middle and New Kingdom ornamental metalwork, notably on pectorals where it is used to simulate the textures of the wings of birds and scarabs and the manes of griffins and apes, and as a decorative motif in its own right. For examples of the use of this technique for applying inlay over a domical surface, see Alix Wilkinson, *Ancient Egyptian Jewellery* (London, 1971), pls. XXVIIA, L, LIVA, LVIA. Fig. 53 shows this technique applied to the hoop of an earring, a portable medium without the culture-specific religious imagery of the pectorals that may have provided a conduit for this technique to extend beyond Egypt.

By the middle decades of the seventh century, imported examples of such scale inlay were probably available in England via the continental connections of the church and the courts, as is evident from the application of the same technique to the tongue shield of the mid-seventh century silver buckle from Crundale, Kent (London, British Museum).[69] That mid-seventh-century Anglo-Saxon metalsmiths were looking to a wider range of models for garnet cloisonné designs may also be seen on the Monkton brooch. Here Sonia Hawkes noted that the design of alternating triangles used for the outer border is rare in the Anglo-Saxon context and suggested that this design, first introduced to central Europe by the Huns, may have come into England from Visigothic Spain.[70] While the earlier Kentish composite disc brooches clearly borrow from Frankish garnetwork designs, the Monkton and Boss Hall brooches may look to a far broader geographic range for their models.

Helen Geake's work on Anglo-Saxon grave-goods of the conversion period has pointed up the extent to which grave-goods deposited in Anglo-Saxon England after 600 demonstrate a shift of interest in material culture increasingly toward the heartland of the Roman Empire, including the Byzantine east. She proposes that this shift be understood as concomitant initially with the development of kingship and later with the conversion of the Anglo-Saxons and the identification of the church with Rome and its Mediterranean empire. This incorporates both a renascence of associations with the Roman past and the development of strong trade connections to the contemporary Byzantine world, connections that appear to be direct rather than channeled through the Frankish Empire, which was influential for the majority of the population primarily in Kent, although elsewhere the highest echelons of society maintained and displayed their Frankish connections as well.[71] A case in point is the range of finds in the recently excavated princely chamber tomb at Prittlewell (Essex) where two Frankish tremisses were found along with two "Coptic" vessels, a lidded flagon ornamented at the neck with a medallion showing a riding saint or emperor and a bronze bowl, both from the Byzantine world, and a folding stool possibly from either Lombard Italy or Asia Minor.[72] The Boss Hall brooch may demonstrate

---

[69] Cathy Haith, "6 Buckle, Crundale, Kent," in *Making of England*, ed. Webster and Backhouse, 24; and Bruce-Mitford, *Sutton Hoo*, 2: 561, 560–33, here 561, figs. 412–414.

[70] Hawkes, "Monkton," 252.

[71] Geake, *Use of Grave-Goods*, 108–9, 123–36, here 130–31.

[72] "Prittlewell: Treasures of a King of Essex," *Current Archaeology* 190 (16, no. 10) (2004): 430–36; Ian Blair, Liz Barham, and Lyn Blackmore, "My Lord Essex," *British Archaeology* 76 (May, 2004): 11–17. The gold foil crosses have late seventh- or eighth-century Lombard and Alamanic parallels (Museum of London Archaeology Service, *The Prittlewell Prince: The Discovery of a Rich Anglo-Saxon Burial in Essex* [London, 2004], 28).

a similar message of prestige through affiliation, not as an import itself but as a local product incorporating an imported design idea. It combines a disc brooch with raised center, echoing Frankish filigree brooches, with a scale or feather-like cloisonné pattern of tiny garnets paralleled in and possibly echoing eastern Europe; here these forms blend with two high-status regional traditions: the composite disc brooches of Kent and the all-over garnetwork of the East An-glian court. That the smith struggled with the production process indicates that the Boss Hall brooch was not business as usual but an unusual commission for a patron with an agenda. The deployment of these mutually alien techniques, de-spite their obvious difficulties for the unfortunate smith given the job of incorpo-rating them into one object, would identify the wearer as a person of exotic and thereby sophisticated tastes, as part of the wealthy and well-traveled elite, part of the class whose authority stemmed at least in part from their self-identification with the full array of power structures on the continent, past and present. In the same grave assemblage, the single regal solidus of Sigebert III, provided with a loop for display as a pendant, is probably intended to send a similar message of elite connectedness to the continent rather than to serve as an index of wealth or ethnic identity.

There is a certain poignant, wishful quality about the Boss Hall brooch that is not present earlier in the Long Wittenham stoup or the Strood mount. The latter may also be about imported rarities conferring prestige, a sensibility of connection at a distance. But by its rough imitation of the prestige display of earlier generations both at Anglo-Saxon elite centers and on the continent, the Boss Hall brooch looks with desire to elite contexts that were neither well known nor truly accessible. It betrays a kind of provincial or colonial angst played out in unconvincing emulation, not of one antique high-prestige tradition but an un-easy recombination of three or four strands of early medieval metalworking. The overwhelmingly sumptuous effect of dark glitter unsuccessfully attempts to sub-stitute for finesse in production; the ambitions of the patron have far exceeded the abilities of the craftsman. Yet this object outlasted its original owner and was worn at length, repaired and patched, and finally buried a generation or two later, enclosed in a leather bag perhaps as a keepsake or family heirloom. This is more than the politics of accommodation or resistance, as hypothesized respec-tively by Wood and Carver for Sutton Hoo. It suggests that continental imports, whether actual objects or design concepts, were understood and expressed in different ways over time in Anglo-Saxon England, and that ultimately the is-sue is not only the politics of centers or politically identifiable units but also the self-projections, ambitions, and desires of individuals, families, and communities with their own agendas.

CHANGING FACES:
LEPROSY IN ANGLO-SAXON ENGLAND

CHRISTINA LEE

In the popular view of the Middle Ages, people lived short and uncomfortable lives. No matter how many contradictory conclusions are deduced by the academic community from evidence such as skeletal remains, which seem to indicate a sizeable elderly population,[1] care for the sick and evidence for rearing children with disabilities, modern media seem to be hooked on the titillating image of the so-called Dark Ages as a period of squalor and adversity. In this "barbaric" society it is taken as self-evident that the diseased and disabled were treated as lesser human beings or even excluded; these ideas may be supported by the superficial study of some diseases, as, for example, leprosy, a disease that is very much associated with the European Middle Ages. Hasty conclusions could be drawn from that fact that by the twelfth century lepers were apparently organized in special communities and even guilds, which enjoyed certain privileges as well as being separated from society. However, should we not ask whether this segregation was compulsory or whether other factors may have played a decisive role in the "seclusion" of lepers?

---

[1] The aging of adult skeletal remains is notoriously difficult, since there are very few bone changes after the age of 25. Currently, paleopathologists work with a number of different factors which focus mainly on age-related decay, including teeth abrasion and changes in the bone, such as the occurrence of arthritis or brittleness of bones. Different methods have given different results. Modern research takes into consideration that aging is influenced by a number of factors (genetic predisposition, occupation, and lifestyle can all influence the process). Traditionally skeletons have been aged by comparisons with modern pathology (where the age was known), which may be misleading, since few modern people will have been exposed to the nutritional and occupational hazards of Anglo-Saxon populations: Andrew Chamberlain, "Problems and Prospects in Paleodemography," in *Human Osteology in Archaeology and Forensic Science*, ed. Margaret Cox and Simon Mays (London, 2000), 101–15, here 105–7. For a more skeptical look see John Hines, "Lies, Damned Lies, and a *curriculum vitae*: Reflections on Statistics and the Populations of Early Anglo-Saxon Inhumation Cemeteries," in *Burial in Early Medieval England and Wales*, ed. Sam Lucy and Andrew Reynolds (London, 2002), 88–102, here 101.

It should be noted, for example, that medieval leper orders often attracted rich patrons, and evidence from the skeletal remains from leper hospitals has shown that a sizeable number of healthy people were buried in their churchyards, which could equally suggest that life as a leper could be fairly comfortable.

Lepers and leprosy in the post-Conquest period have been studied by a number of scholars,[2] but much less is known about the treatment of lepers in the Anglo-Saxon period. Leprosy, however, is a good contender for an examination of attitudes towards disease in early medieval Britain, since it features in literature, and, as evidence from the examination of excavated skeletal remains has shown, occurred throughout the Anglo-Saxon period, albeit in fairly small numbers. For the purpose of this essay I will take a number of different approaches in order to examine possible attitudes towards lepers in Anglo-Saxon England. I will first use evidence from grave archaeology and compare the burials of lepers, in both pagan and Christian contexts, with those of non-diseased populations, and question whether there are any apparent differences. I will then consider descriptions of lepers in textual and linguistic sources.

Hitherto there has been no whole-scale examination of Anglo-Saxon attitudes towards disease, although medicine and medical textbooks of the period have been examined in detail.[3] The existence of such books is an indicator that diseased people were cared for in Anglo-Saxon England, but they tell us little about the status or life of the infected person. It is necessary to ask what attitudes towards diseased people are evident from the period, and whether the conversion to Christianity led to any changes in the treatment of the sick. It is an often overlooked fact that throughout the Middle Ages medical aid and care were available to the wider public, administered by men and women of the church who were trained in a monastic, and therefore Christian environment. While there seems to be some evidence for independent physicians, such as Cynefrith who diagnosed the cancerous tumor of the seventh-century saint Æthelthryth, and who

---

[2] See, for example, Saul Brody, *The Disease of the Soul: Leprosy in Medieval Literature* (Ithaca, NY, 1974), and Peter Richards, *The Medieval Leper and His Northern Heirs* (Woodbridge, 2000).

[3] Most recent publications are Malcolm Cameron, *Anglo-Saxon Medicine* (Cambridge, 1993); Edward Pettit, *Anglo-Saxon Remedies, Charms, and Prayers from British Library Ms. Harley 585: The Lacnunga*, 2 vols. (Lewiston and Lampeter, 2001). Charlotte Roberts, one of the preeminent paleopathologists working on leprosy, has recently deplored that "no collective studies anywhere in the world have been undertaken charting the development and frequency of the disease (incorporating unpublished work), the age and sex distribution of leprous sufferers, and their status . . .". She is referring mainly to late medieval burials, but this could be extended to the Anglo-Saxon period as well: "Infectious Disease and Biocultural Perspective: Past, Present and Future Work in Britain," in *Human Osteology*, ed. Cox and Mays, 145–62, here 150.

also seems to have been present at her autopsy,[4] there is not much evidence for a widespread alternative to the hospitals of monastic foundations. Nevertheless, evidence from skeletal remains shows that even the pagan Anglo-Saxons must have had some skilled physicians, who could set bones and even use trepanning with great success, and we should assume that local healers and leeches existed throughout the period.[5]

If diseased people were cared for in monastic foundations, it should be considered that the views of the church had an impact on the attitudes towards the sick and the way in which treatment was offered. Any examination of disease in medieval texts must make allowances for the fact that some depictions may not be based entirely on indigenous sentiments, but may mirror other sources, such as hagiographies, which were translated into Old English. These sources may not be primarily concerned with the pathological aspects of disease, but may treat illness as an allegory for spiritual health. It is therefore necessary to look towards additional evidence if we want to have a broader understanding of how diseased people were treated by their contemporaries. [6]

Additional evidence for the treatment of diseased people from the pagan to the Christian period may come from the examination of skeletal remains, which give an indication of the existence, frequency, and possible treatment of illnesses in Anglo-Saxon England.[7] Death rituals must be approached with caution, since they may reflect only certain aspects of a person's life and may override whatever other identities this person may have had in life. The display of the dead in the grave is now regarded as an expression of social identity, as well as a ritual. Grave archaeology has given us indications of the spatial arrangements of communities of the dead: for example, burial with certain objects may identify a person as belonging to a certain kin-group, which may be supported by physical features, such as Wormian bones (tiny bone growth along the cranial suture lines), which

---

[4] *Ælfric's Lives of Saints*, ed. and trans. W. W. Skeat, EETS o.s. 76 and 82 (London, 1966), 1: 436-38.

[5] The skeletal remains from various sites show great variation in medical skills: Calvin Wells, "The Results of 'Bone Setting' in Anglo-Saxon Times," *Medical and Biological Illustration* 24 (1974): 215-20.

[6] An as yet untapped source of information is place-name evidence. For example, the name of the Northamptonshire town of Cotterstock, which in its earliest form in the *Domesday Book* (1086) is given as *Codestoche,* may refer to "a hospital or building for sufferers of pestilence" if the first element is derived from Old English *copu,* "disease." However, other interpretations have suggested a derivation from Old English *corper-stoc,* "a place of gathering": J. E. B. Gover, Allen Mawer, and Frank Merry Stenton, *The Place-Names of Northamptonshire* (Cambridge, 1933), 200. I would like to thank Dr. Paul Cavill from the English Place Name Society for this information.

[7] Unfortunately, only a minority of diseases leaves a signature on the bones.

can be genetic in origin.[8] Once such kin groups have been identified, it is possible to observe whether related individuals were buried close to one another and whether there are differences in the burial position or grave-goods. From the objects in the grave the importance that was afforded to the dead person can be assessed. Nevertheless, the social stratification of skeletal material from medieval cemeteries remains complex. For example, pagan Anglo-Saxon burial grounds contain only small numbers of children's graves, and it is assumed that their bodies were disposed of elsewhere.[9] Additionally, certain individuals may have been excluded from Christian burial grounds of post-conversion cemeteries for religious reasons. Others may have chosen to be buried in a special place, such as a monastic foundation.[10] Understanding the social stratification is even more difficult in the post-conversion period, since the custom of placing objects in graves, which allow the dating of the burial, was gradually given up during the seventh and eighth centuries.

Leprosy, or Hansen's Disease, is an infectious disease caused by the *Mycobacterium leprae*, and is contracted via a pulmonary route through droplet infection and possibly also skin contact.[11] The bacterium seems to thrive in conditions below 37° C, and the incubation period can be quite long, lasting between three and five years. The period of latency can be up to forty years. Leprosy develops in two major forms from an intermediate state. One is lepromatous leprosy, which is fatal and manifests itself in lesions on the skin and eventual loss of nerve sensations, especially in the hands and feet, with an additional infection of the palate and the nose, and blindness. The ulceration of the flesh and the subsequent necrosis results in a repugnant smell. The second form of leprosy is the so-called tuberculoid leprosy, which can produce skin lesions and paralysis of the face, as well as an ulceration of the extremities and gradual destruction of tissue. Whether an individual contracts a milder or the more serious form depends on their immune system (which in turn is largely governed by their genetically determined

---

[8] The exact reason for the formation of Wormian bones is unknown. The frequency of their occurrence varies between populations (apparently they occur almost twice as often on Chinese than on Anglo-Saxon skulls) and similar patterns can help to identify family groups. However, it should be noted that suggestions have been made that a high number of Wormian bones may point to a mental disability. For example, high amounts of Wormian bones have been observed in children diagnosed with Trisomy 21 (Down's Syndrome), amongst other congenital diseases: Philippe Jeanty, Sandra R. Silva, and Cheryl Turner, "Prenatal Diagnosis of Wormian Bones," *Journal of Ultrasound Medicine* 19 (2000): 863–69.

[9] Sally Crawford, *Childhood in Anglo-Saxon England* (Stroud, 1999), 14–32.

[10] Simon Mays, *The Archaeology of Human Bones* (London and New York, 1998), 25.

[11] Roberts, "Infectious Disease in Biocultural Perspective: Past, Present and Future Work in Britain," 150.

HLA type)[12] and the degree of exposure to the species of the *Mycobacterium*.[13] A person with high resistance may have contracted leprosy, but will not develop bone changes that are archaeologically detectable.[14]

Scientists are not sure how and why the disease spreads. Factors such as a poor diet, unhealthy living conditions, and genetic dispositions have all been discussed.[15] It is believed that leprosy originated in India and was first brought to Europe by the troops of Alexander the Great,[16] and was most likely spread through trade connections. Some archaeologists have suggested that its occurrence in the British Isles may have been a less welcome byproduct of Christianization. However, the earliest confirmed case of leprosy in Britain has been dated to the fourth century at the Roman cemetery of Poundbury, Dorset.[17] The individual involved was not a native of the British Isles, as examinations of the skeletal remains have shown, and most likely brought the disease with him from elsewhere. There may have been earlier cases, but they are disputed amongst paleopathologists. Archaeologically, leprosy is very hard to detect. A telltale sign of the disease on skeletal remains is the disfigurement of the bones of the hands or feet, but these bones are usually the first to decay. Additionally, the *Mycobacterium leprae* is a first cousin of the tuberculosis organism and many of the early disease characteristics are similar, which makes detection difficult.[18] The criteria for the identification of leprosy on skeletal remains go back to the work of Vilhelm Møller-Christensen, who examined the osteological evidence from a Danish leper cemetery.[19] According to

---

[12] The HLA type determines the blood group of an individual.

[13] Angela Gernaey and David Minnikin, "Chemical Methods in Paleopathology," in *Human Osteology*, ed. Cox and Mays, 239–53, here 248.

[14] Roberts, "Infectious Disease," 150.

[15] Herbert Covey, "People with Leprosy (Hansen's Disease) during the Middle Ages," *Social Science Journal* 38 (2001): 315–21, here 316. The DNA of medieval lepers has recently been studied by Michael Taylor, Stephanie Widdison, Ivor Brown, and Douglas Young, "A Mediaeval Case of Lepromatous Leprosy from 13th–14th Century Orkney, Scotland," *Journal of Archaeological Science* 27 (2000): 1133–38.

[16] Keith Manchester and Charlotte Roberts, "The Paleopathology of Leprosy in Britain: A Review," *World Archaeology* 21 (1989): 265-72, here 266. They state that the earliest written record which describes human leprosy is the sixth-century B.C. *Sushruta Samhita*. See also Johannes Anderson, who writes that the Byzantine writer Oribasios claimed that Alexander brought the disease with him: *Studies in the Mediaeval Diagnosis of Leprosy in Denmark* (Copenhagen, 1969), 45.

[17] R. Reader, "New Evidence for the Antiquity of Leprosy in Early Britain," *Journal of Archaeological Science* 1 (1974): 205–7.

[18] It has been suggested that the sudden drop in leprosy cases in the fourteenth century was the result of a rise in TB. The exposure to the *Mycobacterium tuberculosis* seems to increase the immunological resistance to leprosy: Gernaey and Minnikin, "Chemical Methods," 248.

Møller-Christensen, leprosy can be diagnosed only when there are visible inflammatory changes of the hands and feet, together with marked periostitis of the lower leg,[20] plus changes in the alveolar bone of the palate. Such a strict catalogue is problematic for the Anglo-Saxon period where many skeletons are incomplete because of decay, and therefore only a handful of cases have undoubtedly been identified as lepers.[21] Nevertheless, it is obvious from the scarcity of symptomatic bone changes that there is no evidence for a mass epidemic, in contrast to finds from the twelfth and thirteenth centuries.[22] Recently the genetic code for *Mycobacterium leprae* has been identified, suggesting that future excavation will possibly detect leprous individuals more easily.[23]

There are some further problems for the comparison of individuals identified as infected with leprosy with those of other burials, even after the disease has been clearly identified. There is still no uniform way of recording archaeological data, and the detail in which a site can be reported often depends on the funds available for publication. Not all cemetery excavations have had a paleopathologist at hand (though it is now a regular practice), and in some cases reports focus on only certain burials. For example, a seventh-century leper inhumation from Eccles, Kent, which was examined by Keith Manchester, is described as an individual case study and not placed within a wider grave context.[24] Manchester reports that this was the inhumation of a 25–30-year-old male, who had extensive *cribra orbitalia* (pitting of the eye-sockets) and evidence of enamel hypoplasia (pits or furrows in the tooth

---

[19] His work was the first research in the paleopathology of medieval leprosy, and evidence from burials examined earlier may have been misdiagnosed: Vilhelm Møller-Christensen, "Evidence for Leprosy in Early Peoples," in *Diseases in Antiquity*, ed. Don Brothwell and A. T. Sandison (Springfield, IL, 1967), 295–306.

[20] Periostitis is an infection of the thin outer membrane that covers the bones and is very common in Anglo-Saxon skeletons (more than those of any other period in England). It may be caused by a number of things, including a heavy kick on the shin.

[21] Charlotte Roberts lists only eighteen cases from post-Roman Britain and Anglo-Saxon England, and almost half of them seem to come from pre-Christian burial grounds: "The Antiquity of Leprosy in Britain: The Skeletal Evidence," in *The Past and Presence of Leprosy: Archaeological, Historical, Paleopathological and Clinical Approaches*, ed. eadem, Mary Lewis, and Keith Manchester, BAR Int. Ser. 1054 (Oxford, 2002), 213–21, here 214.

[22] Roberts and Manchester, *Archaeology of Disease*, 148.

[23] Taylor et al., " Leprosy from Orkney," 1137.

[24] The multi-period site at Eccles was excavated over a number of years by Alan Detsicas and is published in a number of reports in *Archaeologica Cantiana* 1963–1973. Manchester does not give the grave number or grave context of the burial, which makes it very hard to identify: "A Leprous Skeleton of the 7th Century from Eccles, Kent and the Present Evidence of Leprosy in Early Britain," *Journal of Archaeological Science* 8 (1981): 205–9, esp. 206.

enamel), which indicates either malnutrition or severe ill-health in childhood. The relation of Anglo-Saxon leper burials to non-diseased inhumations can also be complicated through an unclear chronology at multi-period sites. The densely packed cemetery of Cannington, Somerset, contained burials from prehistory right up to the eighth century. Three skeletons have been identified as being those of lepers, and four others show possible signs of the disease.[25] Of the three identifiable leper graves, only G 159, the inhumation of a young woman at the crowded eastern part of the cemetery, can be attributed to the Anglo-Saxon period. This grave contains no goods, and the dating has been done on the basis of burial sequences at this part of the site. Like so many pagan grave fields, Cannington was no longer complete when excavated, having been partly destroyed by quarrying, so that the relation of G 159 to the others remains tentative.

The first example of a more comprehensive picture is a possible group of lepers from Cemetery A at Beckford, Hereford and Worcester, dated to the fifth to early seventh centuries. There were two cemeteries at Beckford, which were only about 600 meters apart. It has been suggested that cemetery A was the resting place of a leading family or kin group.[26] While bone preservation is good in Cemetery A, the skeletal remains of Cemetery B, according to Calvin Wells, are too decayed to see clear patterns of pathology. The population at Beckford showed evidence of a physically active and strenuous life, and the medial life-span was much lower than at other comparable sites. One sixth-century burial at Beckford A (G 8) has been clearly identified as that of a leper. It contained the remains of a robust male, about 1.82 meters tall, who was buried with a spearhead, an iron-bound bucket, a knife, and some iron and bronze fragments. Buckets are classed as high-status objects, since their occurrence in graves is relatively rare.[27] The Beckford leper was not a healthy man. Slight spina bifida and acute degeneration of the intervertebral disks had led to spinal deformities and so, apart from leprosy, this man suffered excruciating back pain. His burial position at the eastern fringe of the cemetery may suggest some kind of spatial separation, but it should be noted that the other burials with buckets, and therefore possibly also of high status, also occur on the fringes of the cemetery. The two other possible leper burials at Beckford were also placed at the eastern side of the cemetery. These are

---

[25] Don Brothwell et al., "Leprosy (with an Examination of the Skeletal Remains by Keith Manchester)," in *Cannington Cemetery: Excavations 1962–3 of Prehistoric, Roman, Post-Roman, and Later Features at Cannington Park Quarry, near Bridgewater, Somerset*, ed. Philip Rahtz, Sue Hirst, and Susan Wright (London, 2000), 225–36, here 225–26.

[26] *Two Anglo-Saxon Cemeteries at Beckford, Hereford and Worcester*, ed. Vera Evison and Prue Hill, CBA Research Report 103 (York, 1996), 38.

[27] There are two more burials with buckets at Beckford in cemetery B, G 10 and G 81. G10 was possibly a female adult lying on her side, and G 81 a male adult.

the inhumations of an approximately 30-year-old woman (G A11) and a middle-aged man (G A22). It has been suggested that a family connection exists between the man buried in G 8 and the woman in G11. G A11 and G A22 were adjacent to the grave of a child (G A5 and G A10), which may indicate further family members. Both graves were furnished: the woman in G A11 was buried with gilded bronze brooches and the man in G A22 was given a shield and spear, indications that both held respected positions in their society.[28] It appears that for these individuals disease was no impediment to status in death.

At the Anglo-Saxon cemetery of Barrington, Edix Hill, Cambridgeshire (dated to A.D. 500–650), the body of a young woman shows all the indicators of leprosy. This may not have been the cause of death, but her disfigurement would have been clearly visible when she died since her face and extremities showed advanced degeneration of the bones. The most striking feature of her burial is that she was laid out on a bed, which was then lowered into the grave. Bed burials are extremely rare, but at Edix Hill there were two.[29] Along with ship funerals and other unusual practices, they appear to indicate the resting place of an important member of the community. The burial of this leprous woman in G 18 has been dated to the seventh century and is among a group of other highly-furnished inhumations, so that this may be the resting place of a leading family. Her grave-goods confirm her high status: a weaving sword, adapted from a real weapon, a bucket, a possible box containing a number of artifacts, and silver rings from what may have been a necklace. Thus it appears that she had the burial of a princess, despite her disease. There is another possible case of leprosy at Edix Hill, in G 93, which is situated at the western fringe of the excavated area. Here the lepromatous deformations are not as far advanced and do not fulfil the strict criteria established by Møller-Christensen. However, this middle-aged woman too was buried with a range of grave-goods. Two possible leper inhumations were found at Worthy Park, Kingsworthy, Hampshire (G 20 and G 57),[30] but here the deformation is not very far advanced, so that the leprosy may not have been obvious to those who buried the bodies. Interestingly, both graves are unfurnished, and appear in a corridor of dense inhumations in the middle of the excavated cemetery,[31] many of

---

[28] See also Burwell, Grave 111, dated to the seventh century by T. C. Lethbridge, which is unusually big. Here *facies leprosa* is clearly visible: Vilhelm Møller-Christensen and D. R. Hughes, "Early Cases of Leprosy in Britain," *Man* 62 (1962): 177–79, here 178.

[29] Bed burials have so far been found at only six sites. They are predominantly female inhumations and often contain a rich array of goods.

[30] Calvin Wells, Guy Grainger, Bernhard Denston, and Sonia Chadwick Hawkes, "The Inhumations and Cremations," in *The Anglo-Saxon Cemetery at Worthy Park, Kingsworthy, near Winchester, Hampshire*, ed. Sonia Chadwick Hawkes and Guy Grainger (Oxford, 2003), 153–89. Unfortunately, no dating sequences for the site are given.

which seem to be of people with some form of physical impairment, mostly as the result of heavy physical labor. However, this part of the cemetery does not seem to be evidence for a deliberate separation of diseased people; it rather appears to be a plot which contains many unfurnished inhumations, and may indicate an area reserved for the poor or servants of the community.[32]

While it appears that at pagan Anglo-Saxon cemeteries status negates any adverse associations that the disease may have had, the picture is different at post-conversion sites. Recently the skeletal remains from the Norwich cemetery of St. John the Baptist have been re-examined, using a new method which takes radiocarbon dates from stable isotopes of the carbon components in bone collagen.[33] This method allows for a much more accurate dating than traditional techniques, such as dendrochronology, or by using debris from the soil. The cemetery of St. John the Baptist is unusual, since its northern side contains a large number of diseased people, including thirty-five lepers. From the results of the stable isotope analysis, it became evident that they are not Norman, as previously assumed,[34] but are most likely late Anglo-Saxon inhumations. During this period the cemetery of St. John the Baptist was situated outside the city gates, adjacent to one of the main roads approaching from the south.[35] The burial ground contained a disproportionately high number of leper graves, as well as the skeletal remains of individuals with various other diseases. The high number of inhumations of people who had suffered from leprosy at this site, some of which were identified as members of family groups,[36] may be evidence that leper colonies existed in the late Anglo-Saxon period. Despite the fact that leper hospitals have been recorded since the seventh century in continental Europe (the oldest were at Metz, Verdun, and Maastricht), it is assumed that no such institution existed in England before the Conquest. However, the evidence from St. John the Baptist suggests that lepers in the late Anglo-Saxon period were already segre-

---

[31] Again, this site is obscured by subsequent building activity and only a part of the cemetery could be excavated.

[32] We should observe that G 57 is adjacent to G 45, an inhumation of a young male who had either polio or a birth defect, and who nevertheless was buried with a spear, which suggests a respected position in life.

[33] A. Bayliss, E. Shepherd Popescu, N. Beavan-Athfield, C. Bronk Ramsey, G. Cook, and A. Locker, "The Potential Significance of Dietary Offsets for the Interpretation of Radiocarbon Dates: An Archaeologically Significant Example from Medieval Norwich," *Journal of Archaeological Science* 31 (2004): 563–75.

[34] Sue Anderson, "Leprosy in a Medieval Churchyard in Norwich," in *Current and Recent Research in Osteoarchaeology: Proceedings of the 3rd Meeting of the Osteoarchaeological Research Group*, ed. eadem (Oxford, 1998), 31–37, here 31, and esp. 36.

[35] Bayliss et al., "Potential Significance," 568.

[36] Anderson, "Leprosy in a Medieval Churchyard," 36.

gated into special communities, which, at least in death, were placed outside the city gates.[37]

There are also a few Anglo-Saxon leper burials at the Northamptonshire cemetery of Raunds Furnells, which was in use to the mid-tenth to the mid-twelfth centuries. These graves appear to be at the outer fringes of the graveyard.[38] The first possible leper inhumation at this site was G 5256, which was the body of a 25–35-year-old male who was buried during the first phase of the cemetery at what was then the southernmost boundary of graves. Another possible leper burial was G 5178, which contained the inhumation of a mature male. This grave was unusual, since it was positioned near the so-called "eavesdrop" burials (used in cases where baptism may be needed), close to the south side of the first church, an area which contained mainly infant inhumations. This grave was marked with a large stone at the foot-end. Usually, proximity to a church is seen as a privilege, since it allows the dead to be close to the altar and the host, symbols of the resurrection of the dead. However, here the closeness of infant burials and the proximity of another unusual body (a man with cranial cuts) may indicate that this inhumation, which appears to be the last in this phase, was part of a series of atypical interments.[39] To the right of this grave is another bizarre inhumation of a person with cranial cuts. The cuts appear to have been performed post-mortem, and we can only guess why this person was thus mutilated.[40]

The second leper burial at Raunds Furnells is that of G 5046, a young male whose face and extremities had been destroyed by leprosy. The body was buried at the southernmost boundary of the cemetery. The dating sequence at Raunds is not quite clear, but this seems to have been an eleventh-century inhumation. This is not the only diseased burial at the fringes, since G 5218, which contained a person with progressive poliomyelitis, who had a foreshortened right leg and arm and was also afflicted with tuberculosis, is situated at the northernmost boundary of the cemetery.[41] The evidence from Raunds Furnells and St. John the Baptist suggests that by late Anglo-Saxon England lepers and people with

---

[37] This division of lepers from the non-leprous also occurs in contemporary cemeteries in Lund, Sweden. Of the 43 lepers found in the Lund excavation, nearly all of them were buried near the cemetery of Trinitas Wooden Church (dated 990–1100) or Kattesund (1050–1100). In both cemeteries all cases of leprosy (bar one) occur in the outer zones: Caroline Arcini, *Health and Disease in Early Lund: Osteo-pathological Studies of 3,305 Individuals Buried in the Area of Lund 990–1536* (Lund, 1999), 118–21.

[38] F. Powell, "The Human Remains," in *Raunds Furnells: The Anglo-Saxon Church and Churchyard*, ed. Andy Boddington (London, 1996), 113–24, here 123, and microfiche.

[39] Boddington, ed., *Raunds Furnells*, 55.

[40] Powell, "Human Remains," 123.

[41] Victoria Thompson does not think that these inhumations show discrimination towards the diseased, and interprets some of the literary sources cited in this essay differently.

contagious disease were buried away from the non-infected population. However-er, they were still buried in what appears to be common ground, making distinc-tions between diseased and non-diseased populations less visible than they are in the later medieval period when leper burials are associated with leper hospitals.

The spatial separation of lepers and the non-infected population in late An-glo-Saxon cemeteries may mirror changes in attitudes towards the treatment of the diseased in general. For evidence of such changing views we must turn to literature, which is not as straightforward as it might seem. Leprosy features in a number of Anglo-Saxon prose texts, but the question remains *what* exactly was referred to when terms for the disease were employed. There is a confusing ar-ray of vocabulary that seems to refer to leprosy in Old English, as I will show, which may be the result of either linguistic variation or translations from differ-ent sources. The Latin term for leprosy is usually rendered *lepra,* which occurs in a number of biblical passages. References to *lepra* by classical or biblical writ-ers, however, do not describe leprosy, but a variety of skin diseases. Greek *lepros,* "rough and scaly," translates the Hebrew word *za'rat.* [42] The term *lepra* is used variously by medical writers such as Hippocrates, but not to describe leprosy.[43] Similarly, the descriptions of *lepra* in Leviticus 13 and 14 describe a *curable* skin condition, which can be detected within seven days and is mainly concerned with hair loss and pustules, which is certainly not leprosy.[44] It appears that the terms *elephas* or *elephantiasis* were used by Greek writers to portray the lepromatous form of leprosy.

One of the influential sources for Anglo-Saxon literature is the seventh-cen-tury writer Isidore of Seville, who describes a number of diseases that are "appar-ent on the surface of the body" in his *Etymologies.*[45] Isidore differentiates between *scabies* and *lepra.* The latter, in his definition, manifests itself in the roughness of scaly skin, and takes its name from the changing color of the skin, which can vary among black, white, and red. *Lepra* is primarily diagnosed through the examination of skin color and texture, whereas a third disease, *elefantiacus,* is

---

Thompson cautions that we should look at other possibilities for the exclusion of people with a disability, rather than automatically assume that it was the disability itself that ex-cluded them: *Death and Dying in Late Anglo-Saxon England* (Woodbridge, 2004), 122–23. While I share her concern about the often hasty and unsubstantiated claims that are made from observations of graves and skeletal remains, I do think that the position of the Raunds lepers is different from that of other burials.

[42] Gilbert Lewis, "A Lesson from Leviticus: Leprosy," *Man* 22 (1987): 593–612, here 596.

[43] Anderson, *Studies in the Mediaeval Diagnosis of Leprosy in Denmark,* 18.

[44] Lewis, "A Lesson," 596.

[45] "De morbis qui in superficie corporis videntur: Scabies et lepra": *Isidori Hispalen-sis Episcopi Etymologiarum sive originvm libri XX,* ed. W. M. Lindsay (Oxford, 1911), 4.8: 10–12.

described as a disease which results in hardened skin similar to that of an elephant. It is not clear from Isidore's description which of the three diseases refers to leprosy, though two of them, *lepra* and *elefantiacus*, show symptoms that may occur with the disease. Among the first signs of an infection with leprosy are reddish-brown skin lesions. These may have been featured when the disease was depicted in manuscript illuminations. While there are no pictorial depictions of lepers in Britain from the pre-Conquest period,[46] images in continental manuscripts generally show people covered in pustules, as in an illustration in a ninth-century gospel book from Coblenz (Düsseldorf, Landesbildstelle, MS. Cod. B. 113, fol. 5r), which shows Christ healing a leper girded in a loincloth and with his alms horn strapped to his side inside a walled city,[47] while another enters through gates. The caption next to the man reads "leprosus." A similar depiction of a "leper" appears in the gospel book of Otto III (Munich, Bayerische Staatsbibliothek, MS. Latin 4453, fol. 97v), produced 998–1001.[48]

It is debatable how accurately medieval physicians could identify early forms of leprosy, which can appear similar to other skin problems and infectious diseases.[49] Even if they could form a correct diagnosis, it appears that the definition of what constitutes leprosy was made by priests, not physicians, on the basis of biblical references. The example of Christ's miracles as a healer (and in particular the curing of leprosy) was understood by church fathers and medieval writers as a sign that spiritual health and bodily well-being were connected. Christianity introduced the moral obligation of care for the sick.[50] Cassiodorus (ca. 485–589) makes healing and the study of medical writers part of the monastic ministry in his *Institutiones*, written for the monastic community at Vivarium.[51] The interest of religious writers in disease is founded on a long tradition of caring for the sick, which was coupled with biblical examples of ministering to outbreaks of infectious illnesses. It is generally assumed that ideas of exclusion or segregation of lepers by medieval writers is based on Leviticus 13 and 14, where God tells Moses and Aaron how to detect and isolate a "leper." This difficult passage, which seems to describe not one disease, but a variety of different ailments,[52] commands the priest

---

[46] The earliest English depiction of *facies leprosa* is thought to be from the north aisle of the Angel Choir at Lincoln Cathedral: David Marcombe, *The Leper Knights* (Woodbridge, 2003), 138–39.

[47] Such horns led to the name of *hornigbruoder* ["horned brother"] in the Old High German Gospel translation of Otfried and Tatian.

[48] Brody, *Disease of the Soul*, pls. 5, 6.

[49] Manchester and Roberts claim that evidence from medieval leprosia suggests that the diagnosis was accurate in most cases: "Paleopathology of Leprosy," 267.

[50] Daniel W. Amundsen, *Medicine, Society and Faith in the Ancient and Medieval Worlds* (Baltimore, MD, 1996), 13. Also R. Stark, *The Rise of Christianity* (Princeton, NJ, 1996).

[51] Cassiodorus, *Institutiones*, ed. R. A. B. Mynors (Oxford, 1961), 1146.

to decide whether a person should be isolated from the community and when they can be readmitted.

Anglo-Saxon law codes have no provision for lepers, though, as we have seen from archaeological evidence, there must have been cases during the period. Whether this is an accident of preservation, or whether care for the leprous was indeed left to the church, remains to be seen.[53] At the same time there is, however, growing concern about the treatment of lepers in continental laws, both clerical and secular, which eventually culminates in the exclusion of lepers from churches and cemeteries by a decree of the Third Lateran Council in 1179.[54] The procedure of segregation as suggested in the writ *De leproso amovendo* forced lepers to undergo a ritual funeral after which they were declared as "dead to the world, but alive to God." It is debatable how stringently these measures were adhered to,[55] but we know that at least by the end of the twelfth century lepers in England were organized in special communities, which were sustained by charitable bequests, such as the *leprosarium* at Sherburne, Durham, which was founded in 1181.[56]

However, Church injunctions concerning lepers go as far back as the Council of Orleans (A.D. 549), which curbed the social intercourse of lepers with non-lepers.[57] In 583 the Council of Lyon forbade begging and in 643 the Langobardic lawcode known as the *Edictus Rothari* declared the leper "dead to the world."[58] The first admonition given to an English cleric regarding leprosy was the advice from Pope Gregory II to Boniface in 726 to allow lepers to take communion,

---

[52] Elinor Lieber, "Old Testament 'Leprosy', Contagion and Sin," in *Contagion: Perspectives from Pre-Modern Societies*, ed. Lawrence Conrad and Dominik Wujastyk (Aldershot, 2000), 99–136.

[53] It is interesting to note that Scandinavian evidence shows that only the most severely disfigured people were segregated: Charlotte Roberts, "The Paleopathology of Leprosy in Britain," *World Archaeology* 21 (1989): 265–72, here 267. Leprosy spread to Scandinavia from Anglo-Saxon England and one of the earliest laws which mentions a special status for lepers is the tenth-century Norwegian *Gulaþingslög*, which forbids lepers to become part of a military organization: "Nu scal eigi leiðangr gera firi líkþrá menn alla" : *Norges Gamle Love indtil 1387*, ed. Rudolph Keyser and P. A. Munch (Christiana [Oslo], 1846), 1: 97.

[54] Brody, *Disease of the Soul*, 64. Incidentally the Council sought to protect the plight of lepers. The impact of their removal from the community was also discussed at the Councils of Westminster in 1175 and 1200: Friedrich Merzbacher, "Die Leprösen im kanonischen Recht," *Zeitschrift der Savigny-Stiftung für Rechtsgeschichte: kanonische Abteilung* 84 (1967): 27–45, here 29–31.

[55] Brody, *Disease of the Soul*, 63.

[56] Merzbacher, "Die Leprösen im kanonischen Recht," 30.

[57] G. Keil, "Aussatz" in *Lexikon des Mittelalters*, ed. Robert Autry et al., 10 vols. (Munich and Zurich, 1977–1999), 1: 1251.

[58] *Reallexikon der germanischen Altertumskunde*, ed. Johnnes Hoops, 4 vols. (Strassburg, 1911–19), 1: 505.

provided they were Christians, but otherwise to hinder them from taking meals with non-lepers.[59] We would assume that some of the Frankish population suffered from leprosy, since it was made grounds for a divorce by King Pippin III in 757,[60] while Charlemagne ordered that lepers were not to interact with the non-infected population.[61] Recently Françoise Olivier Touati has heavily criticized scholarly perceptions of the exclusion of lepers from medieval society, which she regards as a manifestation of modern prejudice towards the "primitive" Middle Ages.[62] She writes that the notion of the separation of lepers from society on the basis of Levitical rules is "nonsense," and supported by historians who do not realize that in the eyes of medieval theologians the Old Testament was superseded by the New Testament.[63]

Touati's cautionary note is not unfounded. "Leprosy" signifies a number of very different things in medieval literature, as I will show below, and can denote heresy as well as the compassion of Christ towards the afflicted from the early medieval period onwards. One thing, however, is certain: the leprous are different from other people, and they are made different by their disease. The "sliding" of the leprous to the fringes of society that Touati observes in the thirteenth century was prepared for by a long history of interpretation of the disease as "visible sin."[64]

"Leprosy" in Anglo-Saxon literature occurs primarily in religious writings, such as homilies and hagiography, which were often influenced by non-indigenous sources, and also in leechbooks. There is only one mention of the disease in Old English poetry, in the anonymous life of St. Andrew, which is based on a now lost Latin version of the apocryphal *Acta Andreae apud anthropophagos*.[65] Before turning to the interpretations of "leprosy" in Anglo-Saxon literature, it seems useful to look at the vocabulary which appears in the various genres. The

---

[59] *Briefe des Bonifatius: Willibalds Leben des Bonifatius nebst einigen zeitgenössischen Dokumenten*, ed. and trans. Reinhard Rau (Darmstadt, 1968), 92: "Leprosis autem, si fideles Christiani fuerint, dominici corporis et sanguinis participatio tributur; cum sanis autem convivia celebrare negentur."

[60] *Capitula Regum Francorum*, ed. Alfred Boretius, MGH (Hanover, 1883), I, 39.

[61] " De leprosis: ut se non intermisseant alio populo," in *Capitula Regum Francorum*, ed. Boretius, 64.

[62] Françoise Touati, "Contagion and Leprosy: Myth, Ideas and Evolution in Medieval Minds and Societies," in *Contagion*, ed. Conrad and Wujastyk, 179–201, here 180–81.

[63] Touati, "Contagion and Leprosy," 181–85.

[64] Touati, "Contagion and Leprosy," 201.

[65] *Andreas and the Fates of the Apostles*, ed. Kenneth Brooks (Oxford, 1961), line 579, in a passage that refers to the miracles of Christ: "Sealde he dumbum gesprec, deafe gehyrdon, healtum ond hreofum hyge blissode ða þe limseoce lange wæron, werige wanhale,

earliest reference to the occurrence of *lepra* in Anglo-Saxon England in a written source appears to be from the *vita* of the seventh-century Irish missionary St. Fursey.[66] Almost contemporaneous is the use of the Latin term *lepra* in number 94 of Aldhelm's *Enigmata*, where he refers to *ebulus*, "wallwort," as a relief for the "terrible leprosy."[67] The eighth-century Leiden Glossary glosses *lepra* as *ulcus*, "ulcer" or *uncus*, "hooked," and *leprositas* as *morbo regio*, "royal disease," which is not very helpful.[68]

The multiplicity of terms, and consequent difficulties of deciding precisely which disease is referred to, is even more apparent in the Old English glosses to Latin texts and Bible translations into the vernacular. The Gospels of Matthew, Mark, and Luke all tell of Christ's healing of lepers. In the tenth-century gloss to the Lindisfarne Gospels, *leprosi*, "lepers," glosses *hreaf*, and *lepra* is referred to as *hreofl* or *riofl*.[69] *Hreofl* (with spelling variants *hriofol* and *hreofol*) is generally used for translating the Vulgate's *lepra* in most versions of the Old English Gospels. However, it is apparent that there is no consensus on the nature of the disease. In the Old English translation of Bede's *Historia Ecclesiastica*, *hreofl* refers to scabies, in an account of the miracles of John of Beverley.[70] On the other hand, *hreofan adl* in the Cambridge Corpus Christi manuscript of Wærferth's translation of Gregory's *Dialogues* is used to render the *morbo elephantino* of the original.[71] Ælfric uses the Latin elefantinus morbus when he cites a passage from Gregory's

---

witum gebundene" ["he gave speech to the dumb, the deaf had hearing, he made the minds of the lame and the lepers joyful, who had long been crippled, sick, chained by their torments"]. All translations are my own unless otherwise stated.

[66] Fursey was in the service of the East Anglian king Sigebert in 633, and built a monastery at Burghcastle in Suffolk. During his time there it is said that the "debiles et claudos, cecos atque leprosos, vel etiam qui varias habeant iniurias" ["the crippled and lame, the blind and leprous, as well as those who had various injuries"] came to him: *Vita Virtutesque Fursei Abbatis Latinacensis*, ed. Bruno Krusch, MGH, Scriptores Rerum Merovingicarum 4 (Hanover and Leipzig, 1902), 441.

[67] *Aldhelmi Opera*, ed. Rudolf Ehwald, MGH Auctores Antiquissimi 15 (Berlin, 1919), 141.

[68] John H. Hessels, *A Late Eighth-Century Latin Anglo-Saxon Glossary Preserved in the Library of Leiden University* (Cambridge, 1906) 9, 36. It may however be based on a confusion of Isidore's description of jaundice, which apparently can be cured by royal wine: *Etymologiae*, 4.8 :14.

[69] *The Four Gospels in Anglo-Saxon, Northumbrian, and Old Mercian Versions*, ed. W. W. Skeat, 4 vols. (Cambridge, 1871–1874).

[70] *The Old English Version of Bede's Ecclesiastical History*, ed. Thomas Miller, 2 vols., EETS 95, 96, 110 (London, 1898), 2: 388; compare *Bede's Ecclesiastical History of the English People*, ed. and trans. Bertram Colgrave and R. A. B. Mynors (Oxford, 1969), 5.2: "sed et scabiem tentam ac furfures habebat in capite."

Dialogi, which extols one of the miracles of St. Benedict, as a source. Wærferth's translation recounts the poor fortune of Antony's servant who was "geþræd mid þære hreofan adle swa þæt him eallunga þa hær afeollan, ond seo hyd asweoll swa þæt heo ne mihte bedyglan þæt weaxende wyrms ond widle" ["afflicted with leprosy, so that all of his hair fell out, and his skin swelled, so that it could not hide the growing of pus and impurities"].[72] The original passage refers to *morbo elephantino,* and seems to describe a condition which is indicated by hair loss and skin that grows thick and swollen. Nevertheless, the servant could be healed through the intercession of St. Benedict.[73] Skin lesions are characteristic of both forms of leprosy, but it is generally the tuberculoid version of the disease that leads to the destruction of follicles and sweat glands.

Occasionally the term *licðrowere,* which may be translated literally as "someone who suffers on his body," is used to denote biblical lepers.[74] The glossing of the word *leprosus* as *licðrowere* occurs in the *Vocabulary of Ælfric,*[75] and the term seems to be a synonym for "leper," which appears to be used mainly in a religious context. Ælfric's *Grammar* translates *leprosus* as either *licðrowere* or *hreoflig.*[76] He uses both terms indiscriminately again in the *Life of St. Basil,* where a mass priest named Anastasius hides a man who is described as both *licþrowere* and *hreoflian,* in a locked cave.[77] The most intriguing information on this person is that he is *unsprecende fornean,* "almost unable to speak." Lepromatous leprosy affects the alveolar part of the throat, which leads to profound changes in the voice and can result in the loss of speech. In the glossary in London, BL, Cotton Cleopatra A.iii, Latin *callosi* ["thick-skinned" or "gnarled"] is referred to as *hreofe oðða wearihte.*[78] One of the symptoms of leprosy is the loss of sensation in the skin of affected areas and,

---

[71] *Bischof Wærferth von Worcesters Übersetzung der Dialoge Gregors des Großen,* ed. Hans Hecht (Leipzig, 1900–1907), 157.

[72] *Bischof Wærferth,* ed. Hecht, 157.

[73] Gregory, *Dialogi* 2.26, *PL* 66. 183.

[74] See, for example, Luke 4:27, "And manega licþroweras wæron on israhel" ["and many lepers were in Israel"], which translates "et multi leprosi erant in israhel": *The Old English Version of the Gospels,* ed. Roy M. Liuzza, EETS o.s. 304 (Oxford, 1994), 1:107.

[75] *Anglo-Saxon and Old English Vocabularies,* ed. Thomas Wright and Richard Wülker, 2 vols. (Darmstadt, 1968), 1: 162.

[76] *Ælfrics Grammatik und Glossar,* ed. Julius Zupitza (Berlin, 1880), 305.

[77] *Ælfric's Lives of Saints,* 1: 78: "He hæfde ænne lic-ðrowere be-locen on anum clyfan egeslisce to-swollen and un-sprecende fornean, and hine ðær afedde un-afunden oð þæt" ["He had a leper shut away in a cave, who was terribly swollen and almost speechless, and he had fed him there undiscovered until then"]. Basil can open the door of the cave by the power of his word and stays awake all night with "mid þam wædlian hreoflian" ["the poor leper"].

[78] Wright and Wülker, *Anglo-Saxon and Old English Vocabularies,* 1: 375 line 20.

because of a weakening of muscle tissue, fingers and feet become gnarled. It is possible that this term may refer to lepromatous leprosy.

Such variation of terminology also appears in Anglo-Saxon medical texts. For example, the tenth-century *Bald's Leechbook* lists the following, all under one subject heading: Leechdoms against the *yflan blæce* ["evil skin ailment"] and the *hreofum lice* ["leprous body"], the *adedum lic* ["deadened body"], and the *miclan lic*, which has been variously translated as elephantiasis (a hardening of the skin) or erysipelas (a bacterial infection which discolors and lifts the skin).[79] Other skin ailments, such as shingles, have separate entries, and it is not quite clear whether this heading refers to a group of related diseases or to one and the same affliction. Malcolm Cameron has cautioned that *hreofl* does not always refer to true leprosy, but covers a variety of skin diseases.[80] This is certainly the case in two of the late Anglo-Saxon translations of medical texts, the *Old English Herbarium* and the *Medicina de Quadrupedibus*. In the *Herbarium*, *hreofl* translates *elefantiosis* as well as *lepra* and *leprosis*.[81] In the *Medicina de Quadrupedibus*, *hreofl* and *tofleon*, "covered in rashes," are both translations of Latin *peduclosus* (pediculosis, a skin reaction to lice infestation).[82] *Bald's Leechbook* refers to *hwite riefðo*, "white roughness," with the cryptic definition *þe mon on superne lepra het*, "which is called leprosy in the south."[83] The Old English *Lacnunga*, a late tenth-century collection of medical remedies, describes a mixture for *micclan lic* and *blece*, and while the first may be an allusion to the swelling of the face associated with tuberculoid leprosy, the latter term usually refers to the discoloration of the skin that occurs with psoriasis.[84]

Most uses of *hreofla* in Anglo-Saxon homiletic writings are in the context of the miracles that Christ performs for mankind.[85] A typical example is *Vercelli Homily* IV.[86] Christ is here praised as the "blindra mana leoht 7 dumra gesprec 7 deafra gehyrnes 7 hreofra clænsung 7 healtra gang" ["light of the blind and the speech of the dumb and the hearing of the deaf and the lepers' cleansing and the lame people's ability to walk"].[87] The healing of the sick and the lame, where human physicians have failed, is evidently seen as a mark of great powers granted to

---

[79] *Leechdoms, Wortcunning and Starcraft of Early England*, ed. Oswald Cockayne, 3 vols., Rolls Series (London, 1864–1866), 2: 8: *Læcdomas wið þam yflan blæce*.

[80] Cameron, *Anglo-Saxon Medicine*, 96.

[81] *The Old English Herbarium and the Medicina de Quadrupedibus*, ed. Herbert Jan de Vriend, EETS o.s. 286 (Oxford, 1984), 134, 154.

[82] De Vriend, *Old English Herbarium*, 256.

[83] Cockayne, *Leechdoms*, 2: 228.

[84] Pettit, *The Lacnunga*, 1: 118.

[85] Such as described in Matthew 8:3 and Luke 5:12.

[86] *The Vercelli Homilies*, ed. Donald G. Scragg, EETS o.s. 300 (Oxford, 1992).

[87] Scragg, *Vercelli Homilies*, 97.

saints. The curing of lepers is a staple ingredient of hagiography. Ælfric describes the healing of a leper through the powers of St. Martin, who heals the *hreofla wundorlice to-hroren*, "the leper, wondrously diseased," on his way to Paris with a kiss.[88] The characteristic of this leper is someone who lives at the city gates and is a terrible sight to others. The leper may constitute Ælfric's idea of the ultimate outcast, since he has no one who may fetch him the bedstraw of the saint, or a letter from the holy man, for a cure.[89] Whether or not this depiction is based on Ælfric's own experience, or influenced by non-indigenous sources, cannot be determined easily. However, the concept of the leper as an outcast in need of spiritual care, rather than bodily cure, may be based on a tradition which links disease to penance, and which goes back to the understanding that body and soul are connected. One influenced the other, and the body had to be protected from the desires of the soul. Sickness, in the eyes of writers such as Gregory the Great and Bede, allowed the afflicted an opportunity for redemption through suffering.[90] Leprosy came to be seen as the ultimate suffering, a living purgatory endured for sinful living. In King Alfred's Old English translation of Gregory's *Pastoral Care*, leprosy is linked to lust:

> Ðonne bi ðæm sceabbe swiðe ryhte sio hreofl getacnað ðæt wohhæmed. And ðonne bið se lichoma hreof, ðonne se bryne þe on ðæm innoðe bið utaflihð to ðære hyde. Swæ bið sio costung ærest on ðæm mode 7 ðonne færeð utweardes to ðære hyde, oððæt hio utascieð on weorc. Butan tweon gif ðæt mod ær ðæm willan ne wiðbritt, se wilm ðæs innoðes utabirst 7 wierð to sceabbe 7 monega wunda utan wyrcð mid ðæm won weorcum.

> ["The scab of leprosy is a type fornication. The body is leprous when the inflammation of the body spreads to the skin. Thus temptation is first in the mind and then it spreads to the skin until it bursts forth in actions. Doubtlessly, unless the mind oppose the desire beforehand, the internal inflammation breaks forth and becomes scab, causing many external sores with the perverse actions."] [91]

This translation by a king who suffered from a mystery illness for most of his life, which he feared to be "leprosy or blindness,"[92] from the works of a pope who

---

[88] Skeat, *Ælfric's Lives of Saints*, 2: 254.

[89] Skeat, *Ælfric's Lives of Saints*, 2: 254.

[90] Asmundsen, *Medicine, Society, and Faith*, 188–89.

[91] *King Alfred's West Saxon Version of Gregory's Pastoral Care*, ed. and trans. Henry Sweet, EETS o.s. 45 (London, 1871), 70. Both the Cotton and Hatton MSS contain this passage.

[92] "Timebat enim lepram aut caecitatem": *Asser's Life of King Alfred and the Annals of St Neots*, ed. William Stevenson (Oxford, 1959), 55.

suffered excruciating stomach pain at times, draws a clear connection between suffering and sin.[93] Gregory's original text, however, does not use *lepra*, but refers to a "scab":

> Jugem vero habet scabiem, cui carnis petulantia sine cessatione dominatur. In scabie etenim fervor viscerum ad cutem trahitur per quam recte luxuria designatur, quia si cordis tentatio usque ad operationem prosilit, nimirum fervor intimus usque ad cutis scabiem prorumpit; et foris jam corpus sauciat, quia dum in cogitatione voluptas non reprimitur, etiam in actione dominatur.

> ["Those have permanent scabs who are overcome by wantonness of the flesh without respite. Indeed, in the scab the violent inflammation of the innermost organs is drawn to the skin; by which indulgence is rightly indicated, since, if the heart's temptation leaps forth into action, without doubt the secret intoxication breaks out all the way into scabs of the skin: and it now wounds the body outwardly, because, while pleasure is not repressed in thought, it still dominates in activity."][94]

It is interesting that Alfred appears to make a connection between leprosy and lust. The idea that lepers were punished for sexual voraciousness features prominently in the late medieval period, based on a confusion of leprosy and syphilis. Symptoms for both illnesses can look quite similar in the early stages.[95] It is not known if this analogy appears anywhere else in Anglo-Saxon literature. The earliest analogue comes from the works of the second-century Greek writer Aretaios Cappadox, who made a connection between sexual activity and a disease he names *satyriasis* and *elephas*, which appears to be an accurate description of lepromatous leprosy. He claims that this disease leads to an increase of sexual appetite and permanent erections.[96] Whether either Gregory or Alfred was aware of Aretaios's writings is debatable, but it seems that their concepts of scabies or *hreofl* as an indicator for moral depravity prefigures much later attitudes towards leprosy.

It is, however, apparent that disease is interpreted by both Gregory and Alfred as a failure of the spirit, an early warning system which allows the victim to make amends. Gregory again makes use of leprosy as a metaphor for inner

---

[93] Gregory himself mentions that he suffers from a disease of the stomach which causes him much pain: *Moralia*, prol. 5, *PL* 75. 515; ed. M. Adriaen, CCSL 143 (Turnhout, 1979), 6. For an analysis of King Alfred's disease see David Pratt, "The Illnesses of Alfred the Great," *ASE* 30 (2001): 39–90.

[94] Gregory, *Cura Pastoralis, PL* 77.25.

[95] The most prominent example may be Robert Henryson's *Testament of Cresseid.*

[96] Carl Gottlob Kühn, *Medicorum Graecorum opera quae extant: Aretaeus* (Leipzig, 1828), 182; see also Andersen, *Studies*, 30-31.

depravity in the *Moralia*, where he compares it to heresy.[97] A biblical antecedent for such an interpretation can be found in Numbers 12:10, where God punishes Miriam with a snow-white skin disease for opposing Moses' marriage to the Cushite woman.[98] Gregory's interpretation is close to that of Isidore of Seville, who likens Miriam's opposition to the synagogue, which appears leprous on account of slander and grumbling against Christ.[99] Isidore states further that the ten lepers healed by Christ signify the various forms of heretics,[100] a theme taken up again by Hrabanus Maurus in *De Medicina*.[101] Generally, early Christian writers treat the Levitical rules on leprosy as an allegory for sin and divine retribution.[102] Origen, for example, describes in a homily on Leviticus the six types of leprosy mentioned in Leviticus 13, and interprets leprosy of the head as signifying those who do not accept Christ as their head.[103] Tertullian claims that a leper is a person defiled with sin.[104] These exegetical readings were known to Old English writers, but among them, it is Ælfric in particular who makes use of *hreofl* and the *hreofliga menn* as symbols of sin. In his homily on the third Sunday after Epiphany, Ælfric uses the healing of the lepers as described in Matthew 8:1–13 to underline that leprosy is a symptom of the sinful man, an outward sign of inner depravity.[105] Ælfric's main source is Haymo of Auxerre,[106] but the description of the various stages of *lepra* is derived from Leviticus. Ælfric uses the Levitical directive which states that a priest should consider the fate of the afflicted and rebukes those who think that they are virtuous enough to heal themselves. Subsequently, only an ordained man is able to decide whether a leper can be cured or whether he is too degenerate to be saved. Even though leprosy is

---

[97] Gregory, *Moralia*, *PL* 75. 525.

[98] See also the case of Uzziah, King of Judah, who usurps the priesthood and is punished by leprosy: 2 Chronicles 26:16–23.

[99] *Allegoriae quaedam sacrae scripturae*, *PL* 83.109: "Maria, soror Moysi, synagogæ speciem prætulit, quæ leprosa propter detractionem et murmurationem contra Christum existit."

[100] Isidore, *Allegoriae*, 127.

[101] Hrabanus, *De Medicina*, *PL* 111. 502.

[102] Isidore claims that the leper cured by Christ in Matthew 8:1–4 represents the human race defiled with sin: "Leprosus, quem Christus descendens de monte primum curavit, humanum indicat genus delicti contagio maculosum": Isidore, *Allegoriae*, 150, *PL* 83.118.

[103] In *Origenis Opera Omnia*, *PG* 12.492–508.

[104] Tertullian: a leper is a person defiled with sins: *Adversus Marcionem*, *PL* 2.263–556, esp. 403–4 (comment on Luke 5:12–14).

[105] *Ælfric's Catholic Homilies: The First Series*, ed. Peter Clemoes, EETS s.s. 17 (Oxford, 1997), 242.

[106] Malcolm Godden, *Ælfric's Catholic Homilies: Introduction, Commentary and Glossary*, EETS s.s. 18 (Oxford, 2000), 190–91. Godden thinks that Ælfric was personally acquainted with lepers.

used here in an allegorical sense when Ælfric states that "on gastlicum andgite getacnode þes hreoflia man eall mancynn þe wæs atelice hreoflig mid mislicum leahtrum on þam inran menn" [" In a spiritual sense the leprous man signifies all mankind that is horribly leprous with various sins on the inside"],[107] he nevertheless still draws a literal correlation between leprosy and sin. In his Homily 27, *De Natale S. Pauli*, Ælfric further declares "þæt þe he on lichaman geþrowade þæt ðrowað þes on his sawle" ["what he suffered in his body, he suffers in his soul"], in a commentary on Giezi (Gehazi), the servant of Elisha (2 Kings 5), who is punished with *lepra* for his avarice.[108]

Not all of Ælfric's depictions of lepers are negative. The tendency of patristic literature to see disease as a punishment for transgression led to the attitude that the leper is equally cursed and blessed.[109] Attitudes towards leprosy in many cases mirror those towards disability, which can range from punishment for transgression to a blessing, since it will keep the sufferer from cardinal sins such as pride.[110] In his homily for the second Sunday after Pentecost Ælfric uses the leper as a symbol for Christ's mercy.[111] There cannot be a more pitiful image of a leper than in this homily, where the outcast leper, *fram mannum forsewen* ["despised by men"], has his wounds licked by dogs, and yet the leper with his stinking wounds will become a *mundbora* ["guardian"] at the Last Judgment.[112] Ælfric reminds his

---

[107] *Ælfric's Catholic Homilies*, ed. Clemoes, 1: 242.

[108] *Ælfric's Catholic Homilies*, ed. Clemoes, 1: 408. Giezi (Gehazi) is described as *hreofla*.

[109] See for example, Gregory, *Cura Pastoralis,* chap. 12 (*PL* 77.25–26, p. 69).

[110] It seems that Ælfric in particular sees disability as an opportunity for self-improvement.

[111] The leper here is based on the beggar Lazarus of Luke 16:20, and is the lesser of Christ's brothers. His soul is carried to heaven.

[112] *Ælfric's Catholic Homilies,* ed. Clemoes, no. 1: 23, 367–69. See also Vercelli homily 22, which contains a contemplation of what happens to the sinful soul after death. The homily, which according to Donald Scragg is based freely on Isidore's *Synonyma*, gives a colorful picture of the treatment of the soul, which is that of a leper, shunned, despised, and expelled: "Se halga Isodorus cwæð: Eawla þæt sio sawl [hiofeð þonne] hio of ðam lichoman anumen bið. Ealle hie hie swa wundige hyrwað, 7 swa fule stincende hie hie onscunað, 7 swa hreofe hie hie ascufað, 7 se lichoma lið on eorðan isne genearwod 7 mid racentu[m] geðryd 7 mid bendum gebunden 7 mid fetrum gefæstnod, 7 þære synfullan sawle ne beoð þa tintrego gelytlode" ["The holy Isidore said: Alas, that the soul (laments when) she is taken away from the body. They all despise her as an ulcerous (person), and shun her as a foully stinking one, they expel her as a leper, and the body lies in the earth, confined with iron, and punished with fetters, and bound with bonds, and fastened with fetters, and the torments for the sinful soul will not diminish"]: *Vercelli Homilies,* ed. Scragg, 370.

audience: "Manega lazaras ge habbað nu licgende æt eowrum gatum. biddende eowre oferflowednyssa: þeah ðe hi syn waclice geþuhte: þeahhwæþere hi beoð eft eowre þingeras wið ðone ælmihtigan" ["many lazars you have now lying outside your gates, begging for your superfluity. Though they may seem poor, afterwords they will intercede on your behalf with the Almighty"].[113] Malcolm Godden has pointed out that this homily, which is based on Gregory, Haymo, and Smaragdus and is a commentary on Luke 16, has replaced the original *ulceribus plenus*, "full of sores" of Lazarus (Luke 16:20) with the term *licþrowere*, which can refer to a leper, as shown above.[114] It is generally assumed that the name of "Lazars" for lepers was introduced through the Crusader order of the Knights of St. Lazarus of Jerusalem, which was founded as a religious community for lepers and rose to much power in the High Middle Ages. The name itself is based on a confusion between Lazarus the beggar (Luke 16: 20) and Simon the leper, who, after being healed, gave a banquet for Christ (John 12: 1–11). It seems that Ælfric already connects the biblical Lazarus, who is covered in sores, with leprosy, which is even today regarded as a "poor man's disease,"[115] since a life of poverty can result in weakened immunity. While the evidence from early Anglo-Saxon cemeteries does not support such a generalization, it seems that by the time of Ælfric lepers were forced to beg. It is likely that the segregation of lepers from society, and by extension the inability to work, led to the image of the leper as a beggar, which may have already been common in late Anglo-Saxon England. While it is impossible to draw conclusions about the general treatment of lepers from religious texts, which were taken from a variety of sources and interpret leprosy in an allegorical way, we should not forget that homilies and sermons were read from the pulpits of churches to a general public and therefore had reason to use symbols that could be widely understood.

Looking at the evidence from burials, it appears that some fundamental changes in the attitude towards lepers occurred during the Anglo-Saxon period. Pre-Christian burial rites included lepers in the community of the dead, either because their status was more important than the fact that they were diseased, or because the early Anglo-Saxons had little knowledge of the disease, or maybe because they were more tolerant in this respect than their Christian successors. The advent of Christianity brought with it the differentiation of lepers from other social groups, which is evident in the burials of lepers at the fringes of cemeteries, or, as in the case of the St. John the Baptist cemetery, in emerging communities of the diseased, located outside the gates of the city, but also in the literary depiction of leprosy and other skin ailments as diseases of the soul, a visible sign of sin.

---

[113] *Ælfric's Catholic Homilies*, ed. Clemoes, 369.

[114] Godden, *Ælfric's Catholic Homilies: Commentary*, 190–91.

[115] Manchester, "Leprous Skeleton from Eccles," 205.

The change of attitude is vividly expressed in a passage from the *Chronicon Abbatiae Ramesiensis*, which tells of the fate of Bishop Ælfweard, who presided over the see of London but was expelled from his monastery after contracting leprosy, despite having *multis pretiosarum* ["many treasures"],[116] which he subsequently bequeathed to the abbey of Ramsey, where he died in 1044.[117] The *Chronicon* lays the blame for his affliction on his previous act of stealing relics from the tomb of St. Osgith.[118] Despite his being a capable leader, this was not enough to keep him in office or even allow him to remain part of his community.[119] John Cule has recently claimed that the writ *De Leproso amovendo* was in use in England before 1100.[120] I have not yet found a reference to it from the Anglo-Saxon period, but the depiction of lepers in Ælfric's writings as people who are socially inferior and who have to scrape together a living outside of the community cannot be based entirely on just his homiletic sources. It is unknown whether Ælfric ever met a leper in his life, but his characterization of the leprous and diseased in his texts as sinful and despised by society certainly foreshadows attitudes towards leprosy prevalent in literature after the Norman Conquest.[121]

---

[116] *Chronicon Abbatiae Ramesiensis*, ed. Dunn Macray, Rolls Series (London, 1886), 157.

[117] He had formerly been trained at Ramsey.

[118] Macray, ed., *Chronicon*, 157.

[119] The Worcester (D) version of the Anglo-Saxon Chronicle records his death for 1045 and comments on his time as abbot of Evesham: "þæt mynster wel geforðode þa hwile þe he þær wæs" ["the abbey was run well as long as he was there"]: *The Anglo-Saxon Chronicle: A Collaborative Edition*, ed. G. P. Cubbin (Cambridge, 1996), 6: 67.

[120] John Cule, "The Stigma of Leprosy," in *Past and Presence of Leprosy*, ed. Roberts et al., 149–54, here 151.

[121] I would like to express my thanks to Elizabeth Popescu who readily answered questions on the Norwich cemetery of St. John the Baptist. I am also grateful to Judith Jesch and Richard Marsden for their helpful comments on an earlier draft of this essay, to Catherine Karkov for her encouragement, and to The British Academy.

A Map of the Universe:
Geography and Cosmology in the Program
of Alfred the Great

Nicole Guenther Discenza

In early medieval world maps, Britain occupies a small space near the edge of the known world. In early world history, it plays little part. Many ninth-century Anglo-Saxons on the street, or out in the field, might be unaware of their place in the world; as Margaret Bridges writes, "Of course the Anglo-Saxons were no closer to experiencing cosmic liminality than the Antipodeans were ever able to experience what it was like to be suspended upside down."[1] Some few figures — writers such as Adamnán or Bede, religious who went on missions to the Continent or carried on a correspondence across the Channel, and traders who made trips overseas — might realize England's marginal position.

Yet Alfred the Great's late-ninth-century program of education and translation would suddenly bring books rooted in the classical and late antique world to more people. This new audience, likely the future leaders of the nation, would find England relegated to the margins if it appeared at all. Anglo-Saxons probably did not yet think of an "England" *per se*, nor did they feel the unity that the program would help begin to construct, but whether they thought of themselves as Mercians, West Saxons, or even Anglo-Saxons, they would see very little of themselves in most of the program's texts. Perhaps *most* Anglo-Saxons did not experience "cosmic liminality," but for some there must have been a dizzying moment of realizing that they *were* on the edge of the known world.[2] In bringing

---

[1] Margaret Bridges, "Of Myths and Maps: The Anglo-Saxon Cosmographer's Europe," in *Writing and Culture*, ed. Balz Engler (Tübingen, 1992), 69–84, here 72.

[2] King Alfred himself would be aware from personal experience of the great distance between Wessex and Rome: see Asser, chaps. 8 and 11; the Anglo-Saxon Chronicle: A 853; and corresponding entries in other versions of the Chronicle: Asser, *Asser's Life of King Alfred together with the Annals of Saint Neots*, ed. William Henry Stevenson with introductory article by Dorothy Whitelock (Oxford, 1959); and *The Anglo-Saxon Chronicle: A Collaborative Edition*, gen. eds. David Dumville and Simon Keynes (Cambridge,

readers of *englisc* into dialogue with a broader Latin culture, Alfred's program paradoxically risked making the rising new leaders of what was to become England feel insignificant: some of the texts in the program would seem to underscore the country's distance from the heart of culture, religion, and history.

Yet surely this marginality would be contrary to the lived experience of most readers, for whom the center might be wherever the king currently resided, the bounds of their monastery, or where their families held land. Many if not most Anglo-Saxons in the ninth century would have heard of Rome and the pope, and they would know something of that great city's political and religious history. Indeed, Nicholas Howe argues, "the Anglo-Saxons found an intellectual and spiritual *patria* that had Rome as its capital."[3] Though the best-educated Anglo-Saxons may have found a spiritual home in Rome, for most people, even clerics and relatively learned laity, the world was what was around them. Rome could seem far-off and marginal, Jerusalem distant and exotic.[4] Pierre Bourdieu writes,

> Because the dispositions durably inculcated by objective conditions . . . engender aspirations and practices objectively compatible with those objective requirements, the most improbable practices are excluded, either totally without examination, as *unthinkable*, or at the cost of the *double negation* which inclines agents to make a virtue of necessity, that is, to refuse what is anyway refused and to love the inevitable.[5]

At the same time, what was unthinkable to Anglo-Saxons had already been written by Romans and others. What happens when "dispositions durably inculcated" by experience of the Anglo-Saxon world suddenly collide with the expectations of a Mediterranean-centered, late antique disposition?

The translators did not have as calculating a strategy as this analysis might make it appear. To speak of translators' "strategies" is not to endow the translators

---

1983–). My citations refer to the A Chronicle (ed. Janet M. Bately, 1986) unless otherwise specified. See also Simon Keynes, "Anglo-Saxon Entries in the 'Liber Vitae' of Brescia," in *Alfred the Wise: Studies in Honour of Janet Bately on the Occasion of her Sixty-fifth Birthday*, ed. Jane Roberts and Janet L. Nelson with Malcolm Godden (Cambridge, 1997), 99–119, esp. 103, on the difficulties of the journey. On how Rome might have appeared to Anglo-Saxon visitors, see Nicholas Howe, "Rome: Capital of Anglo-Saxon England," *Journal of Medieval and Early Modern Studies* 34 (2004): 147–72, esp. 159–61.

[3] Howe, "Rome," 148.

[4] Howe argues that Alfred's "pedagogical project was in effect a forced program of modernization that sought to reconnect the badly educated and peripheral Anglo-Saxons to the center of Christian belief and culture": "Rome," 158. The "forced" nature of the program reflects the great distance between most Anglo-Saxon and Roman perspectives.

[5] Pierre Bourdieu, *Outline of a Theory of Practice*, trans. Richard Nice (Cambridge, 1977), 77.

with a God-like ability to escape their own dispositions, look down upon both readers and the writers of source texts below, and transfigure the texts into new formations designed to attain a set end such as the unification and glorification of "England."[6] Instead, each translator would constantly mediate between the world from which he (or she) came and the world of Latin texts.

Bourdieu explains "the economy of logic" with the term "'polythesis', the 'confusion of spheres'": the same person or people can overlay two or more contradictory models of the world without being troubled, because they need never put all schemes into practice simultaneously; only in our analysis do they coexist and hence contradict.[7] Thus the same texts that recognize Rome and Jerusalem as political, religious, and cultural centers, and England as a backwater, can *also* redraw the mental map to provide a vision more centered on *Angelcynn* — and a map of the universe in which England, Rome, and Jerusalem are all equally small.

It is at just such moments of cultural contact that *doxa*, "that which is taken for granted," the conventional wisdom that everyone knows, may be exposed as *one* way of thinking among many rather than the *only* possibility.[8] *Doxa* is the conventional wisdom of a society or group that has not (yet) come into question, as when modern scientists still believed that protons and neutrons were the smallest particles of matter, or when society held particular assumptions about women and work that were overturned in the twentieth century.[9] In Alfred's program, Anglo-Saxon *doxa* meets late antique Mediterranean *doxa*. As a result, neither can remain *doxa*. Yet polythesis allows different and conflicting views of the world and the universe to remain in tension in Alfred's program. The workings of these different schemes provide insight into Anglo-Saxon dispositions

---

[6] Kathleen Davis argues that we cannot "assume Alfred's ability to escape and manipulate his own ideological framework" in "National Writing in the Ninth Century: A Reminder for Postcolonial Thinking about the Nation," *Journal of Medieval and Early Modern Studies* 28 (1998): 611–37, here 618. Bourdieu's notions of habitus and strategy prove valuable precisely because they do not require that Alfred and other translators escape ideology, merely that they 'play the game' that they are already playing. At the same time, the collision of Anglo-Saxon and Mediterranean conventional wisdom would make it impossible for *doxa* (for which see below) to remain; no one reading vastly different accounts of the world could continue to assume that his or her own idea of England and the Earth was the only possible viewpoint. No one can fully escape his or her own ideology, but reading and reflection could make Anglo-Saxon thinkers as well as modern ones more aware of ideologies — and more able to respond flexibly to their own and others'.

[7] Bourdieu, *Outline*, 110. For a fuller explanation with several examples of contradictory schemes among the Kabyle people, see *Outline*, 109–24.

[8] Bourdieu, *Outline*, 168.

[9] For *doxa* in modern societies, see Pierre Bourdieu, *The Rules of Art: Genesis and Structure of the Literary Field*, trans. Susan Emanuel (Stanford, CA, 1996), esp. 165–66, 184–86.

and how they might accommodate foreign modes of thought. Alfred and his fellow writers and translators drew upon three strategies to counter England's apparent marginality: a recentering of translated texts around Anglo-Saxon lived experience; a broader, cosmological perspective that reduced the importance of earthly geography; and an emphasis on learning that allowed readers to transcend the limitations of physical place.

Living on the Edge

The marginality of England is immediately evident on world maps. Most medieval maps were not navigation aids but theological and political statements.[10] The simplest and most common maps are called TO *mappae mundi* because they are round maps divided by a T to show the three continents: a circle is divided in half and then half again, with Asia occupying half and Europe and Africa each a quarter. Marcel Destombes estimates that this form made up 60% of extant medieval *mappae mundi*.[11] The East was often although not always at the top, and Jerusalem often represented "the civilized center of the Earth" according to David Woodward, although the convention of putting Jerusalem at the actual center of the map was not set until the early twelfth century or later.[12] Though Greco-Roman models (including some maps transmitted with Orosius's *Historia*) did not center on Jerusalem, Adamnán described a column in the center of Jerusalem as the center of the world and Jerusalem as the "umbilicus terrae" ("navel of the world") in his *De locis sanctis*.[13] Medieval maps and written descriptions tend to

---

[10] Anna-Dorothee von den Brincken, "Europa in der Kartographie des Mittelalters," *Archiv für Kulturgeschichte* 55 (1973): 289–304.

[11] Marcel Destombes, *Mappemondes A.D. 1200–1500*, Catalogue préparé par la Commission des Cartes Anciennes de l'Union Géographique Internationale; Imago Mundi: A Review of Early Cartography, Suppl. 4, Monumenta Cartographica Vetustioris Aevi 1 (Amsterdam, 1964), 19; cited in Bridges, "Of Myths and Maps," 80.

[12] David Woodward, "Medieval *Mappae mundi*," in *The History of Cartography* vol. 1: *Cartography in Prehistoric, Ancient, and Medieval Europe and the Mediterranean*, ed. J. B. Harley and idem (Chicago and London, 1987), 286–370, here 332; for the centering of maps around Jerusalem, see von den Brincken, "Europa," 294. Nicholas Howe argues that for Bede, Jerusalem is central only in a spiritual and metaphorical sense; Rome is the true center of his world. See "An Angle on this Earth: Sense of Place in Anglo-Saxon England," *Bulletin of the John Rylands Library* 82 (2000): 3–27 (a revised version of his 1999 Toller Lecture, 10–11); and idem, "Rome," esp. 150–58.

[13] Reference from Woodward, "*Mappae mundi*," 340; quotation from Adamnán's *De locis sanctis*, ed. Denis Meehan (Dublin, 1958, repr. 1983), 56.27 (bk 1, chapter 11, sec. 4). All translations are my own unless otherwise specified.

put east in a privileged position, "while the western and northern regions come last and least."[14]

Medieval maps almost invariably present the British Isles as small shapes at or near the edge of the map. For instance, Rome, Vatican City, Biblioteca Apostolica Vaticana, lat. 6018, fols. 63v–64r, oddly places west at the top, and labels two islands as if they were seas: "mare mortuorum" ("sea of the dead") and "oceanus occiduus" ("western ocean").[15] Those islands ought to read "Hibernia" and "Britannia"; apparently the cartographers here were working outside what they knew. TO *mappae* typically present Europe as one block and thus often omit the British Isles entirely.[16]

British mapmakers sometimes represented the world a little differently. The earliest extant Anglo-Saxon *mappa mundi*, the Cotton World Map, dates to around 1050 and includes the British Isles.[17] The Cotton World Map is not technically a TO map but has been drawn in a rectangle that nearly fills the manuscript page. It maintains roughly the same organization, however: Asia occupies the top half, Africa the lower right quadrant, and Europe the lower left. Britannia is clearly labeled and relatively large, but very near the edge. The Hereford World Map, drawn over two centuries later, retains much the same shape and still shunts Britannia off into a corner, though the map was clearly produced in England.[18]

Of course, Alfred's people would not have seen these particular maps, but Evelyn Edson notes that Isidore's *De natura rerum* was often called *Liber rotarum* for its diagrams, which included TO *mappae mundi* and other *rotae* or circular diagrams.[19] Three works by Bede now extant in fifteen manuscripts contain *mappae*

---

[14] Bridges, "Of Myths and Maps," 71.

[15] See Evelyn Edson, *Mapping Time and Space: How Medieval Mapmakers Viewed Their World* (London, 1997), 62–63.

[16] See Woodward, "*Mappae mundi*," 297–303, 343–47, and 350–55 for some examples.

[17] London, BL, Cotton Tiberius B.v, fol. 56v. For a good color plate, see P. D. A. Harvey, *Medieval Maps* (Toronto, 1991), plate 19 (p. 26). See also Howe's discussion, "An Angle on This Earth," esp. 11–16.

[18] For the Hereford World Map, see P. D. A. Harvey, *Mappa Mundi: The Hereford World Map* (Toronto, 1996); Naomi Reed Kline, *Maps of Medieval Thought: The Hereford Paradigm* (Woodbridge, 2001); and Scott D. Westrem, *The Hereford Map: A Transcription and Translation of the Legends with Commentary* (Turnhout, 2001).

[19] Evelyn Edson, "World Maps and Easter Tables: Medieval Maps in Context," *Imago Mundi* 48 (1996): 25–42, here 27. For instance, the map from Munich, Bayerische Staatsbibliothek, Clm 10058, fol. 154v, dates to the eleventh century; see Harvey, *Medieval Maps*, 22. For other examples of late antique and medieval maps and *rotae*, see Edson, *Mapping Time and Space*; Harvey, *Medieval Maps*; *The History of Cartography* vol. 1, ed. Harley and Woodward; and James Siebold, "Index of Cartographic Images Illustrating Maps of the Early Medieval Period 400–1300 A.D.," *Index of Early Medieval Maps*, 22 April 1998, www.henry-davis.com/MAPS/EMwebpages/EML.html, accessed 20 May 2005.

mundi: *De temporum ratione*, *De temporibus*, and *De natura rerum*.[20] While we cannot be certain that Alfred and his circle knew such illustrated manuscripts, or even these works, *Fontes Anglo-Saxonici* suggests *De temporum ratione* as a possible source for two lengthy passages in the Old English *Martyrology*, and *De temporibus* as a possible source for one briefer one.[21] Later, Ælfric certainly seems to have made heavy use of *De temporum ratione* and *De natura rerum*, and some of *De temporibus*.[22] Alfred himself may have made use of *De natura rerum* in his *Boethius*; *De natura* may also have informed the Old English *Orosius* and the *Meters of Boethius*.[23]

---

[20] See Woodward, "*Mappae mundi*," 303. Ironically, "Bede himself seems to have had a low opinion of diagrams and tables"; the diagrams postdate Bede and were usually borrowed from Isidore's *De natura rerum*: see Edson, *Mapping Time and Space*, 66. Some figures seem to be from the Carolingian era, and a group circulated together with texts by Bede, Isidore, and others; for details, see Edson *Mapping Time and Space*, 66–71. Several maps from tenth- through twelfth-century manuscripts of *De temporum ratione* (hereafter *DTR*) and *De natura rerum* (hereafter *DNR*) are listed, and a few images can be viewed, at Siebold's website. Destombes, *Mappemondes*, 35–36, lists fifteen manuscripts of Bede's works with maps ranging from the ninth to the twelfth century: from the ninth century, Munich, Bayerische Staatsbibliothek, Clm. 210, fol. 132v (*DTR*); Paris, BN, MS. NAL 1615 (Libri 90), fols. 135 and 170v (*De temporibus* [hereafter *DT*]); Vienna, Nationalbibliothek, Cod. 387, fol. 134 (*DTR*); and Wolfenbüttel, Herzog-August-Bibliothek, Cod. Guelf. 66 Weiss (Cat. no. 4150), fol. 61v (*DNR*). Tenth century: all at Paris, BN: MS. Lat. 5239 (Reg. 5823), fol. 142 (*DT*); MS. Lat. 5543 (Reg. 5961), fol. 136v (*DT*); NAL 456 (Libri 44), fol. 170 (*DTR*). Eleventh century: London, BL, Cotton Tib. B.v (i), fols. 28v–29 (*DNR*; image at Siebold's website, 201D, but listed as *DTR*); Oxford, Bodleian Library, Canon Misc. 560 (S.C. 20036), fol. 3 (*DT*); Paris, BN, MS. Lat. 7474 (Reg. 6582), fol. 84 (*DTR*); Trier, Stadtbibliothek, Cod. 1084, fol. 99 (*DTR*). Twelfth century: three in Paris, BN: MS. Lat. 7418 A (Reg 4346–3–3a), fol. 15v (*DTR*); MS. Lat. 7419 (Reg. 6055–5), fol.16 (*DNR*); MS. Lat. 11130 (S.L. 272 bis), fol. 82 (*DNR*; image: Siebold 205Z); and Rome, Vatican City, Biblioteca Apostolica Vaticana, Vat. Lat. 3123, fol. 112 (*DNR*).

[21] Christine Rauer, "The Sources of the Anonymous Old English *Martyrology* (Cameron C.B.19)," 2000–2002. *Fontes Anglo-Saxonici: World Wide Web Register*, http://fontes. english.ox.ac.uk/. Also available on CD-ROM: version 1.1 (Oxford: 2002).

[22] See *Fontes* for a variety of Ælfrician works, sourced by several contributors, which draw upon Bede's *DTR*, *DT*, and *DNR*.

[23] See Nicole Guenther Discenza, "The Sources of King Alfred's Old English Version of Boethius's *De consolatione philosophiae* (Cameron C.B.9.3)," 2001, *Fontes*; Rohini Jayatilaka, "The Sources of the Old English *Orosius*, *History against the Pagans*," (Cameron C.B.9.2)." 2001–2002, *Fontes*; and Daniel C. Anlezark, "The Sources of the Old English *Meters of Boethius* (Cameron C.A.6)," 2002, *Fontes*.

Thus manuscripts sometimes offered maps of the world. Many more wall maps doubtless graced palaces, churches, and monasteries than now survive.[24] Even if we cannot identify specific maps, some educated Anglo-Saxons probably saw one or more maps and would already be aware of their island's place in the world. Thus, when those who could not read Latin gained learning from the Alfredian translations, perhaps these models of the earth might not come as a complete shock. While no maps appear in extant copies of Alfredian texts, *mappae mundi* and related diagrams that readers might see would only underscore the sense of Britannia as an island near the edge of the world.

Yet Nicholas Howe rightly reminds us that "The surest way to misunderstand the deep engagement in these texts with geography and the ways it constructs culture is to transpose their sense of place to a visual, cartographic form that seems more familiar to us but which in truth largely charts the limits of our own geographic imagination."[25] Some of the audience of Alfredian translations would be familiar with maps and diagrams, but they too would read and hear other kinds of accounts. Those unfamiliar with diagrams would approach geography and cosmology only in the less schematic ways, relying wholly on verbal descriptions.

One of the first translations associated with Alfred's program is the Old English *Orosius*. This text begins with a geography of the world outlining the three continents. Ireland forms the boundary of Europe (9.10 and 19.5); Britannia receives two mentions along the way in the geography derived from the Latin (12.19 and 18.26–27).[26] Then the translator gives more details about each continent: it lists many place- and people-names, all from Orosius's point of view, sometimes expressed by "we" or "Orosius." Many transitions include "we" or use the third person, giving responsibility for the geography to Orosius and not the Old English translator.

The details of Europe include: "From þære ie Danais west oþ Rin þa ea, seo wilð of þæm beorge þe mon Alpis hætt 7 irnð þonne norþryhte on þæs garsecges earm þe þæt lond uton ymblið þe mon Bryttania hætt, 7 eft suþ oð Donua þa ea. . . ." ["From the river Don west until the river Rhine, [Europe] runs from the

---

[24] See Woodward, "*Mappae mundi*," Appendix 18.2 (359–68) for a list of major medieval *mappae mundi*, some of which are no longer extant. Destombes, *Mappemondes*, offers a detailed catalogue of maps to 1500, though the title refers only to the period 1200–1500.

[25] Howe, "An Angle on This Earth," 9.

[26] *The Old English Orosius*, ed. Janet M. Bately, EETS s.s. 6 (London, 1980). Subsequent primary citations will be parenthetical, in the form (page number.line number). For other written traditions marginalizing England, such as Vergil's first *Eclogue* and Gildas's *De excidio Britanniae*, see Howe, "An Angle on This Earth," esp. 9–10.

range which one calls the Alps and runs then to the north and into the arm of
the sea which lies around that land that one calls Britannia, and again south until
the river Danube. . . .": 12.17–20].[27] Britain is nothing to write home about, and
the description at once returns to more central places like Greece and Germania.
Then the *Orosius* goes into a number of specifics that are not from the Latin. As
Bately notes, it "seems to describe the area as it was known in the second half of
the ninth century."[28] Britain reappears in this passage:

> Brittania þæt igland, hit is norððeastlang, 7 hit is eahta hund mila lang 7
> twa hund mila brad. Þonne is be suðan him on oðre healfe þæs sæs earmes
> Gallia Bellica, 7 on westhealfe on oþre healfe þæs sæs earmes is Ibærnia
> þæt igland, 7 on norðhealfe Orcadus þæt igland. Igbernia, þæt we Scotland
> hatað, hit is on ælce healfe ymbfangen mid garsecge, 7 for ðon þe sio sunne
> þær gæð near on setl þonne on oðrum lande, þær syndon lyðran wedera
> þonne on Brettannia. Þonne be westannorðan Ibernia is þæt ytemeste land
> þæt man hæt Thila, 7 him is feawum mannum cuð for ðære oferfyrre.
> (19.11–20)

> ["That island Britain extends to the northeast, and it is 800 miles long and
> 200 miles broad. Then to the south of it, on the other side of the sea's arm,
> is Gallia Belgica, and on the west side, on the other side of the sea's arm, is
> that island Hibernia, and on the north side the island Orcades. Hibernia,
> which we call Ireland, is on each side surrounded by the sea, and because
> the sun sets nearer there than in other lands, the weather is milder there
> than in Britain. Then to the northwest of Hibernia is that outermost land
> that men call Thule, and it is known to few because of the excessive dis-
> tance."]

Yet Britain's peoples are not listed, unlike those of other parts of Europe. The
British Isles, like Thule, appear too distant to be known. The geography then
turns to Africa.

After the geographical introduction, the *Orosius* dives into history. Its focus, unsurprisingly, remains outside England: Book I is largely biblical, involving mainly Assyria, Egypt, and Israel; Book II concerns the founding and early
days of Rome; III still centers on Rome, but it includes Lacedaemon and Persia
and follows the adventures of Alexander the Great for a time; IV and V develop

---

[27] Translations (and any errors therein) are my own, but I am indebted to Janet
Bately's excellent Glossaries for the *Orosius*. For changes to the geographical perspective
in the OE version, see Salvador Insa Sales, "The Treatment of Some Spanish Matters in
the Old English *Orosius*," *Revista de la Sociedad Española de Lengua y Literatura Inglesa
Medieval* 9 (1999): 173–79.

[28] Bately, *Orosius*, notes to 12.23, pp. 166–67.

Rome, its wars, and its foreign affairs. Britain receives a few mentions totaling less than two pages in Bately's 156-page edition of the text.[29]

Throughout, Orosius's theme of four great empires develops. As put succinctly in one passage:

> An wæs Babylonicum, þær Ninus ricsade. Þæt oðer wæs Creca, þær Alexander ricsade. Þridda wæs Affricanum, þær Ptolome ricsedon. Se feorða is Romane, þe giet ricsiende sindon. Þas feower heafodricu sindon on feower endum þyses middangeardes mid unasecgendlicre Godes tacnunge. (36.12–16)

> ["The first was the Babylonian [empire], where Ninus ruled. The second was Greek, where Alexander ruled. The third was African, where Ptolemy ruled. The fourth is Roman, which is yet ruling. These four empires are in the four ends of this earth through the dispensation of the ineffable God."]

God has planned four empires, one in each direction. The last of these, Rome, is contemporary for Orosius; but, as Malcolm Godden writes, the Anglo-Saxons thought that it too had fallen well before the ninth century.[30] There is no room for more empires, and Britain holds no interest for the first three and only slight interest for the fourth. The *Orosius* reduces Britain to a speck, and one inhabited by Britons. England does not exist in world geography, and the Anglo-Saxons do not appear in this world history. The *Orosius*'s presentation of history must come into conflict with the *doxa* of its Anglo-Saxon audience's perceptions of history.

Other texts in the program show a world that seems to *lack* England. The Old English *Boethius* contains a surprising degree of geographical and historical detail, with over thirty place- and people-names.[31] The history is almost purely classical,

---

[29] Julius Caesar's conquest gets ten lines (126.1–10), the later battles of Severus with the Picts and Scots merit almost four (142.11–14), reference to Constantius gains Brittania a little over a page in the edition (147.3–148.9), and Maximianus wins in another two lines (153.28–29).

[30] Malcolm R. Godden, "The Anglo-Saxons and the Goths: Rewriting the Sack of Rome," *ASE* 31 (2002): 47–68, esp. 64.

[31] Alfred copies several place names directly from the Latin: Creca (18.18; for "Lydorum" II pr. ii. 11), Pærsa (18.19), Ætne (34.8), Etne (34.28), Africanas (36.7, 37.6; for "Poenorum" II pr. vi. 11), Caucaseas (43.9), Parðum (43.12), Indeum (67.31), Tyle (67.32), Retie (115.16, an error for Neritii). Many forms of "romana" and "romanisc" occur. Other names which Alfred makes explicit where Boethius implies them, or simply adds to the text, are: Gotan (7.1), Sciððiu (7.1), Italia (7.3), Sicilia (7.4), Amulinga (7.6), Constentinopolim (7.20), Ierusalem (11.18), Sicilia (34.9), Sicilia (34.29), Egyptum (36.29), Nilus (37.3), Trogiaburg (39.20), Sciððeas (43.10), Nensar (99.9), Deira (99.10), Babilonia (99.11), Ðracia (101.23), Creca (101.24), Leuita (102.30), Troiana (115.14),

from an account of the Golden Age (33.20–34.13) to many references to Roman emperors and a few to other Mediterranean powers. Neither England nor Anglo-Saxons ever appear. At the same time, Wærferth's *Dialogues* explores a much more limited geography: Gregory the Great wrote his source text explicitly to demonstrate that saints and miracles can still be found in his day — in Italy.[32] The Verse Preface to the *Pastoral Care* identifies Gregory as "Rome papa" ["pope at Rome," 9.9] and "Romwara betest" ["best of Romans," 9.12], while almost a hundred mentions of two dozen different places and peoples in or near the Holy Land fill the *Pastoral Care*.[33]

Iþacige (115.16), Wendelsæ (115.22–23), Crecum (141.11), Lædenwarum (141.12–13). All these are from *King Alfred's Old English Version of Boethius' De Consolatione Philosophiae*, ed. Walter John Sedgefield (Oxford, 1899). See also Nicole Guenther Discenza, *The King's English: Strategies of Translation in the Old English Boethius* (Albany, NY, 2005), 15–19, for the *Boethius*'s treatment of proper nouns.

[32] *Bischof Wærferths von Worcester Übersetzung der Dialoge Gregors des Grossen*, ed. Hans Hecht (Leipzig, 1900–1907, repr. Darmstadt, 1965).

[33] The best edition of the Verse Preface as verse is in *The Anglo-Saxon Minor Poems*, ed. Elliott Van Kirk Dobbie, ASPR 6 (New York, 1942), 110; I have cited both prose and verse from *King Alfred's West-Saxon Version of Gregory's Pastoral Care*, ed. Henry Sweet, EETS o.s. 45, 50 (London, 1871; repr. as 1 vol., Oxford, 1996) for the sake of convenience. See also Nicole Guenther Discenza, "Alfred's Verse Preface to the *Pastoral Care* and the Chain of Authority," *Neophilologus* 85 (2001): 625–33. While the many mentions of scriptural figures or parties such as David, Saul, Solomon, the Pharisees, Paul, and many others put the minds of readers of the *Pastoral Care* firmly in the Holy Land, specific places receive notice as well: Babylon (267.9, 267.10), Babylonia (39.13); Canonea land (Canaan, 389.32); Corinctheum (211.1, 323.11, 371.18–19, 395.12, 425.31); Ebreas/ebreiscan (205.7, 415.15–16); Egipt (403.33, 405.1, 405.3); Galatas/Galatiscan/Galað (Galatians or Gilead and its inhabitants, depending on context; the forms seem interchangeable; 117.7, 207.13, 207.14, 367.3, 367.5, 367.8, 367.14), Galileum (43.20); Gomorwara (Gomorrah, 427.33); Hierusalem (161.4, 161.10, 161.13, 161.21, 161.25, 163.12, 163.23, 311.6–7, 311.9, 311.11, 385.21, 385.22, 463.23); Idumeas (367.27); Israhel (39.2, 79.5, 79.6, 89.19, 89.21, 113.5, 113.9, 153.22, 157.5, 257.17, 267.14, 267.17, 304.10, 387.26, 389.32, 423.13, 423.17); Iudea/Iudeas (33.14, 101.6, 151.20, 207.8, 241.6, 315.24, 355.24, 403.31, 413.26, 443.3, 443.14); Kolosensum (Colossians, 311.25); Leuis kynn (tribe of Levi, 353.14); Libano/Liuano (Lebanon, 65.24, 433.19, 433.24); Madianiten (353.19); Nazarensican (443.5, 443.23); Salonicensa (Thessalonians, 213.4); Sardis (445.20); Segor (Zoar, 397.33, 399.9, 399.13, 399.14, 399.15); Sidon (409.32, 409.34); Sodoman/Sodome (Sodom, 397.33, 397.34, 399.9, 399.14, 427.28, 427.29, 427.33). Alfred also writes, "Gregorius lærde, se wæs oðrum noman genemned Nanzanzenus" ("Gregory taught, who was named by his other name Nazianzenus," 173.16–17), but it is not at all clear that he recognizes the surname as a place name. In two places English is mentioned, but as a language, not a people: Alfred says "on Englisc" and supplies a translation or synonym for a word or name at 139.15 and 367.5.

Finally, Alfred's prose rendering of the first fifty Psalms refers to seventeen different places and races in the Holy Land, mentioned over eighty times.[34] Many of these references are in the introductions to the Psalms: David's kingdom appears in the introduction to Ps. 7, and his flight from Saul into the wilderness in the introductions to 10, 35, and 38; direct references to Assyria and the Babylonian captivity appear in seventeen introductions.[35] Several other specific historical figures, peoples, tribes, and places appear in the introductions.[36] The Psalms frequently refer to "Israele" or "Israhela"; God's holy mountain or the mountain Sion; Mount Libanus, Cades, Tarsus and Cilicia, Hermon, the River Jordan, and Tyre. The Old English text seems to center God and Christian history in the Holy Land, as many early Latin descriptions and maps did. Adamnán wrote his *De locis sanctis* based on the account of Bishop Arculf, who gave both an oral description and some maps of churches in Jerusalem; Bede later adapted Adamnán's *De locis sanctis* himself in the *Historia Ecclesiastica*. Both, of course, make Jerusalem central to Christian history. Alfred certainly knew Bede, but the Old English *Martyrology* goes further, drawing several passages straight from Adamnán.[37] Though some translations provide more reminders of England's marginality than others, readers can never forget it.

---

[34] *King Alfred's Old English Prose Translation of the First Fifty Psalms*, ed. Patrick P. O'Neill (Cambridge, MA, 2001). Following O'Neill's practice, I cite using the second, parenthetical set of line numbers for ease of matching with the Latin text. Assirie (Introductions to 12, 13, 25, 28, 29, 33, 45); Babilonia (Ints. 14, 22, 24, 25, 30, 39, 41, 42, 50); (tribe of) Beniamin (Int. 45); Cades (28.8); Cilicia (47.8); Cyðþiscan (Hittite; Int. 50); Ermon (Hermon; 41.7); Hierusalem (Int. 14; 9.15, 45.5, 47.13); (River) Iordan (41.7); Israele (Ints. 14, 22, 25, 41, 46, 50; 13.7 (twice), 21.4, 21.22, 24.22, 40.14, 46.2, 49.7); Iude (tribe of Judah; Int. 45; 47.12); Iudeas/Iudas (Ints. 2, 4, 5, 10–13, 16, 17, 25, 28–30, 38–43, 45, 46, 49; 16.14, 17.46, 47.12); Libanus (28.5, 36.35); Syon/Sion (2.6, 9.12, 13.7, 19.3, 47.3, 47.12, 47.13, 49.2); Syria (Int 45); Tarsit (Tharsis, 47.8); Tyrig (Tyre, 44.13). For searches of the Psalms, I used O'Neill's Glossary of Proper Names (346-47) and the Dictionary of Old English Corpus online (http://ets.umdl.umich.edu/o/oec/; access restricted to subscribers). All other word searches and counts were performed with the online Corpus.

[35] See above note for specifics. Other references to difficulties, etc., such as "earfoþum" ("difficulties") in the introduction to 32, remind readers more obliquely of such events as the Babylonian captivity.

[36] Specific references include frequent mention of David and Ezechias; Mathathia and Machabeas under King Antiochus (Int. 43); Machaebeum (Int. 46); the tribes of Judah and Benjamin, along with "Faccees, Rumeles suna, and Rasses, Syria cyncges", "cynincges geearnuncga Achats" (Int. 45); and Uriah being sent against the Hittites (Int. 50).

[37] See Rauer, "The Sources of the Anonymous Old English *Martyrology*."

Recentering

At the same time, several Alfredian texts engage in a strategy of recentering readers on Britannia, England, the land of the Anglo-Saxons. England comes into focus, sometimes even in the very texts which marginalize it.[38] First and foremost, of course, even as "the Latinity of [the source texts] would also have underscored the intellectual preeminence of Rome," the *act* of translation into English validates the vernacular and puts the Anglo-Saxons into contact with a world culture.[39] A geographical recentering takes place as well, the first strategy that Alfred and his fellow translators used to deal with England's insignificance to world history and geography.

While the *Orosius*'s traditional geography places Britannia at the very margin, two inserted interviews suddenly change voice and orientation. At the heart of the extended world geography, instead of the usual "Orosius cwæð" ["Orosius said"], we read, "Ohthere sæde his hlaforde, Ælfrede cyninge. . . ." ["Ohthere said to his lord, King Alfred. . . ." 13.29], and a little later, "Wulfstan sæde. . . ." ["Wulfstan said," 16.21]. The interviews say nothing of England itself, but the shifted viewpoint makes that unnecessary: England becomes the center to which these explorers return after they have gone to *more* marginal lands, and Alfred is their "lord."

Paradoxically, mentions of the distant lands in the main narrative may also help bring England notionally closer to the rest of Europe. In the *Orosius*, Persia, Assyria, and lands even farther to the east take up much of the text; the *Boethius* likewise offers a world bounded by India and Thule. These places lie so distant as to make Francia and Rome seem close, implicitly putting Wessex nearer the centers of politics and religion than the texts explicitly allow. At the same time, the *Orosius* relates Alexander's triumphs in these far-off lands very matter-of-factly; places that in a text like *Marvels of the East* or *Alexander's Letter to Aristotle* would be filled with wondrous peoples and animals are here simply the settings for battles, and it is Alexander's relatively conventional victories that excite admiration.[40] It is quite a big world out there, but the people and places are not

---

[38] For the politics of translation, see esp. Davis, "National Writing," and eadem, "Performance of Translation Theory in King Alfred's National Literary Program," in *Manuscript, Narrative, Lexicon: Essays on Literary and Cultural Transmission in Honor of Whitney F. Bolton*, ed. Robert Boenig and Kathleen Davis (Lewisburg, PA, 2000), 149–70; and Discenza, *King's English*.

[39] Howe, "Rome," 158.

[40] The major exception occurs at 68.24–27, with an extraordinarily cold river. For a key study of such texts as *Wonders of the East*, see Andy Orchard, *Pride and Prodigies: Studies in the Monsters of the 'Beowulf'-Manuscript* (Cambridge, 1995).

so alien. The distances can be traversed, and northerners like Ohthere come to England to find welcome at court. Distant lands can be understood. Moreover, at least one *Orosius* manuscript counterbalanced the focus outside England with a focus inside England: London, BL, Cotton Tiberius B.i begins with the *Orosius* and ends with the Anglo-Saxon Chronicle C.[41] The Anglo-Saxons have their own history, which serves in this manuscript almost as a continuation of the Old English *Orosius*.

Other texts do more to recenter readers' world-view around the land of the Anglo-Saxons. While Alfred's Preface to the *Pastoral Care* shows a clear awareness of the higher status of Latin, Alfred insists on using the *englisc* language, named four times in the Preface and once in the Verse Preface, for readers in *Angelcynn*, a word he uses seven times in the Preface, though it was a new term.[42] In this context, respect for Latin language and culture actually encourages respect for English language and culture, because Alfred positions the Anglo-Saxons as the heirs of ancient culture, establishing a genealogy of authority, in which Hebrew, Greek, and Latin culture culminate in Anglo-Saxon:[43]

Ða gemunde ic hu sio æ wæs ærest on Ebreisc geðiode funden, & eft, ða hie Creacas geliornodon, ða wendon hie hie on hiora agen geðiode ealle, & eac

---

[41] For a full description of the manuscript, see Katherine O'Brien O'Keeffe's edition of the C text in the *Collaborative Edition*, vol. 5 (2001), xv–lvi.

[42] *Angelcynn* appears at 3.3, 3.4, 3.13, 5.10, 5.20, 7.10, 7.16. See Sarah Foot, "The Making of *Angelcynn*: English Identity before the Norman Conquest," *Transactions of the Royal Historical Society* 6th ser. 6 (1996): 25–49, for the term. See also Patrick Wormald, "Bede, the *Bretwaldas* and the Origins of the *Gens Anglorum*," in *Ideal and Reality in Frankish and Anglo-Saxon Society: Studies Presented to J. M. Wallace-Hadrill*, ed. idem, with Donald Bullough and Roger Collins (Oxford, 1983), 99–129; and idem, "*Engla Lond*: The Making of an Allegiance," *Journal of Historical Sociology* 7 (1994): 1–24, esp. 10–18 on terms for the English and their sense of identity from Bede on. *Englisc* appears in the Prose Preface at 3.15, 7.18, 7.19, and 7.24; and in the Verse Preface at 9.13. Alfred also invokes the English language twice in the body of the *Pastoral Care*; see note 33 above.

[43] Kathleen Davis notes Alfred's emphasis on following church tradition: Gregory is his source author, while Continental models such as Charlemagne worked very much in a church context as well ("Performance," 151–54). Davis argues in "National Writing," "Alfred never considers that the vernacular might be inappropriate or inferior, but suggests that Latin was retained only because 'woldon ðæt her ðy mara wisdom on londe wære ðy we ma geðeoda cuðon' [they would have it that the more languages we knew, the greater would be wisdom in this land] (5/24–25). According to this formulation, translation is necessary, but it is not an unfortunate compromise. Rather, the English vernacular stands as one among many legitimate languages . . ." (615). Surely Alfred and his audience both recognized the superior status of Latin; by not explicitly addressing or apologizing for the difference, however, Alfred avoids reinforcing it at the very moment he seeks to legitimate English.

ealle oðre bec. & eft Lædenware swæ same, siððan hie hie geliornodon, hie
hie wendon ealla ðurh wise wealhstodas on hiora agen geðiode. Ond eac
ealla oðræ Cristnæ ðioda sumne dæl hiora on hiora agen geðiode wendon.
(5.25–7.5)

["Then I recalled how the law was first written in Hebrew, and again, when
the Greeks learned it, then they translated it all into their own language,
and also all other books. And again, the Romans did the same: once they
learned them, they translated them all through wise translators into their
own language. And also all other Christian peoples translated some portion of them into their own language."]

The Anglo-Saxons represent the culmination of Hebrew, Greek, and Latin culture. The Verse Preface's description of the *Pastoral Care* touches repeatedly on
its Roman origins, but it also establishes the line of transmission: Augustine of
Canterbury brought it from Rome, from Gregory himself.[44] Many readers must
also have been aware of Bede's famous punning story of Gregory as the great con-
verter of the Angles, which appears both in Bede's Latin text (ed. Colgrave and
Mynors, 132–34) and its Old English translation (12.1; OE *Bede* 96.3–98.12).[45]
Colgrave and Mynors note in their edition that the story appears to be a traditional oral tale; the audience would not necessarily have needed familiarity with
Bede to know that the author of the Latin *Pastoral Care* had a special connection
to the Anglo-Saxons.[46] The Preface simultaneously nods to the importance of
Rome and establishes the importance of *Angelcynn*.

    Taking a slightly different tack, the Psalms, for all their geographical speci-
ficity, invite the reader to identify directly with David. Introductions to most
Psalms list the circumstances under which any righteous man might say these
words. The Psalms' translation by Alfred also suggests an identification between
Alfred, the king beset by Vikings, and David, the future king beset by Saul:
despite the differences between the Israelites and the Anglo-Saxons, and their
respective kings, their circumstances seem parallel, and readers can bring one

---

[44] See Discenza, "Alfred's Verse Preface."

[45] See Howe, "An Angle on This Earth," for Bede's treatment of *Angli* and later ap-
propriations of it.

[46] *Bede's Ecclesiastical History of the English People*, ed. and trans. Bertram Colgrave
and R. A. B. Mynors (Oxford, 1969), 133n: "This story which Bede says is traditional is
found in a shorter and slightly different form in the Whitby *Life*. Both authors are probably quoting from different forms of the oral tradition." Wormald argues that Gregory's
formulation, transmitted through Canterbury and spread by Bede, helped form a single
identity for the mixture of people as the Angles, Saxons, Jutes, et al. converted to Christianity and established ecclesiastical hierarchies: "Bede, the *Bretwaldas*."

world-view to bear in interpreting both sets of experiences.[47] Even the *Boethius* mentions the Germanic Weland the Smith in an otherwise highly classical mythology (46.16–21). The *Boethius*, like the Franks Casket and some of Alfred's coinage, fuses Germanic and Roman traditions to underscore the Anglo-Saxons' continental heritage.[48]

Thus England has much in common with Rome and Israel. Of course, the texts most effective at recentering readers' mental geography are the two histories of and by the English themselves: the Anglo-Saxon Chronicle and the Old English *Bede*. The Chronicle establishes an internal English geography (D and E even start with a geographical preface before the first entry) while supplying a history comparable to the classical histories.[49] Julius Caesar's conquest of the island initiates all Chronicle entries; the birth of Christ follows, while the *Breten* people are mentioned only sporadically (167, 189, 381, 409), all in contexts linked to Rome.[50] After 449 the Anglo-Saxons take center stage, culminating, in the first recension, in Alfred. Yet the Anglo-Saxon Chronicle is decidedly non-insular in some ways: entries tell of the Vikings in Francia while they are not in the British Isles; Alfred's dispatch of messengers with alms to Rome demonstrates close, regular ties to this still-important city and the importance of the

---

[47] See Nicholas Howe, *Migration and Mythmaking in Anglo-Saxon England* (New Haven, 1989) for the Anglo-Saxon self-identity as the heirs of Israel. Alfred himself sometimes identifies with the narrators of the dialogues he translates but often underscores their historical situatedness; see Malcolm R. Godden, "The Player King: Identification and Self-Representation in King Alfred's Writings," in *Alfred the Great: Papers from the Eleventh-Centenary Conferences*, ed. Timothy Reuter (Aldershot, 2003), 137–50. (For a very different reading of Alfred's self-representation that emphasizes identification with his characters, see David Pratt, "The Illnesses of King Alfred the Great," *ASE* 30 [2001]: 39–90.) Bourdieu would describe such identification as a relation of homology; see *Outline*, 86 and *Rules of Art*, esp. 161–66.

[48] Also like the *Boethius*, the Franks Casket treats images of good and bad kingship, both Roman and Germanic, as Catherine Karkov notes (personal communication, August 2004). For detailed examination of the Franks Casket, see Leslie Webster, "The Iconographic Programme of the Franks Casket," in *Northumbria's Golden Age*, ed. Jane Hawkes and Susan Mills (Stroud, 1999), 227–46. In the same volume, James Lang suggests a connection between the Franks Casket and Psalm 68 and its exegesis: "The Imagery of the Franks Casket: Another Approach," 247–55, and Carol Neuman de Vegvar discusses Roman and Anglo-Saxon versions of a classical legend in "The Travelling Twins: Romulus and Remus in Anglo-Saxon England," 256–67.

[49] See Jacqueline Ann Stodnick, "Writing Home: Place and Narrative in Anglo-Saxon England" (Ph.D. diss., University of Notre Dame, 2002), for detailed analysis of geography in the C text of the Chronicle.

[50] Maximianus was born in Britain (A 381), the Goths' sack of Rome ended Roman rule in Britain (A 409), the Romans pulled out in 418, the Britons pleaded for help in 443.

idea of Rome in Alfredian literature.[51] The arrival of monks from Ireland in a boat and mention of the death of the Irish scholar Swifneh (891) show a place and people even more remote than *Angelcynn*. The Anglo-Saxons are *not* isolated, as Orosius's Latin, and even much of its Old English translation, seem to imply. Surely *this* representation of history, centered on England, fits Anglo-Saxon dispositions much more comfortably than do classical histories.

The Old English *Bede* also provides geography and history focused on Britannia.[52] From the sources of information that Bede lists to the dedication to King Ceolwulf of Northumbria, the preface (both in Latin and in the Old English translation) focuses on the land of the Anglo-Saxons.[53] The *Bede* proper, like the Latin *Historia Ecclesiastica*, begins with the geography of the island itself. As in the Chronicle, Julius Caesar and other Roman emperors appear at the beginning, but they have been selected according to their relevance to Britain. The vast majority of the action takes place within England, at specific, often familiar locations, involving first Britons, then Anglo-Saxons. The texts follows some Anglo-Saxons in exile or mission to the continent as well, including kings who give it all up to die in Rome in V.7 (Cædwalla 468–72, OE 404.16–406.8; Ine and others, 472, OE 406.8–17), showing the distance to be great but not insurmountable. England is the new center of this history.[54] The *Bede* may well have been translated after the Chronicle was begun, and it may even have been translated after Alfred's death, but it certainly continues the work of his program.[55]

Thus some of the same texts that seem to make England marginal geographically and historically also shift temporarily to an Anglo-Saxon orientation, while two emphasize England's importance. These changes may seem obtrusive to

---

[51] Susan Irvine, "The *Anglo-Saxon Chronicle* and the Idea of Rome in Alfredian Literature," in *Alfred the Great: Papers from the Eleventh-Centenary Conferences*, 63–77.

[52] The OE version notably deletes documentation, especially that from non-Anglo-Saxon writers; see Nicole Guenther Discenza, "The Old English *Bede* and the Construction of Anglo-Saxon Authority," *ASE* 31 (2002): 69–80.

[53] *Bede's Ecclesiastical History*, 2–6; *The Old English Version of Bede's Ecclesiastical History of the English People*, ed. Thomas Miller, EETS o.s. 95–96, 110–111 (London, 1890), 2.1–6.3.

[54] Howe sees Bede's treatment of Rome and England's missionary activity as making Rome central: "Rome," esp. 152, but the translation's abridgements and deletions serve to make England more focal and Rome less prominent; see Discenza, "Old English *Bede*."

[55] The date of the *Bede* is uncertain and Janet Bately argues that it may well be later; even if Alfred sponsored the translation, it may have been completed after his death. For Bately's dating see "Old English Prose Before and During the Reign of Alfred," *ASE* 17 (1988): 93–138, esp. 97–98 and 103–4. Dorothy Whitelock summarizes dating arguments in "The Prose of Alfred's Reign," in *Continuations and Beginnings: Studies in Old English Literature*, ed. Eric Gerald Stanley (London, 1966), 67–103; and eadem, "Old English Bede," *Proceedings of the British Academy* 48 (1962): 57–90, remains crucial for the study of the text. Foot discusses the *Bede* as part of Alfred's program in some detail in "The Making of *Angelcynn*," esp. 38–41.

modern readers who compare the source texts and translations, but to vernacular readers making first contact with a larger world, for whom *Angelcynn* was always already a central reference point, the shifts would probably be imperceptible.

Specks in the Universe

Yet these geographical and historical strategies remain in constant tension with the program's cosmological bent, which emphasizes the small size and brief life of the world and shifts attention to the larger universe and lasting realms.[56] Such cosmology simultaneously and equally diminishes not only *Angelcynn* but Rome and Jerusalem, a second strategy translators used.

As the geographical place of England was graphically represented by maps, so the place of the earth in the universe was graphically represented by figures called *rotae* (or 'wheels'). Isidore of Seville produced many of these representing the winds, zones of the earth, and seasons. While Bourdieu writes that different schemes can coexist because they come into practical use at different times and there is no "assembling of these meanings in simultaneity,"[57] Isidore and others heap together circular diagrams with very different meanings and sometimes dizzying shifts of viewpoint. Two common Isidorean *rotae* show earth at the center of the planets and the relationship between microcosm and macrocosm. Earth may be central, but it occupies the center of a sphere or disk several times its own size.[58]

---

[56] Bridges notes Augustine's similar strategies, "problematizing the representation of geographical reality through diverting attention away from the map in favour of moralizing allegorizations as well as through his replacement of tribes and nations by communities of believers": "Of Myths and Maps," 79.

[57] Bourdieu, *Outline*, 110–12 and 123; quotation at 123.

[58] For examples, see Edson, *Mapping Time and Space*, pls. 3.1–3.6 on pp. 41–45, and Kline, *Maps of Medieval Thought*, figs. 1.2–1.26, and her discussion in Chapter 1, "The Cosmological Wheel," 7–43. Woodward, "*Mappae mundi*," gives examples of an Isidorean rota (fig. 18.39, p. 337) and a diagram from Bede's *De natura rerum* that maps out the relations among the cardinal directions, the continents, the elements, the seasons, and the properties of matter (18.38, p. 335). Cambridge, Trinity College O.3.7 and Cambridge, University Library Kk.3.21 show *rotae* rather like Edson's 3.1–3.4; these post-Conquest manuscripts present Boethius's *De consolatione philosophiae* with glosses, and their diagrams illustrate the cosmological meter (3 met. 9). Other microcosm-macrocosm diagrams might relate man to the whole universe, as does a somewhat eccentric representation from Byrhtferth's *Computus* (Oxford, St. John's College, MS. 17, fol. 7v); a wonderful color plate can be found in Evelyn Edson and Emilie Savage-Smith, *Medieval Views of the Cosmos: Picturing the Universe in the Christian and Islamic Middle Ages*, with foreword by Terry Jones (Oxford, 2004), fig. 11, p. 27; and *Byrhtferth's Enchiridion*, ed. Peter S. Baker and Michael Lapidge, EETS s.s. 177 (Oxford, 1995), offers a clear diagram with all the Latin inscriptions in Appendix A, p. 374.

In a huge universe, England, Rome, and Jerusalem all become mere specks. The Alfredian texts, even while they make Anglo-Saxon England a place of importance, simultaneously reduce the importance of place in the world to take a more metaphysical stance.

The *Orosius* makes the point historically. While Britain seems minor compared to the four great empires God ordained, just how important are those empires? The text gives us the answer:

> Seo ilce burg Babylonia, seo ðe mæst wæs 7 ærest ealra burga, seo is nu læst 7 westaste. Nu seo burg swelc is, þe ær wæs ealra weorca fæstast 7 wunderlecast 7 mærast, gelice 7 heo wære to bisene asteald eallum middangearde, 7 eac swelce heo self sprecende sie to eallum moncynne 7 cweþe: "Nu ic þuss gehroren eam 7 aweg gewiten, hwæt, ge magan on me ongietan 7 oncnawan þæt ge nanuht mid eow nabbað fæstes ne stronges þætte þurhwunigean mæge." (43.33–44.6)

> ["That same city Babylon, which was the greatest and the first of all cities, it is now the last and most desolate. And now the city is such, which before was the strongest and most wonderful and most famous of all works, [that it is] just as if it were established as an example to all earth, and also as if she herself were speaking to all mankind and said, 'Now I am thus fallen and departed away; look, you may understand and know in me that you have no fastness with you nor strength that can survive.'"]

The text later details God's plan in having four empires, and how long they lasted (132.24–133.28), but ultimately what matters is not the places but the salvation of God's people.

Bede similarly focuses not so much on England as a place, but on "historiae ecclesiasticae gentis Anglorum" ("history of the church of the English people," 8, top of the Latin table of contents);[59] the narrative centers on the conversion of the Anglo-Saxons and their adoption of Roman practice to assume their place as God's people. Of the histories, only the Anglo-Saxon Chronicle has no overt salvific or providential drive, but rather a dynastic drive, as the first recension presents Alfred as the pinnacle of Anglo-Saxon kingship. The Chronicle does, however, occasionally invoke the Deity, as the miraculous healer of Pope Leo

---

[59] Literally, "the race of the Angles." Stodnick argues that Bede uses the term both for all Anglo-Saxons and for Northumbrians, and it is sometimes difficult to tell which he means ("Writing Home," 89–92). Compare Wormald, *"Engla Lond,"* who argues that Bede's use of *Angli* for Angles, Saxons, and other ethnicities helped found a common English identity. Here Bede seems to use *Angli* inclusively. (The Old English offers no equivalent term.)

after his mutilation in 797, and protector of the Anglo-Saxons in 896.[60] The Psalms, while solidly grounded in the physical setting of the Holy Land, unsurprisingly remind readers that God's creation goes beyond earth with five mentions of angels, while Psalm 48 concerns hell.[61] The *Pastoral Care* makes direct reference to heaven thirty-nine times and hell seven times.[62] These texts all construct a greater cosmology, making the space of earth smaller and of secondary importance.

The *Boethius* offers a more complete cosmology than any of the other texts. It situates the earth among the stars, naming constellations (Boeties, 126.8, and Ursa, 135.29) in passing. Frequent references to heaven, hell, angels, and devils reduce the entire earth to a "rondbeag on scelde" ["boss on the shield," 41.25–60] of the cosmos.[63] While central, and not inconsequential, it is a small part of a much larger universe. Finally, in Alfred's famous extended metaphor, God is the center of a wagon wheel; to escape the effects of Fortune, one must move up the spokes to Him (129.19–131.19). The image of an earth-centered universe that the *rotae* present is here replaced by a very similar but God-centered universe in which physical geography becomes almost irrelevant. Wisdom also explains that much of this vast world is uninhabitable, and that fame does not travel widely.[64]

---

[60] I do not include the later addition to 890 that describes Plegmund as "gecoron of Gode" in a hand of the late eleventh or early twelfth century; see Bately's edition of the A Chronicle, note 3 to the 890 annal and Introduction, p. xxxix.

[61] Int. 33; 8.6, 33.8, 34.5, and 34.6.

[62] The *Pastoral Care* mentions angels as intermediaries (or protectors) at 101.20, 251.25, 255.24, 257.8, 379.16, 399.22, 399.30, 405.33, and 445.35. Fallen angels appear at 111.23, 249.18, 301.18, 329.7, 357.16, and 359.1. Other mentions of angels include 261.12 (companions of Christ in heaven) and 385.14 (Christ as teacher of angels). There are 38 mentions of *heofen/heofn* or *hefen/hefn*: 33.13, 59.19–20, 67.15, 81.14, 85.7, 85.8, 99.8, 99.18, 99.23, 101.19, 125.20, 161.17, 169.6, 169.10, 195.18, 203.2, 222.23 (Cotton; passage missing from Hatton), 233.20, 249.15, 255.4, 285.16, 321.7, 347.25, 351.10, 385.14, 393.35, 395.24, 397.16, 401.2, 403.3, 403.26, 411.12, 443.19, 443.27, 449.15, 449.35, 451.9, and 465.34–35. One mention of *neorxna wong* refers to an otherworldly paradise, 99.7 (two others refer to the Garden of Eden). One additional mention of heaven and hell is by implication: 309.2–11 tells the story of Lazarus and the rich man after their deaths without explicitly naming either heaven or hell. Hell appears explicitly at 33.2, 339.3, 391.14, 429.24, 429.26, 429.28, and 443.10.

[63] The *Boethius* repeatedly proclaims that God is Creator and Ruler of a great universe whose complex workings, controlled by His love, are described especially in Alfred's famous translation of 3 met. 9 (79.10–82.17; but see also 48.21–50.7, 57.2–8, 92.16–93.19, 128.27–129.18, 135.23–136.31).

[64] See 41.19–43.26 and 43.27–44.27. Moreover, "Hwæt, ealle men hæfdon gelicne fruman, for þam hi ealle coman of anum fæder 7 of anre meder, 7 ealle hi beoð git gelice acennede" ["Look, all men have a similar origin, for they all came from one father and one mother, and they are all born similarly": 69.17–19].

Transcending Geography

If fame neither spreads far nor lasts long, and earth itself is but a small point in the universe, then England and Rome find themselves in the same position. Those who can read of the greatness of Rome and the Holy Land — and, more importantly, of the divine truths manifested there — are not marginal but privileged no matter where they reside. The Anglo-Saxons need not fear their liminality, but neither should they exult in their local power. The shift from physical geography to mental and spiritual ground allows England to be a place of learning too. Yet readers should recall that their ancestors thought they would never lose Latin, as Alfred said in his Preface to the *Pastoral Care* (5.22–23). Though scholars remain uncertain how much learning had declined, and how much Alfred exaggerated for rhetorical effect, readers must recall that England has suffered much in recent years, and could again lose riches and books.[65] Learning must be pursued to keep England on the map, so to speak.

The importance of place can be recuperated through yet another means of treating the tensions surrounding England. Even as *Angelcynn* claims its place in the tradition of learning, the texts present places that signify symbolically. Real distance from these points is not important as long as the mental distance can be closed by reading the signification correctly. Changing from physical to mental or figurative geography thus represents a third strategy for translators. God's temple and Mount Zion in the Psalms are real historically and geographically, but they are simultaneously metaphorical. The dual meaning begins in the source texts, but Alfred extends the figurative implications in the Psalms and the *Pastoral Care*. His glossing translation method adds to or makes explicit the Psalms' figuration:

> . . . et statuit supra petram pedes meos et direxit gressus meos
> et inmisit in os meum canticum nouum hymnum Deo nostro
>
> ["and he set my feet upon a rock and directed my steps.
> And he put a new canticle into my mouth a song to our God": 39.3–4][66]

---

[65] For a review of scholarship on the topic and a treatment of recent evidence, see Simon Keynes, "The Power of the Written Word: Alfredian England 871–899," in *Alfred the Great: Papers from the Eleventh-Centenary Conferences*, 175–97. Keynes does find evidence of decline, but also some evidence for continuing traditions of Latin literacy in Mercia and Wessex from which Alfred could rebuild.

[66] Quotations from the Latin Psalms are from *Le psautier romain et les autres anciens psautiers latins*, ed. Robert Weber (Vatican City, 1953).

becomes:

> And he asette mine fet on swiðe heanne stan (þæt ys, on swyðe heah setl
> and on swyðe fæstne anweald), and he gerihte mine stæpas, and sende on
> minne muð niwne sang (þæt is, lofsang urum Gode). (39.3–4)

> ["And he set my feet on a very high stone (that is, on a very high seat and
> on a very strong power), and he steadied my steps, and sent into my mouth
> a new song (that is, a praise song for our God)."][67]

Sometimes when the temple is mentioned, it is difficult to tell whether the referent is the earthly or the heavenly temple (26.5–6, 47.8); one so evokes the other,
however, that it hardly matters.

Most of the places named in the *Pastoral Care* also carry more symbolic reso-
nance than literal. Zion is a real place, but that is not always its import. While
the text makes frequent reference to real geographical places, many of those carry
some figurative weight. Ten passages specify real places for an overwhelmingly
figurative sense, as in:

> Ðu ðe wilt godspellian Sion, astig ofer heane munt. Ðæt is ðætte se sceal,
> se ðe wile brucan ðara godcundra ðinga & ðara hefonlicra lara, forlætan ðas
> niðerlican & ðas eorðlecan weorc, forðam he bið gesewen standende on ðam
> hrofe godcundra ðinga. (81.12–16)[68]

> ["You who would preach to Zion, ascend over the high mountain. That is,
> he who would enjoy the divine things and the heavenly lore must abandon
> the lowly and the earthly works, because he must be seen standing on the
> roof of divine things."]

Several are purely figurative: "Ðin nosu is suelc [suel] se torr on Liuano ðæm
munte" ["Your nose is just as the tower on Mount Libanus": 65.23–24] is quoted
to explain that a large nose means "gesceadwisnesse" ["discernment," 65.25; see
also 433.19–29].[69] A metaphor for Christ goes beyond the earthly: "sio sunne,
ðæt is Crist" ["the sun, that is Christ": 285.14].

---

[67] For further examples, see Ps. 10:5 and 18:6.

[68] See also 101.24–103.5, 103.11–105.1, 197.11–201.3, 267.9–16, 385.21–24, 397.32–
399.31, 403.29–405.10, 415.13–417.1, and 427.26–429.2.

[69] See also 311.7–13 and 367.2–22. Vaguer geographical references are to navigating at
sea (59.1–7); the gold and stones of the temple scattered in the street (133.8–135.20); and
the inner city as a retreat from the world (385.4–9). At least two passages have literal and
figurative meaning so intertwined that it is hard to say which dominates: Ezekiel besieges a
model of Jerusalem, with a literal meaning for the city but a lesson about pride for teachers at

In this figurative geography, Rome and Jerusalem are not the only places that signify. In closing the *Pastoral Care*, Gregory uses the image of being lost at sea as a humility topos; Alfred neatly translates it:

> Ðær ic hæbbe getæht hwelc hierde bion sceal. To ðæm ic wæs gened mid ðinre tælnesse, ðæt ic nu hæbbe manege men gelæd to ðæm stæðe full-fremednesse on ðæm scipe mines modes, & nu giet hwearfige me self on ðæm yðum minra scylda. Ac ic ðe bidde ðæt ðu me on ðæm scipgebroce ðisses andweardan lifes sum bred geræce ðinra gebeda, ðæt ic mæge on sittan oð ic to londe cume, & arær me mid ðære honda ðinre geearnunga, forðæmðe me hæfð gehefegad sio byrðen minra agenra scylda. (467.19–27)

> ["There I have taught how a pastor must be. I was compelled to this task by your reproof, that I now have led many men to the shore of perfection in the ship of my mind, and yet I myself still toss in the waves of my guilt. But I pray you that you offer me the board of your prayers in the shipwreck of this present life, that I may sit on it until I come to land, and lift me with the hands of your merits, because the weight of my own guilt so burdens me."]

External geography here becomes vague and non-specific; it exists merely to figure internal space. Whether readers envision the Mediterranean or the much closer North Sea, the result is the same. The focus of the *Pastoral Care* itself on the ruler's disposition and how he directs those is as applicable to Alfred's people as to Gregory's Romans, and the copying of the text indicates that his successors valued it as well.[70]

Alfred's two most introspective works also emphasize internal geography. Though the *Boethius* is packed with historical and geographical references, those references illustrate other points, and its imagery sheds light on *inner* space. That interiority can be figured as a library:

> ne me na ne lyst mid glase geworhtra waga ne heahsetla mid golde 7 mid gimmum gerenodra, ne boca mid golde awritenra me swa swiðe ne lyst swa me lyst on þe rihtes willan. Ne sece ic no her þa bec, ac þæt ðæt þa bec for-stent, ðæt is, þin gewit. (11.26–30)

161.2–165.23; Isaiah tells Sidon that the sea told it to be embarrassed at 409.31–411.1, and a complicated exegesis follows. When Jerusalem is said to be fornicating, the city's inhabitants are literally meant, but so are all believers, just as fornication means not just sexual sin but worshipping false gods: 463.23–465.3. How literally one is to take Satan's "Ic wille wyrcean min setl on norðdæle" ["I will build my seat in the northern part": 111.24] is unclear.

[70] Four of the six extant manuscripts are later copies; see N. R. Ker, *Catalogue of Manuscripts Containing Anglo-Saxon* (Oxford, repr. with supplement, 1990), items 19, 30, 87, and 175.

["Nor do walls worked with glass please me, or high seats ornamented with gold and with gems, nor do books written with gold please me as much as your right will pleases me. I do not seek here books, but what understands the books, that is, your mind."]

Anglo-Saxon libraries had declined over the previous years, but Alfred was trying to rebuild them in England.[71] Surely the image would be highly evocative even for Anglo-Saxons who had never left their homeland or even seen an elaborate library. Similarly, Wisdom describes God as "ælces godes ægðer ge hrof ge flor" ["both the roof and the floor of every good": 110.24–25], an image familiar to every Anglo-Saxon. The opening of this dialogue emphasizes the narrator's physical setting in an Italian prison, but by the end that setting has been virtually forgotten — or transcended.

The mind must be freed to seek its heavenly homeland, as Wisdom repeatedly tells Mod. This internal journey is often described as if external (in a wood, 100.4–6). Turning inward will lead the narrator outward and upward. As the narrator recalls himself more and more, Wisdom encourages him: "þu eart nu fulneah cumen in on ða ceastre þære soðan gesælðe, þe þu lange ær ne meahtest aredian" ["you are now very close to entering into the city of the true good, to which you could not find the way a while before": 96.26–28]. This homeland becomes more clearly linked to heaven when Wisdom offers: "ic sceal ærest ðin mod gefeðeran, ðæt hit mæge hit ðe yð up ahebban ær ðon hit fleogan onginne on ða heanesse, þæt hit mæge hal 7 orsorh fleogan to his earde, 7 forlætan ælce ðara gedrefednesse ðe hit nu ðrowað" ["I must first feather your mind that it may the more easily rise up before it begins to fly into the heights, so that it may whole and untroubled fly to its land, and leave each of those troubles which it now suffers": 104.29–33], and then begins to sing about flying to this homeland. The *Boethius*, for all its detailed classical geography, grounds readers in this world only to move them to a higher one — reached by going inside. The flight begins in the mind, but later the whole being will make the actual transit, whether from Rome or from Wessex.

The *Soliloquies* take this strategy even further, providing a purely mental geography which begins with the image of a man building a house from lumber provided by the wood of the Fathers (47.9–12); their books create the walls and ceiling, reminiscent of the passage from the *Boethius* quoted above (110.22–25).[72] These works of the Fathers will, Alfred hopes,

---

[71] See Keynes, "The Power of the Written Word." For more on the image of the library, see Discenza, *King's English*, 19–20.

[72] Specifically Augustine, Gregory, and Jerome: *King Alfred's Version of St. Augustine's Soliloquies*, ed. Thomas A. Carnicelli (Cambridge, MA, 1969).

hure mines modes eagan to þam ongelihte þæt ic mage rihtne weig aredian to þam ecan hame, and to þam ecan are, and to þare ecan reste þe us gehaten is þurh þa halgan fæderas. sie swa. (48.1–3)

["indeed open my mind's eyes to the light that I may find the right way to that eternal home, and to that eternal honor, and to that eternal rest which is promised us through the holy fathers. Let it be so."]

The narrator's wishes are further detailed in an evocatively domestic image:

he hine mote hwilum þar-on gerestan, and huntigan, and fuglian, and fiscian, and his on gehwilce wisan to þere lænan tilian, ægþær ge on se ge on lande, oð þone fyrst þe he bocland and æce yrfe þurh his hlafordes miltse geearnige. swa gedo se weliga gifola, se ðe egðer wilt ge þissa lænena stoclife ge þara ecena hama. Se ðe ægþer gescop and ægðeres wilt, forgife me þæt me to æðrum onhagige; ge her nytwyrde to beonne, ge huru þider to cumane. (48.6–12)

["He might rest himself there sometimes, and hunt, and fowl, and fish, and in each way tend to the lease, both in the sea and on the land, until that time when through his lord's mercy he win bookland and eternal inheritance. May the wealthy Giver make it so, He who wills both in this borrowed dwelling and the eternal homes. May He who made both and wills both grant that I may be suitable both to be useful here and indeed to come there."]

The forest is a library metaphorically, and perhaps more literally in the wooden boards used as book covers. The exotic lands of the *Orosius* and the *Boethius* are forgotten here in favor of a home that needs no specification. The *Soliloquies* lack any historical context aside from the brief mention that Augustine, Bishop of Carthage, wrote this book, and there is little context within the text itself.[73] The only other specific geographical reference appears near the end of the text: to Augustine, Rome is the greatest city, the center of political and religious power, yet its history cannot be known by personal experience. Significantly, that does not preclude any possibility of knowledge about it (97.5–8). Rome is important

---

[73] "Agustinus, Cartaina bisceop, worhte twa bec," literally, "two books": 48.13. This metaphysical and epistemological investigation begins with an extraordinarily long prayer (50.10–56.9) which makes frequent reference to God as creator of everything in this world and the next. Godden, "The Player King," emphasizes Alfred's distinction between himself as translator, and the narrators as historically situated characters, yet the sparseness of particular geographical and historic references in the *Soliloquies* seems rather to allow readers to conflate Alfred and Augustine as narrators in a relation of homology. For homology in world-views, see Bourdieu, *Outline*, 86 and *Rules of Art*, esp. 161–66; see also note 47 above.

here not as the city itself, but for what the narrator can know about it and *how* he can know it. Geography and cosmology figure greater truths.

All the physical settings, however concrete or abstract, are likewise images. The sun becomes an image of God (69.16–26). The view from a ship crossing the sea parallels how people learn (61.17–22). Coming to the king's home in many different ways, and the king having different residences, figure God's heavenly home to which we all hope to come (77.5–78.2). A discussion of the effects of light from the sun, moon, and stars on healthy and unhealthy eyes, and a later mention of the sun and clouds, lead to the mind's eye (78.2–17 and 92.22–93.6). Climbing a sea cliff to look around — both below at the sea and back down at the land behind — illustrates reaching a new level of understanding (78.17–23). Here too the earthly body is a prison which we will leave (93.14–20). The implications of these many and varied images always point to the heavenly home, and explicit mention of angels (82.15–18, 85.18) underscores the interest of the text. Here *all* the geography and history that matter are mental and spiritual, and the settings appeal to English readers.

Conclusions

In following Alfred's work into his most difficult books, we may seem to have left Britannia far behind. Anglo-Saxon readers, of course, would not. Readers were continually pulled in different directions by the Alfredian texts. England *was* marginal to most of the world, as maps and classical texts represented it. Yet Anglo-Saxons' own dispositions, which, as Bourdieu would argue, "give disproportionate weight to early experiences,"[74] would tell them that their people, be they West Saxons, Mercians, or even transplanted Franks, could not be hanging off the edge of the world or entirely non-existent, as some maps and descriptions seem to portray them.

While Alfred's program of translation brought Anglo-Saxon readers perhaps sometimes uncomfortably close to a Rome-centered viewpoint, none of the Alfredian texts *solely* marginalizes England. Most of the texts recenter themselves, albeit some only temporarily, around Britannia. A second tactic is to take an entirely different perspective, from which all of earth is marginal. Finally, place becomes metaphor, with spiritual significance equally available to readers everywhere.

The program as a whole redirects readers from a marginalization of England, though not to replace Jerusalem, Rome, or Francia with Winchester, Wessex, or *Angelcynn*. Realistically, such replacement could not succeed: everyone

---

[74] Bourdieu, *Outline*, 78.

knew of these centers of religion, power, and learning, and they remained destinations for pilgrims and ambassadors. Spiritually, replacement would conflict with the emphasis that most Alfredian texts placed on divine gifts and responsibilities. Yet the program also did not encourage readers to accept classical views of the world; England's place may be minor in the universe and in the fullness of time, but in the here and now it matters a great deal.

Alfred's program encouraged a dual focus: on duties here in this world, and the eventual destination of one's soul. For the most part, the texts move easily from one approach to another. The translators have been formed by and in turn reproduce in texts a sense of both personal responsibility for one's own soul and social responsibility for one's own world. Despite differences between the late antique world and the Anglo-Saxon one, homologies appear in the translations. *Angelcynn* can be as insignificant *and* as central as Rome. All England needs are the tools of learning and devoted minds. The former Alfred can provide; the latter, the audience must supply. Alfred simultaneously teaches his readers geography and cosmology and asks them to work with him to improve England's place in the world through their efforts — and to work with God to secure their own and each other's place in the next world.[75]

[75] I am grateful to many colleagues whose conversation, questions, and suggestions have helped me in writing this piece and led me to other avenues of investigation I hope to pursue shortly. I should mention especially Katherine O'Brien O'Keeffe and Jacqueline Stodnick; Paul E. Szarmach; Jim Siebold (who answered questions about his website and very generously sent me a CD-ROM containing much information); two anonymous readers for this edited volume; and Nicholas Howe and Catherine Karkov, whose comments and references both when I gave a version of this paper at the 2003 ISAS meeting and when I submitted it for this volume have been most helpful.

"Old Names of Kings or Shadows": Reading Documentary Lists

Jacqueline Stodnick

As Kenneth Sisam described it in 1953, the process of reading Anglo-Saxon documentary lists is fraught with readerly angst: "One soon becomes involved in a tangle of possibilities, where the temptation to be over-ingenious is always present, with the doubt whether time is well spent on these old names of kings or shadows."[1] As Sisam makes clear, what I am labeling "documentary lists" are difficult texts to read because of their lack of context, a lack that the reader seems anxiously compelled to restore. These texts consist simply of names — of bishops, kings, abbots, popes, patriarchs, places — written serially either in vertical columns or in long lines across a manuscript page, and with a bare minimum of, or indeed with no, connective syntactical structure. Appearing in many different versions and manuscript contexts, these lists date from as early as the eighth century and continued to be copied and updated throughout the Anglo-Saxon period.[2]

---

[1] Kenneth Sisam, "Anglo-Saxon Royal Genealogies," *Proceedings of the British Academy* 39 (1953): 287–346, here 288.

[2] For the textual history of these lists, see David N. Dumville, "The Anglian Collection of Royal Genealogies and Regnal Lists," *ASE* 5 (1976): 23-50; idem, "Kingship, Genealogies, and Regnal Lists," in *Early Medieval Kingship*, ed. Peter H. Sawyer and Ian N. Wood (Leeds, 1977), 72–104; idem, "The Catalogue Texts," in *An Eleventh-Century Anglo-Saxon Illustrated Miscellany (Cotton Tiberius B.v Part I)*, ed. Patrick McGurk, idem, Malcolm R. Godden, and Ann Knock, EEMF 21 (Copenhagen, 1983), 55–58; idem, "The West Saxon Genealogical Regnal List: Manuscripts and Texts," *Anglia* 104 (1986): 1–32; idem, "The West Saxon Genealogical Regnal List and the Chronology of Early Wessex," *Peritia* 4 (1985): 21–66. Dumville was of course building here on the work of Sisam in "Anglo-Saxon Royal Genealogies," which his own studies then superseded. For the episcopal lists see R. I. Page, "Anglo-Saxon Episcopal Lists, Parts I and II," *Nottingham Medieval Studies* 9 (1965): 71–95; idem, "Anglo-Saxon Episcopal Lists, Part III," *Nottingham Medieval Studies* 10 (1966): 2-24; and Simon Keynes, "Episcopal Lists," in *The Blackwell Encyclopaedia of Anglo-Saxon England*, ed. Michael Lapidge et al. (Oxford, 1999), 172–74.

While they presumably had a prehistory as independent texts, these lists appear in Anglo-Saxon manuscripts in collections, idiosyncratically comprised of separate regnal lists for the old kingdoms combined with ecclesiastical or territorial material. Even though identifying Latin rubrics precede many of these lists, the lack of an explanatory or connective prose context makes their purpose within Anglo-Saxon textual culture and their evident fascination for copyists frustratingly opaque. Were they intended to be read, or were they copied for reference purposes only? Did copyists (readers? users?) understand the material in these lists? If so, did they understand them only because they were able to "round out" their context, as it were, by the mental addition of supplemental information?

This paper will address these questions, and others dealing with the function of these lists for their Anglo-Saxon readers, by examining one particular list collection: that contained in the eleventh-century manuscript London, BL, Cotton Tiberius B.v fols. 19v–24r.[3] Since we lack any specific discussion from the period of the purpose or use of this type of documentary list collection, I will here reexamine Sisam's instinct that such lists draw in and tempt their readers to make, as he put it, "over-ingenious" tangles of interpretive possibility. In fact, I will suggest here that, rather than being merely a temptation suffered by modern readers of these confusing old texts, this invitation to "reconstruct" a framework of meaning for these decontextualized lists of names was felt also by their Anglo-Saxon users; and was, in fact, a structural component of the list collection format. More than that, I will argue that the form of the list collection functions as an identificatory technology, structuring and producing a certain response in its reader. An important component of my claim will be that list-texts themselves exert an influence on their copyists, causing them to place form above content and display-value above use-value. In other words, I will argue that the lists' production of knowledge about England is not effected through the historical relevance or accuracy of the individual names contained in the lists themselves, but rather through the texts' combined ability literally to exhibit nationality as a complex epistemological construct. As I will show, additions and deletions made in the tenth century to the core material of the list collection contained in Tiberius B.v show a regularizing impetus at work, and reveal a collection which invites its reader to recognize "England" as a multi-faceted historical, ecclesiastical, and territorial category. The bringing together of originally diverse items within the standardizing form of the list "collection" therefore serves to generate a unified, while still rich, historical identity for England.

---

[3] A facsimile of this manuscript is available: *An Eleventh-Century Anglo-Saxon Illustrated Miscellany*, ed. McGurk et al. The manuscript is number 193 in N. R. Ker, *Catalogue of Manuscripts Containing Anglo-Saxon* (Oxford 1957; reissued with supplement, 1990), 255–56.

I. Documentary Listing: Tiberius B.v

Tiberius B.v is a sumptuously illustrated manuscript copied, according to its editor, probably at one time in the second quarter of the eleventh century and at one place, although where exactly this was remains a matter of debate. The presence of entries from the chronicle of Battle Abbey running from the Incarnation to 1206 indicates that the manuscript was at this house by, as David Dumville argues, the early twelfth century, but nothing is known for certain of its earlier provenance.[4] However, because the manuscript is a costly production with three illuminated picture cycles, it is likely to have emerged from a major scriptorium in the period. The pre-Conquest material is copied by one scribe (although a second makes brief contributions) and consists largely of computus texts, such as tables for calculating annual dates of liturgical feasts, a metrical calendar, the text of Ælfric's *De temporibus anni*, and a selection of astronomical texts.[5] Like most computus manuscripts, Tiberius B.v contains an array of materials relating to both time and space, including two maps (a Macrobian zonal diagram and the famous Anglo-Saxon world map) along with texts like a bilingual Latin and Old English version of *The Marvels of the East* and Priscian's translation of Dionysius's *Periegesis*, an account of Rome.

Even though the scope of the computus was broad (as Evelyn Edson comments, it "attempted to depict as a whole the marvellous, meaningful handiwork of an intelligent and beneficent God"),[6] editors and readers of Tiberius B.v seem reluctant to classify it unambiguously as a computus collection — hence the more general title, *An Anglo-Saxon Illustrated Miscellany*, given to the facsimile. This reluctance is perhaps due to the secular nature of some of the items within the manuscript, which fit uncomfortably with the apparent aim and intended audience of a computus collection,[7] or to the apparently careless and uncomprehending copying

---

[4] The chronicle sections have been rebound and are now fols. 238–41r of London, BL, Cotton Nero D.ii. See in particular Patrick McGurk, "The History of the Manuscript," 25–27, and David N. Dumville, "A Note on the Post-Conquest Additions," 104–6, in *Illustrated Miscellany*. For bibliography and a summary of the arguments about the manuscript's origins, in which Winchester and Christ Church, Canterbury dominate, see David N. Dumville, "The Anglian Collection," 27–28.

[5] See Patrick McGurk, "Contents of the Manuscript," 15–24, and "The Astronomical Section," 67–78, in *Illustrated Miscellany*.

[6] Evelyn Edson, *Mapping Time and Space: How Medieval Mapmakers Viewed their World* (London, 1997), 96.

[7] Its editors repeatedly describe Tiberius B.v as a "secular" manuscript (see *Illustrated Miscellany*, 15, 66). For an argument that the world map shows more Roman features, like the borders of provinces, than Christian sites see Catherine Delano-Smith and Roger J. P. Kain, *English Maps: A History* (Toronto, 1999), 34–35. The map's rectangular shape,

of computus materials, which suggests that use-value was not the first aim of the compiler.[8] Patrick McGurk proposes the following general classification of the texts within Tiberius B.v: geographical (*The Marvels of the East*, Sigeric's Roman itinerary, the zonal map, the *Periegesis*, and the world map); scientific (computistical material, Ælfric's *De temporibus anni*, the *Aratea* [Cicero's translation of Aratus's astronomical text]); historical (the lists and genealogies); ecclesiastical (the calendar).[9] He offers no clear suggestion as to the manuscript's purpose, noting that "Tiberius presents a not very clearly defined section of knowledge."[10] Nicholas Howe, on the other hand, sees this lack of definition as a consequence of the manuscript's expansive approach, suggesting that Tiberius is "a collection . . . a miscellany . . . an encyclopedia of the world," in which the texts are "less valuable for their raw information than for their ways of knowing: specifically, for forms of calculating and representing the earth and its inhabitants."[11] The fact that Robert Cotton rearranged the manuscript makes it difficult to do more than generalize about its overall meaning in this way, since we know only what texts it comprised

---

relative accuracy, and the likely Roman provenance of its exemplar cause these authors to set it aside from the tradition of *mappae mundi* in England, the first unambiguous example of which they believe to have been produced in the late twelfth century. While I agree with their overall argument here, I do not think that the representation of the marvels of the East on the map is an unambiguously mythological statement downplaying the Christian element, as the authors note. The wonders were very often included on later *mappae mundi* and, indeed, were a key part of ecclesiastical discussions around the issues of humanity, salvation, creation, and so on. Given the nature of the material in this manuscript overall, I am not sure that it fits comfortably into either of the distinctions "secular" or "ecclesiastic." As Nicholas Howe observes of the manuscript, "it is secular in addressing a lay audience, though much of its material is religious in origin and nature" and, I would add, quite technical (Nicholas Howe, "An Angle on This Earth: Sense of Place in Anglo-Saxon England," *Bulletin of the John Rylands Library* 82 [2000]: 3–22, here 15).

[8] Patrick McGurk not only notes a lack of order in the computus section of Tiberius B.v, but also observes that the scribe has copied his material uncomprehendingly and carelessly, repeating texts and dividing others in an unexpected way. McGurk believes that the material is in fact so unclear that a monk would need extra instruction to use it. He writes, "[t]hat it was carelessly copied and that its Easter tables were clearly out of date says something about the habits and aims of the Tiberius compiler and scribe" ("The Computus," in *Illustrated Miscellany*, 51–55, here 55). Clearly these aims did not include creating the most practically useful and current aid for calculating the date of Easter. This knowledge was preserved (by someone who apparently did not understand it) for another reason.

[9] Patrick McGurk, "Conclusion," in *Illustrated Miscellany*, 107–9, here 107.

[10] McGurk, "Conclusion," 109.

[11] Howe, "An Angle on This Earth," 15–16.

and not their original order.[12] However, as Howe has observed, because even the most exotic texts in Tiberius B.v are involved in a process of "negotiating similarity and difference" in such a way that distant lands and customs are shown to be "at once like and unlike those to be found on the island," the manuscript can in fact be seen as a lengthy attempt to situate (geographically, religiously, ethnographically) and thereby define the English land and people.[13]

Part of this mediatory function is performed by the manuscript's inclusion of a particularly extensive collection of list material, differing in several key respects from its sources and combining secular and ecclesiastical material with both insular and "foreign" elements.[14] The material, contained on fols. 19v–24r, is a well-defined unit connected, according to Patrick McGurk, with the computus calendar and tables following.[15] Following Dumville's numbering of items, the list texts are ordered as follows:[16]

1) 19v. Catalogue of popes, numbered to CXI and entered in columns. Numbers CXII to CXXII have been entered but are not followed by names. Continued on 23v.

2) 19v–20r. List of seventy-two disciples of Christ, numbered I to LXXVII and organized in columns.

3) 20r. List of Roman emperors organized in columns.

---

[12] Patrick McGurk notes that "any reconstruction of the gatherings can only be extremely tentative" ("Palaeography and Illumination," in *Illustrated Miscellany*, 28–39, here 28). Ker records the order that the folios were in when the manuscript was catalogued in the sixteenth or seventeenth century (*Catalogue*, 256).

[13] Howe, "An Angle on This Earth," 14. Mary B. Campbell notes that medieval travel accounts most commonly present difference in terms of similitude in this way, by describing the unknown in terms of the familiar (Mary B. Campbell, *The Witness and the Other World: Exotic European Travel Writing, 400–1600* [Ithaca, NY, 1988], 3).

[14] Nicholas Howe includes the list material as numbers 2 (lists of popes and bishops), 3 (genealogies), and 4 (Sigeric's itinerary) in his own brief list of texts in Tiberius B.v which develop the theme of similarity and difference, and which negotiate the notion of "foreignness" in relation to England and the English (Howe, "An Angle on This Earth," 14–15). A detailed analysis of these texts, however, is beyond the aim of his study here. Thus my own work on the lists is intended to supplement and extend his analysis in this area.

[15] "It was the compiler's deliberate intention to link this computus-calendar with the genealogies, with Ælfric's *De Temporibus Anni*, and with the other secular texts in Tiberius. It was not so linked in any other book" (McGurk, "The Computus," 53).

[16] Dumville, "The Catalogue Texts," 55–57. This list of the texts is largely abstracted from the information given by Dumville (and also by McGurk, "The Contents," 15–24), but also includes my own observations.

4) 20v–21r. List of the patriarchs organized in columns.

5) 21v–22r. Anglo-Saxon bishop lists organized in columns and representing every English see as they were in 990. Unique to this version is the singling out of the name "Swiðun" with capitals and red decoration, and the epithet "Dei amicus" applied to Archbishop Sigeric.[17]

6) 22r, col. 4. West Saxon regnal list from Cerdic to Æthelred, organized in columns and providing lengths of reigns. Headed "CCCCXCIIII," the year in which the list begins.[18]

7) 22v–23r. Anglian collection of royal genealogies and regnal lists, organized in columns and headed "Hæc sunt genealogie per partes Brittanie regum regnantium per diversa loca."[19]

22v. (Top half). This page must be read in two halves horizontally.

Col. 1. Deiran genealogy.

Col. 2. Bernician genealogy.

Col. 3. Bernician genealogy.

22v. (Bottom half).

Col. 1. Northumbrian regnal list.

Cols. 1–2. Mercian regnal list.

Col. 3–23r col. 1. Mercian genealogies.

23r. Col. 1. Lindsey genealogies.

Kent genealogies.

Cols. 1–2. East Anglian genealogies.

8) 23r cols. 2–3. Retrograde genealogy for the kings of Wessex from Edgar back to Adam, entitled "Haec sunt genealogiae regum Occidentalium Saxonum."[20]

9) 23v. In the top left portion of the page, almost marginal, is a list of nineteen abbots of Glastonbury from Hemgils to Ælfweard.[21]

---

[17] Edited by Page, "Anglo-Saxon Episcopal Lists, Part III," 13–17.

[18] Edited by Dumville, "The West Saxon Genealogical Regnal Lists," 30–31.

[19] Edited, with admirable attention to replicating the manuscript layout, by Dumville, "The Anglian Collection," 35–37. This collection is the same as that Sisam had named the "Vespasian Group."

[20] Edited by Thomas Wright and James Orchard Halliwell, *Reliquiae Antiquae: Scraps from Ancient Manuscripts, Illustrating Chiefly Early English Literature and the English Language* (London, 1843; repr. New York, 1966), 2: 172–73.

[21] Edited by J. A. Robinson, "The Saxon Abbots of Glastonbury," in idem, *Somerset Historical Essays* (London, 1921), 26–53, here 41–42.

10) 23v. Written in long lines across the remainder of the page is a continuation, after a thirty-year break, of the list of popes given on fol. 19v. Entries here run from John X (914–928) to John XV (985–996).

11) 23v–24r, 5. Archbishop Sigeric's Roman itinerary of A.D. 990, consisting of a list of churches visited over two days in Rome followed by, after a blank line, a list of seventy-nine stations on the journey back to the Channel coast.[22]

While the precise contours of this collection are unique to Tiberius B.v, individual items within it have complex textual histories that can be only partially reconstructed from the surviving manuscript evidence. What becomes clear from this evidence is that, although several of these texts are already embedded within collections in their earliest surviving versions, links with related material in other manuscripts (such as the *Historia Brittonum*, the Moore Memoranda, and parts of the *Historia Ecclesiastica*) indicate that these items had an existence as separate texts before their incorporation within list collections. Several scholars have demonstrated this fact more concretely. For instance, in a detailed study of the textual history of the episcopal material (item 5), R. I. Page argues that, rather than drawing solely on the *Historia Ecclesiastica*, the list compiler and Bede himself were using earlier lists circulating individually or in collections that have not been preserved. As Simon Keynes notes, the core material in the list of popes could have been transmitted to England from Rome in the eighth or ninth century also in the form of a separate list text, which then received additions in the later ninth century.[23] The list of the seventy-two disciples of Christ was similarly

---

[22] The text has been most recently edited by Veronica Ortenberg, "Archbishop Sigeric's Journey to Rome in 990," *ASE* 19 (1990): 197–246, here 199–200. For identification of the place-names see Francis P. Magoun Jr., "The Rome of Two Northern Pilgrims: Archbishop Sigeric of Canterbury and Abbot Nikolás of Munkathverá," *Harvard Theological Review* 33 (1940): 267–89, and idem, "An English Pilgrim-Diary of the Year 990," *Mediaeval Studies* 2 (1940): 231–52. The itinerary has been compared to a twelfth-century Old Icelandic pilgrim itinerary (preserved in a late fourteenth-century manuscript) by Joyce Hill in "Pilgrim Routes in Northern Italy," *Bollettino del Centro Interuniversitario Richerche sul "Viaggio in Italia"* 5 (1984): 3–22. Hill notes here the brevity of the English itinerary in comparison to the fuller and more personal Old Icelandic pilgrim diary.

[23] Professor Keynes makes this observation in an important study, examining the textual history and historiographical import of the list collection in London, BL, Cotton Vespasian B.vi ("Between Bede and the *Chronicle*: BL Cotton Vespasian B.vi, fols. 104–9," in *Latin Learning and English Lore: Studies in Anglo-Saxon Literature for Michael Lapidge*, ed. Katherine O'Brien O'Keeffe and Andy Orchard, 2 vols. [Toronto, 2005], 1: 47–67). I am most grateful to Professor Keynes for making this piece available to me before its publication.

introduced into England as a freestanding text, probably by Archbishop Theodore in the seventh century.[24] It suffices to note, therefore, that the existence of a wide range of similar list material, both in single instantiations and in collections, indicates that it was common practice in the period to gather lists together into larger textual units even when, as in the combination of papal lists and genealogies, the material brought together was conceptually quite different.

What begins to become evident, and is particularly interesting, then, in tracing the history of these individual list texts, is this swift incorporation into collections of other list material. The manuscript evidence thus demonstrates the antiquity not only of the individual texts, but also of the ongoing practice of collecting and modifying them to which Tiberius B.v contributes. How far back can we trace this process? The age of the items at the core of the list — the so-called "Anglian collection" (item 7), consisting of genealogies for Deira, Bernicia, Mercia, Lindsey, Kent, East Anglia, and Wessex, and regnal lists for Northumbria and Mercia, in addition to the lists of popes, disciples, and English bishops — has been established by Dumville. Preserved in three pre-Conquest manuscripts, it represents "[t]he earliest extant set of English royal genealogies," dating in the oldest manuscript to 805–814.[25] The fact that this earliest version of the Anglian collection, that in London, BL, Cotton Vespasian B.vi, does not include the genealogy for Wessex nor the regnal lists for Northumbria and Mercia present in later manuscripts (such as Tiberius B.v), encourages Dumville to posit that an original version of the collection including these items was compiled between 787 and 796.[26] Vespasian B.vi either lost these regnal lists for Northumbria and Mercia at some point in its history, or it never included them and surviving later manuscripts must have descended from the putative 787–796 original by a different route. Simon Keynes, in an important analysis of the Vespasian B.vi collection, argues in contrast that these Northumbrian and Mercian regnal lists could have been added to later versions of the collection at a ninth- or tenth-century stage (at the same time that the additional Wessex material was added and, possibly, the lists of emperors and patriarchs present in Tiberius B.v), and provide insufficient evidence for the existence of an eighth-century Anglian collection.[27] Whether or not we posit a version of the Anglian collection predating that preserved in Vespasian

---

[24] Keynes, "Between Bede and the *Chronicle*."

[25] Dumville, "The Anglian Collection," 24, 49–50. The manuscripts that contain the Anglian collection are London, BL, Cotton Vespasian B.vi, fols. 104–109; Cambridge, Corpus Christi College 183; and Tiberius B.v itself. For a description of the manuscripts see Dumville, "The Anglian Collection," 24–28. For the list collection in BL Vespasian B.vi, Keynes, "Between Bede and the *Chronicle*" is indispensable.

[26] Dumville, "The Anglian Collection," 39–41.

[27] Keynes, "Between Bede and the *Chronicle*."

B.vi, however, the surviving manuscript witnesses compellingly demonstrate that the practice of collecting list material together, and the existence of this collection in particular, were established at least by the early ninth century when Vespasian B.vi was copied.

The network of relationships among surviving manuscripts containing this material suggests, in fact, that the collection should be approached by scholars as analogous to the Anglo-Saxon Chronicle — that is, as consisting of differing manuscript versions (spanning a lengthy time period) that participate in and contribute to a virtual and singular "text" understood to have coherence and identity (while not being identical with any of its actualized constructs).[28] Reading these list collections will thus, as Thomas Bredehoft has recently articulated of the endeavor of interpreting the Chronicle, always be a procedure imbricated with the determination of their textual history.[29] And, again like the Anglo-Saxon Chronicle, what becomes interesting are of course the changes and idiosyncrasies of the individual version in relation to all the others, changes which are interpreted by scholars as the inscription of a particular historical configuration upon a pre-existing text; that is, as revelatory of a certain vision or aim prevalent at the moment of compilation or copying.

The precise ways in which scholars have interpreted the relationship between changes in list collections and contemporary political concerns are instructive. For many years, of course, these kinds of documentary lists were seen to provide unmediated information about dynastic relationships and ecclesiastical succession, a traditional view that was corrected in the late 1970s by Dumville's extensive studies of such lists as propagandistic. For Dumville, changes in the form of the lists are signs either of scribal mistakes or of deliberate manipulation in favor of the ruling dynasty under the purview of which the collection was composed. For example, the fact that the pedigrees given in the Anglian collection for each of the heptarchic kingdoms — Bernicia, Deira, Lindsey, Mercia, East Anglia, Kent, and Wessex — all go back to Woden and are all of equal length (regardless of chronology) is, for Dumville, politically significant.[30] Whatever the date

---

[28] Thomas Bredehoft comments in his book-length study of the Anglo-Saxon Chronicle that "the Chronicle was recognized to be something more than a single, coherent composition reflected (perhaps imperfectly) in various physical books. In short, the Chronicle was clearly understood to be a cultural document quite literally larger than any one of its manuscripts" (*Textual Histories: Readings in the* Anglo-Saxon Chronicle [Toronto, 2001], 7).

[29] "The Chronicle has always encouraged its readers to become readers of textual history" (Bredehoft, *Textual Histories*, 147).

[30] As Dumville notes, he is here building on an observation originally made by Sisam ("Anglo-Saxon Royal Genealogies," 327).

at which a particular line ends (and bearing in mind that they proceed backwards through time, this is actually where the lists begin), their main lines all contain about fourteen entries back to Woden. Dumville argues that, as the Saxon kingdoms (Wessex, Essex, Sussex) had their own eponymous god Seaxnet, the fact that their genealogies go back to Woden indicates that, when the collection was compiled in the eighth century,

> descent from Woden expresses an Anglian origin, or perhaps — more cautiously — belief in an Anglian origin. When extended to non-Anglian peoples, it reflects a political link: in this case, subjection to Anglian (Northumbrian or Mercian) overlordship.[31]

For Dumville, such tactics of regularizing genealogies are part of "the manipulative and systematic techniques" that make them a form of propaganda for the ruling classes "to present the past (and, by implication, the future) in terms of their own history."[32]

Other idiosyncrasies of the Tiberius collection are interpreted, however, as the result of scribal misunderstanding. Dumville notes that "[a]lthough T is a beautifully produced manuscript, our texts and the related documents give the impression of being very carelessly written."[33] For example, the fact that fol. 22v must be read in two halves has resulted in a displacement of columns which makes eight early Northumbrian kings follow on from the Mercian king Offa (item 7).[34] In other lists, like that of the seventy-two disciples of Christ (which actually numbers seventy-seven), extra entries have appeared at some stage through scribal misreading (item 2).[35] Returning to the suspiciously uniform royal pedigrees, he observes that the Lindsey line is only the same length as the others because it goes back beyond Woden, including another five ancestors who "properly belong with the whole collection" since Woden is a shared ancestor of all the dynasties.[36] Dumville explains this situation as resulting from the fact that, in the exemplar, all the pedigrees were probably set out in columns across a double page with the extra genealogy for Woden at the foot in such a position that it applied

---

[31] Dumville, "Kingship," 79.

[32] Dumville, "Kingship," 82, 83. Of course, by the ninth century Wessex was the dominant kingdom and yet it maintained its genealogy back to Woden. Dumville explains this phenomenon as resulting either from the fact that the West Saxons were now so powerful that they had no need to rewrite the genealogies or that they lacked the knowledge to do so.

[33] Dumville, "The Anglian Collection," 28.

[34] Dumville, "The Anglian Collection," 28.

[35] Dumville, "The Catalogue Texts," 55.

[36] Dumville, "The Catalogue Texts," 90.

to all of them. However, when the exemplar was copied, the extra names were likely "incorporated . . . into the shortest line for the sake of symmetry or into the line beneath which this extension sat on the page."[37] For Dumville, this phenomenon is one of the "contradictions or inconsistencies which . . . give us the opportunity to prise open the holes in the scheme"; it is the imperfection which reveals the deliberate manipulation of the rest.[38] Thus, in Dumville's viewpoint, all changes to the content of the lists are read within the context of a deliberate manipulative scheme — that is, either changes occur as part of a deliberate plan or they occur as a result of mistakes that ultimately serve to identify the deliberate manipulations.

Simon Keynes, in his recent work on the list collection in Vespasian B.vi, nuances the notion of propagandistic change proposed by David Dumville. In a compelling and careful reading, Keynes suggests that the particular form of the Anglo-Saxon episcopal and regnal lists in Vespasian B.vi represents an orthodox ninth-century view of the English church and of kingship. In particular, Keynes notes that the inclusive and orderly nature of the episcopal lists, along with the association of the Anglian dynasties with Woden, both seem to be moves deliberately made by the compiler to exploit Bedan notions of the English church and of English kingship. Preferring the view of these lists as a "historical construct" digesting the material of the *Historia Ecclesiastica* rather than as a form of royal propaganda, Keynes sensitively argues that the Vespasian B.vi collection as a whole (which includes along with the episcopal and regnal material a metrical calendar, the list of popes, and the list of disciples, among other texts) represents a careful attempt to impose order on the world and to provide a distinguished context for the Anglo-Saxon material.[39]

While recent scholarship thus advances a more complicated understanding of the relation of documentary lists to their political moment, it seems profitable to return to the particular collection in Tiberius B.v (a later instantiation of the material in Vespasian B.vi), in order to determine exactly how it modifies this existing historiographical tradition and practice. By taking a more reader-oriented approach to these list texts, moreover, it becomes possible more subtly to outline the boundary between accident and intention in the compilation of these lists, and to show how their historical meaning is not only a result of artfulness but is also, to a certain extent, fortuitous. To clarify, although scholarship on the lists

---

[37] Dumville, "The Catalogue Texts," 90.

[38] Dumville, "The Catalogue Texts," 94. He also observes that "It is knowledge of the possible conventions, and exploitation of the discrepancies in any such scheme, which allows us to make some headway against what may otherwise seem impenetrable lists of names" (82).

[39] Keynes, "Between Bede and the *Chronicle*."

has moved away from a propaganda model heavily dependent on the notion of manipulation, there is nevertheless still an underlying tendency to stress compilatory intent as sole arbiter of meaning and to discount the form of the text itself as shaping its interpretation. And this is not a small distinction: focusing on the primacy of intent allows documentary lists only to reflect a pre-existing political or cultural conception, rather than to generate it. If, to re-orient the question, we strategically read re-production of list-texts *as* reception, what expectations were apparently set up and what pressures exerted by these texts upon their readers, causing them to read and change the texts in the way that they did?

II. List as Genre

Understanding more about how lists work as texts, and the expectations that they generate in their readers, involves bringing together the work of a diverse group of scholars who have addressed the topic.[40] While these scholars would not

---

[40] There is no self-identifying "school" of scholarship on lists. I have therefore brought together in this essay the insights of different scholars whose work addresses the list, or related forms, in various fields and time periods. These scholars would not, I think, recognize themselves as a group; their approaches and methodologies are, in many cases, very different. However, my synthesis of their ideas about lists has been of great assistance in defining and understanding the function of the form in Anglo-Saxon England. This body of scholarship includes Michel Foucault, *The Order of Things: An Archaeology of the Human Sciences* (New York, 1970), esp. xv–xxiv; Martin Irvine, "Medieval Textuality and the Archaeology of Textual Culture," in *Speaking Two Languages: Traditional Disciplines and Contemporary Theory in Medieval Studies*, ed. Allen J. Frantzen (Albany, 1991), 181–210, and idem, *The Making of Textual Culture: 'Grammatica' and Literary Theory, 350–1100* (Cambridge, 1994); Stephen A. Barney, "Chaucer's Lists," in *The Wisdom of Poetry: Essays in Early English Literature in Honor of Morton W. Bloomfield*, ed. Larry D. Benson and Siegfried Wenzel (Kalamazoo, 1982), 189–223; Robert Belknap, "The Literary List: A Survey of its Uses and Deployments," *Literary Imagination: The Review of the Association of Literary Scholars and Critics* 2 (2000): 35–54; William Gass, "And," in *Voicelust: Eight Contemporary Fiction Writers on Style*, ed. Allen Wier and Don Hendrie Jr. (Lincoln, NE, 1985), 101–25; Jack Goody, *The Interface between the Written and the Oral* (Cambridge, 1987), and idem, *The Domestication of the Savage Mind* (Cambridge, 1977); Nicholas Howe, *The Old English Catalogue Poems* (Copenhagen, 1985); Walter Ong, *Orality and Literacy: The Technologizing of the Word* (London, 1982).

Despite the prevalence of lists in the Anglo-Saxon period itself, little scholarship has been directed towards the form in general. With the exception of Howe's *The Old English Catalogue Poems*, which investigates the origin of the catalogue mode and examines its appearance in a number of different texts, such work as has been completed on lists tends to be genre-specific, limited to passing comments in larger studies devoted to riddle or proverb collections. See, for example, Thomas A. Shippey, *Poems of Wisdom and*

necessarily recognize themselves as a group, their combined insights about the form suggest that list-texts are both accretive and regularizing: that they serve to unify and thus suggest, indeed produce, categories of knowledge, and that they do this specifically by offering an interpretative challenge to the reader that provokes, in turn, a recognition and acknowledgement of the "meaning" of the list.

The most elementary form of the list is of course a simple series of words linked together by one of the following: minimal connectives ("and," "or," "either"); marks of punctuation such as, in the modern graphic system, the comma, colon, or semicolon or, in medieval texts, the medial point or *punctus elevatus*; or vertical arrangement on the page in a column (which was by no means as standard a form for the presentation of lists in early medieval culture as it is today). As Robert Belknap defines it, the list is "a framework that holds separate and disparate items together. More specifically, it is a formally organized block of information that is composed of a set of members."[41] Nicholas Howe writes of the catalogue form that it is both "accretive" and "discontinuous" at the same time, qualities which are, however, equally evident in the simple list.[42] In other words, each element within a list both stands alone and is also part of a whole. Moreover, the presence of items within this whole produces a system of conceptual relationships among them, since the form of the list suggests that items "belong" together in particular ways: in this respect, the list is a form "in which an array of constituent units coheres with specific relations generated by specific forces of attraction."[43] The constitution of this whole is characteristically fluid since items can easily be added or removed: the list is "a plastic, flexible structure" with a potentially endless form.[44] Thus the structure of the list offers possibilities for and even encourages expansion and accretion of additional elements. Conversely, items can also easily be lost, dropped, or replaced. This flexible character of lists is especially prevalent in list-texts like the collection in Tiberius B.v which consists of, in Jack Goody's words, decontextualized lists — that is, lists consisting of items of information arranged serially and removed from a situation of action.[45]

Learning in Old English (Cambridge, 1976); Elaine Tuttle Hansen, *The Solomon Complex: Reading Wisdom in Old English Poetry* (Toronto, 1988); Carolyne Larrington, *A Store of Common Sense: Gnomic Theme and Style in Old Icelandic and Old English Wisdom Poetry* (Oxford, 1993); and Paul Cavill, *Maxims in Old English Poetry* (Cambridge, 1999).

[41] Belknap, "The Literary List," 35.

[42] Howe, *Old English Catalogue Poems*, 27.

[43] Belknap, "The Literary List," 35.

[44] Belknap, "The Literary List," 35. Howe, *Old English Catalogue Poems*, 28, notes the endless form of catalogues but, again, this observation is equally applicable to lists.

[45] For example, while giving directions to a place you have visited involves recalling and organizing information in a context of experience, rearranging the names of these places according to alphabetical order in a list removes them from this context (Goody, *The Interface*, 175–90).

Ong, Goody, and other orality-literacy theorists have investigated how different "ways of managing knowledge," such as lists, are not obvious and inevitable but are central to any understanding of human identity.[46] Goody asserts that "the shift from utterance to text led to significant developments of a sort that might be loosely referred to as a change in consciousness," profoundly altering social life and ways of viewing the world.[47] The relevance of much of this work, therefore, expands greatly beyond its initial concentration on a diachronic shift from orality to literacy (which often in practice necessitated gathering synchronic evidence from contemporary oral cultures); this theoretical discipline in fact both provides a methodology for reading texts as socially transformative and also demonstrates exactly how certain written forms engineer particular modes of thought.[48] Lists

---

[46] Ong, *Orality*, 1. Much scholarly work loosely grouped in the field of museum studies comes to very similar conclusions about the cultural functions of collecting as those drawn by orality-literacy theorists about list-compiling, even though the two fields arrive at these conclusions via different approaches. The great majority of what can be labeled "museum theory" concentrates, for obvious reasons, on post-eighteenth-century Europe and develops a Foucauldian methodology to explain the ways that the emergent modern museum participates within and with other contemporary technologies (see, for example, Tony Bennett, *The Birth of the Museum: History, Theory, Politics* [New York, 1995]). While museum and collection theory often moves to historicize modern developments through an examination of medieval relic collections or other "talismanic" objects (see, for example, Susan Pearce, *Museums, Objects and Collections: A Cultural Study* [Washington, DC, 1992], 43–46; Werner Muensterberger, *Collecting: An Unruly Passion* [Princeton, 1994], 29–31), its focus is the function of objects for the alienated subject under capitalism and its conclusions must therefore be applied only with care to early medieval culture. However, the attention given within museum studies to the cultural function of display, the role of looking, the relationship between object and text, between past and present, to name but a few significant themes of the discipline, have fascinating relevance to Anglo-Saxon textual culture. Although I will be exploring this topic more extensively elsewhere, I should note the great relevance to my argument here of Susan Stewart's work on collections in *On Longing: Narratives of the Miniature, the Gigantic, the Souvenir, the Collection* (Baltimore, 1984), esp. 150–69. Stewart's Marxist and psychoanalytical approach subtly engages with and explains the individual and social roles of collecting objects. Many of the conclusions she draws here echo my own in this piece, especially her attention to the ways that the "collection replaces origin with classification, thereby making temporality a spatial and material phenomenon" (153) and her observation, following Baudrillard, that "because of the collection's seriality, a 'formal' interest always replaces a 'real' interest in collected objects" (154).

[47] Goody, *The Domestication*, 75.

[48] Within Anglo-Saxon studies, of course, scholarly works concentrating on what are labeled "orality-literacy" phenomena have revealed the extreme complexity of relationships between oral and literate culture, especially as these manifest themselves in manuscript texts. In fact, a perception of the orality/literacy shift as diachronic and decisive has been

are an important component of this scholarly field, where they are treated as formative of social and economic structures rather than as products of these structures: Goody writes of lists that

> these written forms were not simply by-products of the interaction between writing and, say, the economy, filling some hitherto hidden 'need', but . . . they represented a significant change not only in the nature of transactions, but also in the 'modes of thought' that accompanied them, at least if we interpret 'modes of thought' in terms of the formal, cognitive and linguistic operations which this new technology of the intellect opened up.[49]

It is precisely through their conservatism that lists "open up" new "cognitive and linguistic operations." Because lists at the same time pare down information to a bare minimum, removing extraneous syntax and detail, and also gather data together into a series, they enforce and strengthen relationships between items. In other words, classification is a product of the list rather than a pre-conceived system which the list merely formalizes and represents: "The ordering involved in written lists seems to promote a feed-back effect that reacts upon the definition of categories, in some contexts, by making them more visible."[50] The effect is one, as Goody describes it, of concretization or reification: the list, by including and excluding certain information, brings a concept into being and solidifies it, or makes it "thing-like." It is evident here that this procedure does not simply result from the way in which information is "fed into" the list by its compiler or writer; it is not, in other words, an author-controlled effect, which would necessitate the pre-existence of the categories to be exemplified in the list, but a product of the form itself.[51] Instead, when they are put into writing, lists "acquire a generalized, decontextualized authority" of their own and begin to generate their own systems of categorization.[52] For this reason, even while a list may not appear to have an order, to have been compiled almost by accident and without thought, it cannot help but systematize: "Lists have subjects. They are possessive. Lists are lists of."[53]

---

effectively deconstructed by recent work on this topic. See, to name one prominent example, Katherine O'Brien O'Keeffe, *Visible Song: Transitional Literacy in Old English Verse* (Cambridge, 1990).

[49] Goody, *The Domestication*, 81.

[50] Goody, *The Interface*, 182.

[51] As Goody notes elsewhere, "The arrangement of words (or 'things') in a list is itself a mode of classifying, of defining a 'semantic field', since it includes some items and excludes others" (*The Domestication*, 103).

[52] Goody, *The Interface*, 116.

[53] Gass, "And," 118.

Resistant as his work is to the progressivist model underlying much orality-literacy theory, Michel Foucault's work on systems of knowledge suggests similar conclusions about the function of lists. In fact, as he represents it, it was a moment of list-reading that provoked his meditation on the social nature of knowledge in *The Order of Things*. He describes how he was reduced to laughter by reading one of Borges's lists, said to be given in a Chinese encyclopedia,

> in which it is written that 'animals are divided into: (a) belonging to the Emperor, (b) embalmed, (c) tame, (d) sucking pigs, (e) sirens, (f) fabulous, (g) stray dogs, (h) included in the present classification, (i) frenzied, (j) innumerable, (k) drawn with a very fine camelhair brush, (l) *et cetera*, (m) having just broken the water pitcher, (n) that from a long way off look like flies'.[54]

Foucault's laughter, however, is uneasy since the catalogue brings him up short against a way of thinking so different from our own as to be incomprehensible: he writes that the passage,

> shattered . . . all the familiar landmarks of my thought — *our* thought, the thought that bears the stamp of our age and our geography — breaking up all the ordered surfaces and all the planes with which we are accustomed to tame the profusion of existing things.[55]

The problem with Borges's taxonomy is not that it deals in strange and improbable juxtapositions, but that it removes any conceptual common ground on which these items could meet. The fact that one of the categories, animals "included in the present classification," subsumes all the others destabilizes the "relation of container to contained" and makes it impossible to conceive of the space that could hold them all.[56] It is this that makes Foucault's laughter uneasy: the fear of the "heteroclite," or the state in which "things are 'laid', 'placed', 'arranged' in sites so very different from one another that it is impossible to find a place of residence for them, to define a common *locus* beneath them all."[57]

Foucault's discussion of lists in *The Order of Things* encourages us to read all lists (and not just lists of place-names) as being at one level about place. His problem with Borges's catalogue, as he explains, is caused by its defiance of the

[54] Foucault, *The Order of Things*, xv. Foucault does not provide a bibliographical reference for the passage, drawn from Borges's essay, "The Analytical Language of John Wilkins." Robert Belknap also includes this passage in his personal "A-List of Lists," quoted in Peter Monaghan, "Literary Lists are (1) Interesting (2) Important (3) Everywhere," *Chronicle of Higher Education*, 28 September 2001, 28–29, here 29.

[55] Foucault, *The Order of Things*, xv.

[56] Foucault, *The Order of Things*, xvii.

[57] Foucault, *The Order of Things*, xvii–xviii.

common faculty of lists to produce an imagined place in which their items co-exist. He describes how lists achieve this by bringing together their different elements:

> the mere act of enumeration that heaps them all together has a power of enchantment all its own . . . startling though their propinquity may be, it is nevertheless warranted by that *and*, by that *in*, by that *on* whose solidity provides proof of the possibility of juxtaposition.[58]

As Foucault shows, lists make places by collecting together diverse items into a whole: the form of the list generates a conceptual site in which the individual items belong together. And this site is provided with a certain kind of solidity through the syntax, "that *and* . . . that *in* . . . that *on*," of the list itself.

Foucault alerts us to the ways in which compiling and reading lists is a cultural practice serving to define "all the familiar landmarks of . . . *our* thought, the thought that bears the stamp of our age and our geography."[59] In other words, Foucault's confusion in reading Borges's list makes visible the organizing conceptual parameters and structures of his own world: the fact that he cannot "think" the list forces him to confront and question the underlying systematicity of his own perceptions. The moment of reading the list is thus one of recognition that cultures are constituted through conventional structures that organize and authorize knowledge in certain ways, and condition the thinkability of concepts. These structures, which produce themselves as "natural" and "self-evident," differ from place to place and between times; they are "*our* thought, the thought that bears the stamp of our age and our geography."[60] The practice of compiling and reading lists exercises and replicates these structures, and therefore functions both to create and to define the group (social, ethnic, religious) using the lists.

III. Defining Subjects

Knowing a little more about the effect of decontextualized lists allows us to explain certain aspects of the Tiberius B.v collection and how it might have been read during the Anglo-Saxon period. The first, somewhat obvious, point to be made is that examples of miscopying (such as the misplaced Northumbrian kings or the "extra" disciples), even if they were inherited from the exemplar, illustrate that the Anglo-Saxons experienced the same kinds of "problems" in reading

---

[58] Foucault, *The Order of Things*, xvi.

[59] Foucault, *The Order of Things*, xv.

[60] Foucault, *The Order of Things*, xv.

decontextualized lists as do modern commentators. In other words, the fact that the information has no broader context or explanation made, and makes, for interpretative difficulties, and thus "mistakes." But because these lists *were* copied, regardless of obvious misunderstanding, suggests that they had assumed what Jack Goody names a "decontextualized authority" of their own, which was operating as the source of their value and, to a certain extent, determining changes made by scribes. Unsurprisingly, when we consider the nature of lists as a form, these changes tend to take the form of addition or deletion of elements (or indeed extra texts). Also bearing in mind the nature of list-texts, we would expect these changes to work in the service of focusing and concretizing a category of understanding or a concept: an imagined *locus* or site of connection between the individual texts in the collection. Determining the subject of the Tiberius collection (since it is not explicitly stated) is a writerly act for the reader, an act that effectively erases the difference between "intentional" and "accidental" changes that have been made to the collection being read.

In order to begin to demonstrate some of these points more concretely, I want to return to the oft-noted regular length of the genealogies in the Tiberius collection. Whether or not this phenomenon is the residue of a propagandistic or an accidental change, it suggests a propensity in Anglo-Saxon scribal practice, not only to bring list-texts together, but also to regularize the shape of lists within collections. Sisam noticed this factor in his 1953 study, where he explained the regular length of the heptarchic genealogies in the collection as the result of a procedure of standardization that had occurred when the lists, in an earlier manifestation, were set out in table format:

> The chance agreement in length of two or three important lines, such as the Kentish and the Mercian, would establish a normal length for the columns. Because any irregularity is unpleasingly conspicuous where the columns stand side by side, and perhaps because there seemed to be a certain fitness in having the same number of generations in each trunk line, others of the original collection were made to conform . . . Trunk pedigrees incorporated later, or recorded elsewhere in imitation of the standard collection, would be made to match them. Thus a rigid form was imposed on materials still comparatively fluid.[61]

Thus the regular length of the genealogies is as much a condition of the list-form itself, which encourages the arrangement of text in symmetrical relationships, as it is, in Dumville's terms, a propagandistic alteration. It was the written form itself, rather than overtly partisan or national feelings, that suggested the appropriateness of bringing individual lists together; of adding or deleting items; and

---

[61] Sisam, "Anglo-Saxon Royal Genealogies," 328.

of regularizing the lists' overall shape.[62] The effect of this regularization, how-ever, can ultimately be ideological, since it serves to enhance the impression of unified meaning within the lists. The fact that the genealogies, for instance, are all of a similar length reinforces a sense of their fundamental homogeneity: that they participate in an underlying meaning that the reader must discover. And what the homogeneity in the form of the texts strongly suggests is a correspond-ing homogeneity in the regnal trajectories that they represent; or, in other words, a fundamental sameness in the historical background of England's once-separate kingdoms.

As might now be becoming obvious, the Tiberius collection essentially works to cement the sense of both national inclusiveness and dignification that Simon Keynes has identified as characteristic of the earlier version of the collection in Vespasian B.vi.[63] To make this point, though, it is necessary first to review how the lists in Tiberius B.v differ from other related collections. Even though Tiberi-us is an eleventh-century manuscript, its list collection manifests a set of changes made probably in the mid- and then the late tenth century. To begin with, while it is customary for the Anglian collection (item 7 in my list above) to be accom-panied by episcopal and papal lists, in Tiberius B.v the genealogical core of the Anglian material has been sandwiched between additional West Saxon records. The first part of these consists of a regnal list (item 6) providing reign lengths for the West Saxon kings from Cerdic to Æthelred. As Dumville notes, this list is an abstract of the so-called "West Saxon Genealogical Regnal List," which pref-aces the Anglo-Saxon Chronicle.[64] The Anglian collection is then followed by a lengthier genealogy from Edgar back to Adam "primus homo" (item 8). Both

---

[62] The "mistakes" in the Anglian collection illustrate perfectly that the lists have as-sumed their own decontextualized authority. Sisam finds that "transmission was careless throughout Anglo-Saxon times" across both the West-Saxon and Anglian genealogies, which were not "preserved with ritual precision" ("Anglo-Saxon Royal Genealogies," 325). Thus the authority and value of the list are not felt to be contained in its content. Even if the mistakes were present in the exemplar, they are repeated unrecognized or un-questioned by the Tiberius scribe; if this scribe inserted the mistakes, it is only because he was copying a text valued for the authority of its form and not because it was a historical source for the individual names. The authority of the list as a written form also produces the regularization of content in the list: it is more important that the lists assume a regu-lar shape than that their content remain "true" to an original. The preservation of the Wessex genealogy from Woden, even after Wessex had assumed power and could have "updated" the list by inserting their own eponymous god Seaxnet in place of Woden, also shows that the list has assumed an authorizing value.

[63] Keynes, "Between Bede and the *Chronicle*."

[64] Dumville, "The Catalogue Texts," 56. See also idem, "The West Saxon Genea-logical Regnal List."

of these lists were likely compiled during the reign of Edgar (959–975); Dumville dates the latter more specifically to 969.[65] That the only non-genealogical information included in this list is a reference to Ingeld's founding of Glastonbury abbey, along with the fact that it is followed by a unique list of the abbots of that house (item 9), encourages Dumville to assign a Glastonbury origin to this portion. After the abbot list appear another two items unique to Tiberius B.v (items 10 and 11), namely a continuation of the earlier list of popes and Archbishop Sigeric's Roman itinerary of A.D. 990. These two texts seem to indicate another stage of compilation: Dumville suggests that both were added in 990, at which time the episcopal lists (item 5) were also updated and the name of the current archbishop, Sigeric, singled out with the epithet "Dei amicus," unique to this version of the list.[66] The itinerary, prized as the only complete record of an Anglo-Saxon pilgrim's journey to Rome, consists of a catalogue of twenty-three churches visited by the archbishop over two days in Rome and a list of seventy-nine stopping places on the journey back to the Channel coast.

The particular augmentation of the collection which is represented by Tiberius B.v can be seen to crystallize the concept already suggested by the Anglian collection, namely an idea of "England" as a unified political, historical, and ecclesiastical entity, by means of additions particularly resonant to a tenth-century context (when the substantial revisions to the collection were performed). To begin with the dynastic material, the core of the earlier collection had consisted of genealogical material for all the heptarchic kingdoms (item 7) and thus had enforced a notion of shared history. In Tiberius B.v, however, this suggestion is cemented by the inclusion of extra West Saxon lists (items 6 and 8). This new material encircles the older Anglian collection (item 7), incorporating these northern-oriented lists within West Saxon history just as these territories had been subsumed under the control of Wessex. At the same time, the combination of dynastic material (regnal lists and genealogies) with the list of Roman emperors in Tiberius B.v is redolent of other tenth-century imperializing rhetoric, such as the use of expansive Latinate titles for the monarch in certain charters.[67]

In the case of the bishop lists, the provision in the Anglian collection of bishop lists for every English see already suggested ecclesiastical comprehensiveness

---

[65] Dumville, "The Anglian Collection," 43 and n. 1.

[66] Dumville, "The Anglian Collection," 44.

[67] See H. R. Loyn's analysis of the imperial titles used by the tenth-century Anglo-Saxon kings, in which he aims to discover if they are "fact" or "rhetoric" ("The Imperial Style of the Tenth Century Anglo-Saxon Kings," *History* 40 [1955]: 111–15). Particularly useful is Eric John, " 'Orbis Britanniae' and the Anglo-Saxon Kings," in idem, *Orbis Britanniae* (Leicester, 1966), 1–63. Similar imperializing rhetoric is suggested by the statement that "all the kings in this island" submitted to Æþelstan made in annal 926 of the D-text of the Anglo-Saxon Chronicle.

(item 5) while, through the association of this insular material with the list of the disciples of Christ and the papal list (items 1 and 2), also contextualizing English ecclesiastical identity in relation to salvation history and Roman Christianity. This earlier collection, then, already evoked a spatio-temporal network in which England was defined as a part of Roman Christendom and the Anglo-Saxons were connected linearly in time to Christ. These links with scriptural history are reinforced in Tiberius B.v by the genealogical tract connecting the kings of Wessex back to Christ and Adam (item 8). At the same time the vision of England as a part of Roman Christendom, suggested by the juxtaposition of English episcopal lists with the papal list (items 1 and 5), is forcefully accentuated in Tiberius B.v by the addition of the list of Glastonbury abbots immediately before a continuation of the list of popes (items 9 and 10). The final item of the collection in Tiberius B.v, the itinerary of Archbishop Sigeric's journey to Rome, literalizes this juxtaposition of Roman and English ecclesiastical authority by bringing an English archbishop into Rome itself: in other words, where the positioning of the episcopal and papal lists metaphorically produces England as a part of the Roman church, both historically and administratively Sigeric's itinerary links Rome to England geographically.[68] The unique property of the list format allows the English material (items 5 and 7) to be both a part of and apart from the papal and disciple lists at the same time, producing England both from without as a component of wider Christian geography and history, and from within as a consistent entity with its own unique traditions and regions. And not the least significant effect of this juxtaposition of lists is, as Keynes notes, to aggrandize the particularly Anglo-Saxon material; an effect that is created through the formal equivalence of the texts themselves.[69]

Meaning in the list collection as a whole is produced through the organization of the items, the juxtaposition of which is suggestive of interpretive affinities and relationships. While this effect is achieved most obviously through the juxtaposition of lists, the most important structural principle of the collection in Tiberius B.v is the envelope pattern.[70] At the center of this pattern is the Anglian

---

[68] I am grateful for the observation made by Nicholas Howe, during the discussion of this paper at the 2003 ISAS conference, that Sigeric's itinerary *begins* in Rome and *ends* at the Channel coast, thus bringing the archbishop home to England. While this does not make a substantial difference to my argument, it does reinforce the notion that England is the center and subject of this list collection.

[69] Keynes, "Between Bede and the *Chronicle*."

[70] For description of envelope patterns in Old English poetry, see Adeline Courtney Bartlett, *The Larger Rhetorical Patterns in Old English Poetry* (New York, 1935), 9–29; John D. Niles, "Ring Composition and the Structure of *Beowulf*," *Publications of the Modern Language Association* 94 (1979): 924–35; and Constance B. Hieatt, "On Envelope Patterns (Ancient and — Relatively — Modern) and Nonce Formulas," in *Comparative Research on Oral Traditions: A Memorial for Milman Parry*, ed. John Miles Foley (Columbus, OH, 1985), 245–58.

collection of royal genealogies, surrounded on both sides by thematically-associated material radiating outwards, as it were, in concentric circles: directly preceding and following the northern genealogies are lists relating to Wessex; of these two lists, the genealogical tract matches the earlier list of the disciples of Christ in linking the Anglo-Saxons to biblical history; and the bishop lists for all the English sees are reflected in the list of the abbots of Glastonbury. This principle of envelopment is literalized by the papal list, which breaks off in the first half of the collection on 19v and is then continued on the other side of the genealogies on 23v. Finally, the collection begins and ends in Rome, starting with the papal list and ending with Sigeric's itinerary. Reading the collection in this way as an extended envelope pattern places England at its center in the core of regnal material from the English kingdoms. Again, England is produced here internally, by means of the insular lists at the center of the pattern, while it is also contextualized externally through the surrounding lists relating it to biblical history and Roman Christianity.[71]

The decontextualized mode of presentation of the lists in Tiberius B.v is what makes them at the same time simple to read but difficult to understand, since the reader receives no interpretive instruction. This lack of context is, of course, part of the way in which lists involve and engage the reader by inviting them to reconstruct a context; to become, as Sisam put it, entangled in the possibilities of meaning.[72] The arrangement of the lists in Tiberius B.v suggests such a context, as I demonstrated above, through the associative links that are produced between items. This method of understanding the functioning of the lists fits comfortably within Anglo-Saxon reading practices in general. As Katherine O'Brien O'Keeffe has demonstrated, vernacular manuscripts in the period lacked many of the visual cues of distinctive layout and punctuation which assist us as

---

[71] Reading the list collection in this way shows how it fits in conceptually with other items in Tiberius B.v that serve to define Englishness, as these have recently been interpreted by Nicholas Howe and Martin Foys in particular, but also more generally with Anglo-Saxon textual practices, which often work to incorporate the Anglo-Saxons within world or Christian history — for example, the Ohthere and Wulfstan interpolations in the Old English *Orosius*, or the representation of the Anglo-Saxons as the new Israelites in Bede's *Ecclesiastical History*.

[72] For an interesting analysis of this principle as it works in Gerald of Wales's *Itinerarium Kambriae* see Monika Otter, *Inventiones: Fiction and Referentiality in Twelfth-Century English Historical Writing* (Chapel Hill, NC, 1996), 129–55. Otter argues here that the paratactic structure of this itinerary text opens up horizontal levels of thematic affiliation between episodes, through which Gerald is able to make implicit political comments. The juxtaposed nature of the narrative, however, requires the reader to participate in the text by engaging in a "process of association, cross-reference, and 'sorting-out'" (140).

modern readers in recognizing and processing text.[73] The fact that Old English texts often lack titles and it is sometimes unclear where they begin and end meant that readers had to participate extensively in the text in order to read it: O'Brien O'Keeffe shows how texts with few graphic signals guiding interpretation caused scribes to make "formulaic" guesses as part of the reading process. At the same time, the prevalence of essentially spatial structures like the envelope pattern and interlace in both poetry and prose indicates that readers were attuned to the ways in which contiguity and juxtaposition could be meaningful.

Reading the Tiberius list collection in this way allows us to see it as bringing to fruition meanings suggested by earlier versions of the collection, such as that in Vespasian B.vi, and that must therefore have exerted a powerful historiographical imperative on contemporary readers — at the very least those who felt compelled to preserve and to augment the collection. Understanding the decontextualized authority of lists can also perhaps shed light on the relation of this collection to the rest of the manuscript that contains it. Since the "mistaken" changes made to the Tiberius lists suggest that the scribe understood little more than the casual modern reader about the particularities of what he was copying, it seems that (at least by the eleventh century) the significance of the material was more iconic than it was specific. In other words, the list collection in Tiberius B.v seems to be more important for what it displays than for the details it gives. And, as I have argued above, what it displays is an imagined locus — that is, the concept of "England" as a multilayered territorial, historical, and ecclesiastical category. Given the apparent practical uselessness of some of the other materials in the manuscript, such as the computus texts, we have to wonder if other portions might share this largely iconic function. Rather than being preserved as a container for information, the manuscript (and the lists it contains) seems primarily to have been valued by its Anglo-Saxon users for its transformation of text into display — and the representation it is thus able to perform of knowledge, of history, and of place.

---

[73] O'Brien O'Keeffe, *Visible Song*, 4–5.

COLONIZATION AND CONVERSION IN CYNEWULF'S *ELENE*

HEIDE ESTES

Cynewulf's *Elene*, a poem about Helen's discovery in Jerusalem of the True Cross, is uniquely preserved in the Vercelli book, a manuscript of the late tenth century, along with another of Cynewulf's poems, *The Fates of the Apostles*. Cynewulf's other two poems, *Christ I* and *Juliana*, are preserved in the Exeter Book. Both manuscripts are dated on paleographical and codicological grounds to the second half of the tenth century; the Exeter Book was probably written quite near 1000, Vercelli perhaps somewhat earlier.[1] History records several men named Cynewulf during the Anglo-Saxon period, but the author of the poems has not been convincingly associated with any of them,[2] and the dates assigned to the works bearing Cynewulf's signature have ranged from 750 to 1000. Scholarly consensus has generally settled on a ninth-century date.[3] However, it has recently been argued that textual details concerning the poems and their sources indicate that Cynewulf composed them in the tenth century. In addition, historical particulars suggested by the language of *Elene* and the changes made to the Latin source of that poem evoke events specifically of the early part of the century.

---

[1] *The Vercelli Book*, ed. George Philip Krapp, ASPR 2 (New York, 1932), xvi; *The Exeter Book*, ed. George Philip Krapp and Elliott van Kirk Dobbie, ASPR 3 (New York, 1936), x. N. R. Ker, *Catalogue of Manuscripts Containing Anglo-Saxon* (Oxford, 1957; repr. 1990), 153, 460; and Helmut Gneuss, *Handlist of Anglo-Saxon Manuscripts: A List of Manuscripts and Manuscript Fragments Written or Owned in England up to 1100* (Tempe, AZ, 2001), 54, 14, concur with Krapp and Dobbie's dates for the manuscripts.

[2] Earl R. Anderson, *Cynewulf: Style, Structure and Theme in His Poetry* (Rutherford, NJ, 1983), 17; Alexandra Hennessey Olsen, *Speech, Song, and Poetic Craft: The Artistry of the Cynewulf Canon* (New York, 1984), 24; and R. D. Fulk, "Cynewulf: Canon, Dialect, and Date," in *Cynewulf: Basic Readings*, ed. Robert E. Bjork (New York, 1996), 16.

[3] P. O. E. Gradon argues for an early ninth-century date in *Cynewulf's 'Elene'* (Exeter, 1958; repr. 1996), 22–23; this view is accepted by Stanley B. Greenfield and Daniel G. Calder, *A New Critical History of Old English Literature* (New York, 1986), 164.

Patrick Conner has recently argued that Cynewulf's poem *The Fates of the Apostles* depends upon a version of Bede's *Martyrology* written by the Benedictine monk Usuardus of Paris, or upon a somewhat later recension of Usuardus's text containing additional details. Usuardus died around 875[4] and dedicated his manuscript to Charles the Bald, who reigned from 875 to 877; his recension can, therefore, be dated quite precisely.[5] The Venerable Bede had composed a version of the *Martyrology* that was for many years taken as Cynewulf's source; Bede's text survives only in later manuscripts with substantial additions. As Conner recounts, textual scholars of the early twentieth century were able to separate Bede's text from the later accretions, and it was observed that the details included in Cynewulf's *Fates* overlapped considerably with those in Usuardus's version of the *Martyrology*. However, since scholars were convinced that Cynewulf had written earlier than the late ninth century, the correspondences were largely ignored.[6]

Conner has examined several recensions of the *Martyrology* and points out that Usuardus's version of the *Martyrology* has the greatest number of parallels to Cynewulf's *Fates of the Apostles*. For example, the name "Egias" appears only in *Fates* and in Usuardus's *Martyrology*. Usuardus's recension is also the earliest Latin text to locate the narrative of Egias in the province of Achaiae, a detail also appearing in the Vercelli poem *Andreas*. Moreover, the disciples Simon and Thaddeus are described in both *Fates* and Usuardus's *Martyrology* as working together in Persia and dying on the same date, details not found elsewhere. Conner has identified several passages in *Fates* as close paraphrases of the Usuardian *Martyrology*.

A few details in the *Fates of the Apostles* are not found in Usuardus's "pure" *Martyrology*, but are found in later recensions based on his version. For example, Usuardus's text reports that Matthew preached among the Ethiopians, a detail shared with *Fates*, but Cynewulf also includes the detail that Matthew was killed by the king Irtacus, who appears not in the "pure" Usuardus but in the augmented Usuardian tradition. Three manuscripts of Usuardus's *Martyrology* have survived from Anglo-Saxon England, though no "augmented" text survives.[7] Nevertheless, Conner's surmise that a text of an extended version was available to Cynewulf, even though a manuscript of it does not survive, is plausible given the sheer volume

---

[4] Patrick W. Conner, "On Dating Cynewulf," in *Cynewulf: Basic Readings*, 23–56. For biographical detail on Usuardus, see *The New Catholic Encyclopedia*, 2nd ed. (New York, 1967), 14:498.

[5] Conner, "On Dating Cynewulf," 56 n. 83.

[6] Conner, "On Dating Cynewulf," 37. Conner's discussion, of which the following is a summary, appears on 36–47.

[7] Conner, "On Dating Cynewulf," 43.

[8] "Martyrologies would have been among those texts with which the Benedictine Revolution flooded England in the second half of the tenth century": Conner, "On Dating Cynewulf," 47.

of records lost from the period.[8] Conner points out that some years would have to pass while Usuardus's *Martyrology* was first disseminated, and then augmented and further transmitted. Therefore, in order to be able to use such an extended text, Cynewulf must have written "somewhat later than the last quarter of the ninth century."[9] Cynewulf might also have used the "pure" Usuardian *Martyrology* in combination with another source for the added details, in which case this would still place his composition some years after 875.

Conner's argument, it must be acknowledged, has occasioned debate. John McCulloh has written the most substantial rebuttal of Conner's proposal for an earlier date for Cynewulf.[10] According to McCulloh, Cynewulf cannot have used the Usuardian *Martyrology* because several details in *Fates* are absent from Usuardus's text, and the information appears in different sequence. McCulloh proposes, instead, a lost *Martyrology* or *Breviarium* as Cynewulf's source. McCulloh, however, does not address Conner's suggestion that Cynewulf could have used a text from the augmented Usuardian tradition, nor does he accept the possibility that Cynewulf could have used (as he formulaically claims to do in the opening to his poem) a variety of sources. McCulloh reviews several points of similarity among *Fates of the Apostles*, Usuardus's *Martyrology*, and two earlier, more extended versions of the *Martyrology* by Florus of Lyon and Ado of Vienne, and concludes that the Usuardian text "has fewer parallels with the *Fates* than does either Florus' or Ado's."[11] McCulloh argues based on the absence of certain details from all three of these versions of the *Martyrology* that "none of them seems especially appropriate as a source for Cynewulf's poem."[12] However, as Conner notes, while these details do not appear in the "pure" text of Usuardus's *Martyrology*, they are present in later texts based on the version produced by Usuardus.

Conner's argument is controversial;[13] however, he makes a credible case for a tenth-century date for the Cynewulfian canon which is also supported by other details in the poem. Stacy S. Klein has argued that the language of queenship used for Helen in the poem reflects cultural practices current in England in the

---

[9] Conner, "On Dating Cynewulf," 47.

[10] See John McCulloh, "Did Cynewulf Use a Martyrology? Reconsidering the Sources of the *Fates of the Apostles*," *ASE* 29 (2000): 67–83.

[11] McCulloh, "Did Cynewulf Use a Martyrology?", 73.

[12] McCulloh, "Did Cynewulf Use a Martyrology?", 80.

[13] Though Fulk agreed with Conner's dating in his 1996 article, "Cynewulf: Canon, Dialect, and Date" (see esp. 1–18), he accepts McCulloh's objections and a Usuardian *Martyrology* as Cynewulf's source. Most recently, he has suggested that Cynewulf must have used "an as yet unidentified passionary," examples of which were available in England as early as the eighth century. See R. D. Fulk and Christopher M. Cain, *A History of Old English Literature* (Malden, MA, 2003), 134, 254 n. 33.

[14] Stacy S. Klein, "Reading Queenship in Cynewulf's *Elene*," *Journal of Medieval and Early Modern Studies* 33 (2003): 47–89.

tenth century, but not in the ninth.[14] Klein notes that the Latin source for *Elene* seldom refers to Helen as "regina," instead using her proper name in most cases. Cynewulf, however, frequently replaces these mentions of her name with references to "cwen" or compounds including the word "cwen."[15] Klein points out that "it was in the mid-tenth century that the first English queen was formally granted the title *regina*."[16] That *Elene* is referred to repeatedly as "cwen," then, would resonate especially with readers familiar with the increased prestige and power attained by queens later in the Anglo-Saxon period. As I argue in the pages that follow, *Elene* also contains other thematic links to the historical events of the late ninth and early tenth centuries that could suggest a date of composition later than those events.

During much of the ninth century and the first half of the tenth, the Anglo-Saxons were preoccupied with an extended series of battles with the Scandinavians in which northern attackers harried, plundered, and eventually settled areas of Britain. In the 880s, King Alfred codified the existence of the Danish colony in England through a treaty of peace with the Danish leader Guthrum, establishing the boundaries between the Danish and English kingdoms, but this was by no means the end of the hostility.[17] In subsequent decades the Anglo-Saxons sought to recover the land settled by the Danes. This re-conquest was begun after Alfred's death in 899 by his son Edward and daughter Æthelflæd, and was continued in turn by Edward's sons, Æthelstan, Edmund, and Eadred, who reigned in sequence after Edward's death. During the long period of battles between the English and the Danes, the Church suffered significant losses. Several bishoprics were interrupted, forced to move, or completely destroyed; churches were plundered and abandoned; and religious communities were forced to move or disbanded altogether. Monastic life was severely disrupted, almost to the point of complete destruction, and the libraries of the clerical communities were demolished.[18]

Joanna Story discusses the paucity of books surviving from ninth-century England in comparison to other places or times, as well as the sorry state of Latin learning in England in the ninth century.[19] This decline, and the tenth-cen-

---

[15] Klein, "Reading Queenship," 56.

[16] Klein, "Reading Queenship," 58. See also Pauline Stafford, *Queen Emma and Queen Edith: Queenship and Women's Power in Eleventh-Century England* (Oxford, 1997), whom Klein cites here and elsewhere in her discussion of the construction of queenship in *Elene*.

[17] Frank Stenton, *Anglo-Saxon England*, 3rd ed. (London, 1971), 260 n.

[18] *King Alfred's West-Saxon Version of Gregory's Pastoral Care*, ed. Henry Sweet, EETS o.s. 45 (London, 1871; repr. 2001), 2–3.

[19] Joanna Story, *Carolingian Connections: Anglo-Saxon England and Carolingian Francia, c. 750–870* (Aldershot, 2003), 13–14.

tury renewal of learning, provides another argument for a tenth-century dating for Cynewulf. For a monk to be able to acquire sufficient learning to read Latin texts, translate them, and adapt them into several substantial Old English poems during a period of such severe monastic disruption would be quite striking. For someone to command the resources for the manuscript preservation of those poems into the next generation in a period of such monastic disruption would also be remarkable.

The political recovery of Danish territory was accompanied by religious renewal, and the two movements were viewed by participants and contemporary commentators as tightly intertwined, if not identical. In characterizing the attackers repeatedly as "heathens," the Anglo-Saxon Chronicle makes clear that the imperative for the English to fight back was not merely to contain the invading forces and, later, to recover lost territory, but also to re-establish a Christian hierarchy of both secular rulers and religious leadership. A condition of Alfred's negotiations for peace with the Danes was that Guthrum be baptized, a move justified by the belief that Christianity was the only true faith and enacted in the multiple narratives of colonization and conversion in Cynewulf's *Elene*. As lands once held by the English were reconquered, churches could be recovered and bishoprics re-established. In 954, with the defeat of the last Scandinavian ruler of York, Eric Bloodaxe, the Worcester manuscript of the Chronicle reports that Wulfstan was able to resume his position as archbishop of York.[20]

The clear message in *Elene* that Christian faith itself is sole justification for martial conquest and cultural imperialism justifies the conquest of Danish-held areas of England in the tenth century under the children and grandsons of Alfred. Constantine's victory as a Christian king several centuries earlier would give encouragement and legitimacy to the Christian kings in England,[21] first in fighting off pagan Danes, and later in battling to conquer the lands that the Danes had settled. Moreover, as the first Christian emperor, Constantine was of critical importance to the spread of Christianity through the Roman Empire.

---

[20] According to the entry for 954, "Her Norðhymbre fordrifon Yric, 7 Eadred feng to Norðhymbre rice. Her Wulfstan arcebiscop onfeng eft biscoprices on Dorceceastre" ["In this year the Northumbrians expelled Eric, and Eadred acceded to the Northumbrian throne. In this year Archbishop Wulfstan received once again the bishopric in Dorchester"]: *The Anglo-Saxon Chronicle: A Collaborative Edition: MS D*, ed. G. P. Cubbin (Cambridge, 1996), 45. Swanton notes that this is a reference to Wulfstan's re-installation as archbishop of York in a ceremony at Dorchester: *The Anglo-Saxon Chronicle*, ed. and trans. Michael Swanton (New York, 1998), 113n.

[21] See Nicholas Howe, "Rome: Capital of Anglo-Saxon England," *Journal of Medieval and Early Modern Studies* 31 (2004): 147–72, here 163.

The belief that Constantine had been born in Britain while his father, Constantius, was ruling the island in the third century may well have added to the legend's appeal to the Anglo-Saxons. This legend is apparently first mentioned by Aldhelm, who died in 709, in his prose *De Virginitate*, in which he mentions in passing that Constantine was born of Helen in Britain.[22] The widespread awareness of Aldhelm's work is attested by its survival in no fewer than twelve manuscripts still extant from the period, including eight containing continuous or substantial glosses in Old English.[23] According to the Old English version of Bede's *Ecclesiastical History of the English People*, translated in the late ninth century, "Writeð Eutropius þæt Constantius se casere wære on Breotone acenned" ["Eutropius writes that the emperor Constantine was born in Britain": 1.8].[24] The survival of six manuscripts of the Old English *Ecclesiastical History* indicates that it was also well known.[25] The idea of Constantine's British birth remained current in England; it was expressed again, with the additional claim that Helen was a daughter of Coel, king of the Britons, rather than a continental visitor to England at the time of Constantine's birth, in Geoffrey of Monmouth's *History of the Kings of Britain*.[26]

The late tenth-century Vercelli book context for *Elene* coincides chronologically with Ælfric's composition of a homily on the same subject, "Inventio Sanctae Crucis," between 989 and 995.[27] However, the two works differ significantly in focus, suggesting links with different historical events and thus differ-

---

[22] ". . . Constantius Constantii filius in Britannia, ex pellice Helena genitus": *De Laudibus Virginitatis Sive de Virginitate Sanctorum*, PL 89.148B. See also *Aldhelm: The Prose Works*, ed. and trans. Michael Lapidge and Michael Herren (Cambridge, 1979), 115. Antonina Harbus reviews Anglo-Saxon references to Helen in *Helena of Britain in Medieval Legend* (Woodbridge, 2002), 28–43.

[23] Gneuss, *Handlist*, 11, 151.

[24] *The Old English Version of Bede's Ecclesiastical History of the English People*, ed. Thomas Miller, EETS o.s. 95 (Oxford, 1890; repr.Woodbridge, 1997), 42. According to the Latin text at this point, "Eutropius quod Constantinus in Britannia creatus imperator patri in regnum successerit" ["Eutropius writes that Constantine was created emperor in Britain and succeeded to his father's kingdom"]: *Bede's Ecclesiastical History of the English People*, ed. and trans. Bertram Colgrave and R. A. B. Mynors (Oxford, 1969), 36–37.

[25] Gneuss, *Handlist*, 156.

[26] Geoffrey of Monmouth, *The History of the Kings of Britain*, trans. Lewis Thorpe (New York, 1966), 132.

[27] Ælfric, "Inventio Sanctae Crucis," in *Ælfric's Catholic Homilies, The Second Series*, ed. Malcolm Godden, EETS s.s. 5 (London, 1979), 174–76. Ælfric also makes reference to the legend in one of his saints' lives, "Exaltatio Sancte Crucis," in *Ælfric's Lives of Saints*, ed. W. W. Skeat, EETS o.s. 94, 114 (London, 1890; repr. 1966), 2: 144–58, here 144. For Ælfric's dates of composition, see Greenfield and Calder, *New Critical History*, 75.

ent literary concerns at their respective dates of composition. Ælfric's homily on
the discovery of the cross is significantly shorter than *Elene* and differs in several
important details. It resembles *Elene* in its broad outlines: both works open with
a description of Constantine's vision of the cross, his victory over the much larger opposing army, and his subsequent conversion to Christianity. Both versions
continue by narrating Helen's journey to Jerusalem to recover the True Cross, her
verbal wrangling with the Jews, and the Jews' conversion.

Cynewulf and Ælfric, however, chose different Latin traditions upon which
to base their works, reflecting different contemporary, historical, and literary
concerns. In Ælfric's account of the legend, the emperor Constantine, attacked
by the warrior chieftain Maxentius with a powerful army, has a vision of the
cross, with which, he is told by a contingent of angels, he can defeat his enemy.
He immediately orders the production of a golden cross and, using this as his
battle-standard, decisively defeats Maxentius and his army on the morning following his vision. Ælfric, who cites Jerome as his authority, is accurate in terms of
the historical record in representing Constantine and Maxentius as rival claim-
ants to the Roman throne.[28]

However, several Latin versions of the narrative which circulated in the early
Middle Ages made an important shift in this narrative. While it has been argued that Cynewulf used details from several sources,[29] the Latin text generally
taken to be most similar to Cynewulf's poem is the *Acta Quiriaci*, which appears
in the *Acta Sanctorum* for May 4.[30] In any event, the Latin versions proposed as
sources for *Elene* share the details relevant to this discussion. Rather than battling another Roman general for kingship, Constantine is in these Latin versions
harried by a large army of foreigners ["gens multa barbarorum"][31] against whom
he must defend Rome and the Roman people. Another Old English text of the
legend survives in only two manuscripts, one of the eleventh century and one of
the twelfth. This prose version is based on a Latin version of the legend quite

---

[28] Eusebius, *Life of Constantine*, 1. 33–38, ed. and trans. Averil Cameron and S. G.
Hall (Oxford, 1999), 82–85, 213–15.

[29] John Gardner, "Cynewulf's *Elene*: Sources and Structure," *Neophilologus* 54 (1970):
65–76.

[30] *Cynewulf's 'Elene,'* ed. Gradon, 15. See also *Sources and Analogues of Old English Poetry: The Major Latin Texts in Translation*, trans. M. J. B. Allen and Daniel G. Calder (Cambridge, 1976), 59. The Latin versions depend upon a Syriac original, which was translated
into Greek and thence into Latin; the Syriac text, probably composed in the fourth century,
concerns only Helen's journey, and does not include the narrative of Constantine's vision
and battle. See Johannes Straubinger, *Die Kreuzauffindungslegende* (Paderborn, 1912).

[31] *The Old English Finding of the True Cross*, ed. Mary Catherine Bodden (Cambridge,
1987), 60. Allen and Calder translate as "a large barbarian host": *Sources and Analogues*,
60.

similar to that used by Cynewulf, and shares this detail about the identity of the foreign army, translating the Latin phrase as "micel ælþeodig folc" ["a large foreign people"].[32] Cynewulf, however, makes a further change in the narrative, in that he names specific tribes — Huns, Hrethgoths, and Franks — as attackers upon Rome (*Elene* lines 20–21, 58).

Cynewulf's use of this description is curious, since the Franks were Christianized and had been traditional allies of the English. In 855, the year the Anglo-Saxon Chronicle records as the first in which the heathen Danes remained on English lands over the winter, King Æthelwulf (father of Alfred) had married Judith, a granddaughter of Charlemagne. Yet Cynewulf makes it clear that the various attacking tribes are "hæðene" ["heathens," line 126]. The Anglo-Saxon Chronicle repeatedly uses the same term to characterize the Danes who harassed the Anglo-Saxons throughout the ninth century.[33] In their status as pagans, those who attack Constantine are analogous to the pagans who attacked England. By the early tenth century, the alliance with the Franks would have faded into the background, overshadowed in importance by the ongoing conflict between the Anglo-Saxons and the residents of the Danelaw. For a writer to refer to the Franks as one of several tribes of heathen enemies is less jarring in the later context.

Cynewulf describes the massed armies of "elþeodige" ["foreigners," line 57] as enormous, threatening Constantine's small retinue: "Modsorge wæg / Romwara cyning, rices ne wende / for werodleste, hæfde wigena to lyt" ["the king of the Romans bore heart-sorrow; he did not expect to rule, for lack of fighters: he had an army too small": lines 61b–63]. Cynewulf makes it clear that Constantine's small fighting force can vanquish the vast foreign army only due to his faith in his vision of the cross: "Þa wæs gesyne þæt sige forgeaf / Constantino cyning ælmihtig / æt þæm dægweorce, domweorðunga, / rice under roderum, þurh his rode treo" ["It was seen at that day's work that Constantine, mighty king, was given victory and honor, might under heaven, through the wood of his cross": lines 144–147].

Cynewulf's description of Constantine's encounter with the angel who grants him a vision of the cross is expanded considerably beyond the brief account in the Latin versions. The angel bringing news of Christianity to Constantine promises victory if Constantine will give faith to the "sigores tacen" ["token of victory," line 85] sent by "cyning engla" ["the king of angels," line 79]. Both phrases appear exclusively in religious contexts. "Cyning engla" is used in several poems to refer to God.[34] The relatively unusual phrase "sigetacen" refers to the

[32] *True Cross*, ed. Bodden, 61.

[33] See, for example, the entries for 832, 855, and 865: *Two of the Saxon Chronicles Parallel*, ed. John Earle, rev. Charles Plummer (Oxford, 1965), 62–63, 66–67, 68–69.

[34] "Cyning engla" appears in *Genesis*, lines 1210, 1497, etc., *Andreas* line 1517, *Fates of the Apostles* line 115, and *Christ* line 712. The phrase "cyning engla" may be read as a pun on "cyning angla." The *Anglo-Saxon Chronicle* poem "The Death of Edgar" refers to the eponymous king as "Engla cyning" (l. 2); see *The Anglo-Saxon Minor Poems*, ed. Elliott van Kirk Dobbie, ASPR 6 (New York, 1942), 22.

cross in one of the Blickling homilies,[35] as it does in *Elene*. In other texts, the phrase is also used with religious connotation. In *Guthlac*, "sigores tacen" appears as an alternative for "godspel" ["gospel," line 1116]; in the Paris Psalter, sigetacen refers to the plagues against Pharaoh while the Israelites are enslaved in Egypt (134.9); and in *Genesis*, "sigores tacen" is used as a euphemism for circumcision.[36] In contrast to Constantine's warriors, the enemy troops in *Elene* carry an unspecified "herecombol" ["battle standard," line 25], and they flee immediately in the face of the "halige treo" ["holy cross," line 128] raised by Constantine's army. Through these linguistic details, then, Cynewulf associates Constantine very strongly with victorious Christianity in opposition to the pagan foreigners he defeats.

The angel who brings the message of Christianity to Constantine is referred to as "friðuwebbe" ["peace-weaver," line 88]. This compound appears elsewhere only in *Beowulf* and *Widsith*, where it denotes women of high status who give gifts and speak publicly in an effort to make peace among an assembly of warriors.[37] The use of the term in *Elene* to refer to an angel is unique; it emphasizes Constantine's association with ideals of Germanic lordship. The idea that Constantine was born in Britain seems to lie behind the tenth-century accounts, and reinforces the link between his victory and conversion and contemporary events in Anglo-Saxon England.[38] The reference to the angel, rather than to Helen, as "friðowebbe" marks an interesting shift from the poems based upon Germanic traditions to this Latin-based work. That Helen is not the poem's "peace-weaver" highlights her martial and commanding function in her interaction with the Jews in the poem, a role bracketed and thus emphasized by her subordination to Constantine at the beginning of the narrative and to Judas (renamed Cyriacus after his baptism) by its end.[39]

---

[35] "Homily VIII," in *The Blickling Homilies*, ed. and trans. R. J. Kelly (New York, 2003), 58.

[36] Where the biblical narrative states that Abraham circumcises all the men of his tribe (Gen. 17:10–14 and 23–27), in the poem God tells him that he must "sete sigores tacn soð on gehwilcne wæpnedcynnes" ["place the token of victory truly on each man," lines 2313–2314]. *Guthlac* is preserved in the *Exeter Book*. For the *Paris Psalter*, see *The Paris Psalter and the Meters of Boethius*, ed. George Philip Krapp, ASPR 5 (New York, 1932); for *Genesis*, see *The Junius Manuscript*, ed. George Philip Krapp, ASPR 1 (New York, 1931).

[37] For a discussion of the term, see L. John Sklute, "*Freoðuwebbe* in Old English Poetry," in *New Readings on Women in Old English Literature*, ed. Helen Damico and Alexandra Hennessey Olsen (Bloomington, 1990), 204–10.

[38] Interestingly, both *Beowulf* and *Widsith*, like *Elene*, involve legends built around kings whose existence as historical figures can be independently verified.

[39] Joyce Tally Lionarons notes that Helen is referred to with the warlike terms "guð-cwen" ["war-queen," line 254] and "sigecwen" ["victory-queen," line 260], but after Judas has converted and become the spiritual leader in Jerusalem, her role changes to a more traditionally feminine one. See "Cultural Syncretism and the Construction of Gender in *Elene*," *Exemplaria* 10 (1998): 51–68, here 59.

In addition to its focus upon Constantine as a Christian ruler, *Elene* uses language and imagery familiar to Old English heroic poetry to align Constantine with Anglo-Saxon traditions. The Latin versions narrate Constantine's vision and victory quite tersely, with no description of Constantine, who is given simply the title "Rex."[40] Cynewulf, however, opens the poem with this description: "Wæs se leodhwata lindgebeorga / eorlum arfæst. Æðelinges weox / rice under roderum. He wæs riht cyning, / guðweard gumena" ["The valiant prince of shield-warriors was gracious to earls. The prince's power grew under heaven. He was a just king, lord of warriors": lines 11–14a]. Cynewulf includes several other passages describing Constantine in which he uses terminology that echoes the vocabulary of poems about Germanic and English heroes. Where Constantine is "leodhwata," Beowulf is "leodcyning" (line 54) and Hrothgar is "leodgebyrga" (line 269); both terms also mean "prince" or "king." Constantine's "lindgebeorga" are paralleled in *Beowulf* by "lindgestealla" ["shield-companions," line 1973], "lindhæbbende" ["shield-bearers," lines 245, 1402], and "lindwiga" ["shield warrior," line 2603]. Constantine is "riht cyning," recalling Beowulf's noble ancestor Scyld Scefing, who is "god cyning" (line 11).[41] Cynewulf drew upon the same stock of poetic vocabulary used by the *Beowulf*-poet in developing his portrait of Constantine as a warrior chieftain in the Anglo-Saxon tradition.

In a further departure from the Latin tradition, Constantine and his warriors in *Elene* adorn themselves with the traditional Anglo-Saxon image of the boar: on the night of his vision, Constantine meditates on the upcoming battle "eoforcumble beþeaht" ["protected by a boar-emblazoned banner," line 76]. Later, the Roman warriors who travel with Helen to Jerusalem bear the same standard (line 259). While boars also appear on Roman arms and armor, they are not mentioned in the Latin analogues to Cynewulf's poem, so the detail appears borrowed from the Anglo-Saxon tradition: boar imagery appears on helmets from the Anglo-Saxon period discovered in archaeological sites;[42] and the warriors of Beowulf's retinue wear helmets topped with golden boars.[43]

In a further addition to the Latin texts, and a parallel that suggests a specifically tenth-century context for the composition of *Elene*, Constantine is described

---

[40] *True Cross*, ed. Bodden, 60, 64; Allen and Calder, *Sources and Analogues*, 60–61.

[41] For quotations from *Beowulf*, see *Beowulf and the Fight at Finnsburh*, ed. F. Klaeber, 3rd ed. (Lexington, MA, 1950).

[42] Catherine M. Hills, "*Beowulf* and Archaeology," in *A Beowulf Handbook*, ed. Robert E. Bjork and John D. Niles (Lincoln, NE, 1997), 291–310, here 304.

[43] "Eoforlic scinon ofer hleorborgan gehroden golde" ["Figures of boars shone over helmets decorated in gold": *Beowulf*, lines 303–304]. For further discussion of boar imagery in Old English poetry, see Maximino Gutiérrez Barco, "The Boar in *Beowulf* and *Elene*: A Germanic Symbol of Protection," *Revista de la Sociedad Española de Lengua y Literatura Inglesa Medieval* 9 (1999): 163–71.

as "beorna beaggifa" ["ring-giver to warriors," lines 100, 1198]. This phrase is unusual, as is the compound "beaggifa" itself, and both appear almost exclusively in works of late date. Other than in *Elene*, the phrase "beorna beaggifa" appears only in two poems datable definitively to the tenth century. In *The Battle of Brunanburh*, the Anglo-Saxon Chronicle entry for 937, the expression describes King Æthelstan (line 2).[44] *Brunanburh* concerns attempts to defend English land from pagan attackers, in direct parallels to the poetic portrayal of Constantine as fighting against a pagan army. In *The Death of Edgar*, the entry for 975, the phrase is used for the dead king (line 10). Aside from *Elene* and the tenth-century Chronicle poems, the compound "beaggifa" occurs on its own only four more times in the Old English corpus: in the *Preface* to the Old English translation of Gregory's *Dialogues*, written in the last decade of the ninth century; in *The Battle of Maldon*, which commemorates a battle fought in 991; in *Maxims II*, a poem which prefaces the eleventh-century manuscript C of the Anglo-Saxon Chronicle;[45] and in *Beowulf*, which is preserved only in a copy written down about 1000, though the question of its dating has prompted intense controversy. This distribution of appearances of the term suggests that, although the concept of generous giving of treasure as a means to cement bonds between lord and retainer is familiar from a very early date, the compound "beaggifa" might possibly be a late coinage (though later texts could also imitate a much earlier usage).

The use of Anglo-Saxon heroic diction familiar from *Beowulf* and from poems describing English warriors to describe Constantine suggests that, for the English in the tenth century, he was seen as a potent and desirable model because his martial prowess was combined with and enabled by his acceptance of Christianity. The tradition that he had been born in England eases his assimilation as a forebear and as an exemplary figure simultaneously religious and secular. The idea that Constantine was born in Britain seems to lie behind the three Old English accounts of his victory and conversion, and certainly provides a stronger link between Constantine's exploits and Anglo-Saxon political and religious affairs.

Constantine's conversion to Christianity is a crucial part of Cynewulf's version of the narrative. Writing at the end of the tenth century, after the Danelaw had been integrated into the English political and Christian orders, Ælfric sees no reason to give any rationale for or explication of Constantine's conversion. In his homily he passes over it very briefly, commenting only that after defeating Maxentius and ascending to the imperial throne, Constantine "mid sige gesæt.

---

[44] Both poems appear in the Parker Chronicle (manuscript A), to which entries were added throughout the tenth century. See *The Anglo-Saxon Chronicle*, ed. Swanton, xxi–xxii.

[45] For the C-Text of the Chronicle, see *The Anglo-Saxon Chronicle: A Collaborative Edition, Ms. C*, ed. Katherine O'Brien O'Keeffe (Cambridge, 2001).

siððan his cynestol. gefullod on criste" ["with victory, afterward occupied his
throne in victory, baptized in Christ"].[46] The Latin analogues for *Elene* are likewise fairly laconic about the conversion, though they note that Constantine was
educated in key aspects of the significance of the symbol of the cross before becoming Christian and asking his mother to seek the original cross in Jerusalem.

In *Elene*, however, Cynewulf adds detail to the material found in his Latin
source, suggesting that conversion of the Danes was a current concern while he
was writing. Cynewulf expands his account of Constantine's conversion and adds
parallels between Constantine's search for Christian truth and Helen's search
for the "True Cross" that bring both parts of the narrative into focus. Cynewulf
narrates Constantine's conversion as a quest in which Constantine first seeks a
teacher and then undergoes a period of education before being baptized. Since
Constantine's mother is already Christian, it seems an unlikely detail that, after
defeating the pagans, he must search widely for someone who can explain the
meaning of the cross. Yet Cynewulf emphasizes the process of conversion by describing Constantine as returning home from battle and then summoning from
his kingdom "þa wisestan" ["the wisest ones," line 153] learned in both ancient
writings and men's counsels ["fyrngewrito," line 155, and "hæleða rædas," line
156]. Cynewulf describes the assembly as at first unable to answer his questions,
until the wisest among the wisest reveal that the cross is "heofoncyninges tacen"
["the sign of the king of heaven," lines 170–171]. This sets the stage for a lesson about the Trinitarian nature of God; about Jesus' identity as the son of God;
about the crucifixion and ascension; and about Jesus' redemption of the souls of
men from "locan deofla" ["the devil's stronghold," line 181]. Constantine's teachers then tell him that those souls received grace from the same "sigores tacen"
(line 184) that he had seen in his vision before battle. According to Cynewulf,
Constantine is then immediately baptized, and he devotes himself to God's service, worshiping "dæges ond nihtes" ["day and night," line 198] for the rest of his
life. (In fact, Constantine did not actually receive baptism, and formally convert,
until he was on his deathbed in 337.)[47] The expansion of the scene in which Constantine learns about Christianity indicates Cynewulf's enhanced emphasis on
the importance of conversion in the narrative. The Anglo-Saxons' focused desire
to conquer and convert the Danes in the tenth century provides a powerful argument for reading the poem within this context.

Following his conversion, Constantine sends his mother, Helen, to Jerusalem to search for the True Cross. In Cynewulf's depiction, Helen functions less
independently than in the Latin versions of the legend, following the lead of

---

[46] *Ælfric's Catholic Homilies*, ed. Godden, 175, lines 36–37. The punctuation is as
printed in Godden's edition.

[47] Eusebius, *Life of Constantine* 4. 61–64 (117–79, 342–43).

Constantine to a much greater extent than in the Latin analogues.[48] Moreover, she is able to assert power over the inhabitants of Jerusalem because her Christianity elevates her in status over the Jews,[49] but as soon as Judas converts to Christianity (upon which he is renamed Cyriacus), she becomes subordinate to him. Helen's limited power as a woman within the universe of the poem is suggested by the legend's emphasis on visions and prayer. The poem opens, as noted above, with Cynewulf's vision; when Helen arrives in Jerusalem to recover the True Cross, she does not herself pray for revelation, but depends upon a Jew to do so. Helen undertakes no direct communion with God, nor is she granted visions from God.[50]

Helen's interrogation of the Jews in Jerusalem resembles Constantine's questioning of his advisors in structure, but contains nuanced differences in language. Whereas Constantine assembles the wisest of the Romans, Helen demands audience with "þam snoterestum" ["the cleverest," line 277] among the Jews. Constantine's wise men are knowledgeable in both book learning and oral counsels; the Jews assembled by Helen know about "dryhtnes geryno / þurh rihte æ" ["God's mystery through the true law," lines 280–281], but are limited to explaining "Moyses æ" ["the law of Moses," line 283]. As Andrew Scheil suggests, Helen's repeated invocations of the "wisdom" of the Jews finally "begin to ring hollow."[51] Constantine learns from Christians among his advisors of Jesus' Crucifixion; Helen taunts the Jews with the accusation that they were responsible for the Crucifixion: "Ge mid horu speowdon / on þæs ondwlitan þe eow eagene leoht, / fram blindness bote gefremede" ["You spat with filth upon the face that offered you light for your eyes, a cure from blindness": lines 297–299]. Constantine politely asks for help and information; Helen harangues and insults the Jews. As Scheil argues, this reference to the Jews' spitting in Jesus' face "links the Jews to the base fluids of the body and heightens the emotional cathexis of the Passion narrative: they add insult to injury with the expectoration of a foul fluid."[52] The

---

[48] This observation has been developed most recently by Karin Olsen in "Cynewulf's Elene: From Empress to Saint," in *Germanic Texts and Latin Models: Medieval Reconstructions*, ed. eadem, Antonina Harbus, and Tette Hofstra (Leuven, 2001), 141–56. See also Anderson, *Cynewulf*, 103–25; and Gordon Whatley, "The Figure of Constantine the Great in Cynewulf's 'Elene'," *Traditio* 37 (1981): 161–202. Klein links Helen's reduced stature in Cynewulf's poem to an expression of a "traditional Pauline social vision of both rank and gender": "Reading Queenship," 75.

[49] Joyce Tally Lionarons has shown that patristic theology represents Jews as feminized by their unbelief: see "Cultural Syncretism," 62.

[50] Klein notes that Helen "is the only major character in the poem who does not herself convert": "Reading Queenship," 61.

[51] Andrew Scheil, *The Footsteps of Israel: Understanding Jews in Anglo-Saxon England* (Ann Arbor, 2004), 222.

"blindness" from which the Jews will not be cured is spiritual; it is their inability to recognize Jesus' divinity. The Christological tradition of Jewish blindness is explicated more fully in one of the homilies of the Vercelli Book alongside which *Elene* is preserved. In that context, this passing reference carries the full weight of the Christian anti-Judaic exegetical tradition.[53]

Jews play an important part in Cynewulf's *Elene* in terms of both their role in the Christian exegetical tradition and their function in structuring the category of "Christian" in tenth-century Anglo-Saxon England. Emphasizing the role of the Jews as external to Christianity allows Cynewulf to signal that Danes and Anglo-Saxons could become a single community as Christians, transcending their history as members of opposing armies. Helen schools the Jews on Christian interpretation of the Hebrew scriptures. In presenting Helen's lectures to the Jews, the poem incorporates biblical exegesis without presenting it as a direct lesson, suggesting that the poem may be directed in part at recent Danish converts with little Christian education.[54]

Notably, as a woman, Helen is empowered to explicate Christianity to the Jews, though her own son Constantine had sought his Christian education from other, presumably male, authorities. She tells them, "Hwæt, ge witena / lare onfengon, hu se liffruma / in cildes had cenned wurde, / mihta wealdend" ["See, you received the teaching of prophets, how the source of life, the mighty ruler, would be born in the person of a child": lines 334b–337a]. She further states that Moses said that Jesus "modor ne bið / wæstmum geeacnod þurh wiges frige" ["(his) mother will not grow pregnant with offspring through the love of a man": lines 340b–341]. Helen goes on to explain the Christian interpretation of the words of Solomon and the prophecy of Isaiah to the Jews.

At length, the Judas of *Elene* reveals to his people that his father, while dying, instructed him about the Crucifixion and its import for the new religion. In this revelation, Judas exemplifies Christian teaching about all post-biblical Jews: not only did he know about Jesus, despite his denials of such knowledge, and not

---

[52] Scheil, *Footsteps of Israel*, 212.

[53] Scheil, *Footsteps of Israel*, 213. For discussion of medieval Christian attitudes toward Jews, see also James Parkes, *The Conflict of the Church and the Synagogue: A Study in the Origins of Anti-Semitism* (New York, 1961); Rosemary Radford Ruether, *Faith and Fratricide: The Theological Roots of Anti-Semitism* (Minneapolis, 1974); and Gavin Langmuir, *History, Religion, and Anti-Semitism* (Los Angeles, 1990). For the Pauline origins of the trope of Jewish blindness, see for example Romans 2:25–29; Galatians 3:2–3 and 3:14.

[54] Cynthia Zollinger notes the didactic function of the poem in "Cynewulf's *Elene* and the Patterns of the Past," *JEGP* 103 (2004): 180–96, here 191. Ellen F. Wright also takes the poem to be didactic in purpose: see "Cynewulf's *Elene* and the 'Singal Sacu'," *Neuphilologische Mitteilungen* 76 (1975): 538–49.

only had he learned the Christian interpretation of Jesus' life and death from his father, but he resisted admitting to his knowledge for fear that, should the cross become known, "ne bið lang ofer ðæt / þæt Israhela æðelu moten / ofer middangeard ma ricsian" ["it will not be long after that, that the lineage of Israel may reign over middle-earth": lines 432–434].

Ælfric's homily focuses upon Christian faith as that which legitimizes kingship, as it is only Constantine's acceptance of Christianity which differentiates him from his rival Maxentius. In Ælfric's version of the legend, Helen arrives in Jerusalem and is led to the location of the cross by a divine symbol ("þurh heofonlicere gebicnunge"),[55] and there is no reference to Jews or other inhabitants of Jerusalem. Again, Ælfric is correct in the historical particulars; Jerusalem had ceased to exist as a Jewish city early in the second century, when, following Jewish revolts against high Roman taxation, the emperor Hadrian (A.D. 132–135) had the city razed and rebuilt as "Aelia Capitolina." Jews were forbidden by imperial edict from living in the city; they were permitted to visit only once a year.[56] The absence of Jews from Ælfric's narrative gives his version of the tale a focus very different from Cynewulf's emphasis on conversion. Ælfric concludes by exhorting Christians to honor the cross and give thanks to Jesus. His homily, then, takes a Christian community as its audience and appears designed to encourage deepened faith among those already belonging to the community.

By the time Ælfric was writing, at the end of the tenth century, the intense concern with the conversion of the Danes that had motivated the churchmen of the late ninth and early tenth centuries was no longer current. Churches and bishoprics in the Danelaw had been re-established; once again, England faced external threats rather than internal ones. The focus in Ælfric's homily on the Invention of the Cross upon conflict between pagans and Christians allows him to streamline his message of faith.

Cynewulf's poem, however, follows a different tradition of Latin versions by including the Jews as a third group in *Elene*, and it exploits this addition in the depiction of the Jews' reluctance to aid Helen in finding the cross. In his expansion and opposition of the two conversion narratives, Cynewulf effects a significant shift in the meaning of the legend. Cynewulf's poem concerns the education and conversion of non-Christians. Those like Constantine who accept Christianity easily are celebrated; for those who resist Christian faith, the poem legitimizes the use of force in accomplishing conversion. Cynewulf portrays Judas accepting Christianity only after being tortured, and the other Jews in Jerusalem as requiring intensive persuasion before they convert.

---

[55] *Ælfric's Catholic Homilies*, ed. Godden, 175, lines 41–42.
[56] *A History of the Jewish People*, ed. H. H. Ben-Sasson (Cambridge, MA, 1976), 332–33.

Unlike Constantine, whose vision of the cross is immediately accompanied by faith in its power even though he does not yet understand its meaning, Judas is aware of the prophecy that a savior is to be born of Jewish people, yet does not believe that Jesus is that savior. In *Elene*, Judas is the only individual with this knowledge, even though medieval Christian theology held that all Jews were presumed to be stubborn in possessing the knowledge of Jesus' divinity but unwilling to acknowledge it. As Scheil argues, the poem suggests that "[b]y hiding the location of the cross, the Jews are, in a sense, reenacting the crucifixion, extending their original crime."[57] Danish pagans among the original audience for *Elene*, therefore, are oddly redeemed by their lack of knowledge about Christianity. Like Constantine, they may be presumed to be genuinely ignorant of Christianity yet willing to learn, in contrast to the Jews, with their hidden knowledge and their reluctance to accept Christianity even when they observe miracles.

Helen's spoken battles with the Jews occur in a series of scenes that resemble other Anglo-Saxon representations of strong female characters: verbal skill is expected of women in the Anglo-Saxon poetic tradition, in contrast to the martial power that characterizes men. Helen's vocal prowess is contrasted to the speechlessness of the Jews as a group in her first several encounters with them; in their lack of any capacity for speech, they are somehow less than human. However, Helen's verbiage is ultimately unsuccessful. Cynewulf repeatedly states that in her spoken assaults upon the Jews, Helen "begins" to address them. In her first encounter with them, "ongan þa leoflic wif / weras Ebrea wordum negan" ["the lovely woman then began to attack the Hebrew men with words": lines 286–287].[58] In her succeeding addresses to the Jews, she is unable to make progress: each is another beginning, prefaced with a clause similar to and echoing this first one.[59]

Ultimately, she is not able to persuade the Jews to turn Judas over with words. Only when Helen threatens them with annihilation by fire do the Jews give Judas up to her. Helen is likewise unable to use words to persuade Judas to reveal the information he knows; he denies that Jesus is divine until she confines him for a week in a dry desert well. Bowed by hunger and thirst, he promises to reveal what Helen wants to know if she will release him. Yet still he equivocates, asking God in prayer to reveal the location of the cross only "[g]if þin wille sie, wealdend engla / þæt ricsie se ðe on rode was" ["if it be your will, ruler of angels, that he should rule who was on the cross": lines 772–773]. Judas is finally con-

---

[57] Scheil, *Footsteps of Israel*, 226.

[58] One wonders if the terms "wif," "wer," and "leoflic" should all be read as vested with irony in this passage.

[59] "Hio sio cwen ongan / wordum genegan" ["the queen began to attack them with words": lines 384–385]; and "þa sio cwen ongan / weras Ebresc wordum negan" ["then the queen began to attack the Hebrew men with words": lines 558–559].

vinced of Jesus' divinity by the resulting sign indicating the location of the cross. By the end of the poem, the Jews of Jerusalem convert to Christianity, but not until they have witnessed with their own eyes the miraculous revelation of the cross's location; its use to raise a dead man back to life; and a sign showing the location of the nails with which Jesus was nailed to the cross. In stark contrast to Constantine's willing belief, the conversion of the Jews is represented as a difficult and protracted matter complicated by bad faith and misplaced will.

After her verbal battle with Judas, Helen is given only one additional passage of direct speech in the poem, when she requests that Judas/Cyriacus seek the nails from the cross. Her deferential manner of addressing him, in direct contrast to her earlier commanding language, shows that Judas has taken his rightful place in the gendered hierarchy of Christianity, and now outranks Helen despite her status as queen. This fact is underlined by Judas/Cyriacus' elevation as bishop of Jerusalem — a position permanently unavailable to Helen because she is female. Helen's position has not shifted: she has remained static, still Christian, still female, while Judas has converted from Jew to Christian and has been elevated to the power of the bishopric. Moreover, as soon as Judas accepts Christianity, his linguistic power becomes greater than Helen's: he attains the capacity to pray directly to God, with repeatedly favorable results. While the poem presents repeated examples of the alteration of religious affiliation, gender is fixed, as expressed by Helen's stasis throughout the poem. Her status shifts with changes in Judas's religious position, but only in response to his changing position.[60]

The attention in *Elene* to its dual conversions sets up a complicated dynamic in which various groups are contrasted, sometimes explicitly and sometimes implicitly. Through these narratives of conversion, the poem provides powerful precedent for the English insistence on the Danes' conversion to Christianity. Constantine is a former pagan who converts to Christianity early in the narrative. The pagans he defeats in battle at the start of the legend disappear, and Cynewulf makes no further reference to them in the poem. The reality in England was that paganism was difficult to eliminate. Guthrum and the inhabitants of the Danelaw had officially become Christian in 878, yet nearly three-quarters of a century later, the bishopric at York was still under the control of pagans. Moreover, place names attest to the survival of pagan temples and pagan burial practices, even in Christian areas and especially at the boundaries between political

---

[60] Lionarons points out that gender is "neither a static nor an essentialized characteristic" in *Elene*, but "a relationally constructed category based upon the cultural norms of two divergent social and literary traditions": "Cultural Syncretism," 68. Helen's status appears to shift in the poem depending upon the status of those she encounters; within a Christian hierarchy, however, her position remains unchanged throughout, fixed by her status as a woman.

regions and on the margins of bishoprics.[61] The narrative of *Elene* suggests that if they will not convert, the pagans will disappear, written out of history and legend, as do Constantine's opponents after their defeat.

Elene enacts the fantasy of the conversion of the entire Jewish community, and the conversion of even the Jews may parallel the desired conversion of pagans in the Danelaw. Yet even as the narrative insists upon Jewish conversion, its references to Jews register the existence of the non-converted Jewish community remaining within Christian Europe yet apart from Christianity, still disagreeing with the Christian interpretation of Hebrew scripture. If the conversion of the Danes was not very thorough, if pagan practices remained, at least the Danes were not Jews, obstinately opposed to Christian "truth." Like the Jews, the Danes were external to Anglo-Saxon society, but unlike the Jews, who remained definitively outside the fabric of Christendom, they could become assimilated to Anglo-Saxon Christianity through conversion. The figures of Helen and Constantine are absorbed into the Anglo-Saxon cultural matrix, while the people of Jerusalem become the Other, colonized and converted through force in the imagined universe of the poem, but utterly excluded from the Christian social order in the poem's actual historical context.

In its intertwined narratives of conversion and battle, *Elene* suggests that difference in religious affiliation legitimates the attack of a neighboring people protected by treaty. In the initial battle, *Elene* opposes Romans and pagans; the pagan army is defeated militarily through the adoption of a Christian battle-standard. The pagan Huns and Hrethgoths attacking Rome are, although a large army, ultimately an insignificant force, vanquished easily by Constantine once he sees a vision of the cross and adopts it as his standard even without understanding its significance. The battle is fought on poetically familiar ground, with the sounds of shields and humans mingled in battle-song with the cries of wolf and eagle. The physical conquest of the pagans by the Christianized Constantine is rendered a simple matter enabled by faith rather than by ferocious fighting. English Christians might be encouraged to go to battle against the Danes by the poem's implied promise that conquering pagan opponents is effortless. The people of Jerusalem, on the other hand, are a bitter foe, against whom Helen must wrangle words at length; their communal theological capitulation is completed only by a series of divine interventions.

The story that Constantine effected a significant victory immediately after his vision of the cross and his decision to devote himself to whatever it might

---

[61] Margaret Gelling, "Further Thoughts on Pagan Place-Names," in *Otium et Negotium: Studies in Onomatology and Library Science Presented to Olof von Feilitzen*, ed. Folke Sandgren (Stockholm, 1973), 109–28, and eadem, *Signposts to the Past: Place-Names and the History of England* (London, 1978), 154–61.

symbolize is a potent enough narrative juxtaposition of politics and religion, with its suggestion that the God of Christianity could give temporal power to human rulers. In addition to justifying force by Christian kings, however, *Elene* also subtly suggests that their authority as Christian monarchs also gives them the responsibility to support the Church. Yoking the narrative of Constantine's victory and conversion to the legend of Helen's successful search for the cross and subsequent founding of a church in Jerusalem depicts Constantine as not only personally committed to Christianity, but also committed to putting the resources of the Roman Empire behind its dissemination. By promoting the two ideals in conjunction, Cynewulf suggests to English kings that if faith should support them in battle against Danish warriors, they should in turn give financial and legal support to the Church in its appeal for the conversion of Danish pagans.

Making Women Visible: An Adaptation of the *Regularis Concordia* in Cambridge, Corpus Christi College MS. 201

Joyce Hill

The *Regularis Concordia*, the defining, authoritative, central text of the English Benedictine Reform, confidently proclaims itself to be a text of national standing: *Regularis Concordia Anglicae Nationis Monachorum Sanctimonialiumque, The Monastic Agreement of the Monks and Nuns of the English Nation.*[1] It is probably not too far-fetched to imagine that the authors saw it, when it was issued in the early 970s, as a text of iconic significance, successfully embodying the traditions of the continental reform, declaring the unity of church and king in furthering that reform, and — in something of a triumph of hope over reality — signaling uniformity of practice within the monastic life throughout the entire English nation. In fact, as the historical sources reveal, the impact of the Reform on monastic life was in practice somewhat limited: it was confined to the south; it was more patchy than the Reform's promotional texts would have us believe; and we know that, as evidenced by Ælfric's *Letter to the Monks of Eynsham*[2] and the text under present discussion,[3]

---

[1] *Regularis Concordia Anglicae Nationis Monachorum Sanctimonialiumque: The Monastic Agreement of the Monks and Nuns of the English Nation*, ed. Thomas Symons (London, 1953). See also "Regularis Concordia Anglicae Nationis," ed. Thomas Symons, Sigrid Spath, Maria Wegener, and Kassius Hallinger, in *Corpus Consuetudinum Saeculi X/XI/ XII, Monumenta Non-Cluniacensia*, ed. Kassius Hallinger, Corpus Consuetudinum Monasticarum 7.3 (Siegburg, 1984), 61–147. The Latin text referred to in this article is the 1953 edition because it is more widely available and is provided with a full introduction in English and a facing translation.

[2] *Ælfric's Letter to the Monks of Eynsham*, ed. Christopher A. Jones (Cambridge, 1998).

[3] The present text includes variations from the *Regularis Concordia* other than those making adaptations for female use. For discussion of some of these, see Joyce Hill, "Lexical Choices for Holy Week: Studies in Old English Ecclesiastical Vocabulary," in *Lexis and Texts in Early English: Studies Presented to Jane Roberts*, ed. Christian J. Kay and Louise M. Sylvester (Amsterdam, 2001), 117–27, and eadem, "Rending the Garment and Reading by the Rood: *Regularis Concordia* Rituals for Men and Women," in *The Liturgy of the Late Anglo-Saxon Church*, ed. Helen Gittos and M. Bradford Bedingfield, HBS Subsidia 5 (Woodbridge, 2005), 53–64.

variations in practice quickly developed. But the universalist position was adopted, and we can see it visualized in the miniature which precedes the text in London, BL, Cotton Tiberius A.iii (see fig. 3.1, p. 178), where, in the upper register, there is the crowned figure of the king flanked by Dunstan and Æthelwold and beneath them a monk, all united by a long scroll representing the text which binds them in one agreement.[4]

The continental consuetudinaries, to which the *Regularis Concordia* is so closely related,[5] differ from the Anglo-Saxon text in one important respect: they were written for particular monastic houses (Fleury, St. Emmeram, Fulda, Verdun, and so on), having no pretensions to universal authority, and were written in all cases, as far as I know, for houses of monks. But in England the situation was different — and novel. National uniformity is emphatically proclaimed, in the title, in the Cotton Tiberius miniature, and in comments in the contextualizing and explanatory proem and epilogue. Yet, in common with its continental sources, the consuetudinary proper is written as if for a male community. Its linguistic exclusivity is obvious in its choice of male nouns and pronouns; and its practical exclusivity is evident in its underlying assumption that the community includes deacons and priests, with the result that it describes rituals which thus can readily be performed in male houses but not female ones, and gives directions which women could not necessarily execute. Women are thus invisible within the main body of the text. Female religious appear only in the proem and epilogue — that is, the adjunct parts of the text — and such references as there are in proem and epilogue do nothing to explain how women might occupy the space that the *Regularis Concordia* defines. In the proem's account of how the Reform was fostered and the *Regularis Concordia* produced, male and female religious, abbots and abbesses, are referred to together, without drawing any distinctions between them, except for the provision that men are put under the protection of the king, and women under the queen, and that there is an absolute ban on any monk or any man of whatever rank entering or frequenting the places set apart for nuns.[6] The avoidance of scandal and the preservation of religious rectitude are implicit issues

---

[4] The miniature is examined by Benjamin Withers, who also provides a bibliography of previous discussions: "Interaction of Word and Image in Anglo-Saxon Art II: Scrolls and Codex in the Frontispiece to the *Regularis Concordia*," *OEN* 31 (1997): 38–40.

[5] On the sources, see Thomas Symons, "Sources of the *Regularis Concordia*," *Downside Review* 59 (1941): 14–36, 143–70, 264–89, and idem, "*Regularis Concordia*: History and Derivation," in *Tenth-Century Studies: Essays in Commemoration of the Millennium of the Council of Winchester and Regularis Concordia*, ed. David Parsons (London and Chichester, 1975), 37–59. There is also information about sources in the two editions referred to in note 1 above.

[6] *Regularis Concordia*, ed. Symons, 2 (protection of the queen); 4–5 (limitations of access).

for women, but no reference is made to how the monastic agreement itself — the ordering of community life and the reformist elaborated ritual of liturgical and para-liturgical observance set out in the text — might be implemented in female houses. The epilogue is similarly uninformative. In discussing the heriot and the management of wealth, abbots and abbesses are referred to together, but then, in the concluding sentence setting out what happens if the superior dies with a superabundance of goods, there is reference only to abbots and brethren.[7] We might conclude from this that women were less likely to be worldly, and less likely to be rich, but again there is no recognition of the difficulty women might have in relating to the *Regularis Concordia* proper.

Yet it was certainly the case that, given the universal status of the *Regularis Concordia* and its function in establishing uniform observance, the male orientation of the text would inevitably have presented problems, requiring the communities of women who followed its provisions to make their own adjustments here and there. For most of the non-sacramental liturgy, such as the daily hours, and for most of the regulation of community life, this adjustment would have been minimal: the prescriptions of the Latin text as written would have served perfectly well, provided that the male-oriented language was understood to subsume the female, since there was nothing in these areas of activity that the church prevented women from doing. The prescriptions of the sacramental rites likewise presented no particular difficulty, because although female houses had to be served by male priests, the conduct of the sacramental liturgy would not have been affected: male language was the correct language to use in describing the activities of the priest, and the church admitted no other option. But there were gray areas, most obviously in connection with special ceremonies for feast days, where communities of nuns would have needed guidance, whether in confirming that they could carry out the ceremonies as described, or in establishing what modifications were necessary, especially if there were aspects of the ceremonial where those performing particular functions were identified in the *Regularis Concordia* text in terms of the orders of the church (for example, priest or deacon, for which there is no female alternative), rather than the offices of the community (such as abbot or prior, which have female equivalents).

The obvious way of responding to this problem was to adapt the *Regularis Concordia* — as indeed the Benedictine Rule was also adapted during the Reform period[8] — and it may be that a number of female houses had copies of the text, in Latin or Old English, separately adapted for their own use. But the only

---

[7] *Regularis Concordia*, ed. Symons, 69.

[8] Mechthild Gretsch, "Æthelwold's Translation of the *Regula Sancti Benedicti* and its Latin Exemplar," *ASE* 3 (1974): 125–51; Rohini Jayatilaka, "The Old English Benedictine Rule: Writing for Women and Men," *ASE* 32 (2003): 147–87.

surviving textual evidence for such a response is the tantalizing translation of the *Regularis Concordia* into Old English, which survives on pages 1–7 of Part A of Cambridge, Corpus Christi College, 201, in a hand of the early eleventh century.[9] What we have on these few pages is that part of the *Regularis Concordia* dealing with the period from Palm Sunday to part way through Good Friday.[10] The text stops abruptly in mid-sentence on line 19 of a fully ruled-up page, with the rest of the page remaining blank, as if awaiting further work by the scribe. But it seems clear that what survives was part of a larger stint of copying, presumably planned as a copy of the whole, since the "tidy" beginning with the start of the Palm Sunday passage in the extant manuscript, near the bottom of page 1, was a creation of Archbishop Parker, who erased the first thirty-eight lines of the page in order to make space for his list of what the manuscript contained. Page 1 is the beginning of a quire. We can deduce that what Parker erased was "untidy" in his eyes because textually imperfect — a mere continuation, quite probably in mid-sentence, from the previous page (the last of the previous quire), which no longer survived. It would be reasonable to suppose that the whole text of the Old English translation of the *Regularis Concordia* up to the point where it now breaks off had once existed, but had been lost by the sixteenth century, when Parker obtained the manuscript from Edward Cradock, Lady Margaret Professor of Divinity at Oxford. We know nothing of the manuscript's origins: on linguistic grounds it has been assigned to the southeast, perhaps Canterbury; on the grounds of content a case can be made for York or Worcester (although York would not have been the source of the *Regularis Concordia* text, or a locale in which the CCCC 201 copy would have been needed); and there is palaeographical

---

[9] I am grateful to the Master and Fellows of Corpus Christi College, Cambridge, for permission to consult this manuscript. The Old English *Regularis Concordia* text on pp. 1–7 was published by Julius Zupitza, "Ein weiteres Bruchstück der *Regularis Concordia* in altenglischer Sprache," *Archiv für das Studium der neueren Sprachen und Literaturen* 84 (1890): 1–24. Line references will be to Zupitza's text. It should be noted, however, that Zupitza's line numbers are problematic: they are given in increments of five, but are often incorrectly printed at four-line and occasionally six-line intervals. Since it would be too confusing to correct this, where it is necessary to give line references in this article, I have invariably counted from the preceding printed line-number (even if this is at odds with the next printed line-number). For the following account of the manuscript's origins and provenance, see N. R. Ker, *Catalogue of Manuscripts Containing Anglo-Saxon* (Oxford, 1957), 82–83, 90, and the discussion in *The Old English Poem Judgement Day II: A Critical Edition with Editions of De Die iudicii and the Hatton 113 Homily Be domes dæge*, ed. Graham D. Caie (Cambridge, 2000), 1–5 (description of the manuscript), 7–9 (provenance), 9–10 (dating).

[10] The Old English text corresponds to p. 34 "Dominica die Palmarum" to p. 42 "et dicat primam" in Symons's 1953 edition of the *Regularis Concordia*.

evidence to indicate that it was in Winchester by the middle of the eleventh century. As Sarah Foot has recently reminded us, it was at best only in a handful of West-Saxon royal foundations for female religious that liturgical and community life organized along the elaborate lines set out in the *Regularis Concordia* could have been sustained,[11] but beyond that we cannot go in determining where or for whom the translation into Old English was made, in which house the female adaptations originated, or which house was intended to have the CCCC 201 copy.

Short as the surviving passage is, however, relative to the length of the whole, there is enough to learn something about the translator: he was a good Latinist, an accomplished, rather formal stylist in Old English, of a scholarly frame of mind, but yet sensitive to the audience's needs and intent on making the Old English version helpfully accessible through occasional explanatory comments, while still remaining faithful to the authoritative original, with which he was clearly very familiar, albeit in a form that was in some details different from the Latin text known to us. There is also enough here to let us see that the lexical choices point to the Winchester school, and that the vocabulary is markedly different from that used in the corresponding interlinear gloss to the *Regularis Concordia* in Cotton Tiberius A iii.[12] Yet the adaptations for female religious, while fairly extensive, are not quite systematic, and most of the adaptations, though fully incorporated into the text in scribal terms (so that they are not visually evident as textual disturbances in the surviving manuscript), are incorporated awkwardly in terms of grammar and syntax. It is obvious that the adaptations for female use were not integral to the original translation, and the grammatical and syntactical awkwardnesses indicate that they were not incorporated by the original translator, who was far too careful. My supposition is that they began as marginalia (or perhaps interlineations in the case of the short phrasal adjustments) and that they were incorporated rather mechanically into the main text, possibly by the scribe of CCCC 201, or in an immediate exemplar. They are, then, striking examples of how women were able, in practice, to colonize the essentially male space defined in the *Regularis Concordia* by converting the all-male text so that the female presence and participation was explicitly acknowledged. In terms of manuscript history, this was done initially by colonizing the interlinear spaces and margins, and then by incorporating these additions into a more integrated

---

[11] Sarah Foot, *Veiled Women I: The Disappearance of Nuns from Anglo-Saxon England* (Aldershot, 2000), particularly chap. 4 (85–110), chap. 6 (145–98), and chap. 7 (199–208).

[12] For a summary of the evidence, see Hill, "Lexical Choices for Holy Week," 117–18, and in more detail Walter Hofstetter, "Winchester and the Standardization of Old English Vocabulary," *ASE* 17 (1988): 139–61, here 153, 156. For the interlineated Cotton Tiberius text, see *Die 'Regularis Concordia' und ihre altenglische Interlinearversion*, ed. Lucia Kornexl (Munich, 1993).

textual conversion for women when a later copy was made. The nature and extent of these acts of textual colonization and conversion, reflecting lived experience, deserve detailed examination, which they have not hitherto received.[13]

The first adaptation in the surviving text is for the maundy of the poor (lines 122–131), where female communities are catered for by the simple addition of "oððe abodyssan" and "oððe þære abbodyssan" alongside the two references to the abbot, and "oððe þa geswysterna" alongside the one reference to brothers. The translation is otherwise very close to the Latin.

Shortly after, at lines 157–166, there is a similar adaptation of the special maundy and the first part of the general maundy,[14] although here there is grammatical evidence that the additional phrases were not integral to the original text. As with the maundy of the poor, the abbess and the sisters are specified as alternatives to abbot and brothers, but the attempt to adjust the grammar produces an illogicality. In the Latin text the subject is singular, "abbas," with the verbs "uoluerit" and "peragat" naturally being singular also. However, the inclusion of the reference to the abbess as an alternative creates what might be taken at a glance to be a multiple subject, "se abbod oððe seo abbodisse," and it is then treated collectively as a plural subject, resulting in adjustments to the verbs "hi wyllen" (cf. "uoluerit") and "gan . . . to heora syndrian mandatum" (cf. "peragat mandatum"), a shift to the plural which is further reinforced by "hi to þam gecorene habbað," an explanatory phrase that has no equivalent in the Latin. The care taken here is misplaced: the abbot and abbess would each be acting separately, so that there is no justification for treating them together as a plural, and in any case Old English syntax normally uses a singular verb for two singular subjects linked by "oððe."[15] The plural constructions probably reflect colloquial usage, which can

---

[13] They are not discussed by Zupitza, "Ein weiteres Bruchstück der *Regularis Concordia*"; and Mary Bateson, "Rules for Monks and Secular Canons after the Revival under King Edgar," *English Historical Review* 9 (1894): 690–708, simply noted in passing that "It seems to have been intended for the use of nuns, as 'abbess' is inserted as an alternative to 'abbot'" (707), a comment which falls far short of describing the nature and extent of the textual adaptations.

[14] For the corresponding Latin, see *Regularis Concordia*, ed. Symons, 40 (first part of § 42).

[15] Bruce Mitchell, *Old English Syntax*, 2 vols. (Oxford, 1985), 1: 637–38, § 1525. However, in the phrases "gif hit munecas synd" and "gif hit þonne munecas syn," to which attention is drawn elsewhere in this article (pp. 163, 165), the change between singular subject "hit" and a plural verb and complement is an extension of the standard practice whereby the number of the verb is governed by the number of the complement, and not by a formal neuter demonstrative subject (varied here as pronoun, functioning similarly, perhaps with some sense of the unexpressed referent being "þæt gefer" ["the community"]). On this usage, see Mitchell, *Old English Syntax*, 1. 131, §§ 325–326.

be paralleled in modern English in such circumstances. The sense is clear, but in mixing singular and plural in this colloquial fashion the adaptation is at odds with the distinctly formal style of the translation as a whole.

The description of the general maundy continues at lines 167–170 following the same pattern: abbess is given as an alternative to abbot and the following clauses are then plural: "on heora setlum sitten" and "hi . . . arisen . . . and . . . gesellen" (cf. Latin "resideat abbas in sede sua," ". . . surgens det . . .").[16] In this context, "him" (lines 168 and 170), which would have operated as masculine dative singular "him" when only the abbot was the subject, must now be interpreted as dative plural (all genders) "them," since the pronominal reference is to abbot or abbess, whose actions are given in plural verbs. Again, the sense is clear, but the illogicality of the plural sequence is obvious: if taken literally, it would suggest that the abbot and abbess are acting together, rather than in parallel in their separate communities. "Gebroðrum" (line 169) has no female parallel. Zupitza emended the text editorially by adding "oððe geswysternum," evidently making the reasonable assumption that the omission was a scribal error. This is indeed possible, but the omission could be an instance of imperfect adaptation, which characterizes even the small amount of surviving text.

The description of the special form of the *collatio* comes next (lines 170–197), and it stands out in the extant portion of the text as the most elaborate adaptation for a female house, even giving us a rare description of a woman reading aloud in an ecclesiastical — if not quite liturgical — context. Yet, even here, the adaptation is not well controlled throughout: the practices in male and female houses are at first clearly distinguished, but are then progressively conflated in a way which gives a misleading priority to the female. What is being described is the special form of the *collatio* as normally carried out in male houses on Saturdays and which, in common with the general maundy, was also carried out on Maundy Thursday. This form of the *collatio* is thus described twice in the *Regularis Concordia*, first in connection with the usual Saturday practices (not covered in the partially surviving Old English translation under discussion) and subsequently in connection with Maundy Thursday.[17] According to the Latin text of the *Regularis Concordia*, there was also a normal weekday *collatio*,[18] but this took place in the refectory, with the length of the reading being determined by the prior. No information is given about what the reading might be, which suggests that it was discretionary, and would not necessarily be biblical. On Saturdays,

---

[16] See *Regularis Concordia*, ed. Symons, 40.

[17] For the Saturday *collatio*, see *Regularis Concordia*, ed. Symons, 22–23, §26. For the Maundy Thursday *collatio*, which is the source of the Old English passage under discussion, see 40–41 (second half of § 42).

[18] See *Regularis Concordia*, ed. Symons, 23, § 27.

however, there was more formality: the *collatio* or reading — again subject un-specified — was begun in the church and continued in the refectory, with the moment for the procession from church to refectory being signaled by the ring-ing of a small bell. Once in the refectory, the reading continued while the com-munity carried out the *caritas*, a weekly custom that was intended to strengthen the sense of community life. It required the abbot to kiss the hands of each mem-ber of the community and to offer him a drink, with the abbot then being simi-larly treated by the senior monk present, as a representative of the community as a whole. It was this more elaborate Saturday ceremony that was used on Maundy Thursday as one of the ways of marking the special nature of the day. However, on Maundy Thursday there seems to have been more formality still. The deacon and other hebdomadary ministers put on priestly vestments, the reading — be-gun in the church as on Saturdays — is from St. John's Gospel (John 13.1–15: Christ washing the disciples' feet), the reader is the deacon, and there is a formal procession from church to refectory, with acolytes and thurifer, where the read-ing continues simultaneously with the *caritas*.

This is a classic example of where female religious would have needed ex-plicit guidance. What is described is not a sacramental act, so that it is not neces-sary to use a priest; it involves movement from the church (where female activity is highly circumscribed) into the community proper (in this case the refectory) where, as we know from the proem of the *Regularis Concordia*, even monks were forbidden to go in female houses; *and yet* it is described in the *Regularis Concor-dia* as a ceremony in which the leading figure is identified not by his community role, but as a deacon, vested in a dalmatic and supported by other priestly min-isters in albs. Furthermore, what is to be read is a gospel text and, as Ælfric ex-plains in his Pastoral Letter for Wulfsige, the lector of the scriptures in church (which is where this reading begins) must be in orders because he is in effect preaching God's word.[19] What, then, were women supposed to do?

For the first part of the *collatio*, the adapted text in CCCC 201 makes very clear distinctions. The Old English version has characteristic minor variations from the Latin which tend to clarify particular details, but the only substantive deviation is the phrase "mid munecum" (lines 170–171), which carefully limits the

---

[19] *Die Hirtenbriefe Ælfrics in altenglischer und lateinischer Fassung*, ed. Bernhard Fehr (Hamburg, 1914), reissued with a supplementary introduction by Peter Clemoes (Darm-stadt, 1966), 9–10. In commenting on the seven orders of the church, Ælfric explains that the lector reads in church and is ordained for the purpose (i.e. in minor orders) because he preaches God's word (§ 31), and that one of the particular duties of a deacon (ordained, of course, although not specified here by Ælfric) is to read the gospel in the divine ser-vice (§ 36).

application of what is to follow and distinguishes it from the immediately preceding inclusive ceremony of the general maundy, where execution was identical in female houses and could be affirmed simply by adding "or" phrases to make explicit the applicability to women. Having followed the Latin text, with the added restrictive caveat of "mid munecum," the Old English text then provides a substantial female alternative, beginning at lines 176–177 with a similar distinguishing phrase "mynecena þonne," followed by an immediate explanation that female communities cannot adopt the same practices as male communities because they cannot vest. In addition, they differ from men in that they cannot read the gospel in church. This would not need to be spelled out, of course, but as a way of addressing the problem the Old English text takes care to specify that one of their number is to read "swylce him þearflic sy to gehyrenne" ("such a thing as may be profitable for them to hear" [lines 179–180]), i.e. something suitable for the occasion, chosen presumably at the discretion of the abbess, but not a biblical lection. At the same time, it is stated that candles and incense are used "for arwyrðnesse þæs mæran dæges," ("for the honor of this special day" [lines 177–178]). The implication is clear: reading in church, together with the use of candles and incense, was, in female houses, a special Maundy Thursday event. In this respect, it differed from what was happening in male houses where, for Maundy Thursday, the *collatio* was a particular version of the *collatio* practiced each Saturday. This in turn implies that, with the exception of Maundy Thursday, the *collatio* in female houses was always in the refectory, as the *Regularis Concordia* describes for days other than Saturdays. We can thus see that communities of nuns did not enjoy the weekly variation of added solemnity experienced by the men, when the *collatio* was begun in church and continued in the refectory after a formal procession. Yet, despite the differences on Maundy Thursday, which are explicit in the Old English text, and the differences of weekly community practice in respect of the Saturday *collatio*, which the Old English text allows us to deduce, the Latin text of the *Regularis Concordia* allows for neither variation.

The description of the Maundy Thursday *collatio* continues with the transfer from the church to the refectory, where the ceremony continues in a non-liturgical setting, although in male communities the deacon and ministers would still be vested. At this point the Latin text states that the deacon continues with the reading of the gospel. But the Old English translation makes no reference to this. Instead, attention is focused exclusively on the practices of the female house. We are told that "seo rædestre" ("the female reader / lectrix") enters the refectory in procession and lays the book on the lectern, that the acolytes bearing candles stand "on twa healfe hyre" ("on both sides of her"), and that the abbot or abbess, "se abbod oððe seo abbodysse," offers a drink to all the brothers or sisters ("eallum gebroðrum oþþe geswysternum") and kisses their hands, "onmang þan þe heo standende ræde" ("while she stands and reads" [lit. "while she standing reads"]).[20] The awkwardness of this substitution of the feminine noun ("seo rædestre") and pronouns ("hyre," "heo . . . ræde") in what is otherwise a close translation of the Latin text is particularly in evidence at the point when the previously employed alternatives of "abbot or abbess" and "brothers or sisters" are resumed, since the abbot and brothers are as usual the dominant elements in each pair in a sentence which nevertheless begins with references to a female reader. The use of the feminine forms can be accounted for, if not justified, as a continuation of the appropriately female-only description in the immediately preceding lines, but it is misleading because feminine forms do not conventionally represent both sexes, so that their use wrongly implies a continued exclusivity, when in fact what takes place (apart from the use of the deacon and reference to the gospel) is exactly the same as in a male house. The male practice is thus suppressed and the treatment is consequently at odds with the other parts of the adaptation, where women are specified in addition to men when their ceremonies are substantially the same. Here, if the adapter were to have been consistent in method and logical within the passage, one would have expected that the part of the *collatio* within the refectory and the concurrent *caritas* would have been described in male terms, following the source, with brief phrasal indicators to show that at this point the practices of male and female houses run in parallel, except in respect of what is read, who reads it, and the act of vesting.

Following the reading, and as a reciprocal part of the *caritas*, the one who is the most senior in the community offers a drink to the abbot or abbess. "Se" in "se þe" ("the one who") is the masculine singular form (compare feminine "seo"), but since the recipients of the action in the Old English text are explicitly the abbot or abbess, the phrase must be interpreted as a return to the convention whereby masculine forms subsume the feminine. While this is the linguistic norm — and the method used throughout the Latin text — it conflicts with the use of the feminine forms a few lines earlier and so adds to the sense of awkwardness in this part of the adaptation. The description concludes with the reminder that, if it is a male community, "gif it munecas synd," those who formed the reader's procession must unvest in order that compline may be said as an act of community worship in which all are equal.

The adaptations examined thus far provide confirmation that there are special acts, marking special days, that women could indeed carry out. They are, however, for the most part community acts, rather than liturgical ones, not carried out in the church, and not requiring the leading participants to be vested. Furthermore, the references to the participants in the original Latin are to community

---

[20] The bizarre numbering of Zupitza's text at this point renders unworkable even the compromise stated in note 9 above. All of the words and phrases referred to in relation to the *collatio*'s continuation in the refectory are in the first twelve lines of p. 14.

members designated by community roles ("abbot," "brothers"), for which there are, in any case, female equivalents. The exception is the special *collatio* from Maundy Thursday, for which elaborate explanatory adaptations had to be made in order to overcome the problems posed by the initial location being in the church, the reader and other ministers being robed, and the reading itself being from the gospel. But the conversion of the *Regularis Concordia* into a text usable in a female house, achieved through the text being colonized by interlinear or marginal adaptations, also shows that the role of female religious in special ceremonies carried out wholly within the church was more akin to that of the witnessing laity than to the participatory community of monks. The Mass itself is not at issue here, because when this is celebrated almost all of those present have identical roles as worshippers and communicants, whatever the nature of the congregation. The instances for consideration are, rather, special rituals such as the Ceremony of the New Fire on the last three days of Holy Week, or the ceremonies that followed none on Good Friday and preceded the Mass of the Presanctified, i.e. the symbolic deposition and burial, and the veneration of the cross.

The Ceremony of the New Fire is fully described in the Old English text, closely following the Latin.[21] The brethren vest and gather at the door of the church, where one of their number (a different, specified senior person on each day) holds a staff in the shape of a serpent. The abbot strikes fire from the flint and blesses it, the candle in the mouth of the serpent-staff is lit, and the procession moves to the choir, led by the bearer of the staff, where a single candle is lit from the candle in the mouth of the serpent-staff. In the Latin, of course, the language for the New Fire Ceremony is inevitably male, but it is striking that in the Old English translation this is reinforced, since the opening comments include the statement "the brothers shall vest, if they are monks" ("gescrydan hi ða gebroðra gif hit munecas synd"). The direction that the brothers shall vest is given in the Latin ("induant se fratres"), but "gif hit munecas synd" is an addition which sets up a contrast with the immediately preceding lines. These lines, in the Old English translation, had described the maundy of the poor in *inclusive* language, achieved by the simple expedient of adding "oððe abbodyssan" ("or the abbess") to the original reference to "abbot"; and "oððe þa geswysterna" ("or the sisters") to the original reference to "brothers." By contrast with the Maundy Thursday *collatio*, which is discussed above,[22] the additional phrase "gif hit munecas synd," which introduces the Ceremony of the New Fire, is not paralleled later in the Old English text by a phrase pointing to what nuns do, so that the translation reads as if it is specifying what is done in male houses only. The *Regularis Concordia* says

---

[21] The ceremony is described in Zupitza's text on pp. 11–12. For the Latin, see *Regularis Concordia*, ed. Symons, 39–40, §41.

[22] Pp. 159–62.

that this ceremony is optional, and if it is the case that female houses — by virtue of being female and thus not being able to carry out what one might call a "vested ceremony" — did not observe the Ceremony of the New Fire on Maundy Thursday, Good Friday, and Holy Saturday, it would be another instance where their rituals were simpler than those of the men. An alternative possibility is that, with men being necessary for the Mass that immediately followed, they simply carried out the ceremony, already vested, before they celebrated Mass — thus something done by men for the women as witnesses. However, if this were the case, the ceremony would not have had the same kind of community dimension that it had in male houses, where members of the community were participants; the nuns would have been witnesses in exactly the same way as the laity, who were certainly present for the Mass that followed on each day. For the Mass itself, of course, the directions necessarily focus on the duties of the celebrant, where no adaptation was possible, but it is here, and only here, that the sisters are referred to in the Old English text, "ge geswysternum" (line 153), as communicants, alongside brothers (following the Latin) and the laity (also following the Latin).

On Good Friday there are further special ceremonies which similarly require distinctions to be made.[23] According to the Latin text, the community goes to the church at the hour of none, but none is not recited in the usual way. Instead, the abbot and ministers pray silently at the altar without being vested and then proceed to vest in readiness for the following formal sequence of readings, prayers, and obligatory rituals which lead directly into the Mass of the Presanctified. In addition, the Latin text describes the optional symbolic enactment of the deposition and burial, in which the cross is wrapped in a napkin and laid in the sepulcher. If it is performed, this takes place directly after the veneration of the cross and immediately before the Mass. The laity are evidently present throughout, since they venerate the cross and communicate at the Mass. Furthermore, the intervening symbolic deposition and burial is expressly offered "ad fidem indocti uulgi ac neophytorum corroborandam" ["for the strengthening of the faith of unlearned common persons and neophytes"],[24] which both confirms that the laity were present and that the reform tradition recognized the value of witnessing symbolic events as well as enacting them.

The Old English translation does not preserve the descriptions of the veneration of the cross or the deposition and burial, so that we do not have the references they provide to the presence of the laity. We know, however, that the laity communicated at the Mass, because this was already anticipated at lines

---

[23] The ceremony is described in Zupitza's text on pp. 14–16, at which point the Old English text ends abruptly. For precisely this passage in the Latin, see *Regularis Concordia*, ed. Symons, 41–42, § 43, although the extensive Good Friday ceremonies continue in the Latin text to 46, § 47.

[24] *Regularis Concordia*, ed. Symons, 44.

151–156, following the Latin text. Here, as noted above,[25] the Old English text also specifies that nuns would communicate. The implication of this passage is that the laity could attend services in female as well as male houses and that the role of female religious, as communicants only, was inevitably the same as that of the laity. Thus, if the laity were present at the hour of none on Good Friday in order to witness the full sequence of ceremonies which followed, to kiss the cross and to observe the deposition and burial (if performed), as well as communicate at Mass, we must assume that this sequence could have been performed in female houses as well as male. The difference would be that in female houses the officiants would have been the attendant priests and that the sisters' role for these rituals, as for the Mass itself, would have been the same as that of the laity.

This seems to be the implication of the Old English translation, where, at the hour of none (as in the Latin), the community goes to the church but does not proceed with the usual recitation of the office, which is in effect replaced by the special ceremonies. The adaptation is rather confusing, however, because "abbess" and "sisters" are substituted for the "abbot" and "brothers" of the Latin text in a statement which is in fact applicable to male and female alike: "On þam selfan dæge to rihtes nones gange seo abbodysse to cyricean mid hyre gewysternum, and ealle endemes þæt gewunelice gebed singan, þe is foreboda ælces tidsanges" ["On that same day, at the time of none, the abbess shall go to the church with her sisters and all together they shall sing the customary prayer which is the preface to each hour"]. There is nothing to indicate whether men do anything different; they are simply not mentioned. The Latin states that the abbot and brethren go to church and pray, although it is not made explicit that this is the customary prefatory prayer for each of the Hours — if indeed it is in their case: the phrase is simply "dum peracta oratione." Yet despite exclusively female references in the Old English sentence noting the movement to the church, attention shifts immediately to the vested members of the priestly orders, introduced by the phrase "gif hit þonne munecas syn" ["if it is then monks"]. The requirement to vest at this point is noted in the Latin, and clearly women could not be involved in this, as the exclusionary phrase "gif hit munecas syn" indicates; the women in the translation, of whom we were reminded only one sentence earlier, where they replace male references, are apparently left poised at the preface to the office. It may be that matters would have been clearer if the text had continued, and we must allow for the fact that, by their very nature, rules and consuetudinaries do not always make explicit what was obvious to contemporary users. But even so, the adaptation, here as elsewhere, is intrinsically confusing. Probably what is meant to be indicated is that the nuns remain in their places as worshippers and onlookers, just as the laity would do, while the monks, by contrast, robe for special rituals in which they can be directly involved.

---

[25] P. 164.

Alongside these examples, variously informative and tantalizing, are others where there is a surprising absence of adaptations for female use. For example, the Palm Sunday ceremonies describe how all members of the community vest in albs for the procession of palms, and both here and on Maundy Thursday there are details about how boys shall sing various antiphons and responses. But these are translated — and even elaborated on — in the Old English text without any indication of how female communities should proceed, given that they cannot vest in albs, and presumably do not have boy singers to hand.[26] It is clear from Ælfric's homily for Palm Sunday in the First Series of Catholic Homilies (homily XIV) that it was normal for the laity to join in the procession carrying palms and to offer the palms to God at the offertory, as described for monks in the *Regularis Concordia*.[27] Nuns would presumably have participated in the same way as the laity. But no guidance is provided in the Old English text, even though the adjustments that would have been needed were of the same order as those made for the ceremonies later in the week. In this earlier part of the extant Old English text "ða gebroðra" are also referred to without the female alternative being supplied, and at no point before we get to the maundy of the poor part way through Maundy Thursday are there any confirming phrases to show that for certain observances nuns could act in parallel with monks.

As previously noted,[28] there is evidence to suggest that the surviving text is an incomplete copy of what once existed as a translation of the whole of the *Regularis Concordia*. Given that the scribal hand is of the early eleventh century, what we have cannot be very far removed in time from the date of the original translation, since this shows an intimate familiarity with the *Regularis Concordia* and provides evidence that there had been some local evolution of practices in male houses, both of which indicate a passage of time since it was first introduced. The female adaptations could have been virtually contemporaneous with the translation, although equally they could have come a little later — but not much, given the time-span available. We are left with two unanswerable questions: Why are the adaptations not consistent? And which community was responsible for the adaptations being made?

The *Regularis Concordia* may have been directed at all the religious in England, but the realities of experience within male and female houses were more

---

[26] For Palm Sunday, see Zupitza, "Ein weiteres Bruchstück," 2–5, corresponding with *Regularis Concordia*, ed. Symons, 34–36, § 36; for the relevant part of the Maundy Thursday celebration, see Zupitza, "Ein weiteres Bruchstück," 5–7, corresponding with *Regularis Concordia*, ed. Symons, 36–37, § 37.

[27] *Ælfric's Catholic Homilies: The First Series. Text*, ed. Peter Clemoes, EETS s.s. 17 (Oxford, 1997), 290–98, 297, lines 195–209.

[28] See above, p. 156.

varied than this all-embracing document seems to imply. Although it stands as a pivotal authoritative text, the women who were invisible in the Latin text would have been well aware that it was not quite the universal consuetudinary that its episcopal and royal sponsors found it convenient to claim. We are fortunate in having a surviving textual fragment which gives us at least a glimpse of their attempts to convert and colonize a text which itself set out to 'convert' and 'colonize' the monastic life of the tenth century.

Architectural Metaphors and Christological Imagery in the Advent Lyrics: Benedictine Propaganda in the Exeter Book?[1]

Mercedes Salvador

1. Introduction

In Lantfred's *Translatio et Miracula S. Swithuni*, composed 972–974, the first chapter narrates the conversion to Benedictinism of Eadsige, an unreformed canon, through St. Swithun's mediation.[2] Eadsige had been informed by a smith who had witnessed the saint's miraculous appearance that he should seek Æthelwold to tell him to look for the bishop's remains and move them to the cathedral. The cleric, who was one of those who had been previously expelled from the Old Minster, was first logically reluctant to do so, but he eventually delivered the message and became a monk, entrusted with the keeping of St. Swithun's shrine.[3] This account is

---

[1] I would like to thank Setmaní Valenzuela, Rebecca Stephenson, Frederick Biggs, Michael D. C. Drout, Juan Antonio Prieto Pablos, and Mª José Mora for their valuable help with various aspects of this article. I also had the opportunity to discuss some of the ideas presented in a shorter version of this essay at ISAS 2003 with Hugh Magennis, Thomas N. Hall, and Patrick W. Conner, whose enlightening comments have been useful for the writing of this piece.

[2] For a discussion on the dating of the *Translatio et Miracula S. Swithuni* (henceforth *Translatio*), see *The Cult of St Swithun*, ed. Michael Lapidge (Oxford, 2003), 235–37.

[3] This event is overtly celebrated by Lantfred in the *vita*: "idem clericus qui nuper erat biotticus, huius uitae relictis uanitatibus, pompis ac uoluptatibus, factus est coenobita religiosus multumque Deo dilectus" ["this same cleric, who recently had been secular, abandoned the vanities, prides, and pleasures of this earthly life and became a devout monk much beloved of God"]. The edition and translation of this passage and of all further hagiographic works related to St. Swithun cited in this essay are from *The Cult*, ed. Lapidge; this passage is from 264–65. A parallel account is found in Wulfstan Cantor's *Narratio Metrica de S. Swithuno* (henceforth, *Narratio*), in *The Cult*, ed. Lapidge,

no doubt charged with political connotations, and its relevance lies in the fact that the saint is here presented as an intermediary who successfully manages to reconcile representatives of the reformed and unreformed parties. In a nutshell, the episode reveals one of the major concerns of the Anglo-Saxon Reform movement: the unification of the Church through compliance with Benedictinism.

Æthelwold's Benedictional is another late tenth-century text in which Benedictine propagandistic elements are easily observed.[4] The work has been thoroughly analyzed by Robert Deshman, who has shown that its iconography was devised in a way that favored both the monarchy and monastic Reform. The persistent emphasis on Christ's kingly nature in the manuscript has been interpreted by Deshman as "a form of political propaganda for Edgar," which may have served to consolidate the latter's position as Christ's earthly representative after his coronation in 973.[5] The Benedictional imagery, which was most likely supervised by Bishop Æthelwold, thus mirrors the intricate political maneuvers intended to establish Edgar's legitimacy as (imperial) ruler, given his essential contribution to the Reform cause as the major patron of Benedictine monasticism.

497–503. Interestingly, this poetic version of the *vita* includes a panegyric of Eadsige (lines 134–150) that is not present in Lantfred's. Eadsige's conversion also appears in Ælfric's condensed version of Lantfred's *Translatio* (*Epitome translationis et miraculorum S. Swithuni*) and in his vernacular version of St. Swithun's life, in which Eadsige is said to be a relative of Æthelwold's. He is likewise alluded to in Wulfstan Cantor's account in *Vita S. Æthelwoldi*; see *Wulfstan of Winchester: The Life of St. Æthelwold*, ed. Michael Lapidge and Michael Winterbottom (Oxford, 1991), 32–33. See also Robert Deshman's comments on the significance of this episode in "St Swithun in Early Medieval Art," in *The Cult*, ed. Lapidge, 182–83.

[4] It is generally assumed that the date of Æthelwold's Benedictional should be between 971 and 984, the years of Swithun's translation and Æthelwold's death respectively. See Andrew Prescott's discussion of this in his facsimile edition in *The Benedictional of St. Æthelwold: A Masterpiece of Anglo-Saxon Art* (London, 2002), 6. Deshman proposed 973 as the possible date of compilation, since he considered the iconographic elements in the book to form part of the preparations for Edgar's coronation that year. See Robert Deshman, *The Benedictional of Æthelwold* (Princeton, NJ, 1995), esp, 212–14, 260–61. However, Lapidge has recently cast doubt on this assertion since, as he points out, there are no blessings for the translation of St. Swithun (15 July 971) in the manuscript. As he argues, "The absence of such blessings in a book which was written within a year or two of the translation might imply that the book was designed . . . before the translation itself had taken place": *The Cult*, ed. idem, 88.

[5] Robert Deshman, "*Christus rex et magi reges*: Kingship and Christology in Ottonian and Anglo-Saxon Art," *Frühmittelalterliche Studien* 10 (1976): 367–405, here 403. He also provides a thorough study of this in *The Benedictional*, 192–214.

In its current decapitated state, the sequence known as the Advent Lyrics or *Christ I* opens the Exeter Book, a manuscript whose compilation dates roughly from 950–975 and was therefore probably coeval with Lantfred's *Translatio* and Æthelwold's Benedictional.[6] On the basis of this chronological affinity, we could infer that the Advent Lyrics, having been issued in a period in which drastic political measures were enforcing a general conversion to Benedictinism, might equally be connected to reformist ideology.[7] Suffice it to mention that the lyrics clearly dwell on the notion of the unity of the Church through Christ's Advent, a topic of paramount significance in the context of the Reform, as will be discussed later in this essay. Christ in turn is described in the sequence as a king whose power and skill are crucial to attaining communal unity. Besides, the different lyrics derive from the Advent antiphons of the Divine Office.[8] In this light, it is hard to conclude that a collection of lyrics with these characteristics could be alien to the political climate of the Reform. For these reasons, this essay sets out to consider the possibility that, like the *Translatio* and the Benedictional, the Advent sequence might be permeated with Benedictine influence. Beyond a mere rewriting of liturgical pieces, the lyrics might have been either adapted from an

---

[6] On paleographical grounds, Flower points out that the script of the Exeter Book resembles that of London, Lambeth Palace, MS. 149 and affirms that both manuscripts were written "early in the period 970–990": *The Exeter Book of Old English Poetry*, ed. R. W. Chambers, with introductory chapters by Max Förster and Robin Flower (London, 1933), 90. More recently, Conner claims that the script suggests a date between 950 and 970: Patrick W. Conner, *Anglo-Saxon Exeter: A Tenth-Century Cultural History* (Woodbridge, 1993), 76. This issue is however far from being settled as Muir, the latest editor of the Exeter Book, proposes a time span between 965 and 975: *The Exeter Anthology of Old English Poetry: An Edition of Exeter Dean and Chapter MS 3501*, ed. Bernard J. Muir, 2 vols. (Exeter, 1994), 1: 1.

[7] In a comparative analysis of the Advent Lyrics and the Benedictional, Raw has also recently pointed out the temporal proximity and the liturgical parallelisms of the two works: "The Benedictional and *The Advent Lyrics* are not only contemporary with each other: they derive from a similar liturgical background": Barbara Raw, "Two Versions of Advent: The Benedictional of Æthelwold and *The Advent Lyrics*," *Leeds Studies in English* 34 (2003): 1–28, here 1.

[8] As pointed out by Hall, "The first ten of the twelve lyrics owe their themes and much of their imagery to a group of Latin antiphons that in the medieval Roman church were chanted at Vespers on the days during Advent called the Greater Ferias, from 17 December to 23 December": Thomas N. Hall, "*Christ I*," in *Medieval England: An Encyclopedia*, ed. Paul E. Szarmach, M. Teresa Tavormina, and Joel T. Rosenthal (New York, 1998), 182. See also James W. McKinnon, *The Advent Project* (Berkeley, CA, 2000).

earlier work or even—we may tentatively conjecture—expressly designed as a re-form-oriented work to be included in the Exeter anthology.[9]

I am not alone in suspecting a late tenth-century date for the composition of the lyrics, since Gatch, Woolf, Conner, and Raw have already suggested that the Advent sequence might be contemporary with the Benedictine revival.[10] Deshman in turn has used the Advent Lyrics as part of the battery of proofs supplied to demonstrate the reformist background of the Benedictional's iconography. However, to my knowledge a study focusing solely on the Advent sequence as a work showing an affinity for Benedictine ideology has never been carried out. I will therefore provide evidence of this by considering two particular aspects, architectural metaphors and Christological imagery, the reformist bias of which has already been studied by Deshman in the Benedictional but has not yet

---

[9] Conversely, on linguistic grounds, Campbell proposed a late ninth-century dating for the Advent sequence, but this hypothesis has not received much scholarly support: *The Advent Lyrics of the Exeter Book*, ed. Jackson J. Campbell (Princeton, NJ, 1959), 36-42. Rankin has similarly argued that the composition of the lyrics antedates by far the Benedictine revival, since most of the antiphons that served as models for their composition seem to derive from Roman tradition rather than Gallican: Susan Rankin, "The Liturgical Background of the Old English Advent Lyrics: A Reappraisal," in *Learning and Literature in Anglo-Saxon England: Studies Presented to Peter Clemoes on the Occasion of his Sixty-Fifth Birthday*, ed. Michael Lapidge and Helmut Gneuss (Cambridge, 1985), 317–40, here 334. Rankin's early dating of the sequence has been accepted by Peter Clemoes in *Interactions of Thought and Language in Old English Poetry* (Cambridge, 1995), 383 and Hall, *"Christ I,"* 182. Despite this, we cannot rule out the possibility of a late tenth-century adaptation of earlier material to the necessities generated by the monastic Reform. Besides, even though the introduction of Gallican liturgy ran parallel to the implantation of the Benedictine system, this did not imply the immediate dismissal of Roman tradition. The Royal Psalter (London, BL, Royal 2.B.v), a mid-tenth-century *psalterium romanum*, with glosses attributable to Æthelwold, as Gretsch has demonstrated, is a good instance of the continuing significance of Roman liturgy in Benedictine circles, since the undisputed leader of the Reform would not spend so much effort studying an old-fashioned or unacceptable version of the psalter. Also, for evidence of the use of Roman psalters postdating the mid-tenth century, see Mechthild Gretsch, *The Intellectual Foundations of the English Benedictine Reform* (Cambridge, 1999), 282–83.

[10] Milton McC. Gatch, *Loyalties and Traditions: Man and his World in Old English Literature* (New York, 1971), 96, and idem, review of Mary Clayton, *The Cult of the Virgin Mary in Anglo-Saxon England*, *Speculum* 68 (1993): 733–35, here 735. Cf. also Rosemary Woolf's review of Burlin, *The Old English Advent: A Typological Commentary*, *Medium Ævum* 40 (1971): 60–61; Conner, *Anglo-Saxon Exeter*, 163; Raw, "Two Versions of Advent," 1. I have elsewhere supported the hypothesis of a late tenth-century dating for the Advent Lyrics in *The Literary Encyclopedia* (www.litencyc.com), ed. Robert Clark, Emory Elliott, and Janet Todd (London, 2004).

been analyzed in depth with regard to the Advent Lyrics. Paying special attention to lyric 1 as the piece basic to an understanding of the whole sequence, my contention is that contemporary readers of the poems might have viewed these metaphors and images—together with the concept of Advent—as characteristic of Benedictine iconography and propaganda. I intend to prove this by comparing the elements occurring in the lyrics with parallel images and concepts found in late tenth- and eleventh-century literary and pictorial works whose affinities with reformist ideology are blatantly manifest.

2. The Cornerstone, the Two Walls, and the Ruinous Building: Architectural Imagery and Metaphors in the Advent Lyrics

The surviving lines of lyric 1 lead us into a thought-provoking reflection on the significance of Advent:

> . . . cyninge.
> Ðu eart se weallstan   þe ða wyrhtan iu
> wiðwurpon to weorce.   Wel þe geriseð
> þæt þu heafod sie   healle mærre,
> ond gesomnige   side weallas
> fæste gefoge,   flint unbræcne,
> þæt geond eorðb[yr]g eall   eagna gesihþe
> wundrien to worlde.   Wuldres ealdor,
> gesweotula nu þurh searocræft þin sylfes weorc,
> soðfæst, sigorbeorht,   ond sona forlæt
> weall wið wealle.   Nu is þam weorce þearf
> þæt se cræftga cume   ond se cyning sylfa,
> ond þonne gebete—   nu gebrosnad is—
> hus under hrofe.   He þæt hra gescop,
> leomo læmena;   nu sceal liffrea
> þone wergan heap   wraþum ahreddan,
>   earme from egsan,   swa he oft dyde.

> [". . . king.
> You are the wall-stone that the workers of old
> Rejected from the work; it is (now) most fitting
> That You be the head of that great hall
> And bring together the vast walls,
> Indestructible flint, in firm conjunction,
> That throughout earth's cities, all those with eyes to see
> May gaze for ever. Prince of glory,
> Disclose now with skill Your proper work,
> Fast in truth, bright with victory, and at once let

The wall unite with wall. Now there is need of such work:
That the Craftsman come, the King Himself,
And then restore—it is now in ruin—
The house beneath the roof. He created the body,
The limbs of clay; now must the Lord of Life
Release from the wrathful this weary throng,
These helpless from terror, as He often has."][11]

Through architectural images, the lyric compares Christ with the wall-stone or the cornerstone ("weallstan," line 2a) of a building ("healle mærre," line 4b), which is clearly meant to be the church or any Christian community.

The reference to Christ as the cornerstone uniting Gentiles with Jews in the final accomplishment of the universal Church is presented in a condensed form in the antiphon from which lyric 1 clearly derives: "O Rex gentium et desideratus earum, lapisque angularis! Qui facis utraque unum, veni, salva hominem quem de limo formasti" ["O King of the nations and object of their longing and the cornerstone which makes both parts one: come and save man, whom you formed out of clay"].[12] This motif was well known in biblical and patristic literature. It is, for example, fully expounded in St. Paul's Epistle to the Ephesians:

So then you are no longer strangers and sojourners, but you are fellow citizens with the saints and members of the household of God, built upon the foundation of the apostles and prophets, Christ Jesus himself being the cornerstone, in whom the whole structure is joined together and grows into a holy temple in the Lord; in whom you also are built into it for a dwelling place of God in the Spirit.[13]

---

[11] Robert B. Burlin, *The Old English Advent: A Typological Commentary* (New Haven, CT, 1968), 56–57. All citations and translations in this essay are from this edition.

[12] Burlin, *The Old English Advent*, 58; trans. in *Anglo-Saxon Poetry*, ed. and trans. S. A. J. Bradley (London, 1981), 205. Cook was the first scholar to notice the liturgical sources of the Advent sequence, as most of the lyrics are based on the so-called "Antiphonae majores" or "'O' antiphons," usually employed in the liturgy of Advent or Christmas. See *The Christ of Cynewulf*, ed. Albert C. Cook (Boston, 1900), esp. xxv–xliii. For a reprinted version of Cook's work with a preface by John C. Pope, see *The Christ of Cynewulf* (Hamden, 1964). A comprehensive study of the connection between *Advent* and its liturgical sources is found in Edward Burgert, *The Dependence of Part I of Cynewulf's Christ upon the Antiphonary* (Washington, DC, 1921).

[13] Ephesians 2:19–22. All citations from the Bible in this essay are from *The New Oxford Annotated Bible with the Apocrypha*, ed. Herbert G. May and Bruce M. Metzger (New York, 1977). Cavill has analyzed the presence of this motif in Paris Psalm 117 (lines 54–57a): ("Ðone sylfan stan þe hine swyðe ær / wyrhtan awurpan, nu se geworden is / hwommona heagost . . ." See Paul Cavill, "Children and the Rock: The Ending of the Old English Metrical Psalm 136," *English Studies* 80 (1999): 89–105, here 102–3. Also,

As in the biblical passage, the cornerstone metaphor in the Old English lyric alludes to Christ as the only one capable of uniting the two walls—"side weallas" (line 5b) and "weall wið wealle" (line 11a)—, i.e. Jews and Gentiles. In turn, the "wyrhtan iu" (line 2b), or "the workers of old" who rejected Christ the cornerstone, refers to the Jews as they were held responsible for his crucifixion.[14]

The lyric thus displays a set of architectural images centering on the idea of building. As pointed out by George Brown, the poet "emphasizes the metaphor of construction throughout this lyric by his repetitions of some form of 'weorce': 'wyrhtan' (2), 'to weorce' (3), 'weorc' (9), 'þam weorce þearf' (11)."[15] The poem also describes the house in a ruinous state (line 13b), which suggests "a communal slackening of faith, humanity in a condition of sin, seeking restoration in the Advent of Christ," as Robert Burlin has noted.[16] It then focuses on the necessity of Christ's coming as "se cræftga" (line 12a) who will reconstruct the church. From line 15b to the end, the speaker asks Christ to protect the community—the "wergan heap" (line 16a)—that is threatened by sinners, pagans, or enemies—the "wraþum" (line 16b).

The traditional allegorical reading does not explain the full significance that these images might have had in the cultural milieu of the Exeter manuscript.[17]

---

see Raw's comments on the use of the cornerstone image in this passage in "Two Versions of Advent," 19-20. The cornerstone metaphor is also well known in patristic literature. As pointed out by Cook, it occurs in Gregory the Great's *Moralia in Job*. See Cook, *The Christ*, 75. Burlin also notes the employment of this motif in Jerome's *In Epistolam ad Ephesios* (a commentary on the Pauline text mentioned above) and Bede's homily no. 23 on Palm Sunday. See Burlin, *The Old English Advent*, 59–60.

[14] Ælfric also used this metaphor in his homily on Epiphany (no. 7): "Soðlice se sealmsceop awrat be criste þæt he is se hyrnstan þe gefegð þa twegen weallas togædere. for þan ðe he geþeodde his gecorenan of iudeiscum folce. 7 þa geleaffullan of hæþenum: swilce twegen wagas to anre gelaðunge." ["For the psalmist wrote concerning Christ, that he is the corner-stone which joins the two walls together, because he united his chosen of the Jewish people and the faithful of the heathen, as two walls, to one church"]: *Ælfric's Homilies: the First Series*, ed. Peter Clemoes, EETS 17 (Oxford, 1997), 233–34; trans. Benjamin Thorpe, *The Homilies of Ælfric*, 2 vols. (London, 1844–1846; repr. 1971), 1: 106–7. For similar occurrences of the cornerstone image in Ælfric's homilies, see Burlin, *The Old English Advent*, 60–62.

[15] George Hardin Brown, "Old English Verse as a Medium for Christian Theology," in *Modes of Interpretation in Old English Literature: Essays in Honour of Stanley B. Greenfield*, ed. Phyllis Rugg Brown et al. (Toronto, 1986), 15–28, here 20.

[16] Burlin, *The Old English Advent*, 64.

[17] Several critics have noted that the typological commentary offered by Burlin and the traditional source-hunting approach are not enough to capture the originality and textual peculiarities of the Advent Lyrics. See, for example, Woolf's comments in her review of Burlin's *The Old English Advent*, in *Medium Aevum*, 60–61. Also, see Edward B. Irving, Jr., "The Advent of Poetry: *Christ I*," *ASE* 25 (1996): 123–34, here 123–24.

However, if we provide a contextualized reading, we will notice that this lyric may encapsulate the propagandistic discourse used by the Benedictine movement. If the text is reread in this light, we will gain a deeper insight into some of the textual aspects that have already received comment. To begin with, the corner-stone image points to Advent as the only means to achieve unity in the Christian community. Thus lines 5 and 6 allude to the uniting of the two walls as "inde-structible flint, in firm conjunction," an idea that is taken up again in lines 10b and 11a in which Christ is urged to "unite wall with wall." Similarly, the allusion to the "wrathful ones" suggests a community which is continuously threatened with dissension. Given the constant menace of political rupture due to foreign in-vasion, these images could have conveyed contemporary overtones which would have been easily grasped by a late tenth-century audience. Also, it would not be far-fetched to suspect that the reference to the cornerstone uniting the two walls might have summoned up the idea of the ecclesiastical Reform attempting to pro-vide cohesion in a society in which reformed and unreformed factions coexisted.

Accordingly, in Advent lyric 1 the work of Christ uniting the two walls at best echoes Edgar's skillful policy of bringing together the divided kingdom after the crisis in which Mercia and Northumbria separated from Wessex dur-ing his predecessor's reign.[18] In the tract known as "King Edgar's Establish-ment of the Monasteries," most likely composed by Æthelwold as a preface to the Old English translation of St. Benedict's *Rule*, King Eadwig's misgovernment is harshly criticized as he is said to have "dispersed this kingdom and divided its unity . . ." ("þis rice tostencte 7 his annesse todælde . . .").[19] By contrast, Edgar is praised as having "brought back to unity the division of the kingdom" ("þæs rices twislunge eft to annesse brohte . . .").[20] These two passages clearly focus on the significance of political unity, as the repetition of the term "annesse" and the presence of several words alluding to rupture illustrate—notably, "tostencte," "todælde," and "twislunge." Similarly, in the proem to the *Regularis Concordia* (ca. 973), the foremost document of the Benedictine Reform, there is a clear ref-erence to Edgar's encouraging the acceptance of the *Rule*, urging all "to be of one mind as regards monastic usage . . . and so, with their minds anchored firmly on

---

[18] Plummer comments that "the later biographers of Dunstan" refer to this event "as if something like a civil war had taken place . . .": *Two Saxon Chronicles Parallel*, ed. Charles Plummer, 2 vols. (Oxford, 1899), 2: 151 (note on the entry for year 957).

[19] *Councils and Synods with other Documents Relating to the English Church I: A.D. 871–1204*, ed. and trans. Dorothy Whitelock, M. Brett, and C. N. L. Brooke (Oxford, 1981), 142–54, here 146–47. Although this document appears in an early twelfth-century manuscript — London, BL, Cotton Faustina A.x (fols. 148–151v) — its connection with the Benedictine Reform period is undeniable.

[20] *Councils*, ed. and trans. Whitelock et al., 46–47.

the ordinances of the Rule, to avoid all dissension, lest differing ways of observ-
ing the customs of one Rule and one country should bring their holy conversation
into disrepute" ("ut concordes aequali consuetudinis usu . . . regularia praecepta
tenaci mentis ancora seruantes, nullo modo dissentiendo discordarent; ne impar
ac uarius unius regulae ac unius patriae usus probrose uituperium sanctae con-
versationi irrogaret").[21]

A wellknown image of the king and two of the Reform leaders symboliz-
ing the driving forces producing political and monastic cohesion is extant in the
frontispiece to the *Regularis Concordia* contained in London, BL, Cotton Tiberius
A.iii (fol. 2v), a mid-eleventh-century manuscript, whose affinities with tenth-
century Benedictinism are undisputed (see fig. 3.1).[22] In an architectural setting
that clearly distinguishes two stages, the miniature shows Edgar, Dunstan, and
Æthelwold holding the scroll of the *Regularis Concordia* while the kneeling monk
represents the submission of the Church to the *Rule*.[23] Just as the cornerstone
motif of lyric 1 refers to the union of Gentiles and Jews, the scroll, held by the
four figures, symbolizes the cohesion produced by the monastic Reform in which
monarchy and clergy worked side by side.

Even though the cornerstone metaphor is a wellknown convention, Deshman has argued that it formed part of a group of architectural images that were
akin to the propagandistic iconography of the Reform movement.[24] He thus offers
proof of the common identification of the leading reformers with architectural

---

[21] *Regularis Concordia Anglicae Nationis Monachorum Sanctimonialiumque: The Monastic Agreement of the Monks and Nuns of the English Nation*, ed. Thomas Symons (London, 1953), 2–3.

[22] Among other texts undoubtedly associated with the Reform movement, this codex contains one of the only two extant copies of the *Regularis Concordia*, and a version
of St. Benedict's *Rule*. For a review of the manuscript contents, see Robert Deshman,
"*Benedictus Monarcha et Monachus*: Early Medieval Ruler Theology and the Anglo-Saxon Reform," *Frühmittelalterliche Studien* 22 (1988): 204–40, here 229. Also see Helmut
Gneuss, "Origin and Provenance of Anglo-Saxon Manuscripts: The Case of Cotton Tiberius A.III," in *Of The Making of Books: Medieval Manuscripts, Their Scribes and Readers.
Essays Presented To M. B. Parkes*, ed. P. R. Robinson and Rivkah Zim (Aldershot, 1997),
13–48.

[23] For an analysis of this picture, see Benjamin C. Withers, "Interaction of Word
and Image in Anglo-Saxon Art II: Scrolls and Codex in the Frontispiece to the *Regularis
Concordia*," *OEN* 31 (1997): 36–40. Also see Catherine E. Karkov, *The Ruler Portraits of
Anglo-Saxon England* (Woodbridge, 2004), esp. 93–99.

[24] See Robert Deshman's comments on this image in "The Image of the Living
Ecclesia and the English Monastic Reform," in *Sources of Anglo-Saxon Culture*, ed. Paul
E. Szarmach with V. D. Oggins (Kalamazoo, 1986), 261–82, here 262–72, and in idem,
The Benedictional, 19–23.

Fig. 3.1. London, BL, MS. Cotton Tiberius A.iii, fol. 2v. By permission of the British Library.

objects such as a column or a cornerstone.[25] In an excerpt from Adelard's *Vita S. Dunstani*, the reformer's steadfast character and the etymology of his name give rise to his likening to a mountain rock and, more importantly, to a cornerstone: "Hic Dunstanus iuxta interpretationem nominis sui, montanus utique lapis, ut mons immobilis, ut lapis angulari lapidi affixus, moueri non potuit . . ." ["This Dunstan, according to the interpretation of his name, that is, mountainous stone, or unmovable mountain, or a cornerstone fixed to the stone which is impossible to move . . ."].[26] In Byrhtferth's *Vita S. Oswaldi* the analogy is also present, as the saint's glorious chants are compared to "precious cornerstones": "Fuerunt in angulis sanctae domus suae lapides pretiosi positi, qui eam ne cadere valuisset sustentabant firmiter, ut nullus vis pessimorum ventorum agitari posset" ["They were the precious stones placed in the corners of his own holy house, which (stones) supported it firmly, so that it was not in a condition to fall, so that not one (stone) was able to be shaken by the most dire force of wind"].[27]

On the other hand, we may assume that architectural imagery might have also applied to the figure of the king as the major promoter of the Reform, but there seems to be no textual identification of Edgar with a pillar or a cornerstone as far as I am aware. However, in the description of Edgar's coronation in Byrhtferth's *Vita S. Oswaldi* there is a passage which echoes lines 2 and 3 of lyric

---

[25] As for the column motif, in Wulfstan Cantor's *Vita S. Æthelwoldi*, the reference to Dunstan's long productive bishopric prompts his comparison with an unmovable pillar ("columna inmobilis"). See *Wulfstan of Winchester*, ed. Lapidge and Winterbottom, 24–27. All further citations and translations from this work are from the same edition. A similar reference can be found in Ælfric's abridged version of this *vita* (74). In Adelard's *Vita S. Dunstani*, the same reformer is likewise described as a "column of light" ("columnam lucis"), "God's column" ("columna Dei"), and even "column of monastic religion" ("columen religionis monasticae"): *Memorials of Saint Dunstan Archbishop of Canterbury*, ed. William Stubbs (London, 1874; repr. Wiesbaden, 1965), 59, 66, 56. See Deshman's comments on this motif in "The Living *Ecclesia*," 276–77. The image was not restricted only to the Reform leaders, since St. Swithun, the chief patron of the Benedictine movement, is said to appear in the form of a shining column ("rutilans columna," line 107) ascending to heaven in Lantfred's *Translatio*. A parallel description is found in Wulfstan Cantor's *Narratio*, chap. 3, lines 703–704: *The Cult*, ed. Lapidge, 282–83, 444–45. The reference to St. Swithun as a column is also observed in some liturgical pieces of the Winchester liturgy (78–79, 98–99). Deshman has similarly pointed out the resemblance of St. Swithun's figure in the Benedictional to a column (*The Benedictional*, pl. 32, and comments on 138–39, 151–52).

[26] *Memorials*, ed. Stubbs, 67. My translation.

[27] *The Historians of the Church of York and its Archbishops*, ed. J. Raine, 3 vols., Rolls Series (London, 1879–1894), 1: 419; trans. Deshman, "The Imagery of the Living *Ecclesia*," 276.

1: "Non enim ita ad eum confluxerat suæ gentis admirabilis et gloriosus exercitus ut eum expellerent, vel consilium facerent ut eum morti traderent, vel ligno suspenderent, sicut olim infelices Judæi benignum gesserunt Ihesum" ["And the marvelous and glorious army of his people did not attend (the ceremony) to expel him (Edgar), nor to court-martial him nor to sentence him to death, nor to hang him on a rood, as once did the unhappy Jews with good Jesus"].[28] Although the reference to the cornerstone is not explicit, the identification of Edgar with Christ, together with the occurrence of the verb "expellerent," equivalent to Old English "wiðwurpon" (line 3a) in lyric 1, is at least highly suggestive.

In this light, the reference to the workers that rejected ("wiðwurpon") the cornerstone (Ps. 118:22; Matt. 21:42, Mk. 12:10, Lk. 20:17) gains further significance. The fact that the Advent poet was aware of the central meaning of this passage in lyric 1 is supported by the recurrence of the notion in lyric 3 with the term "wyrpe" (line 67a). The word—which can be translated as revolution, change, recovery, relief, or improvement—was surely selected by the poet because it echoes preceding "wiðwurpon."[29] Interestingly, "wyrpe" appears in a passage in which Christ's Coming is explicitly associated with his rejecting (or rather transforming, undoing, or improving) the work of the Jews: "Nu is þæt bearn cymen, / awæcned to wyrpe weorcum Ebrea . . ." ["Now is the Child come, born to transform the work of the Hebrews"].[30] As Campbell notes, the "wyrhtan iu" of lyric 1 could also refer to "churchmen who make the Church a thing devoid of Christ's spirit . . ." but, given that "wiðweorpan" is the emphatic form of "weorpan" (meaning to expel, throw out, or cast away), we may take the reference a step further, since the workers might likewise suggest the idea of unreformed canons like the ones that were expelled and replaced by monks.[31] Interestingly, a further emphatic variant of this verb is employed in a passage from Ælfric's *Prayer of Moses* which, together with other Old Testament pieces from the *Lives of Saints*, has been associated with late

---

[28] *The Historians*, ed. Raine, 1: 436. My translation.

[29] See Joseph Bosworth and T. Northcote Toller, *An Anglo-Saxon Dictionary* (London, 1898); *Supplement* by T. Northcote Toller, 1921, with *Revised and Enlarged Addenda* by Alistair Campbell, 1972.

[30] Lines 66b–67; Burlin, *The Old English Advent*, 80–81.

[31] *The Advent Lyrics*, ed. Campbell, 12. Note the occurrence of synonymous *utdrifan* in the E-version of the Anglo-Saxon Chronicle (963): "On þes oðer gear syððon he wæs gehalgod, þa makode he feola minstra 7 *draf ut* þa clerca of þe biscoprice, forþan þet hi noldon nan regul healden, 7 sætta þær muneca." ["In the next year after he (Æthelwold) was consecrated he founded many monasteries, and drove the clerks out of the bishopric because they would not observe any rule, and set monks there"]: *The Anglo-Saxon Chronicle: A Collaborative Edition*, vol. 7, ed. Susan Irvine (Cambridge, 2004), 57 (emphasis added); trans. Michael Swanton, *The Anglo-Saxon Chronicle* (London, 1996), 115.

tenth-century political circumstances by Godden:[32] "Hu wæs hit ða sißðan ða þa man towearp munuclif . / and Godes biggengas to bysmore hæfde . / buton þæt us com to cwealm and hunger . / and siðða hæðen here us hæfde to bysmre ." ["How was it then afterward when men rejected monastic life and held God's services in contempt, but that pestilence and hunger came to us, and afterward the heathen army had us in reproach?"][33] Even though this work may be later than the Exeter Book—as part of Ælfric's *Saints' Lives*, it is dated to ca. 995—the use of "towearp" as referring to the dismissal of monasticism and its disastrous consequences therefore supports the idea that the rejection of the cornerstone in lyric 1 may be interpreted as being consonant with Benedictine ideology. By the same token, in lyric 3 the presence of the term "wyrpe"—which can also refer to the idea of transformation or change—might allude to the fact that Christ's Advent would profoundly change the world and bring a new era for mankind, a notion which was probably close to the radical renewal promoted by Benedictinism.

Apart from the suggestive nuances of the pair "wißwurpon/wyrpe" and the proofs supplied by Deshman with regard to the cornerstone motif, in pro-Reform texts there is further evidence of the metaphorical allusion to contemporary key events like the expulsion of unreformed canons and the propagandistic use of concepts such as Advent or the Second Coming.[34] For example, in the "New Minster Refoundation Charter" and the so-called "Peniarth Diploma" there is an account of the fall of the angels which has been associated by David F. Johnson with

---

[32] See Malcolm Godden, "Experiments in Genre: The Saints' Lives in Ælfric's *Catholic Homilies*," in *Holy Men and Holy Women: Old English Prose Saints' Lives and their Context*, ed. Paul E. Szarmach (Albany, NY, 1996), 261–87, and idem, "Ælfric's Saints' Lives and the Problem of Miracles," *Leeds Studies in English* 16 (1985): 83–100.

[33] *Ælfric's Lives of Saints*, ed. and trans. W. W. Skeat, EETS, o.s. 76, 82, 94, 114, 4 vols. (London, 1881–1900; repr. in two vols. 1966), 1: 294–95.

[34] As Lapidge notes, "Æthelwold's expulsion of the secular clerics from the Old Minster, and their replacement by his own monks from Abingdon, was seen by contemporaries as a crucial event in the establishment of reformed Benedictine monasticism in tenth-century England": *The Cult*, ed. idem, 260 n. 42. Also see Lapidge and Winterbottom's comments in *Wulfstan of Winchester*, xlv–xlviii. For Wulfstan's account in his *Vita S. Æthelwoldi* see 30–31, 32–33. This event is recorded in the different versions of the Anglo-Saxon Chronicle. Note, for example, this passage in the A-version (year 964): "Her dræfde Eadgar cyng þa preostas on Ceastre of Ealdanmynstre 7 of Niwanmynstre 7 of Ceortesige 7 of Middeltune 7 sette hy mid munecan." ["In this year King Edgar drove the priests in the city from the Old Minster and from the New Minster; and from Chertsey and from Milton (Abbas); and replaced them with monks"]: *The Anglo-Saxon Chronicle: A Collaborative Edition*, vol. 3, *MS A*, ed. Janet M. Bately (Cambridge, 1986), 75–76; trans. in *English Historical Documents c. 500–1042*, ed. and trans. Dorothy Whitelock (London, 1979), 226.

Æthelwold's ejection of the secular clerks.[35] According to him, the apocryphal allusion in the two documents might have been intended to justify the severe measures imposed by the reformers to achieve monastic unity. Thus, in the "New Minster Refoundation Charter," issued in 966 to provide a written testimony to the refoundation of the New Minster effected by King Edgar and Æthelwold in 964, there is a reference to the expulsion of the angels from heaven and God's creation of man in order to replace them (chap. i). Man's descendants are in turn said to be wiped out by the Flood (chap. iv). The first part of the charter is thus devoted to illustrating God's undisputed authority in bestowing heaven on the angels and Paradise/earth on mankind, and later depriving both angels and man of those privileges. The outline of salvation history in the charter ends with a reference to Christ's Advent, Crucifixion, Harrowing of Hell, and Ascension (chap. v), which all add to the plan of God's conferring a right (Christ's presence on earth and redemption) and later taking it away (with the Crucifixion). Further in the text, this cyclical sequence of granting and depriving is clearly echoed by the subsequent allusion to Edgar's banishing the canons and replacing them with monks (chap. vii): "uitiosorum cuneos canonicorum . e diuersis nostri regiminis coenobiis Christi uicarius eliminaui. . . . auidus inquisitor aduertens . gratos Domino monachorum cuneos qui pro nobis incunctanter intercenderunt . nostri iuris monasteriis deuotus hilariter collocaui ." ["I, the vicar of Christ, have expelled the crowds of depraved canons from the various monasteries of our kingdom. . . . I, a keen investigator, turning my attention to these matters, have joyously installed, in the monasteries within our jurisdiction, throngs of monks pleasing to the Lord, who might intercede unhesitatingly for us"].[36] Thus, like God in the first chapters of the charter, Edgar is legitimized to grant and remove a particular privilege, no matter how convulsive the effect is.

Similarly, in the proem to the "Peniarth Diploma" the allusion to the fall of the angels reaches its climax with an explicit reference to Advent as a new era, offering mankind the possibility of redemption, and as part of God's compensation for eradicating the tenth order of angels—the metaphorical reference to the unreformed faction—thus giving rise to Satan's envy and man's subsequent downfall:

---

[35] See David F. Johnson, "The Fall of Lucifer in Genesis A and Two Anglo-Latin Royal Charters," *JEGP* 97 (1998): 500–21, esp. 512–16. The "New Minster Refoundation Charter" (S 745) is included in fols. 2v–33v of London, BL, Cotton Vespasian A.viii, a late tenth-century manuscript from Winchester that is best known for the presence of a deluxe illustration of King Edgar offering Christ the grant attesting the foundation of the monastery at New Minster (see fig. 3.4 in this essay). The "Peniarth Diploma" is contained in Aberystwyth, National Library of Wales, Peniarth 390 (late tenth century).

[36] *Property and Piety in Early Medieval Winchester: Documents Relating to the Topography of the Anglo-Saxon and Norman City and Its Minsters*, ed. and trans. Alexander R. Rumble (Oxford, 2003), 81.

formatu*mq*u*e* pr*o*thoplastum serpentin*us* liuor ad mortem usq*ue* p*er*duxit. Omneq*ue* human*um* gen*us* post illum. Et qu*an*do dei inmensa mis*ericor*dia hoc p*er*spexit. condoluit, unicu*mque* filiu*m* suu*m* mittens satu*m* de intemerata uirgine Maria p*er* crucis mortem om*n*e humanu*m* genus piissime redemit.

["And serpentine envy brought the first created man unto death, and the entire human race after him. But when God in His boundless mercy perceived this, He sympathized, and, sending His only son, begotten of the inviolate Virgin Mary, He righteously redeemed the entire human race through death on the cross."][37]

On the basis of the combined use of the fall-of-the-angels motif and the topic of Advent with suggestive political implications in the "New Minster Refoundation Charter" and the "Peniarth Diploma," it might not be rash to assume that the allusion to Advent as mankind's longed-for era in the Exeter poetic sequence could likewise be charged with contemporary overtones. In this light, the reference to the cornerstone and the two walls in lyric 1 might be read by a late tenth-century audience as a further indirect allusion to the unity effected by the Reform and the tension between unreformed and reformed factions, respectively.

There are other architectural images that are worth analyzing in Advent lyric 1, one of them being the notion of the ruinous building that needs to be reconstructed as found in lines 11b–14a. Again, this passage seems to be endowed with a contemporary coloring, since, for tenth-century readers, the description of the ruinous house in lyric 1 might evoke not only the image of a physically dilapidated building but also probably the decadence of the unreformed church and its members. It is well known that the Reform was characterized by (re)building activity, the royal city of Winchester being a good example of this.[38] The recovery

---

[37] Johnson, "The Fall of Lucifer," 515–16. Johnson in turn uses the text found in C. R. Hart, *The Early Charters of Northern England and the North Midlands* (Leicester, 1975), 187. Editorial italics in this passage follow Johnson's spelling of the words that appear in an abbreviated form in Hart's edition.

[38] As explained by Biddle, the archeological remains in Winchester bear witness to the dramatic changes affecting the monastic communities there: "Between 963 and 975 Edgar ordered that fences or walls should be erected to separate the three monasteries from the rush and disorder of the town. Within this framework the three communities followed a way of life that had been profoundly altered both inwardly and externally by the reform of their houses in 964. Even the setting of their daily lives had been changed, their churches rebuilt or enlarged, and their convent buildings regularized to conform with the requirements of a rule that had itself been promulgated in the most ancient of their churches": Martin Biddle, "Felix Urbs Winthonia: Winchester in the Age of Monastic Reform," in *Anglo-Saxon History: Basic Readings*, ed. David A. E. Pelteret (New York, 2000), 302–16, here 308. Lapidge offers a summary of the (re)construction program undertaken in Winchester after St. Swithun's translation (971) in *The Cult*, ed.

of monasticism therefore necessarily implied a period of architectural restoration that is frequently reflected in contemporary literature.

Accordingly, the description of ruinous monasteries and churches needing reconstruction seems to have become a commonplace in the hagiographies related to saints and leaders connected to the Reform. Interestingly, this convention occurs in Wulfstan's *Vita S. Æthelwoldi*, in which there is a description of poorly-endowed and derelict Abingdon before Æthelwold undertook its restoration when he was appointed abbot of that monastery: "In quo modicum antiquitus habebatur monasteriolum, sed erat tunc neglectum ac destitutum, uilibus aedificiis consistens et quadraginta tantum mansas possidens" ["Here there had of old been a small monastery, but this had by now become neglected and forlorn. Its buildings were poor, and its estate consisted of only forty hides of land"].[39]

By the same token, there are frequent allusions in hagiographies to building activity being carried out by different saintly characters. Accordingly, Æthelwold was characterized in his *vitae* as strongly determined to reconstruct English monasticism in both the literal and the figurative dimensions that this task implied.[40]

---

idem, 236–37. For a hypothetical drawing of Winchester Cathedral in the wall-painting found in the Morley Library, see John Crook, "King Edgar's Reliquary of St Swithun," *ASE* 21 (1992): 177–202. Also, on the basis of the references to buildings and furniture as found in the *Regularis Concordia* and Ælfric's *Letter to the Monks of Eynsham*, Mark Spurrel provides a detailed reconstruction of a contemporary monastery in "The Architectural Interest of the *Regularis Concordia*," *ASE* 21 (1992): 161–76.

[39] *Wulfstan of Winchester*, ed. Lapidge and Winterbottom, 18–19. The E-version of the Chronicle offers a parallel description of the ruinous monastery at Peterborough before Æthelwold restored it: "Ne fand þær nan þing buton ealde weallas 7 wilde wuda" ["(Æthelwold) found nothing there but old walls and wild woods"]: *The Anglo-Saxon Chronicle*, ed. Irvine, 57; trans. Swanton, *The Anglo-Saxon Chronicle*, 115, lines 80-82; *The Cult*, ed. Lapidge, 636–37.

[40] St. Swithun is similarly depicted as a staunch builder and restorer of churches and monasteries in the anonymous *Vita S. Swithuni* (second half of the eleventh century): "Ipse amator et cultor sancte uniuersalis ecclesie ecclesias quibus in locis non erant studio ardentissimo pecuniis large contraditis fabricabat; que uero semirutis et infractis parietibus destructe iacebant, dominicis cultibus desiderantissime reparabat" ["St Swithun, the patron and supporter of the Catholic Church, was possessed of the burning desire to construct churches by the generous provision of funding in those places where they previously did not exist; and where churches lay in ruins, their walls collapsed and dilapidated, he very eagerly restored them to the service of the Lord"]. For Goscelin of Saint-Bertin as a possible author of this *vita*, see *The Cult*, ed. Lapidge, 611–22. As noted by this editor, "It is unfortunately not possible to verify the hagiographer's statement [in this passage]: no record of Swithun's building activity survives in contemporary charters" (636 n. 32). However, as pointed out by Lapidge, the saint is credited with the construction of a bridge at the East Gate of Winchester in a poem that was probably composed in the early tenth century: "Idem namque pastor almus et prouisor strenuus / forte pontem extruebat geminasque ianuas / per quas urbis Winthonie adeuntur moenia" ["This same holy bishop, being a

Thus, as bishop of Winchester, his (re)construction activities at the Old Minster to furnish an appropriate place for St. Swithun's remains are lavishly described in Wulfstan Cantor's *Narratio*: "Istius antiqui reparauit et atria templi / moenibus excelsis cluminibusque nouis, / partibus hoc austri firmans et partibus arcti / porticibus solidis, arcubus et uariis" ["Æthelwold also rebuilt the building of the Old Minster with lofty walls and new roofs, strengthening it on its southern and northern sides with solid side-chapels and arches of various kinds"].[41] Similarly, in Wulfstan's *Vita S. Æthelwoldi*, there is a reference to the bishop's active involvement in the construction of buildings: "Erat namque sanctus Aetheluuoldus ecclesiarum ac diuersorum operum magnus aedificator, et dum esset abbas et cum esset episcopus" ["St Æthelwold was a great builder of churches and other buildings, both as abbot and as bishop"].[42] This excerpt might be pointing to the fact that the reformer's zealous building endeavor goes beyond the sheer physical improvement of the monastic communities. Also, it significantly relates Æthelwold's monastic and episcopal activities to those of a builder or "aedificator," a term that echoes line 12 of lyric 1, in which Christ is characterized as "se cræftga," who will restore the ruinous church.[43]

---

vigorous provider, was by chance constructing a bridge with twin gates through which one gained access to the walled town"], *The Cult*, ed. Lapidge, 795–96, lines 5–7.

[41] *The Cult*, ed. Lapidge, 374–75, lines 45–48 from the dedicatory letter to Ælfheah, Æthelwold's successor in the episcopal see at Winchester. For further passages in the *Narratio* alluding to Æthelwold as builder and restorer of monasteries, see lines 35–41, 61–65, 115–120, and 276–278. Deshman also comments on Æthelwold's building tasks in this work, arguing that "the rebuilding of the cathedral to house the relics was an external sign of the internal moral renewal of the Church by monasticism": Deshman, "St Swithun in Early Medieval Art," in *The Cult*, ed. Lapidge, 183. For the description of Æthelwold's reconstruction of the Old Minster, also see Wulfstan's *Vita S. Æthelwoldi*, in *Wulfstan of Winchester*, ed. Lapidge and Winterbottom, 54–57.

[42] *Wulfstan of Winchester*, ed. Lapidge and Winterbottom, 28–29. The extent of Æthelwold's involvement in the reconstruction of Abingdon was certainly remarkable, as in the same chapter he is said to have been miraculously saved from an accident when working in the monastery. Actually, the connection between Æthelwold's episcopal tasks and the restoration of monasticism is pervasive in Anglo-Saxon texts. For instance, the entry for year 963 of the E-Chronicle clearly alludes to this: "Syððan þa com he to se cyng Eadgar, bed him þet he scolde him giuen ealle þa minstre þa hæðene men heafden ær tobrocon, fordi þet he hit wolde geeadnewion, 7 se kyng hit bliþelice tyðode." ["Then afterwards he (Æthelwold) came to the king Edgar (and) asked him that he would give him all the monasteries the heathen men had broken up earlier, because he wanted to restore it (Swanton's note: 'i.e. the monastic life'); and the king happily granted it"]: *The Anglo-Saxon Chronicle*, ed. Irvine, 57; trans. Swanton, *The Anglo-Saxon Chronicle*, 115.

[43] Christopher A. Jones has also detected monastic resonances in "bytla" (lines 148, 733), one of the epithets describing Guthlac "as a holy founder or *aedificator*," and other building terms employed in *Guthlac A* in his "Envisioning the *Cenobim* in the Old English *Guthlac A*," *Medieval Studies* 57 (1995): 259-91. here 273; see esp. 271-78.

The literary production of the second generation of Benedictine authors also reflects this interest in the metaphorical use of architectural imagery. An example of this is Ælfric's *Life of St. Maurus*, in which there is a passage narrating the saint's miraculous intervention when one of the clerics had been injured while supervising the construction of a monastery:

> On ðæs scyppendes naman . þe ge-sceop mann of eorðan .
> aris þu gesund . and ardlice gang
> to ðinum weall-geweorce and hit wél ge-enda. . . .
> þelæs þe hit beo gelet to lange þurh ðe.

> ["In the Creator's name who created man out of the earth, arise thou sound, and go out quickly, to thy wall-building, and finish it well. . . . lest it be hindered too long through thee."][44]

In the speech of Maurus, a saint of wellknown Benedictine affiliation, the term "weall-geweorce" no doubt implies that the cleric is also working to improve the community in a moral and spiritual sense.[45]

The parallel metaphorical handling of architectural imagery in pro-Reform saints' lives and Advent lyric 1 is therefore significant, but this feature is not restricted to only hagiographic works, since Edgar's zealous concern with monastic restoration is also alluded to in "King Edgar's Establishment of the Monasteries": "he . . . began georne mynstera wide geond his cynerice to rihtlæcynne, & Godes þeowdom to aræenne" ["He began zealously to set monasteries in order widely throughout his kingdom, and to set up the service of God"].[46] Similarly, the "New Minster Refoundation Charter" provides further evidence of the remarkable role of building metaphors in the Benedictine context. At the beginning of this document, God's creative power is compared to that of a skilled craftsman: "OMNIPOTENS TOTIUS MACHINAE CONDITOR ineffabili pietate uniuersa mirifice moderatur quae condidit . Qui coaeterno uidelicet uerbo quaedam ex nichilo edidit . quaedam ex informi subtilis artifex propagauit materia ." ["THE ALMIGHTY CREATOR OF THE WHOLE SCHEME

---

[44] *Ælfric's Lives of Saints*, ed. Skeat, 1: 58–59, lines 171–173. This passage is cited and discussed by E. Gordon Whatley, "Pearls before Swine: Ælfric, Vernacular Hagiography, and the Lay Reader," in *Via Crucis: Essays on Early Medieval Sources and Ideas in Memory of J. E. Cross*, ed. Thomas N. Hall, Thomas D. Hill, and Charles D. Wright (Morgantown, WV, 2002), 158–84, here 178–79.

[45] See also Ælfric's *Life of St. Thomas*, esp. lines 67–68 and 71–73: *Ælfric's Lives of Saints*, ed. Skeat, 2: 402–5. In line 103 Thomas is called "cræftga", and in line 104 he is "cristes wyrhtan"; both nouns are likewise employed in Advent lyric 1.

[46] *Councils*, ed. and trans. Whitelock et al., 148–49.

OF THINGS guides marvellously with ineffable love everything which He has created. He, through the co-eternal Word, so to speak formed certain things 'out of nothing' and, like a fine craftsman, created certain other things out of shapeless matter"].[47] The nouns "conditor" (builder, founder, preserver, or creator) and "artifex" (referring to a craftsman, author, or maker), together with the verbs "condidit" and "edidit," thus recall the terms employed in the preceding citations from hagiographic works as well as the vocabulary used by the Advent poet.

As in the charter's passage, it is noteworthy that the reference to Christ's reconstruction of the ruinous building is likewise juxtaposed to the notion of God's creation of man in lyric 1:

> Nu is þam *weorce* þearf
> þæt se *cræftga* cume   ond se cyning sylfa,
> ond þonne *gebete*—   nu *gebrosnad* is—
> hus under hrofe.   He þæt hra *gescop*,
> leomo læmena. (11b–16a)[48]

---

[47] *Property and Piety*, ed. Rumble, 74 (capitalization preserved).

[48] Burlin, *The Old English Advent*, 56–57. I have highlighted the terms related to building, ruins, restoration, and creation with italics. As pointed out by Brown in "Old English Verse as a Medium for Christian Theology," 20, the term "gebrosnað" interestingly reappears in lyric 4, this time "to describe Mary's unsullied maidenhood (84b)." As with lyric 1, *The Ruin* dwells on the description of derelict buildings and the need to restore them, as observed in the following passages (note the use of parellel words which have been highlighted):

> Wrætlic is þes *wealstan*,   wyrde gebræcon;
> burgstede burston,   *brosnað* enta geweorc.
> *Hrofas* sind gehrorene,   hreorge torras,
> hrungeat berofen,   hrim on lime,
> scearde scurbeorge   scorene, gedrorene,
> ældo undereotone . . .
> wurdon hyra wigsteal   westen staþolas,
> *brosnade* burgsteall.   *Betend* crungon
> hergas to hrusan. (Lines 1– 6a; 27– 29a)

["Wondrously ornate is the stone of this wall, shattered by fate; the precincts of the city have crumbled and the work of giants is rotting away. There are tumbled roofs, towers in ruins, high towers rime-frosted, rime on the limy mortar, storm-shielding tiling scarred, scored and collapsed, undermined by age. . . . Their fortress became waste places; the city rotted away: those who should repair it, the multitudes, were fallen to the ground"]: *The Exeter Book*, ed. George Philip Krapp and Elliott van Kirk Dobbie, ASPR 3 (New York, 1936), 227–28; trans. *Anglo-Saxon Poetry*, ed. Bradley, 402. The remarkable lexical parallelisms found in *The Ruin* and lyric 1 therefore suggest that the former might also probably be related to the Benedictine orbit.

Also significantly, the word "cræftga" is linked by means of alliteration to the term "cyning" (line 12). This association of kingship and the notion of (re)construction in turn recalls Edgar's firm commitment to building as described in chapter vi of the "New Minster Refoundation Charter." Hence, paralleling God's authority at banishing the rebellious angels from heaven and expelling man from Paradise, the building terminology subsequently applies to Edgar who, as a just destroyer and builder, is thus legitimized to banish the canons from the New Minster and install monks in their place: "Quosdam igitur suasionibus inuitans ad premia . quosdam terroribus compellens ad gloriam . bona edificans . mala ut Domino faciente potui dissipaui ." ["Attracting certain people to rewards therefore by ex-hortations, driving others on to glory by terrible threats, building up good things, I have destroyed bad things, so far as I have been able, at the Lord's doing"].[49]

All the passages discussed so far support the hypothesis that to a late tenth-century monastic audience the architectural images and metaphors offered by Advent lyric 1 would certainly conjure up themes and ideas that would be akin to Benedictine ideology. The parallel use of the cornerstone, the two walls, and the ruinous buildings, as employed in reform-oriented hagiographies, charters, and other texts, might therefore be pointing to the possible metaphorical reading of these images in lyric 1, thus evoking the key concepts of ecclesiastical unity and monastic restoration, as promoted by the Reform movement.

3. The Shepherd, the King, and the Priest:
Christological Imagery and the Significance of Advent

In the Advent sequence there are several Christological images that are worth analyzing in the context of the Benedictine reform. One of them is the commonplace comparison of Christ with the Good Shepherd protecting the

---

[49] *Property and Piety*, ed. Rumble, 80. The passage continues the use of building and destruction imagery in a subsequent justification of Edgar's decisions due to his fulfilling God's order as found in Jeremiah 1:10: "Ecce constitui te super gentes et super regna ut euellas et destruas et disperdas et dissipes et edifices et plantes" ["Lo, I have set thee this day over the nations, and over kingdoms, to root up, and to pull down, and to waste, and to destroy, and to build, and to plant"]: The association of Edgar's ruling task with that of the reconstruction of monasticism is equally recorded in hagiographic works. In Wulf-stan Cantor's *Narratio*, for example, there is a digressive passage in which Edgar is credi-ted with the rebuilding of monasteries that had been destroyed during his predecessors' reigns: "[regis Eadgari] in cuius regni sunt tempore cuncta / regibus antiquis regnanti-bus eruta quondam / limina sacrorum reparata monasteriorum." ["(King Edgar), during whose reign all the edifices of sacred monasteries, left in ruin while earlier kings were reigning, were restored"]. See *The Cult*, ed. Lapidge, 544–45, lines 1069–1077.

Christian flock, as subtly hinted at in the final lines of lyric 1: "nu sceal liffrea / þone wergan heap wraþum ahreddan, / earme from egsan, swa he oft dyde" ["now must the Lord of Life release from the wrathful this weary throng, these helpless from terror, as He often has"].[50] The motif recurs in lyric 8, in which the sheep clearly represent innocent helpless Christians and the wolf symbolizes the devil or the enemy of the flock:

> Us is þinra arna þearf.
> Hafað se awyrgda   wulf tostenced,
> deor dædscua,   dryhten, þin eowde,
> wide towrecene.   Þæt ðu, waldend, ær
> blode gebohtes,   þæt se bealofulla
> hyneð heardlice,   ond him on hæft nimeð
> ofer usse nioda lust.

> ["We have need of Your mercy.
> The malignant wolf, the beast of the shadow-deeds,
> Has scattered, Lord, Your flock,
> Now widely dispersed. What You, Ruler, once
> Bought with blood, the evil one
> Oppresses fiercely, and takes in his bondage
>   Against our desires"].[51]

The employment of this image in lyric 8 is particularly meaningful, since it not only resumes and expands the pastoral motif that was vaguely presented in the opening lyric but also constitutes a notable divergence from its antiphonal source.[52] Besides, the verb "tostenced" (line 256b) is also significantly used in the reference to Eadwig's misrule as provoking political dissension and favoring lack

---

[50] Burlin, *The Old English Advent*, 56–57, lines 15b–17.

[51] Burlin, *The Old English Advent*, 130-31, lines 255b–258b. The idea of the wolf scattering the flock reappears further in lyric 8: "ær . . . se swearta gæst / forteah ond fortylde" ["the black spirit once / Misled and withdrew us . . .": 130–31, lines 269b–70]. This metaphor mainly derives from a New Testament parable (John 10:11–17). Interestingly, Magennis points out that in *Andreas* the Mermedonians are described as "wælwulfas" (line 149) or "wolves of slaughter." He thus compares that occurrence with this passage from lyric 8. See Hugh Magennis, *Anglo-Saxon Appetites: Food and Drink and their Consumption in Old English and Related Literature* (Dublin, 1999), 66.

[52] "O Rex pacifice, Tu ante saecula nate: per auream egredere portam, redemptos tuos visita, et eos illuc revoca unde ruerunt per culpam" ["O King of peace, born before the ages: come forth through the golden gate, visit your redeemed ones and fetch them back to the place whence, through sin, they fell"]: Burlin, *The Old English Advent*, 132; trans. *Anglo-Saxon Poetry*, ed. Bradley, 211.

of unity in the excerpt from "King Edgar's Establishment of the Monasteries" quoted above.[53]

In this light, the assumption that to contemporary readers the reference to the wolf scattering the flock in lyric 8 could stand for unreformed and reformed factions seems fairly reasonable. These metaphorical implications might also affect the antithetical reference to the longing-for-Advent prisoners and the tormentor menacing them, as presented further in the poem:

> Forþon we, nergend, þe
> biddað geornlice   breostgehygdum
> þæt þu hrædlice helpe   gefremme
> wergum wreccan,   þæt se wites bona
> in helle grund   hean gedreose . . .

> ["Therefore, to You, Savior,
> We eagerly pray in our innermost thoughts
> That You may quickly bring help
> To the weary exiles, that the tormenting murderer
> To the abyss of hell may fall abject . . ."][54]

The oppositional dichotomies occurring in both lyric 1 and 8 thus gain significance in a contextualized reading:

> Lyric 1
> weallstan (2a) / wyrhtan (2b)
> weall wið wealle (11a)
> wergan heap (16a) / wraþum (16b)

> Lyric 8
> wulf (256b) / eowde (257b)
> wergum wreccan (264a)[55] / wites bona (264b)
> leodsceaþan (273a, "the enemy of man") / lifgende god (273b, "living God")

An idea that supports the author's awareness of the antithetical role of these pairs is the presence of alliteration affecting their constituents—with the exception of the "wulf/eowde" couple occurring in different lines. This suggests that the Advent poet had those dichotomies in mind and that a contemporary audience might have interpreted them as hinting at real clashing factions at that time.

---

[53] It there appears as "tostencte" (see p. 176 of this essay).
[54] Burlin, *The Old English Advent*, 130–31, lines 261b–265.
[55] Note also the parallelism with the phrase "wergan heap" in lyric 1.

Although pastoral imagery as found in lyric 8 is actually a wellknown rhetorical convention throughout the Middle Ages, the topos seems to have enjoyed a special popularity during the Benedictine revival. To begin with, it is pervasive in St. Benedict's Rule, since, as explained by Deshman, this text "applied this pastoral metaphor to the abbot who, as the vicar of Christ in the 'sheep-fold' of the monastery, is also a 'shepherd' who must account for his governance of his flock as well as himself to the 'Shepherd' Christ after the Second Coming."[56] The analogy was thus often associated with the abbot and the monks but it could also apply to canons, as observed in the following passage from the *Enlarged Rule of Chrodegang*, the Old English translation of which has been recently linked to the Glastonbury circle of Æthelwold and Dunstan during the 940s and 950s by Michael D.C. Drout.[57]

> wel manege synt þe Cristes scep, na for Cristes lufe, ac for heora worold-wuldre and for hlafordþrimme and for gestreona þingum healdað. Soðlice þa hyrdas sceolon þa eorðlican helpas him georne don, and freflice sceal him ætywan rihte drohtnunge ge mid godum bysnum, ge eac mid wordpre-dicungum.

> ["there are too many who look after Christ's sheep not out of love for Christ but because they strive for worldly glory and power and riches. Truly the shepherds shall grant them earthly help and willingly and carefully teach them the correct conduct through good examples as well as through preaching"].[58]

Here the term "hyrdas" is employed for the priests who are urged to supply their "scep" (parishoners) with both material and spiritual assistance.[59]

The prominence of pastoral imagery is also attested to in visual art, as illustrated in a picture from Oxford, St. John's College, MS. 28 (fol. 2r), which dates

---

[56] Deshman, *The Benedictional*, 206. For a list of occurrences of this metaphor in the *Rule*, see 206 n. 88.

[57] See Michael D. C. Drout, "Re-Dating the Old English Translation of the *Enlarged Rule of Chrodegang*: The Evidence of the Prose Style," *JEGP* 103 (2004): 341–68; idem, *How Tradition Works: A Meme-Based Analysis of the Anglo-Saxon Tenth Century* (Tempe, AZ, 2006), chap. 7. My thanks to the author who pointed me to the presence of pastoral imagery in this passage and kindly provided a pre-publication copy of this book.

[58] *The Old English Version of the Enlarged Rule of Chrodegang, Edited together with the Latin Text and an English Translation*, ed. and trans. Brigitte Langefeld (Frankfurt am Main, 2003), 283, 379.

[59] The pastoral metaphor was also consonant with the role of abbesses, as attested to in "King Edgar's Establishment of the Monasteries," in which they are alluded to as "hyrdum": *Councils*, ed. Whitelock et al., 153.

from the mid-tenth century and contains a Latin version of Pseudo-Linus' *Passio Petri*.[60] In this miniature (fig. 3.2), Christ is holding a book, in which the term "pastor," from the phrase "O bone Petre, pastor et pater," has been deliberately isolated from the text so as to highlight this concept.[61] The insertion of the word in the book was most likely effected to enhance Christ's role as shepherd, an assumption that is quite reasonable, since the text is an apocryphal work dealing with Peter, the first "pastor" after Christ.[62]

   In Anglo-Saxon literature, the specifity of pastoral imagery in the Benedictine context is not easy to track, since the reference to an abbot or bishop as "pastor" was actually a cliché before the Reform.[63] However, Christopher A. Jones has pointed out the probable monastic significance of the term "hyrde" appearing in *Guthlac A*, an assumption that suggests a connection of the text with the Reform movement.[64] Besides, as stated by Michael Lapidge, "The conventions of

---

   [60] In fact this codex is the result of binding together two different manuscripts. The first one, which includes the *Passio Petri*, dates from the mid-tenth century. The second, from the turn of the century, interestingly contains a Latin version of Gregory's *Cura Pastoralis*. In this light, the two manuscripts may have been bound together due to their sharing of the pastoral leitmotif. The binder's possible acknowledgement of the common topic of the two manuscripts in turn supports my conjecture that the inclusion of the term "pastor" within the picture might have been prompted by an initial desire to highlight the pastoral motif, which was probably evident in the first manuscript when it was still independent. Furthermore, as pointed out by John, "most of the manuscript . . . is from St Augustine's, Canterbury, but the drawing itself may be from Glastonbury": Eric John, "The Age of Edgar," in *The Anglo-Saxons*, ed. James Campbell et al. (Harmondsworth, 1991), 181, note to fig. 156. If John's assumption is correct, the Glastonbury provenance suggests a Benedictine affiliation of the picture that may corroborate the significance of the enhancement of the term "pastor." My thanks to Frederick Biggs who kindly helped me to find out information about the contents of the first manuscript.

   [61] In the picture the word "pastor" (in black ink as the rest of the text) is enhanced due to the contrast given by the reddish color of both Christ and the book's outline.

   [62] *Acta Apostolorum Apocrypha*, *Acta Petri*, ed. Ricardus Adelbertus Lipsius (Hildesheim, 1959), 1–22, here 6.

   [63] Not surprisingly, Swithun is labeled "pastor" in different passages from his Latin *vitae* and the liturgical pieces commemorating this saint. For the characterization of St. Swithun as "pastor" in liturgy, see *The Cult*, ed. Lapidge, 76–77, 96–97, 132–33. As for the employment of the epithet "pastor" in hagiographic works, see Wulfstan Cantor's *Narratio* (408–9, line 173) and the anonymous *Vita S. Swithuni* (330–31, line 1) in the same edition.

   [64] Note, for example, the occurrence of "hyrdes" (line 217b), and "hyrde" (lines 318a and 789a) in *Guthlac A*. See Christopher A. Jones, "Envisioning the *Cenobium* 271. See also Patrick W. Conner, "Source Studies, the Old English *Guthlac A* and the English Benedictine Reformation," *Revue Bénédictine* 103 (1993): 380–413; idem, *Anglo-Saxon Exeter*, 162–63.

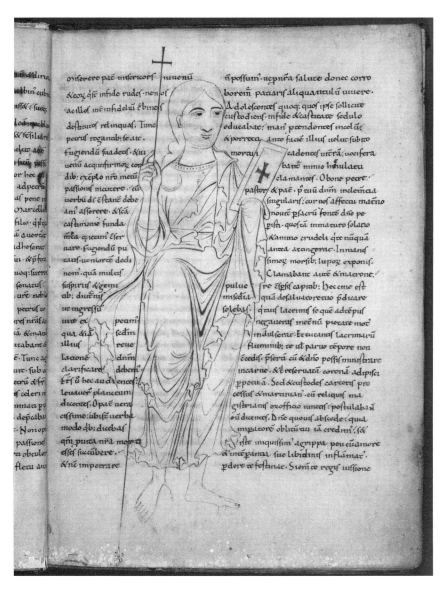

Fig. 3.2. Oxford, St. John's College, MS. 28, fol. 2r. By permission of the President and scholars of St. John the Baptist College in the University of Oxford.

describing Æthelwold and his pupils in terms of shepherd/flock and father/children are frequently found in the Latin writings produced at late tenth-century Winchester."[65] Also, there are particular passages in which the employment of this topos displays a clear contemporary stamp. An example of this is observed in Godemann's metrical preface to Æthelwold's Benedictional:[66]

> craxare hunc sibi prescriptus fecit boanerges
> idcirco ut soteris populum in biblo potuisset
> sanctificare, deoque preces effundere sacras
> pro grege commisso, nullum quo perdat ouilis
> agniculum paruum, ualeat sed dicere laetus:
> 'memet ego adsigno ecce tibi pueros quoque quos tu
> seruandos mihi iam dederas; nullum lupus audax
> exillis rapuit lurcon temet faciente.
> Sed simul adstamus uitam cupimusque manentem
> percipere, in caelisque frui cum principe summo
> cuius membra sumus . . .'

["This book the Boanerges aforesaid (Æthelwold) caused to be indited for himself and in order that he might be able to sanctify the people of the Saviour by means of it and to pour forth holy prayers to God for the flock committed to him, and that he may lose no little lambkin of the fold, but may be able to say joyfully, 'Lo, I present to thee myself and the children whom thou didst give me to keep; by thy aid not one of them has the fierce ravening wolf snatched away (cf. John 17:12), but we stand together and desire to

---

[65] Michael Lapidge, "Æthelwold as Scholar and Teacher," in *Bishop Æthelwold: His Career and Influence*, ed. Barbara Yorke (Woodbridge, 1988), 89–117, here 107. The Alençon liturgical pieces, which were most likely specifically composed for Æthelwold's cult by Wulfstan Cantor, attest to the presence of this commonplace image applying to the figure of Æthelwold. Notably, the sequence opens with a hymn for Vespers: "Inclitus pastor populique rector, / Cuius insignem colimus triumphum, / Nunc Adeluuoldus sine fine letus / Regnat in astris" ["Æthelwold, the excellent shepherd and ruler of the people, whose glorious triumph we celebrate, now rules joyous in heaven without end"] (lines 1–4). In a subsequent hymn Æthelwold is styled as "sancte pastor ecclesie" ["Shepherd of Holy Church"] (line 2): *Wulfstan of Winchester*, ed. Lapidge and Winterbottom, cxiii–cxiv. The manuscript (Alençon, Bibl. Mun. 14) dates from the twelfth century but these devotional compositions (on fols. 34v–36r) are most likely linked to tenth-century Winchester. For Lapidge's arguments in favor of Wulfstan's authorship for the Alençon pieces, see "Æthelwold as Scholar," 116–17. For further examples of this metaphor in the Alençon pieces and in the "Portiforium of St. Wulstan" (CCCC 391), see *Wulfstan of Winchester*, ed. Lapidge and Winterbottom, cvi–cxxi.

[66] This poem is a good illustration of the so-called "Hermeneutic Style." For a survey of the characteristics of this trend, see Michael Lapidge, "The Hermeneutic Style in Tenth-Century Anglo-Latin Literature," *ASE* 4 (1975): 67–111.

receive abiding life and to enjoy it in the heavens with the supreme sovereign whose members we are . . ."].[67]

In this poem, the reference to the community standing together despite the wolf's attacks is a significant element that bears witness to the possible reformist bias of this rhetorical convention.

A further interesting example occurs in author B's *Vita S. Dunstani*, in which the saint is alluded to as a shepherd furnishing the Glastonbury monastery with high walls so that his sheep are brought together and protected from external dangers: "Tunc ergo perprudens opilio, primum scepta claustrorum monasticis ædificiis cæterisque inmunitionibus . . . ex omni parte firmiter munivit; ubi oves Dominicas longe lateque gregatim collectas, ne a lupo invisibili dilaniarentur, includeret" ["Then, as a very prudent shepherd, he first fortified firmly the fences of the precincts on every side with monastic buildings and other defences. . . . There he enclosed the Lord's sheep, gathered in flocks from far and wide, that they might not be torn to pieces by the invisible wolf"].[68] Here the pastoral metaphor effectively merges with the allusion to the saint's involvement in the construction task, thus illustrating again the idea of communal unity as an essential Benedictine principle. There is also a passage from Wulfstan Cantor's *Vita S. Æthelwoldi* that is worth noting: "Exinde superna pietas sancto pontifici tantam contulit gratiam ut sublimes illi saecularium potestatum principes, duces, tyranni atque iudices et omnes qui ei hactenus contrarii et in uia Dei resistere uidebantur subito uelut oues ex lupis efficerentur . . ." ["Furthermore, God in his love gave such grace to the holy bishop that those high lay dignitaries, ealdormen, potentates, and judges, and all who had previously seemed his enemies, standing in God's path, were suddenly made, as it were, sheep instead of wolves . . ."].[69] In this ex-

---

[67] Lapidge, "The Hermeneutic Style," 106, lines 15–25 (see also lines 1–5); trans. in *The Benedictional of St Æthelwold, Bishop of Winchester 963–984*, ed. G. F. Warner and H. A. Wilson (Oxford, 1910), xii–xiii.

[68] *Memorials*, ed. Stubbs, 25; trans. in *English Historical Documents*, ed. Whitelock, 899.

[69] *Wulfstan of Winchester*, ed. Lapidge and Winterbottom, 60-63. In this work the identification of Æthelwold with the Good Shepherd occurs frequently: "Pater erat et pastor monachorum, peruigil sanctimonialium protector et uirginum, uiduarum consolator, peregrinorum susceptor, ecclesiarum defensor . . ." ["He was a father and a shepherd to his monks, an unsleeping champion of nuns and virgins, consoler of widows, receiver of pilgrims, defender of churches"] (44–45). The image reappears in the description of his funeral (62–63). The reference to Æthelwold as a shepherd is also present in Wulfstan's *Narratio*: "Summus et antistes, patrie decus, altor egentum, / spes peregrinorum, splendor honorque patrum, / noster Aðeluuoldus, pastor, pater atque magister" ["And there too is the greatest of bishops, the glory of his country, the sustainer of the poor, the hope of pilgrims, a celebrity and eminence among the fathers, Æthelwold, our own shepherd, father and teacher"]: *The Cult*, ed. Lapidge, 394–95, lines 271–273.

cerpt the analogy is interestingly used to refer to the opponents of the Reform as wolves that have miraculously been turned into sheep thanks to the bishop.

Pastoral imagery did not apply only to the leading reformers, since there is evidence that Edgar's role as monarch was also compared to that of a shepherd. The convention is famously employed in the preface to the *Regularis Concordia*: "Regali utique functus officio ueluti Pastorum Pastor sollicitus a rabidis perfidorum rictibus, uti hiantibus luporum faucibus, oues quas Domini largiente gratia studiosus collegerat muniendo eripuit" ["Thus, in fulfilment of his royal office, even as the Good Shepherd, he carefully rescued and defended from the savage open mouths of the wicked—as it were the gaping jaws of wolves—those sheep which by God's grace he had diligently gathered together"].[70] As in the preceding passage from the *Vita S. Æthelwoldi*, the enemies of the Reform are here presented as ravenous wolves threatening God's flock, whereas Edgar, as the Good Shepherd, is said to be the only one capable of holding the community together.[71]

The passages discussed so far suggest that the pastoral metaphor effectively applied to Christ, Æthelwold, Dunstan, and Edgar alike, thus possibly revealing its tight connection to Benedictine ideology. But pastoral imagery was not restricted to the literature appearing in the first stages of the Benedictine revival, since it was also employed by the second generation of Reform-era writers. For example, Ælfric devotes the whole of Catholic Homily 17 (*Dominica secunda post pascha*) to expounding the significance of the biblical passage (John 10:11–17) from which the pastoral metaphor derives.[72] Furthermore, in Homily 2 of the same collection he makes use of the wolf/sheep cliché: "Þam lareowe gedafenað þ[æt] he symle wacol sy ofer godes eowede. þ[æt] se ungesewenlica wulf godes scep ne tostence." ["It is fitting that the preacher be watchful over God's sheep so that the invisible wolf does not scatter God's sheep"].[73] The passage significantly

---

[70] *Regularis Concordia*, ed. Symons, 2. For further comments on this passage, see Deshman, "*Benedictus Monarcha et Monachus*," 225–28, and idem, *The Benedictional*, 205–6. See also Karkov, *Ruler Portraits*, 100–1.

[71] A further noteworthy example of this metaphor is found in the "New Minster Refoundation Charter," in which the role of Edgar's successors is equated with that of shepherds watching their flock: "Reges itaque quicumque nostri fuerint successores . . . in nullo a reguli preceptis discordantes . Domini gregem non mercenarii sed pastores fidissimi . luporum rictibus eximentes intrepidi defendant." ["Whichever kings therefore shall be our successors . . . dissenting in no respect from the commands of the Rule, not as hirelings (cf. John 10: 12–13) but as most faithful shepherds let them, intrepid, defend the Lord's flock, delivering it from the jaws of the wolves"]: *Property and Piety*, ed. Rumble, 88.

[72] For further occurrences of the wolf/sheep topos in Anglo-Saxon literature, see Magennis, *Anglo-Saxon Appetites*, 66–67.

[73] *Ælfric's Catholic Homilies*, ed. Clemoes, 313–16 and the passage from Homily 2 on 193–94. My translation. Brackets supply abbreviated words.

appears in the homily for Christmas (*Nativitas domini*) and the phrasing closely parallels the excerpts of Advent lyric 8 discussed above. Pastoral images are also frequently employed by Wulfstan the Homilist in his *Institutes of Polity*, an early eleventh-century treatise that opens with a description of the characteristics of ideal kingship: "Cristenum cyninge gebyreð on cristenre þeode, þæt he sy, ealswa hit riht is, folces frofer and rihtwis hyrde ofer cristene heorde." ["It behoves the Christian king in a Christian nation to be, as is right, the people's comfort and a righteous shepherd over the Christian flock"].[74] This passage therefore attests to the continuity of pastoral imagery in the pre-Conquest reformist milieu.

In any event, the pastoral metaphor is an old commonplace that cannot be associated with the Reform period alone. For Anglo-Saxons, the analogy was well known from Gregory the Great's *Cura Pastoralis*, a central piece in Alfred's educational program.[75] It was also popular in Carolingian poetry, in which pastoral imagery was frequently applied to Charlemagne, who was usually compared to Christ and David.[76] However, it may be assumed that the image gained special prominence in late tenth- and early eleventh-century texts as a result of reformist interests in the revival of Alfredian and Carolingian topoi.[77]

A further remarkable aspect of the Advent sequence is the conspicuous emphasis placed on Christ/God's kingship, as pointed out by Earl R. Anderson, who notes that "Multiple epithets for Godhead are also a characteristic of the

[74] *Die 'Institutes of Polity, Civil and Ecclesiastical'*, ed. Karl Jost (Bern, 1959). *Anglo-Saxon Prose*, ed. Michael Swanton (London, 1993), 188. In *The Institutes* the pastoral metaphor also applies to bishops, priests, and reeves (see Jost's edition, sections 6 and 10). The image is also employed by Wulfstan in Homily XVIb, lines 35–36. See *The Homilies of Wulfstan*, ed. Dorothy Bethurum (Oxford, 1957), 241. For a discussion of pastoral metaphors applying to bishops and priests in the latter homily, see Jonathan Wilcox, "The Wolf on Shepherds: Wulfstan, Bishops, and the Context of the *Sermo Lupi ad Anglos*," in *Old English Prose: Basic Readings*, ed. Paul E. Szarmach (New York, 2000), 395–418, esp. 398–400.

[75] For a discussion of late tenth-century pastoral imagery as being inherited from the Alfredian period, see Karkov, *Ruler Portraits*, 100–1.

[76] Murray notes that "The Carolingian age perhaps read that image more completely and more historically than any earlier or subsequent age, and expressed its meaning more successfully": Oswyn Murray, "The Idea of the Shepherd King from Cyrus to Charlemagne," in *Latin Poetry and the Classical Tradition: Essays in Medieval and Renaissance Literature*, ed. Peter Godman and Oswyn Murray (Oxford, 1990), 1–14, here 14.

[77] Alfredian revival during the Reform period is also attested to in Edgar's adoption of some of Alfred's coin types. I thank Catherine E. Karkov for kindly pointing this out to me. See her comments in *Ruler Portraits*, 102–5. Also see Kenneth Jonsson, *The New Era: The Reformation of the Late Anglo-Saxon Coinage* (London, 1987).

Advent Lyrics . . .".[78] Indeed, despite the poem's fragmentary form, in lyric 1 the term "cyning" is employed twice (lines 1b and 12b); also, "wuldres ealdor" (line 8b) stresses Christ's royal status in the same poem. Similarly, two of the lyrics start with a forceful statement of Christ's kingship; lyric 2 thus reads "Eala þu reccend ond þu riht cyning . . ." ["You, O Ruler and rightful King . . . ," line 1] and lyric 8 in turn refers to Christ as "ealra cyninga cyning" (line 251a), an epithet that establishes his imperial nature and recurs in lyric 6 (line 136a). Lyric 11 deploys a significant set of kingly epithets as, for example, "sigores frea" ("Prince of victory," line 404a) and "dryhtna dryhten"(line 405a). Finally, lyric 12 alludes to Christ as being a consecrated king, "se gehalgoda" (line 435a).

Despite the pervasive occurrence of some of these epithets in medieval religious poetry, the insistence on Christ's royal and imperial character in the Advent sequence has been associated by Deshman with pro-Reform pictures in which Christ's role as king and emperor is similarly underlined. In Æthelwold's Benedictional (fol. 9v), for instance, the miniature of the Second Coming (fig. 3.3) is particularly revealing because Christ's mantle presents a golden-lettered inscription proclaiming him as "Rex regum et Dom(i)n(u)s dominatiu(m)."[79] In the frontispiece to the "New Minster Refoundation Charter" (fig. 3.4) the christological role assigned to Edgar has been thoroughly studied by Deshman who affirms that the cross and the key, held respectively by the Virgin Mary and St. Peter, were connected to the notion of the *clavis David*, "which signified Christ's power to open or close the gates of heaven, earth, and hell . . ." (197).[80] This symbol was employed in Æthelwold's Benedictional and the second coronation *ordo*, the service used in Edgar's coronation ceremony.[81] As noted by Deshman, the *clavis David* motif is precisely the central idea of the antiphon that was used by

---

[78] Anderson has also noted the relevance of this characteristic in *Christ II*: "Among the epithets for Godhead, the most prominent semantic category is the group attesting to God's rulership or kingship — 55 references, 41 epithets": Earl R. Anderson, *Cynewulf: Structure, Style, and Theme in His Poetry* (London, 1983), 56. For an account of the differences in the use of epithets related to kingship in the Advent Lyrics and *Christ II*, see 58–59.

[79] As pointed out by Deshman (*The Benedictional*, 64), this picture paraphrases Revelation 19:16: "On his robe and on his thigh he has a name inscribed, King of kings, and Lord of lords." For a full commentary on this miniature see 64–69.

[80] See Deshman, *The Benedictional*, 197. Also, as pointed out by Karkov, "The typological relationship between Christ and Edgar [in the Charter frontispiece] is reinforced by the purple background against which the scene is set. Purple was a colour which symbolised both royalty and the blood of Christ, and one which had definite imperial connotations": *Ruler Portraits*, 86.

[81] See Deshman's comments on fol. 56v (The Doubting of Thomas, plate 21) in *The Benedictional*, 197. See also Janet L. Nelson, "The Second English Ordo," in eadem, *Politics and Ritual in Early Medieval Europe* (London, 1986), 361–74.

Fig. 3.3. London, BL, MS. Add. 49598, fol. 9v. By permission of the British Library.

Fig. 3.4. London, BL, MS. Cotton Vespasian A.viii, fol. 2v. By permission of the British Library.

the Advent poet to compose lyric 2, whose initial lines develop this motif: "Eala þu reccend ond þu riht cyning, / se þe locan healdeð, lif ontyneð, / eadga[an] upwegas . . ." ["You, O Ruler and rightful King, Who guard the lock, Who open life, the blessed ways to heaven . . ."].[82] Lyric 2 therefore betrays a further possible link with the propagandistic symbols of the Reform.

On other hand, the panegyric known as "King Edgar's Coronation," contained in the A-version of the Chronicle (year 973), is also particularly helpful for demonstrating the contemporary coloring of the Christological images employed in the Advent sequence:

> Her Eadgar wæs,   Engla waldend,
> corðre micelre   to cyninge gehalgod
> on ðære ealdan byrig,   Acemannesceastre;
> eac hi igbuend   oðre worde
> beornas Baðan nemnaþ.   Þær wæs blis micel
> on þam eadgan dæge   eallum geworden,
> þon(n)e niða bearn   nemnað 7 cigað
> Pentecostenes dæg.   Þær wæs preosta heap,
> micel muneca ðreat,   mine gefrege,
> gleawra gegaderod.   7 ða agangen wæs
> tyn hund wintra   geteled rimes
> fram gebyrdtide   bremes cyninges,
> leohta hyrdes,   buton ðær to lafe þa (a)g<e>n
> wæs wintergeteles,   þæs ðe gewritu secgað,
> seofon 7 twentig;   swa neah wæs sigora frean
> ðusend aurnen,   ða þa ðis gelamp.
> 7 him Eadmundes   eafora hæfde
> nigon 7 .xx.,   niðweorca heard,
> wintra on worulde,   <þa> þis geworden wæs,
> 7 þa on ðam .xxx. wæs   ðeoden gehalgod.

["In this year Edgar, ruler of the English, with a great company, was consecrated king in the ancient borough, *Acemannesceaster*—the men who dwell

---

[82] Burlin, *The Old English Advent*, 68–69, lines 1–3a. For a study of this passage, see Stanley B. Greenfield, "Of Locks and Keys–line 19a of the OE *Christ*," *Modern Language Notes* 67 (1952): 238–40. See also Burlin's comments on lyric 2: *The Old English Advent*, 70–77. The antiphon on which lyric 2 is based reads "O Clavis David, et sceptrum domus Israel, qui aperis et nemo claudit, claudis et nemo aperit, veni et educ vinctum de domo carceris, sedentem in tenebris, et umbra mortis." ["O key of David and sceptre of the house of Israel, you who open and no one closes: you who close and no one opens (Rev. 3:7): come and lead out of the prison-house the captive who sits in darkness and the shadow of death"]: 70; trans. in *Anglo-Saxon Poetry*, ed. Bradley, 205. The metaphor of the keys and the doors (or locks) reappears in lyric 8 (lines 250–255).

in this island also call it by another name, Bath. There great joy had come
to all on that blessed day which the children of men call and name the day
of Pentecost. There was assembled a crowd of priests, a great throng of
learned monks, as I have heard tell. And then had passed from the birth of
the glorious King, the Guardian of Light, ten hundred years reckoned in
numbers, except that there yet remained, by what documents say, seven and
twenty of the number of years, so nearly had passed away a thousand years
of the Lord of Victories, when this took place. And Edmund's son, bold in
battle, had spent twenty-nine years in the world when this came about, and
then in the thirtieth was consecrated king."][83]

This magnificent piece of royalist propaganda contains some of the images that
have been discussed so far. Edgar's role as consecrated king is clearly stressed, as
the term "gehalgod" is mentioned twice (lines 2b and 20b). His sacerdotal condition is likewise suggested, since he is said to have reached the canonical age
(30 years) for priestly consecration.[84] In addition, Christ, to whom the monarch
is indirectly likened, is alluded to as "leohta hyrdes" (line 13a) or "Shepherd of
Lights," which connects with the pastoral imagery discussed above.[85]

Interestingly, Advent lyric 6 introduces the notion of Christ as king of kings
and as partaking of both royal and priestly condition in a passage that is worth
analyzing:

> Swa þæt gomele gefyrn
> ealra cyninga cyning   ond þone clænan eac
> sacerd soðlice   sægdon toweard,

---

[83] *The Anglo-Saxon Chronicle*, ed. Bately, 76–77; trans. in *English Historical Documents*, ed. Whitelock, 227–28. The poem is also in Manuscripts B and C.

[84] As pointed out by Magennis, "the congregation is of ecclesiastics and wise men,
a fact which emphasizes the coincidence of religious and secular in Edgar's rule": Hugh
Magennis, *Images of Community in Old English Poetry* (Cambridge, 1996), 196.

[85] Karkov has noted the significant employment of the well-known paronomastic
pair *angelorum/anglorum* in the "New Minster Refoundation Charter," which alludes to
both angels and Edgar: "The charter begins with a reference to angelic (*angelica*) creation, and to the fall of the angels (*angelorum*), and the fact that men enjoyed the fellow-
ship of the angels (*angelorum*), and it ends with Edgar's subscription as king of the English (*Anglorum basileus*)": Karkov, *Ruler Portraits*, 88. She has pointed out a similar playful
use of "engla" in *The Death of Edgar*, contained in the A-B-C versions of the Chronicle
(year 975). In this poem the king is styled "Engla cyning" (line 2a) at the start and is later
referred to as "Brego engla" (36a) at the end: (88 n. 17). Furthermore, Edgar is alluded
to as "Engla waldend" (1b) in the coronation poem. In this light, the presence of the epithet "heahengla brego" ("chief of the archangels," line 403b) applying to Christ in Advent
lyric 11 is therefore highly suggestive.

swa se mæra iu,   Melchisedech,
gleaw in gæste   godþrym onwrah
eces alwaldan.

["As sages of former times accurately foretold
The King of all Kings and immaculate Priest,
So, too, of old the great Melchisedech,
Wise in spirit, revealed the divine majesty
Of the eternal Ruler"].[86]

Here the reference to Christ's Advent as being prefigured by Melchisedech represents a remarkable departure from the original antiphon, in which the term "Legifer" (law-giver), from "O Emmanuel, Rex et Legifer noster," has also been changed for Old English "sacerd" (line 137a).[87] As Burlin comments, the replacement of the antiphonal word "enables the poet to include Melchisedech, 'rex Salem, sacerdos Dei summi' (Heb. 7:1)."[88] Indeed, the presence of this Old Testament figure in the lyric can be explained on the basis of the allusion to Melchisedech in St. Paul's Epistle to the Hebrews (7:2–3):

He is first, by translation of his name, king of righteousness, and then he is also king of Salem, that is, king of peace. He is without father or mother or genealogy, and has neither beginning of days nor end of life, but resembling the Son of God he continues as priest for ever.

Campbell adds that Melchisedech was viewed "as a prefiguring of the priesthood of Christ" while "the epithet 'King of Salem' was taken as a foreshadowing of Christ's title, 'Prince of Peace.'"[89] The latter aspect must have been particularly

---

[86] Burlin, *The Old English Advent*, 106–7, lines 135b–140a.

[87] The complete antiphon on which lyric 6 is based reads as follows: "O Emmanuel, Rex et Legifer noster, exspectatio gentium et salvator earum: Veni ad salvandum nos, Dominus Deus noster" ["O Emmanuel, our King and Lawgiver, Hope of the nations and their Saviour: come to save us, Lord our God"]: Burlin, *The Old English Advent*, 108; trans. in *Anglo-Saxon Poetry*, ed. Bradley, 208. The term "Legifer" is used later in the lyric with the phrase "æ bringend" (140b). Campbell has likewise pointed out the original handling of the antiphonal source, as he affirms that lyric 6 "is a good example to use in order to demonstrate how the poet could take one or two suggestions from the antiphon *O Emanuhel*, bring in other material from the Bible and standard Christian belief, and eventually create something which is entirely new": Jackson J. Campbell, "Structural Patterns in the Old English Advent Lyrics," *English Language Notes* 23 (1956): 239–55, here 242.

[88] Burlin, *The Old English Advent*, 109.

[89] Campbell, "Structural Patterns," 243.

appealing to the Advent poet, as it would clearly connect with lyric 3 that is devoted to reflecting on the special status of Jerusalem as the sacred city receiving Christ's Advent. Not surprisingly, this lyric opens with an allusion to the traditional etymology of Jerusalem ("visio pacis"): "Eala sibbe gesihð, sancta Hierusalem."[90] Lyric 8 returns to the idea of Christ as supreme ruler of peace: "Eala þu soða ond þu sibsuma / ealra cyninga cyning, Crist ælmihtig . . ." ["You, O true and You, O peaceable King of all kings, almighty Christ . . ."].[91] In this light, it is quite clear that for the Advent poet the figure of Melchisedech, the concept of Jerusalem as the *visio pacis*, and the notion of Christ as king of peace were interconnected.

According to this, we may tentatively consider the possibility that Melchisedech could have enjoyed a prominent position in Benedictine mythography. To begin with, Melchisedech would surely have been known to a monastic audience well-trained in the singing of the psalter, since he is mentioned in Psalm 109 [110]:4: "You are a priest for ever after the order of Mechisedech."[92] As stated in Genesis 14:17–20, he was a Canaanite priest-king who honored Abraham on his return from battle by offering him bread and wine.[93] For a pro-Reform audience the episode might have been particularly enlightening, since Melchisedech, like

---

[90] Burlin, *The Old English Advent*, 80–81, line 50. The myth of the New Jerusalem, which is present in lyric 3, as a symbol of the renewal of the Church was also particularly akin to Benedictine concerns. Note, for example, the description of Winchester as the New Jerusalem in which the Reform would succesfully flourish in the dream account found in Wulfstan's *Vita S. Æthelwoldi*: *Wulfstan of Winchester*, ed. Lapidge and Winterbottom, 4–7. A contextualized analysis of lyric 3 would thus be reasonable here but the limits of this essay do not allow me to provide one. See also Deshman's discussion of this aspect as part of the Benedictine program in *The Benedictional*, 198–200; Paul E. Szarmach, *"Visio Pacis*: Jerusalem and Its Meanings," in *Typology and English Medieval Literature*, ed. Hugh T. Keenan (New York, 1992), 71–87.

[91] Burlin, *The Old English Advent*, 128–29, lines 214–15.

[92] For example, the Royal Psalter (London, BL, Royal 2.B.v), the Old English glosses of which have been convincingly attributed to Æthelwold by Gretsch, gives the following reading for that psalm verse: "Swor & na hreoweð hine þu sacerd on ecnesse æfter endebyrdnesse melchisedec": *Der altenglische Regius-Psalter*, ed. F. Roedor (Halle, 1904: repr. Tübingen, 1973), 212. For the Æthelwoldian authorship of the Royal Psalter glosses, see Gretsch, *The Intellectual Foundations*, 261–331.

[93] As stated in the Old English *Genesis* (14:18), "Þær com eac Melchisedech, se mæra Godes man, se wæs cyning 7 Godes sacerd; 7 he brohte hlaf 7 win" ["There also came Melchisedech, God's renowned man, who was king and God's priest; and he brought bread and wine"]: *The Old English Version of the Heptateuch: Ælfric's Treatise on the Old and New Testament, and his Preface to Genesis*, ed. S. J. Crawford, EETS 160 (London, 1969), 120. My translation.

Eadsige in Swithun's hagiographies, would possibly offer an interesting example of a conversion to "canonical" religion. This assumption may be supported by the allusion to Melchisedech as a prototype priest in some of the liturgical pieces composed for St. Swithun's cult. Notably, in the so-called "Winchester tropers"—contained in Oxford, Bodleian Library, Bodley 775 and Cambridge, Corpus Christi College 473—the saint is directly equated to Melchisedech in the first piece for the Introit commemorating his deposition:[94]

> Ecce patronus adest meritis signisque refulgens;
> de quo dulcisonum personat officium.
> STATVIT EI <DOMINUS TESTAMENTUM PACIS>
> Quod maneat solido firmum per secula pacto.
> ET PRINCIPEM <FECIT EUM>
>   Ordine Melchisedech libamina sacra ferentem.
> VT SIT ILLI <SACERDOTII DIGNITAS>
> O Suuithune tuos defende benignus alumpnos.
> IN AETERNUM.

> ["Behold, our patron saint is present, gleaming with accomplishments and miracles; in his honour a sweet service resounds. Let it remain forever fixed through a firm agreement. Melchisedech, bearing the sacred offerings from his order (the priesthood). O gentle Swithun, protect your followers"].[95]

Following this item, a subsequent trope introduces the idea of peace, no doubt connected to the figure of Melchisedech as commented on above:

> Aurea lux hodie rutilat Suuithunus in orbe,
> qui quia pacificus fuerat mitissimus atque
> STATVIT EI <DOMINUS TESTAMENTUM PACIS>
> gentibus Anglorum pacem mittendo per illum
> ET PRINCIPEM <FECIT EUM>
>   pontificale decus concessit eique benignus.
> VT SIT ILLI <SACERDOTII DIGNITAS>
>   Huius nos meritis Christus conscribat in astris.
> IN AETERNUM.

---

[94] The two manuscripts most likely originated at the Old Minster, Winchester. As noted by Lapidge (*The Cult*, 90), Bodley 775 dates from the mid-eleventh century but was "possibly based on an earlier Winchester exemplar"; CCC 473 in turn was written ca. 1000, "apparently for the use of the precentor there (presumptively Wulfstan of Winchester himself)."

[95] *The Cult*, ed. Lapidge, 90–91. Capitalization (upper-case letters for the chants and lower-case for the tropes) and punctuation follow Lapidge.

["A golden light—Swithun—shines in the world today, who, because he was peaceful and gentle, by sending peace through him to the English peoples, He, the Kindly One, granted to him pontifical distinction. May Christ enrol us in the heavens through his merits"].[96]

The third trope in the introit sequence again insists on Swithun's belonging to Melchisedech's order, this time paraphrasing the Greek Septuagint version of Psalm 109 [110]:4:

Os ky hereos kata tin taxin Melchisedech
STATVIT EI <DOMINUS TESTAMENTUM PACIS>
ut uigeat summus stola uernante sacerdos
ET PRINCIPEM <FECIT EUM>
inter primates regni celestis heriles.
VT SIT ILLI <SACERDOTII DIGNITAS>
Grex tuus, Suuithune, petit memorare tuorum.
IN AETERNUM.

["You are a priest according to the order of Melchisedech, so that this high priest might flourish with his radiant stole amidst the lordly princes of the heavenly realm. O Swithun, your flock requests that you remember your own"].[97]

The thematic pattern of the three tropes thus strikingly recalls the description of Christ as a priest, belonging to Melchisedech's order, and as a harbinger of peace in the Advent Lyrics. However, the occurrence of this image cannot be ascribed to English Benedictine circles alone, since the third piece of the introit sequence, as pointed out by Lapidge, "is preserved in many continental tropers, especially from Saint-Gallen in Switzerland and Saint-Martial of Limoges in Aquitaine."[98] Besides, he adds that the same trope "is used to commemorate numerous saints, including Saint-Martin and Saint-Martial, and was apparently adapted at Winchester to commemorate Saint-Swithun."[99] Even if the reference

---

[96] *The Cult*, ed. Lapidge, 91.

[97] *The Cult*, ed. Lapidge, 91–92. For further comments on the third trope, see Susan Rankin, "Saint-Swithun in Medieval Liturgical Music," in *The Cult*, ed. Lapidge, 191–213, here 192–99; for a general discussion of the Swithun tropes, see A. E. Planchart, *The Repertory of Tropes at Winchester*, 2 vols. (Princeton, NJ, 1977), 1: 105–7.

[98] *The Cult*, ed. Lapidge, 91 n. 77.

[99] *The Cult*, ed. Lapidge, 91 n. 77. Indeed, the prominence of the figure of Melchisedech as a type of Christ is also attested to in Carolingian illumination. In the *Drogo Sacramentary*, a text whose strong influence on the iconography of Æthelwold's Benedictional has been pointed out by Deshman, the figure of Melchisedech appears in the crossing of

to Melchisedech in lyric 6 and the tropes is simply a rhetorical formula deriving from Frankish sources, it is currently assumed that Carolingian influence on the English Benedictine Reform was strong.[100] Also, we should take into account that the first two tropes of the sequence appear only in the two Winchester manuscripts cited above, so that it may be inferred that they are English compositions, as observed by Lapidge.[101] This gives us a cue to suspect that Swithun's identification with Melchisedech in the first trope and his characterization as a harbinger of peace for the English in the second might point to the popularity of these images in the cultural milieu of tenth-century Winchester.[102] Consequently, the description of Christ as Melchisedech's type in lyric 6 seems to betray a Benedictine bias.

The pre-eminence of the Advent theme in the Reform period is beyond doubt. As discussed above, the notable role of Advent as a topic in the "New Minster Refoundation Charter" and the "Peniarth Diploma" shows that this concept had a special meaning in pro-Reform works. The popularity of this topic is probably related to the fact that, after his coronation, Edgar was acknowledged as *Christus domini* (the Lord's anointed), in other words, as an earthly counterpart

---

the initial "T" in the phrase "Te Igitur" of fol. 15v. The sacramentary, issued for Bishop Drogo's personal use, is contained in Paris, BN, MS. lat. 9428 (ca. 850, Metz). For this picture, see Deshman, *The Benedictional*, 245 and fig. 187.

[100] As for Carolingian influence, Gretsch (*The Intellectual Foundations*, 427) discusses the continental background of Æthelstan's court circle, which "provided the formative experiences" for young Æthelwold and Dunstan that would later give rise to Æthelwold's school at Winchester.

[101] *The Cult*, ed. Lapidge, 91 notes 75, 76.

[102] Actually, there are other liturgical pieces in which the analogy is present. See *The Cult*, ed. Lapidge, 82–83, 124, 128. The continuing popularity of Melchisedech in monastic circles is also attested in texts postdating the Benedictine revival. For example, this Old Testament character is alluded to among other saints in a list of relics from the New Minster: "And of Melchisedech, and of sanct Uedaste, and of sancte Ypolite": *Liber vitae: Register and Martyrology of New Minster and Hyde Abbey, Winchester*, ed. W. De G. Birch (London, 1892), 162. In *Adrian and Ritheus* — an Old English dialogue contained in BL, Cotton Julius A.ii, whose script is dated by Ker as mid-twelfth century — Melchisedech is also mentioned:

Saga me hwilc bisceop wære ærest on þare ealdan æ ær Cristes tokyme.
Ic þe secge, Melchisedech and Aaron.

["Tell me which bishop was first in the old law before the advent of Christ. / I tell you, Melchisedech and Aaron"]: *The Prose Solomon and Saturn and Adrian and Ritheus*, ed. and trans. James E. Cross and Thomas D. Hill (Toronto, 1982), 36 (no. 13). As pointed out by the editors (139), Melchisedech represents "the first named priest of the Gentiles," and Aaron that "of the Israelites." Related to the *Joca monachorum* genre, *Adrian and Ritheus* might have circulated in the monastic milieu. It is therefore significant that Melchisedech is described as prototype bishop before Christ's Advent in this text.

of Christ. As such, the concepts of Advent and the Second Coming possibly achieved great relevance, since they served to propagandize Edgar's position as king of kings. In "King Edgar's Coronation," cited above, the allusion to the proximity of the coronation date to the completion of the first millennium (lines 10b–15a) thus underlines the monarch's role as Christ's representative on earth and the event's connection to Christ's Second Coming. Apart from the king, the concept was applied to the leading reformers with similar propagandistic aims. The E-version of the Chronicle (year 963), for example, records that Æthelwold's consecration as bishop took place "on the first Sunday of Advent."[103]

Manuscript illumination also bears witness to the importance of Advent and the Second Coming in the Reform program. In the picture from "St. Dunstan's Classbook" (fig. 3.5) the archbishop is shown prostrate before a gigantic Christ characterized, as in the Second Coming, as ready to administer justice with his rod.[104] The miniature which, together with the distich above the saint's figure, has been attributed to Dunstan, is an ostensible display of Benedictine propaganda, since the book held by Christ contains a psalm verse related to the *Timor domini* motif, which is a central Benedictine concept cited at the beginning of the preface to the Rule.[105] As explained by Lapidge, "Monks are frequently referred to by Benedict as those who are *timentes Deum*."[106] The prostrate figure of Dunstan, significantly smaller than that of Christ, may have been intended to illustrate the fear of the Lord as exteriorized by the saint, who is clearly depicted as a monk, tonsured and wearing a cowl.[107]

---

[103] "on þe fyrste Sunnondæg of Aduent": *The Anglo-Saxon Chronicle*, ed. Irvine, 57. The A-B-C versions of the Chronicle similarly allude to this event as taking place on the vigil of St. Andrew (i.e., 29 November), in other words, at the beginning of Advent. This date is confirmed by Wulfstan Cantor in his *Vita S. Æthelwoldi*; see *Wulfstan of Winchester*, ed. Lapidge and Winterbottom, 30–31. As indicated by Lapidge (30 n. 2), "it is true that in 963 the first Sunday of Advent fell on 29 Nov., the vigil of the feast of St Andrew (30 Nov.) . . ."

[104] From Oxford, Bodleian Library, MS. Auct. F.4.32 (fol.1r), a composite manuscript in which items related to St. Dunstan are of Glastonbury provenance (tenth century). The picture and the distich below are attributed to Dunstan himself, as the text above reads that the text was written "de propia manu s[an]cti dunstani" (by St Dunstan's own hand). For the distich and its possible Dunstanian authorship, see Lapidge, "The Hermeneutic Style," 108.

[105] The text inserted in Christ's book is from Psalm 33 [34]:12 [11]: "Venite, filii, audite me, timorem Domini docebo vos" ["Come, sons, listen to me; I will teach you the fear of the Lord"]. (My translation.) The phrases at the two ends of the rod ("Virga recta est virga regni tui") are from Psalm 44 [45]: 7 [8].

[106] Michael Lapidge, "Byrhtferth and Oswald," in *St Oswald of Worcester: Life and Influence*, ed. Nicholas Brooks and Catherine Cubitt (Leicester, 1996), 64–83, here 82.

[107] In this train of thought, the phrase "earme from egsan" — designating the pious Christians anxiously awaiting Christ's Advent to be released from their long torment — in lyric 1 (line 17a) might be read by monastic readers as a reference to themselves as the *timentes Deum* fervently awaiting Advent.

Fig. 3.5. Oxford, Bodleian Library, MS. Auct. F.4.4.32, fol. 1r. By permission of the Bodleian Library.

By the same token, in Æthelwold's Benedictional the fact that the miniature of the Second Coming (fig. 3.3), together with that of the Annunciation (fol. 5v), serves as a heading of the liturgical section of the Benedictional confirms the prominence of Advent in the reformist milieu. A couplet facing the Annunciation miniature supports this idea: "Quisqu(e) caput cernis presto est benedictio p(re)s(u)l / Libri huius nati aduentus tibi nam patris almi" ["You, O bishop, whoever you are who looks upon this heading, a blessing of this book of the advent of the Son of the Loving Father is at hand for you"].[108] The presentation of the Benedictional as the "book of the advent of the Son" thus illustrates the outstanding pre-eminence granted to this concept during the Benedictine revival.

4. Conclusions

This study has suggested the skillful fusion of architectural metaphors such as the cornerstone, the two walls, and the ruinous building in lyric 1, and Christological images, especially those of the shepherd, king, and priest, as found in the different pieces of the Exeter Advent sequence.[109] All these images seem to highlight essential concepts related to the Reform movement—such as the urgency of communal unity, peace, and church restoration—that find echo in late tenth- and eleventh-century texts and pictures. Similarly, the notable relevance of Advent as one of the propagandistic concepts of the Reform movement has also been sufficiently illustrated in literary and pictorial works.

The Advent poet's dextrous handling of the liturgical material contributes to the hypothesis of a late tenth-century dating of the lyric sequence. The analysis offered in this essay has proved that the poet had an excellent command of the diction, imagery, and rhetorical devices employed in liturgical composition.[110] As

---

[108] On fol. 6r: *The Benedictional*, ed. Warner and Wilson, 2; trans. Deshman, *The Benedictional*, 16.

[109] In this light, the images applying to the Virgin Mary in the Advent sequence might be equally meaningful. Indeed, lyrics 4, 7, and 9 center on the active involvement of the Virgin in the mystery of the Incarnation. The extent to which Mary is celebrated as an autonomous figure in the Advent sequence leads Clayton to conclude that her prominent role in these lyrics largely surpasses that observed in other Old English works. See Mary Clayton, *The Cult of the Virgin Mary* (Cambridge, 1990), 202. Also, Raw affirms that "the range of the exegetical material used by the author of *The Advent Lyrics*, in particular the emphasis on the role of Mary, fits most easily into the period of the monastic revival": Raw, "Two Versions of Advent," 1. As the analysis of Christological and Marian imagery in the Advent sequence is too wide to be dealt with in a single essay, I intend to provide a separate contextualized study of images and metaphors applying to the figure of the Virgin in the future.

[110] Instead of merely reproducing the antiphonal sources, "The poet of *Christ* tends to create psalms out of the antiphons which inspired him," as observed by Patrick W.

discussed above, the lyrics greatly expand upon the rhetorical and thematic components of the brief antiphons.[111] In fact, the marked idiosyncrasy of the poems is evidence that the Advent author was interested in departing from the original models and adapting them to a new ideological frame which seems to be strongly akin to that of the Benedictine revival. Indeed, the ostensible contemporary stamp of the images and metaphors found in the lyrics would not have escaped a well-versed audience from the Reform period.

All this inevitably links the Advent poet with the great burst of liturgical composition under the auspices of the Reform. During this period, English Benedictinism required a newly-created pantheon that led to the rapid sanctification of the three leading reformers—and before them, Swithun. This in turn gave new impetus to the composition of hagiographies, hymns, antiphons, and all sorts of liturgical pieces needed for the cult of the recently-canonized figures.[112] In this light, a lyric collection based on the antiphons employed in the Divine Office and included in a late tenth-century manuscript might have originated in one of those monastic centers in which liturgical learning and composition were strongly promoted. Since the Advent Lyrics appeared in this milieu, it is therefore not far-fetched to assume that they could have been selected, and even probably "edited," to head a magnificent poetic anthology in the vernacular like the Exeter Book.[113]

Conner, "Religious Poetry," in *A Companion to Anglo-Saxon Literature*, ed. Phillip Pulsiano and Elaine Treharne (Oxford, 2001), 251–67, here 265. Clayton's analysis of lyric 9 leads her to conclude that "The poem is clearly the work of a learned, sophisticated poet, versed in liturgy and theology . . .": Clayton, *The Cult of the Virgin Mary*, 203. Rankin similarly affirms that "the lyrics show their author to have been thoroughly steeped in Christian thought and learning: obviously he was a member of a Christian community, quite possibly a monk": Rankin, "The Liturgical Background of the Old English Advent Lyrics," 318.

[111] For an analysis of the structural differences between Latin antiphons and the Advent lyrics, see Clemoes, *Interactions of Thought*, 371–80.

[112] Lapidge offers an enlightening survey of the liturgical demands that a recent canonization would generate at that time: "if the saint was thought worthy of special veneration, it was necessary to compose afresh the various pieces used in liturgical celebration: for the mass, mass-sets (consisting of prayers called the *collecta*, *secreta*, *prefatio*, and *post-communio*) and tropes (especially for the *Introit*); for the office, a hymn would be needed (the liturgical lections which were also needed could be supplied from the saint's *uita*)": Lapidge, "Æthelwold as Scholar," 114.

[113] On codicological evidence, Conner states that no more than 46 manuscript lines must have been lost in the extant initial lacuna, and that fol. 8r, containing fragmentary lyric 1, seems to have constituted the beginning of the manuscript for some time. This tentatively suggests that the collection of lyrics might have been the introductory work of the anthology, a notion that would also fit the cultural context of the Reform, in which the topic of Advent was certainly a central concept: Conner, *Anglo-Saxon Exeter*, 98.

END TIME AND THE DATE OF *VǪLUSPÁ*:
TWO MODELS OF CONVERSION

RICHARD NORTH

Vǫluspá is usually considered to be a heathen poem, yet it reveals traces of Christian influence, and most readers must wonder at some stage how far its poet really was heathen.[1] Was he (or she; but henceforth "he") a convert, lapsed or unorthodox, and if so, how and when did his conversion take place? The prerequisite for an answer to these complex questions is to ask when *Vǫluspá* was composed. The date of this work has been set as widely as 935 x 1050, but is now usually put in the year in which the Icelandic parliament voted to accept Christianity, perhaps because *Vǫluspá* reaches its climax via the death of Norse gods such as Óðinn, Þórr, and Freyr.[2] Although the Icelanders dated this decision in 1000, it has been persuasively argued that the vote was actually taken in June 999.[3] That the poet is an Icelander seems clear enough from his imagery of volcanic action before the

---

[1] *Vǫluspá*, ed. and trans. Ursula Dronke, in *The Poetic Edda, Vol. II: Mythological Poems* (Oxford, 1997); line numbers within stanzas are given by the half-line. An old controversy: with late classical, and Christian, influence first suggested by A. C. Bang, "Vøluspaa og de Sibyllinske Orakler," *Christiania Videnskabsselskabs Forhandlinger* 9 (Christiania [Oslo], 1879): 1–23; and strongly opposed by Viktor Rydberg, "Sibyllinerna och Vǫluspá," *Nordisk tidskrift* (1881): 1–29, 113–64. More recently, Kees Samplonius suggests that the poet modified the native tradition with some knowledge derived from Latin sibylline literature, in "*Sibylla borealis*: Notes on the Structure of *Vǫluspá*," in *Germanic Texts and Latin Models: Medieval Reconstructions*, ed. Karin E. Olsen, Antonina Harbus, and Tette Hofstra (Louvain, 2001), 185–229.

[2] Wolfgang Butt, "Zur Herkunft der *Vǫluspá*," *Beiträge zur Geschichte der deutschen Sprache und Literatur* 91 (1969): 82–103, esp. 82. On the background, see Dag Strömbäck, *The Conversion of Iceland: A Survey*, trans. Peter Foote (London, 1975), 27–67.

[3] Ólafía Einarsdóttir, *Studier i kronologisk metode i tidlig islandsk historieskrivning* (Lund, 1964), 72–90. Endorsed in *Íslendingabók — Landnámabók*, ed. Jakob Benediktsson, Íslenzk fornrit 1 (Reykjavik, 1968; repr. 1986), xxxiii–xl and 14–18 (*Íslendingabók*, chap. 7).

end of the world (sts. 25, 34–35, 50).[4] The aim of this essay is to strengthen the case for the year 1000 as the poem's *terminus ad quem*: first, by presenting ten parallels between *Vǫluspá* and the ideas and structure of the Book of Revelation; second, by suggesting that *Vǫluspá* was composed in reaction to a millennarial subculture associated with Revelation which spread to Iceland from Europe in the 980s. My conclusion will attempt to throw light on Iceland in this period as subject to two models of conversion: one based on an apocalyptic form of Christianity, which led to confrontation and violence; and an older model, working slowly by inculturation, which the fear of End Time suppressed.

    Vǫluspá is a long narrative poem of supreme imaginative power, in which one sibyl (*vǫlva*), aided by others, relates the history of the creation, from its distant beginnings to the world's end, through a series of visionary tableaux depicting Norse gods, giants, aspects of time, and men. The gods in these visions make, regulate, and then slowly lose their universe in an escalation of error which most commentators regard as a moral decline because of the death of Baldr, the young blameless son of Óðinn, half way through (*Vǫluspá* 31–33). Baldr is slain apparently by a spear tipped with mistletoe that Loki has given to Baldr's blind brother Hǫðr. Baldr's grievous death leads the gods to punish Loki by chaining him beneath a poison-dripping serpent under the earth (st. 34), whereupon the poet describes mortal sinners being punished in hell (sts. 35–38).[5] The world draws to its end and after Ragnarǫk, an Armageddon between gods and giants, all the gods die, the sky catches fire, and earth sinks blazing into the sea (sts. 39–54). But the sibyl goes on: a new world rises from the sea, green and full of game, where the gods meet, the past is discussed, and relics of antiquity are found in the grass (sts. 56–58); cornfields will sow themselves, *bǫls mun allz batna* ["all harm will be healed"], and Baldr and Hǫðr will come back to be reconciled (st. 59); and worthy warrior bands will dwell on for evermore in a hall brighter than the sun (st. 61). The poem ends with the vision of a flying dragon rising up from below with corpses beneath its wings (st. 62). Thus *Vǫluspá* conveys images of damnation and celestial reward, Christianizes Baldr in the manner of his death and characterizes Loki, it has been argued, in Judas's role even before he assumes the mantle of the homilists' Antichrist.[6] Other Old Norse-Icelandic Eddic poems do not invoke the same pathos. So far the many traces of Christianity in

---

    [4] As argued by Sigurður Nordal in his first edition of *Vǫluspá* (1923): see *Vǫluspá*, ed. Nordal, trans. B. S. Benedikz and John McKinnell (Durham, 1980), 72–73 (n. to his st. 35).

    [5] For example, John McKinnell, *Both One and Many: Essays on Change and Variety in Late Norse Heathenism*, with an Appendix by Maria Elena Ruggerini (Rome, 1994), 107–28.

    [6] *Edda II*, ed. Dronke, 55, 95–96.

Vǫluspá have been cited as evidence for one of two things: either the poet lived in the only Scandinavian area, the British Isles, where Norse mythology could be slowly Christianized; or he met missionaries from the Danelaw who could have fed his imagination in Norway or Iceland.[7]

The problem, however, with classifying the poet as Christianized is to explain why there is such respect in his poem for the gods of a heathen cult.[8] Ursula Dronke, an authority on *Vǫluspá* for more than forty years, treats this poet as a heathen but with an awareness of Christian forms, including sibylline poems such as the *Cantus Sibyllae*, part of the Christmas Office from the ninth to eleventh centuries in England, or the *Prophetiae Sibyllae magae*, a poem which was known in the ninth century in Alcuin's abbey of Tours, possibly therefore in York, a town which was ruled by Norwegians in the mid-tenth century. These sibylline texts show some likeness with *Vǫluspá*, but Dronke's view is that the poet's sibylline tradition remains essentially that of heathen Scandinavia, in which the world was in any case imagined to end at periodic intervals.[9] Dronke's reading of the evidence is surely right, but does not emphasize the millennial context of sibylline poetry in the tenth-century Christian world. Not the mystic Latin poems but the apocalyptic texts of the Bible were influential in the doctrine which day to day would have educated the clergy in the Danelaw or elsewhere. Dronke, noting these tendencies in *Vǫluspá*, relegates them as "external effects (. . .) that could come from eschatological homilies or apocalyptic visions of sinners

---

[7] Butt, "Zur Herkunft der *Vǫluspá*," 99. Hans Kuhn, "Das nordgermanische Heidentum in den ersten christlichen Jahrhunderten," *Zeitschrift für deutsches Altertum* 79 (1942): 133–66; repr. in idem, *Kleine Schriften*, 2 vols. (Berlin, 1971), 2: 296–326. See also Kuhn, "Rund um die *Vǫluspá*," in *Mediaevalia Litteraria: Festschrift für Helmut de Boor zum 80. Geburtstag*, ed. Ursula Hennig and Herbert Kolb (Munich, 1971), 1–14, esp. 7. John Lindow inclines to the second view, in "Norse Mythology and Northumbria: Methodological Notes," *Scandinavian Studies* 59 (1987): 308–24, esp. 313–23; also published in *Anglo-Scandinavian England: Norse-English Relations in the Period before the Conquest*, ed. John D. Niles and Mark Amodio (Lanham, MD, 1989), 25–40. Lindow's view is endorsed in John McKinnell, "Norse Mythology and Northumbria: A Response," *Scandinavian Studies* 59 (1987): 325–37, esp. 336.

[8] Helmut de Boor, "Die religiöse Sprache der Vǫluspá," in *Deutsche Islandforschung, Bd. I: Kultur*, ed. Walther Heinrich Vogt (Breslau, 1930), 68–142, esp. 130–31.

[9] Ursula Dronke, "*Vǫluspá* and Sibylline Traditions," in *Latin Culture and Medieval Germanic Europe*, ed. Richard North and Tette Hofstra (Groningen, 1992), 3–23; cf. *Edda II*, ed. Dronke, 93–104. Her conclusion is accepted, with reservations and some changes, by Samplonius, in "*Sibylla borealis*," 188–203. Many biblical parallels, with Revelation and Genesis among others, have been claimed by John McKinnell, "*Völuspá* and the Feast of Easter," in *Scandinavian and Christian Europe in the Middle Ages: Papers of the 12th International Saga Conference, Bonn/Germany, 28th July–2nd August 2003*, ed. Rudolf Simek and Judith Meurer (Bonn, 2003), 366–72.

in hell."[10] To the extent of the relevance of these effects to men, Dronke is right: they are external. Yet in relation to gods the Christian Apocalypse is an internal mechanism in *Vǫluspá*. As the number of parallels grows, after Baldr, a sequence emerges in these which points to the Revelation of St. John as the poet's greatest single Christian source. It is this book that provides the most striking Christian parallels with divine imagery in *Vǫluspá*.

The Book of Revelation was probably written ca. A.D. 90 by an author other than the Apostle to whom the title refers. It was conceived within a tradition of biblical prophecy of which the more important older instances are the Book of Daniel 11–13 (written at the time of a Greek-Syriac tyranny over Israel in ca. 168 B.C.), and some texts from the end of the first century: St. Paul's 1 Thessalonians 4:13–5:11 and 2 Thessalonians 2 (ca. A.D. 51); St. Peter's 1 Peter 4:17 and 2 Peter 3 (especially 3:10–11); and the "Little Apocalypse" from Mark 13, Matthew 24–25, and Luke 21. Taken together, these other texts show the Day of Judgment prophesied for an undisclosed time, after the blowing of a heavenly trumpet, the Lord's descent from heaven, and the resurrection of the dead. To this orderly view of the future the lurid imagery of Revelation offers a startling contrast. Its combination of Judaic symbolism, Babylonian mythology, and contemporary political reference make Revelation, in the words of one authority, "the most powerful apocalyptic work ever written."[11] It begins as a pastoral letter to seven churches around the Aegean, after which the author, said to be John on Patmos, recounts a divinely-inspired vision in which he reveals both some history of recent times (around Christ's birth) and the future Day of Judgment (on the destruction of the Roman Empire). His vision takes an often incoherent form, but keeps an obsessive eye on the Aegean churches whose low standards had earned them the letter. Seven churches; (Christ) the Lamb with seven horns and seven eyes; seven seals on the heavenly scroll, which are broken by the Lamb to reveal the Last Days; seven angels blowing trumpets to reveal the incremental means of the world's destruction; seven visions, through which the birth of Jesus and his combat with Satan are mystically portrayed with reference to the Devil as a "Dragon" which the archangel Michael throws down to hell; seven bowls of plagues; and then comes the Whore of Babylon, astride the Beast whose seven heads were probably meant to recall the seven hills of Rome. More visions follow, leading to the climactic battle between good and evil, in which the narrator says:[12]

---

[10] *Edda II*, ed. Dronke, 93.

[11] Bernard McGinn, *Visions of the End: Apocalyptic Traditions in the Middle Ages*, 2nd ed. (New York, 1998), 14. See also Norman Cohn, *The Pursuit of the Millennium: Revolutionary Millenarianism and Mystical Anarchists of the Middle Ages*, 2nd ed. (London, 1970).

[12] *Biblia Sacra iuxta Vulgatam Clementinam*, ed. Alberto Colunga and Laurentio Turrado, 7th ed. (Madrid, 1985). Translations from *The Revised English Bible with Apocrypha* (Oxford and Cambridge, 1989).

1 Et vidi angelum descendentem de caelo, habentem clavem abyssi, et catenam magnam in manu sua. 2 Et apprehendit draconem, serpentem antiquum, qui est diabolus, et Satanas, et ligavit eum per annos mille: 3 et misit eum in abyssum, et clausit, et signavit super illum ut non seducat amplius gentes, donec consumentur mille anni: et post haec oportet illum solvi modico tempore. (Rev. 20:1–3)

["1 I saw an angel coming down from heaven with the key to the abyss and a great chain in his hand. 2 He seized the dragon, that ancient serpent who is the Devil, or Satan, and chained him up for a thousand years; 3 he threw him into the abyss, shutting and sealing it over him, so that he might not seduce the nations again till the thousand years were ended. After that he must be let loose for a little while."]

Thereafter we are introduced to the hell-bound fate of those who failed to see the light in time, and to the coming of the Heavenly Jerusalem with the hosts of God's elect.

The question here is how much of *Vǫluspá*'s Christian material is grounded in apocalyptic tradition. Among several parallels with biblical texts, some with Revelation have already been noted; I shall try to add more and systematize them.[13] To begin with, *Vǫluspá* moves through the gods' history without denunciation, portraying their setbacks as mistakes rather than moral errors. In due course Baldr's death is portended through Óðinn's insistent questioning of the sibyl's informant (another sibyl, in sts. 27–29). After describing this disaster and its irresistible aftermath (Óðinn's revenge on Hǫðr, in sts. 32–33, and Loki's punishment, in st. 34), the poet of *Vǫluspá* undertakes a vision of heathen End Time, beginning with a vision of hell (sts. 35–38). We can start with the second sibyl's vision of hell. In Dronke's text and translation:[14]

Sal sá hón standa   sólo fiarri,
Nástrǫndo á,   norðr horfa dyrr.
Fello eitrdropar   inn um lióra.
Sá er undinn salr   orma hryggiom. (st. 37)

["A hall she saw standing remote from the sun on Dead Body Shore. Its door looks north. There fell drops of venom in through the roof vent. That hall is woven of serpents' spines."]

---

[13] Cf. Lindow, "Norse Mythology and Northumbria," 319–20; McKinnell, "*Vǫluspá* and the Feast of Easter," 370–72.

[14] *Edda II*, ed. Dronke. I follow Dronke's translation, but with extra commas and with my deviations from her translation noted.

Sá hón þar vaða   þunga strauma
menn meinsvara   ok morðvarga,
oc þannz annars glepr   eyrarúno.
þar saug Níðhǫggr   nái framgengna,
sleit vargr vera.   Vitoð er enn, eða hvat? (st. 38)

["She saw there wading onerous streams men perjured and wolfish murderers and the one who seduces another's close-trusted wife. There Malice
Striker sucked corpses of the dead, the wolf tore men. Do you still seek to
know? And what?"]

In this image of hell the poet's dead Norse sinners resemble the murderers, whore-
mongers, and liars (among others) whom Paul catalogues in 2 Tim. 3:1–5 and in
whose damnation John rejoices in Rev. 21:8.[15] The poet's immediate source may
be a sermon performed in a literal translation from Old English: it has been suggested that this was a sermon on Easter Day.[16] It has long been noted that his
phrase *menn meinsvara ok morðvarga* ["men perjured and wolfish murderers"]
resembles the alliterative pair *mansworan 7 morþ(or)wyrhtan*, which Archbishop
Wulfstan of York used a number of times from 1002 onwards, most famously in
what appears to be his third version of the *Sermo Lupi*, written probably around
1018.[17] Yet this resemblance, close as it is, does not mean that Wulfstan transmitted his terms directly to the poet of *Vǫluspá*.[18] It seems more plausible that the
poet of *Vǫluspá* based his language in this stanza on the homiletic words of an
English preacher, either in England or Norway or Iceland, who drew them from
a common stock of formulae. Wulfstan re-used and varied words, sentences, and

---

[15] Malcolm Godden, "Apocalypse and Invasion in Late Anglo-Saxon England," in
From Anglo-Saxon to Early Medieval English: Studies Presented to Eric Gerald Stanley, ed.
idem, Douglas Gray, and Terry Hoad (Oxford, 1994), 130–62, esp. 147; McKinnell, *Both
One and Many*, 123.

[16] McKinnell, "*Vǫluspá* and the Feast of Easter," 370.

[17] Butt, "Zur Herkunft der *Vǫluspá*," 87–89. *The Homilies of Wulfstan*, ed. Dorothy
Bethurum (Oxford, 1952), 163 (VII.130: *De fide catholica*, cf. 299), 183 (VIIIc.158–60:
Sermo de baptismate), 192 (Xa.11–12: *De regula canonicorum*), 231 (XIII.93: *Sermo ad pop-
ulum*) and 273 (XX(IE).162–63: *Sermo Lupi*). On the dates of *Sermo Lupi*, see Godden,
"Apocalypse and Invasion," 145–58.

[18] *Contra* Butt, Lindow, "Norse Mythology and Northumbria," 315–16. On Wulfstan's aims and the character of his writing, see Jonathan Wilcox, "The Wolf on Shepherds: Wulfstan, Bishops, and the Context of the *Sermo Lupi ad Anglos*," in *Old English Prose: Basic Readings*, ed. Paul E. Szarmach with Deborah A. Oosterhouse (New
York and London, 2000), 395–418, esp. 408–11. See also Patrick Wormald, "Archbishop
Wulfstan and the Holiness of Society," in idem, *Legal Culture in the Early Christian Medieval West: Law as Text, Image and Experience* (London, 1999), 225–51.

even paragraphs from one sermon to another; and he may have derived some expressions from contemporaries or preachers before him.[19]

In his next stanza, the Icelander introduces us to the mother of Norse monsters. Probably this is Angrboða ("grief-boder"), the *gýgr í Jǫtunheimum* ("ogress in the giants' world") with whom Snorri Sturluson, the thirteenth-century Icelandic mythographer, said Loki gets three children: the wolf Fenrir, who will kill Óðinn; the World Serpent, who will kill Þórr; and Hel herself, the goddess and location of the Norse underworld.[20] In the poet's words:

> Austr sat in aldna   í Iárnviði,
> ok fœddi þar   Fenris kindir.
> Verðr af þeim ǫllom   einna nøkkorr
> tungls tiúgari   í trollz hami. (st. 39)

["In the east she sat, the old one, in Iron Wood, and bred there the broods of Fenrir. There will come from them all one of that number to be a moon-snatcher in troll's skin."]

> Fylliz fiǫrvi   feigra manna,
> rýðr ragna siǫt   rauðom dreyra.
> Svǫrt verðr sólskín   of sumor eptir,
> veðr ǫll válynd.   Vitoð er enn, eða hvat? (st. 40)

["It sates itself on the life-blood of fated men, paints red the powers' homes with crimson gore. Black become the sun's beams in the summers that follow, weathers all treacherous. Do you still seek to know? And what?"]

Despite several differences, a second parallel emerges between this ominous creature and the Whore of Babylon in Revelation, whose monstrous image triggers the first of John's battles between good and evil:

> 1 Et venit unus de septem angelis, qui habebant septem phialas, et locutus est mecum, dicens: Veni, ostendam tibi damnationem meretricis magnae, quae sedet super aquas multas, 2 cum qua fornicati sunt reges terrae, et inebriati sunt qui inhabitant terram de vino prostitutionis eius. 3 Et abstulit me in spiritu in desertum. Et vidi mulierem sedentem super bestiam coccineam, plenam nominibus blasphemiae, habentem capita septem, et cornua decem.

---

[19] Andy Orchard, "Crying Wolf: Oral Style and the *Sermones Lupi*," *ASE* 21 (1992): 239–64, and idem, "Oral Tradition," in *Reading Old English Texts*, ed. Katherine O'Brien O'Keeffe (Cambridge, 1997), 101–23, esp. 109–13.

[20] *Snorri Sturluson: Edda: Prologue and Gylfaginning*, ed. Anthony Faulkes (Oxford, 1982), 27 (*Gylfaginning*, chap. 34).

4 Et mulier erat circumdata purpura, et coccino, et inaurata auro, et lapide pretioso, et margaritis, habens poculum aureum in manu sua, plenum abominatione, et immunditia fornicationis eius. 5 Et in fronte eius nomen scriptum: Mysterium: Babylon magna, mater fornicationum, et abominationum terrae. 6 Et vidi mulierem ebriam de sanguine sanctorum, et de sanguine martyrum Iesu. Et miratus sum cum vidissem illam admiratione magna. (Rev. 17:1–6)

["1 One of the seven angels who held the seven bowls came and spoke to me: 'Come,' he said, 'I will show you the verdict on the great whore, she who is enthroned over many waters. 2 The kings of the earth have committed fornication with her, and people the world over have made themselves drunk on the wine of her fornication.' 3 He carried me in spirit into the wilderness, and I saw a woman mounted on a scarlet beast which was covered with blasphemous names and had seven heads and ten horns. 4 The woman was clothed in purple and scarlet, and decked out with gold and precious stones and pearls. In her hand she held a gold cup full of obscenities and the foulness of her fornication. 5 Written on her forehead was a name with a secret meaning: 'Babylon the great, the mother of whores and of every obscenity on earth.' 6 I saw that the woman was drunk with the blood of God's people, and with the blood of those who had borne their testimony to Jesus. And when I saw her I wondered greatly."]

The ogress breeding monsters in an iron wood in *Vǫluspá* recalls the whore of Babylon mounted on her Beast within a desert, another sterile place (*desertum*), in Rev. 17: she seems to answer John's image of *mulierem sedentem super bestiam*; as the beast is *coccineam*, and the Whore is seen *ebriam de sanguine sanctorum*, so the ancient female's offspring *rýðr ragna siǫt rauðom dreyra* ("paints red the powers' homes with crimson gore").[21] In a third parallel, Kees Samplonius suggests that *Gullveig* ("golden-cup"), a name for a sibyl whom the Æsir try to destroy early in their history in *Vǫluspá* 21, might refer to the *poculum aureum* which the Whore of Babylon proffers in Rev. 17:4.[22]

One by one the sirens of the Norse world go off, with opaque images of a harping giant named Eggþér, happy at the ensuing chaos, of cockerels rousing Óðinn's armies and Hell's denizens, and a Cerberus-like dog named Garmr baying in a cave-mouth in expectation of the End (sts. 41–43). Humanity soon comes to grief:

Brœðr muno beriaz   ok at bǫnum verða[z],
muno systrungar   sifiom spilla.

---

[21] Endorsed by McKinnell, "*Vǫluspá* and the Feast of Easter," 370. This was an idea I first put forth in "*Vǫluspá* and the Book of Revelation," in the Leeds International Medieval Congress, University of Leeds, Monday 8 July 2002 (paper 108.b).

[22] Samplonius, "*Sibylla borealis*," 226–27.

Hart er í heimi,   hórdómr mikill,
skeggǫld, skálmǫld, — skildir ro klofnir —
vindǫld, vargǫld,   áðr verǫld steypiz.
Mun engi maðr   ǫðrom þyrma. (st. 44)

["Brothers will fight and kill each other, sisters' children will defile kin-
ship. It is harsh in the world, whoredom rife, an axe age, a sword age —
shields are riven — a wind age, a wolf age, before the world goes headlong.
No man will have mercy on another."]

The family feud, fratricide, and incest here recalls Wulfstan's expressions of
doom, particularly *ne byrhð broðor oþrum* ("no brother will help another") in
Secundum Marcum (Bethurum, homily V) and its variant in *Secundum Lucam*
(Bethurum, homily III). It is also worth comparing *brœðr muno beriaz* with all
three versions of Wulfstan's *Sermo Lupi* (Bethurum, homily XX), particularly
with his remark on these abuses after they have taken place: *ne bearh* (. . .) *hwilum
bearn his agenum fæder, ne broðer oðrum* ("nor did at times a child save his own father, or one brother another").[23] Although this sentiment is expressed in Luke
21:16, Wulfstan, like the Icelandic poet's presumed clerical informant, is most
likely to have taken it from Mark 13:12: *Tradet autem frater fratrem in mortem, et
pater filium* ("Brother will send brother to his death, and father his son").

As war leads to war, Heimdallr, the gods' sentinel, announces the long-pre-
dicted giant assault on Ásgarðr, and Loki slips his bonds (to lead a seaborne assault on the gods' world in st. 46):

Leika Míms synir,   en miǫtuðr kyndiz
at en[o] galla   Giallarhorni.
Hátt blæss Heimdallr   — horn er á lopti —
mælir Óðinn   við Míms hǫfuð.
Skelfr Yggdrasils   askr standandi,
ymr it aldna tré   en iǫtunn losnar. (st. 45)

["Mímr's sons [giants?] sport, but fate's measure is lit at the sound of the
clear-ringing Clarion Horn. Loud blows Heimdallr — the horn points to
the sky — Óðinn talks with Mímir's head. Yggdrasill shivers, the ash, as it
stands. The old tree groans, and the giant slips free."]

Three more parallels with Revelation have been noted, to add to the three suggestions we have already. John McKinnell has seen two allusions to the Christian

---

[23] *The Homilies of Wulfstan*, ed. Bethurum, 125 (homily III.54–55), 140 (homily
V.98–99); 257 (homily XX (BH).57–58), 263 (homily XX(C).71) and 269 (homily XX
(EI).61–63). The past tense is noted in Godden, "Apocalypse and Invasion," 147.

Apocalypse in *Vǫluspá* 45 and one a little later in this poem: the blowing of Heimdallr's horn, a sign of Ragnarǫk, is like that of the first six of seven angels boding
doom with their trumpets in Rev. 8:6–9 and 19; and Loki bursts his chains rather
as Satan is allowed to break out of his chains in Rev. 20:7; moreover, the poet's image of dwarfs and humans, tramping the road from mountains and underworld in
sts. 49–50, resembles that of the dead rising to face judgment in Rev. 20:12–13.[24]
In this way, the last battle between good and evil is a theme common to *Vǫluspá*
47–53 and Rev. 20:8–10.

Loki now sails to Ásgarðr with a fleet of giants and other monsters all ready
to destroy the Æsir. One by one the gods Freyr, Óðinn, and Þórr step out to die
in battle against Surtr the fire-demon, the wolf Fenrir, and the World Serpent,
although Víðarr avenges Óðinn on Fenrir and Þórr appears to kill the Serpent
before he dies (st. 53) and the world sinks in flames (st. 54). But this is not the
End, for now the sibyl from whom the future is known promises a transcendental
future to the sibyl speaking at this point of *Vǫluspá*:

> Sér hón upp koma   ǫðro sinni
> iǫrð ór ægi   iðiagrœna. (st. 56)

["She sees come up, a second time, earth, out of ocean, once again green."]

In heathen terms, the earth's renewal in *Vǫluspá* is probably a motif which stems
from the seasonal rise and fall of the year and which is still plain to see in the
self-sown acres of *Vǫluspá* 59.[25] Yet the poet seems to base his expression for this
renewal, seventhly, on John's statement in Rev. 21:1: *Et vidi caelum novum et ter-
ram novam. Primum enim caelum, et prima terra abiit* ["I saw a new heaven and a
new earth, for the first heaven and the first earth were passed away"], even if he
goes on to say *et mare iam non est* ["and the sea is now not"].

A new generation of Æsir find each other and their ancestors' artifacts on
Iðavellir, and Baldr returns to make peace with his slayer Hǫðr and to dwell in
Hroptz sigtóptir "Hroptr's victory mounds" (Dronke: "walls of triumph", st. 59).
At this time also the god Hœnir re-emerges to pick out the twigs of (heathen)
lots, while apparently the sons of Baldr and Hǫðr live gloriously together in the
vindheim víðan ("wide wind realm." st. 60). The scene becomes celestial:

> Sal sér hón standa   sólo fegra,
> gulli þakðan,   á Gimlé.

---

[24] *The Homilies of Wulfstan*, ed. Bethurum, 136–37 (homily V.40–477); McKinnell,
Both One and Many, 124.

[25] *Edda II*, ed. Dronke, 59–60, 94–96, 101; Jens Peter Schjødt, "*Vǫluspá*: cyklisk tid-
sopfattelse i gammelnordisk religion," *Danske Studier* 76 (1981): 91–95.

Þar skolo dyggvar   dróttir byggia
ok um aldrdaga   ynðis nióta. (st. 61)

["A hall she sees standing, brighter than the sun, roofed with gold, on Jewel Clearing [Dronke: "Refuge from the Flames"]. There shall the worthy warrior bands dwell and all their days of life enjoy delight."]

As McKinnell notes, this celestial hall would be a Christian commonplace, but for a parallel in Rev. 22:5.[26] Indeed the verses in Rev. 21:9–11 come closer:

9 (*cont.*) dicens: Veni, et ostendam tibi sponsam, uxorem Agni. 10 Et sustulit me in spiritu in montem magnum et altum, et ostendit mihi civitatem sanctam Ierusalem descendentem de caelo a Deo, 11 habentem claritatem Dei: et lumen eius simile lapidi pretioso tanquam lapidi iaspidis, sicut crystallum.

["9 'Come,' he said [Seventh Angel to St. John], 'and I will show you the bride, the wife of the Lamb.' 10 So in the spirit he carried me away to a great and lofty mountain, and showed me Jerusalem, the Holy City, coming down out of heaven from God. 11 It shone with the glory of God; it had the radiance of some priceless jewel, like a jasper, clear as crystal.]

John dwells for longer on the jewels and gold of his Heavenly City in Rev. 21:18–21. But already it seems that this is the basis of the image of Gimlé. Dronke translates the elsewhere unattested *Gim-lé* as "Fire-Lee'" or "Fire-shelter," "Refuge from the Flames."[27] The first element of *Gim-lé* means "fire," but as it is formally traceable to Latin *gemma* through OE *gimm* ("jewel"), it also means "gem."[28] This word occurs in *Vǫlundarkviða* 6, where Wayland *sló gull rautt við gim fastan* ("beat red gold round the firm-set gem").[29] *Vǫlundarkviða* is recognized to have been composed in the ninth or tenth century, either in England or by a poet whose language incorporated Old English (and German) loanwords.[30]

---

[26] McKinnell, *Both One and Many*, 125.

[27] *Edda II*, ed. Dronke, 152.

[28] *Edda: Die Lieder des Codex Regius nebst verwandten Denkmälern*, ed. Gustav Neckel and Hans Kuhn, 3rd ed., 2 vols. (Heidelberg, 1968) 2: 75: "*n. feuer od. *gimr (ags. gim) m. 'gemme', Edelstein.*"

[29] *Edda II*, ed. Dronke, 245, 276–79, esp. 277 and 308 (note).

[30] John McKinnell, "The Context of *Vǫlundarkviða*," *Saga-Book of the Viking Society* 23 (1990–1993): 1–27; idem, "Eddic Poetry in Anglo-Scandinavian Northern England," in *Vikings and the Danelaw: Select Papers from the Proceedings of the Thirteenth Viking Congress, Nottingham and York, 21–30 August 1997*, ed. James Graham-Campbell, Richard Hall, Judith Jesch, and David N. Parsons (Oxford, 2001), 327–44, esp. 331 (2. *gim*): "the scribe fails to recognize the word, producing a meaningless compound *gimfastan*."

Here the second element *lé* is hard to explain as a place-name suffix (*ljár* means "scythe"), unless as a loan of Old English *leah*, with the general meaning "place."[31] Both the prefix and topographical suffix of the name *Gimlé*, if foreign, appear to reflect the translation of Old English words into the language of the poet of *Vǫluspá*. Not only does his image capture the *civitas sancta* in Revelation, as an eighth suggested parallel, but the name Gimlé might tell us that the poet learned this from an English missionary.

Here the *Hauksbók* text of *Vǫluspá*, but not that of the better *Konungsbók*, provides a couple of lines which Dronke leaves out of her main text:

Þá kømr inn ríki   at regindómi,
ǫflugr, ofan,   sá er ǫllo ræðr. (*Hauksbók* st. 62 [H 62])

["Then the Mighty One comes to the court of Judgement, powerful, from above, He who rules all."]

Gro Steinsland regards these lines as a heathen part of the original poem;[32] McKinnell, as a heavily Christianized part of the first *Vǫluspá*.[33] Dronke treats them as Christian interpolation, rejecting this stanza "basically on the grounds that it is saying in overt Christian terms what the poet has already subtly expressed in [sts.] 61, 62 [on the dragon]."[34] Of these alternative views, McKinnell's seems the most plausible. The language here is just as covert as previously, for there is still no mention of Christ's name. Moreover, the adjective *ǫflugr* ("powerful") in this verse repeats an earlier divine use in *Vǫluspá* 17 in which three of the Æsir, namely Óðinn, Hœnir, and Lóðurr, are called *ǫflgir* when they create the first man and woman. Also, the word *ofan* ("from above") in this stanza appears to be answered by *neðan* ("from below") in the following stanza, the last in the poem. *Vǫluspá* H62 gives us yet another parallel, with Rev. 20:4–6, and is possibly the poet's ninth allusion to Revelation in his heathen sibylline creation poem on the end of the world.

[31] Margaret Gelling, *Place-Names in the Landscape: The Geographical Roots of Britain's Place-Names* (London, 1984), 198–207, esp. 199: "used by English speakers to denote sites where settlements in forest clearings were flourishing when they arrived."

[32] Gro Steinsland, "Religionskiftet i Norden og *Vǫluspá* 65," in *Nordisk Hedendom: Et Symposium*, ed. eadem (Odense, 1991), 335–48.

[33] McKinnell, *Both One and Many*, 122–25; idem, "*Vǫluspá* and the Feast of Easter," 369.

[34] *Edda II*, ed. Dronke, 87, 152. A view also held by Klaus von See, in *Altnordischer Rechtswörter: Philologische Studien zur Rechtsauffassung und Rechtsgesinnung der Germanen* (Tübingen, 1964), 122 and n. 77.

Þar kømr inn dimmi   dreki fliúgandi,
naðr fránn, neðan   frá Niðafiǫllom.
Berr sér í fiǫðrom   — flýgr vǫllr yfir —
Níðhǫggr, nái.   Nú mun hón søkkvaz. (st. 62)

["There comes the shadowy dragon flying, glittering serpent, from below [Dronke: 'up'] from Dark of the Moon Hills. He carries in his pinions — he flies over the field — Malice Striker, corpses. Now will she sink."]

Thus we end with an image of heaven and hell, a Christian admixture to the heathen plot. This *dreki* ("dragon"), tenthly, looks like the *draco* in Revelation which, according to Rev. 20:1–3, will rise again from the abyss at the end of the thousand years. The context in both Revelation and *Vǫluspá* is the Lord's Judgment of good and bad souls. *Vǫluspá* H62, the stanza above this one, seems to describe the Second Coming, the descent of the Supreme Judge from on high. Preserved by chance in *Hauksbók*, H 62 seems to be an integral part of *Vǫluspá* which fell out of the copying of the R-text from its exemplars, probably because the compiler of the Codex Regius (*Konungsbók*) manuscript, in which the best text of *Vǫluspá* is found, wished to create a collection of heathen works.[35]

In all, these ten parallels with Revelation might show that the poet of *Vǫluspá* not only borrows ideas from this book, but also more or less follows the course of its chapters 17–21. The progress of his Christianized apocalyptic ideas corresponds to Rev. 17:4, 21:8, 17:1–6, 19, 20:7, 20:12–13, 21:1, 21:9–11, 20:4–6 and 20:1–3 (schematically this is A-H-AB-EFG-I-D-C). The waywardness of his progress through the core of Revelation, if the parallels are accepted, suggests that the poet of *Vǫluspá* is more likely to have learned of Revelation from listening to sermons than from reading it in a book. More likely than not, the fairly close resemblance between his unique *menn meinsvara ok morðvarga* (st. 38) and Wulfstan's expression *mansworan 7 morporwyrhtan* ("perjurers and murderers") tells us that his preacher came from England.[36]

The stronger the influence of Revelation on *Vǫluspá*, the more likely it is that this poem was composed at the latest around 1000, for the *dreki* of the last stanza, in the narrative present, shows that the poet thinks the End is nigh.[37] In the late tenth century Revelation was understood to date Armageddon to the end of the first thousand years after Christ's birth. Ælfric, in ca. 995, announces that *Þes tima is ende-next and ende þyssere worulde* ("This time is nearest to the End

---

[35] For the stemma, see *Edda II*, ed. Dronke, 65.

[36] *The Homilies of Wulfstan*, ed. Bethurum, 273 (XX(IE).162–63); *Vǫluspá*, ed. Dronke, 17 (st. 38) and 142 (note).

[37] McKinnell, "A Response," 327: "the first symptom that the future just prophesied by the vǫlva is beginning to come about."

and is the end of this world"), although he does not indicate a date.[38] Wulfstan allows for a date amid evidence of a widespread fear of End Time in his *Secundum Marcum* (Bethurum, homily V), which he probably wrote as archbishop of York in 1002:

> Nu sceal hit nyde yfelian swyðe, forðam þe hit nealæcð georne his timan, ealswa hit awriten is 7 gefyrn wæs gewitegod: *Post mille annos soluetur Satanas.* Þusend geara 7 eac ma is nu agan syððan Crist wæs mid mannum on menniscan hiwe, 7 nu syndon Satanases bendas swyðe toslopene, 7 Antecristes tima is wel gehende, 7 ðy hit is on worulde a swa leng swa wacre.[39]

> ["Now things must of necessity become very bad, because it is fast approaching his time, just as is written and was formerly prophesied: 'After a thousand years Satan will be let loose.' A thousand years and more has now passed since Christ was among men in human form, and now Satan's bonds are very frayed, and the time of Antichrist is very close, and so the longer the world goes on the worse it is."]

Although the subject of this sermon is truly Mark 13:12, Wulfstan quotes the thousand years from Rev. 20:7. This is the only time he provides a date for the Apocalypse.[40]

In his reticence about this date, Wulfstan follows patristic orthodoxy.[41] After the sack of Rome in 410, St. Augustine confirmed in his *De civitate Dei* that Rome henceforth stood for a spiritual, not earthly, city of God. Literal readings of Revelation were to be abandoned, for the Second Coming might arrive at any moment, rather like one's own apprehension of grace; and in Revelation the struggle between the Lamb and the Antichrist should now be read as symbolic of a common choice. St. Augustine did not reject the ideas of Revelation entirely, for in *De civitate Dei* (18.23) he quotes the *Cantus Sibyllae* ["Sibyl's song"], a poem which was translated from a Greek original (*Oracula sibyllina* VIII) and which consists of twenty-seven acrostic verses on the Signs of Judgment.[42] But by the end of

---

[38] *Ælfric's Lives of Saints*, ed. W. W. Skeat, 2 vols., EETS, o.s. 76, 82 (Oxford, 1881–1885, repr. 1966), 1: 304 (XIII: *De Oratione Moysi*, lines 290–300, esp. 294). My translation. Godden, "Apocalypse and Invasion," 133.

[39] *The Homilies of Wulfstan*, ed. Bethurum, 136–37 (homily V.40–7), 290; Patrick Wormald, "Archbishop Wulfstan: Eleventh-Century State-Builder," in *Wulfstan, Archbishop of York: The Proceedings of the Second Alcuin Conference*, ed. Matthew Townend (Turnhout, 2004), 9–27, esp. 17.

[40] *The Homilies of Wulfstan*, ed. Bethurum, 291, n. 44.

[41] *Sermo Lupi ad Anglos*, ed. Dorothy Whitelock, 2nd ed. (London, 1952), 24, n. 8. *The Homilies of Wulfstan*, ed. Bethurum, 278–82.

[42] Dronke, "*Vǫluspá* and Sibylline Traditions," 5–6.

the tenth century the doctrine of the thousand years was officially deprecated as a hindrance to the thief-in-the-night Second Coming which is disclosed in 1 Thess. 5:2 and indicated more fully in Mark 13:33–37 and 2 Thess. 2. Chiliasm (the belief in the doctrine of the thousand years before Judgment) lived on in popular belief, as a subculture which fixed the date for the Second Coming in or after the year 1000. In this frame, which Wulfstan briefly acknowledges in *Secundum Marcum*, Satan's ascent from the abyss in Rev. 20:3, *modico tempore* ("for a little while") as the narrator says, heralds Armageddon just before Doomsday.

The Icelanders probably converted officially in June 999, as we have seen, although A.D. 1000 is the year according to Ari Þorgilsson's *Íslendingabók* ("Book of Icelanders," ca. 1125), the earliest surviving account.[43] The years leading up to this conversion were fraught with tension. The missionary "bishop" Friðrekr who arrived in 980 was threatened, outlawed, and nearly burned alive in his house, until after four years he left Iceland with Þórvaldr Koðránsson, his part-Irish minder, splitting up with him in Norway and returning to *Saxland* ("Saxony") whence he is said to have come.[44] The name *Friðrekr* shows him to have been either a Saxon or Frank.[45] There is apparently some German vernacular influence in *Vǫluspá*, where it has been noted that the poet borrows the notion of 'Muspell' (as a giant, st. 48) from the name 'Muspilli' which appears to denote the Apocalypse in an Old High German fragment from ca. 850.[46] This name is also found in *Lokasenna* (st. 42), a satirical work probably of the early Christian period in the eleventh century. Perhaps, then, the word *Muspell* came into *Vǫluspá* from Friðrekr. About eleven years after this abortive mission, King Óláfr Tryggvason is said to have sent to Iceland an Icelandic lay preacher named Stefnir Þorgilsson, who found his own family unwelcoming, his society hostile, and their idols too tempting: when he started to destroy them, a law was passed in the *Alþing* ("general assembly") the following summer, probably in June 997, specifically to outlaw Stefnir for *frændaskǫmm* ("the shame of his kin").[47] Other Icelanders took up the Christian cause: probably

---

[43] See note 2. *Íslendingabók*, ed. Jakob Benediktsson, 18 (chap. 7): "Þat vas þremr tigum vetra ens annars hundraðs eptir dráp Eadmundar, en þúsundi eptir burð Krists at alþýðu tali" ["That was one hundred and seventy winters after the killing of Edmund, and a thousand after Christ's birth by the common reckoning"].

[44] Named as an early visitor in *Íslendingabók*, ed. Jakob Benediktsson, 18 (chap. 8). His visit is dated in annals as "981" (for 980) in *Annálar og Nafnaskrá*, ed. Guðni Jónsson (Reykjavik, 1981), 3 (*Konungsannáll*), 79 (*Lǫgmannsannáll*). His story is told in *Kristni Saga*, ed. B. Kahle (Halle a.S., 1905), 1–17 (*Þórvalds þáttr Koðránssonar*).

[45] Frankish a little more than Saxon, according to Ian McDougall, "Foreigners and Foreign Languages in Medieval Iceland," *Saga-Book of the Viking Society* 22 (1987–1988): 180–233, esp. 187.

[46] *Edda II*, ed. Dronke, 146–47; McGinn, *Visions of the End*, 80–81.

[47] *Kristni Saga*, ed. Kahle, 19 (chaps. 6–7); Kirsten Hastrup, *Culture and History in Medieval Iceland: An Anthropological Analysis of Structure and Change* (Oxford, 1985), 182.

in June 998, Hjalti Skeggjason, son-in-law of a chieftain of Skálholt named Gizurr *inn hvíti* ("the white") Teitsson, was sentenced to three years' outlawry for blaspheming the Norse gods. His one surviving ditty hints that he had promised to reform after a bout of this sort of trouble before; also that he was sexually conservative, like the clergy (and like the author of *Vǫluspá* 38):

Vil ek eigi goð geyja;   grey þykki mér Freyja.[48]

["I don't want to blaspheme the gods (/ the gods to bark); Freyja seems a bitch to me."]

Hjalti's portrait of Freyja as a bitch with dogs resembles a simile from the longest, probably the third, version of *Sermo Lupi* (ca. 1018), in which Wulfstan condemns men who buy a female slave *7 wið þa ane fylþe adreogað, an æfter oðrum, 7 ælc æfter oðrum, hundum geliccast, þe for fylþe ne scrifað* ["and with that one woman carry out filth, one after the other, and each man after the other, most like dogs, that have no care for filth"].[49] Loki alleges in *Lokasenna* 30 that each god has been Freyja's *hór* ("bed-fellow"); and this language, too, is reminiscent of Wulfstan's denunciation of *fule forlegene horingas manege* ("many foul jaded fornicators") immediately after the *mansworan 7 morþorwyrhtan* in the same version of *Sermo Lupi*.[50] So there is a hint in Hjalti's provocative line that he had learned the language of English preachers. Ari says of both Hjalti and Gizurr, his father-in-law, that *svá er sagt, at þar bæri frá, hvé vel þeir mæltu* ("it is said that there was wonder at how well they spoke").[51] Gizurr built a church, and in due course in 1056 his son Ísleifr Gizurarson, Hjalti's brother-in-law, was appointed the first bishop of Skálholt.

The most vividly remembered activist in Iceland before the conversion was a Saxon or Flemish nobleman named Þangbrandr, whom Tryggvason made court chaplain and dispatched to Iceland probably in 996.[52] Þangbrandr sought

---

[48] *Íslendingabók*, ed. Jakob Benediktsson, 15.

[49] *The Homilies of Wulfstan*, ed. Bethurum, 270 (homily XX(EI).88–89). On Hjalti's sense of humor, see Richard North, *Heathen Gods in Old English Literature* (Cambridge, 1997), 310–11; idem, "*Goð geyja*: The Limits of Humour in Old Norse-Icelandic Paganism," *Quaestio* 1 (2000): 1–22, esp. 1–5.

[50] *The Homilies of Wulfstan*, ed. Bethurum, 273 (homily XX(EI).161–64); Butt, "Zur Herkunft der *Vǫluspá*," 93–94.

[51] *Íslendingabók*, ed. Jakob Benediktsson, 16 (chap. 7).

[52] The son of Vilbaldus *greifa af Brimum* ("Count of Bremen"), thus a Saxon, in *Kristni Saga*, ed. Kahle, 14 (chap. 5) and in *Brennu-Njáls saga*, ed. Einar Ól. Sveinsson, Íslenzk fornrit 12 (Reykjavik, 1954), 256 (chap. 100); but "Theobrandus" was a Fleming, according to the monk Theoderic's early-twelfth-century *Historia de antiquitate regum Norvagiensium*, ed. Gustav Storm, *Monumenta Historica Norvegiæ: Latinske kildeskrifter til Norges historie i middelalderen* (Christiania [Oslo], 1880 [repr. 1973]), 15.

confrontation, as the epithets *snjallr siðreynir* ("brave-eloquent tester of the old ways") and *goðvargr* ("despoiler of the gods"), in two contemporary verses about him, show.[53] Although Þangbrandr is said to have converted some chieftains, the "Burnt" Njáll among them, he became notorious for dueling with reactionaries. Clearly he would always win, killing only two or three in Ari's estimation, but his violence led to failure on a wider scale, and in about 998, if we follow Ari's context rather than his dating, Þangbrandr returned to Óláfr empty-handed.[54] Enough survives about him, particularly in *Kristni saga* (1380s) and *Njáls saga* (ca. 1390), to show that the style was the message, that Þangbrandr fought duels with pagans because he preached of Armageddon. In *Kristni saga* (chap. 6) and *Njáls saga* (chap. 100), it is said that while Þangbrandr, shortly after arrival, pre-pared to sing mass one morning for St. Michael (i.e. on 29 September 996), his host Hallr of Síða asked him about the archangel Michael. When Þangbrandr answered that Michael weighs up good and evil deeds, Hallr asked to be put into Michael's protection. St. Michael is commemorated in this role on runic monu-ments in Sweden; he was known elsewhere in Scandinavia as the protector and conveyor of souls.[55] Three out of four canonical biblical instances of Michael concern his generalship in Armageddon (the exception is Jude 9): in Dan. 10:13 and 12:1, Michael fights against the Antichrist from whom he protects man at the end of history; in Rev. 12:7, when the war breaks out in heaven, Michael du-els with Satan the dragon and throws him into the abyss.

Also in *Kristni saga* (chap. 8) and in *Njáls saga*, when Þangbrandr hears Steinunn, a pagan diehard, claim that Þórr challenged Christ to a duel without answer, he says that he has *heyrt* ["heard"] that *Þórr væri ekki nema mold ok aska, þegar guð vildi eigi, at hann lifði* ["Þórr would be nothing but dust and ashes if God did not permit him to live"].[56] In this exchange Þórr is cast as Christ's opponent as if he were the Beast or Dragon. These words are consistent both with the idea of God's restraining hand, which is known both in Revelation and in 2 Thess. 2:11, and with the fire and brimstone promised in Rev. 20:9.[57] But the story that these sagas preserve is really about Þangbrandr's willingness to take on heathen oppo-nents. Þangbrandr, whether from Flanders or Saxony, could have learned to fight pagans from a text such as the widely-known *libellus* which Adso of Montier-en-Der, probably in ca. 950, wrote as a letter to Queen Gerberga, sister of Emperor

---

[53] *Brennu-Njáls saga*, ed. Einar Ól. Sveinsson, 260–61 (vs. 6: anon.), 262 (vs. 7: Þor-valdr inn veili).

[54] *Íslendingabók*, ed. Jakob Benediktsson, 14 (ch. 7); Strömbäck, *The Conversion of Iceland*, 13–17, 25–37.

[55] Sven B. F. Jansson, *Runes in Sweden*, trans. Peter Foote (Stockholm, 1987).

[56] *Brennu-Njáls saga*, ed. Einar Ól. Sveinsson, 265 (chap. 102).

[57] Ian Boxall, *Revelation: Vision and Insight: An Introduction to the Apocalypse* (Lon-don, 2002), 24.

Otto I of Saxony: his *De Ortu et Tempore Antichristi*.[58] Adso opens by saying that Antichrist may be expected to call himself God and has already sent out Antiochus, Nero, and Domitian as his ministers of evil:

> Nunc quoque nostro tempore multos Antichristos nouimus esse. Quicumque enim siue laicus, siue canonicus siue monachus contra iustitiam uiuit et ordinis sui regulam inpugnat et quod bonum est blasphemat, Antichristus est et minister satane.[59]

> ["In our own time we know there are many Antichrists. Any layman, cleric, or monk, who lives in a way contrary to justice, who attacks the rule of his order of life, and blasphemes the good, is an Antichrist, a minister of Satan."]

In this fanatical light, one could be forgiven for thinking that Þangbrandr's true purpose was to find Antichrists in Iceland.

Þangbrandr is said, in *Kristni saga* (chap. 5), to have visited Canterbury, so in principle he could have influenced those expressions in *Vǫluspá* that are regarded as being of English origin. In practice, however, this seems unlikely, and Sigurður Nordal discounted Þangbrandr's influence when he identified the author of *Vǫluspá* with Vǫlu-Steinn, a poet of this period.[60] A better candidate for this type of sermonic influence would be a priest named Þormóðr whom Óláfr Tryggvason is said to have brought with him from England; Þormóðr is said to have accompanied Gizurr and Hjalti to Iceland (in 999).[61] If England was his country of origin, then Þormóðr is the Danelaw man we are looking for: an English preacher of Danish or Norwegian descent who could have mediated phrases such as Wulfstan's *mansworan 7 morþ(or)wyrhtan* to the poet of *Vǫluspá*. Yet since these words are about men, not gods, it remains quite unlikely that either Þormóðr or Þangbrandr or Hjalti inspired the poet of *Vǫluspá*. This poet blends the mythology of his heathen gods with the Christian language of the Last Days without the slightest trace of antagonism. He represents Þórr positively, giving him a triumph over the World

---

[58] McGinn, *Visions of the End*, 84. Wulfstan made use of some of this: Godden, "Apocalypse and Invasion," 153.

[59] Adso Dervensis, *De Ortu et Tempore Antichristi*, ed. D. Verhelst, Corpus Christianorum Continuatio Mediaevalis 45 (Turnhout, 1976), 22.

[60] Sigurður Nordal, "Vǫlu-Steinn," *Iðunn* 8 (1924): 161–78, esp. 166; trans. B. S. Benedikz, "The Author of *Vǫluspá*," *Saga-Book of the Viking Society* 20 (1978–1979): 114–30, esp. 119.

[61] *Kristni Saga*, ed. Kahle, 38, n. 10 (chap. 12), cited in *Íslendingabók*, ed. Jakob Benediktsson, 15 (chap. 7). Called "Thermo" in Theoderic's *Historia de antiquitate regum Norvagiensium*, ed. Storm, 19. English origin implicit in the Norwegian *Ágrip*, of the early twelfth century, in *Ágrip af Nóregskonungasǫgum*, ed. Matthew J. Driscoll (London, 1995), 30 (chap. 19) and 95 n. 61.

Serpent which, far from identifying him with the Beast or Dragon, recalls St. Michael's victory against the Dragon in Rev. 12:7. As "St. Michael and the Dragon," the story of Michael's generalship enjoyed particular popularity in Ireland from the sixth to the tenth century, from where versions were exported to England and Normandy.[62] There is a possibility that in Iceland, long before the end of the tenth century, an Irish form of this story influenced the tale of Þórr's fight with the World Serpent, postponing Þórr's destruction of this monster in the story of his fishing trip with Hymir (as announced in Úlfr Uggason's *Húsdrápa* of the late tenth century), to his combat with giants in Ragnarǫk (as in *Vǫluspá* 53).[63]

Any allusions to Revelation in *Vǫluspá* should be considered a top-surface over older layers of Christian influence. Baldr, in particular, seems Christ-like probably because before their conversion the Icelanders knew more than a century of trade with Christendom and had seen the Irish *papar* ("fathers") for themselves, along with later Irish settlers from the British Isles.[64] Witness the vocabulary of a verse in the creation section of *Vǫluspá*:

> Sól varp sunnan, sinni mána,
> hendi inni hægri um himiniǫður.
> Sól þat né vissi, hvar hón sali átti,
> stiǫrnor þat né visso, hvar þær staði átto,
> máni þat né vissi, hvat hann megins átti. (st. 5)[65]

---

[62] Maria Elena Ruggerini, "St Michael and the Dragon from Scripture to Hagiography," in *Monsters and the Monstrous in Medieval Northwest Europe*, ed. Karin E. Olsen and Luuk A. J. R. Houwen (Louvain, 2001), 23–58, esp. 31–43.

[63] For the view that the *Vǫluspá*-version of the Serpent's death is a later development, see Kurt Schier, "Die Húsdrápa von Úlfr Uggason und die bildliche Überlieferung altnordischer Mythen," in *Minnjar og Menntir: Afmælisrit helgað Kristjáni Eldjárn, 6 desember 1976*, ed. Guðni Kolbeinsson (Reykjavik, 1976), 425–43, esp. 434–35; and Edith Marold, "Kosmogonische Mythen in der *Húsdrápa* des Úlfr Uggason," in *International Scandinavian and Medieval Studies in Memory of Gerd Wolfgang Weber: ein runder Knäuel, so rollt' es uns leicht aus den Händen*, ed. Michael Dallapiazza, Olaf Hansen, Preben Meulengracht Sørensen, and Yvonne S. Bonnetain (Trieste, 2000), 281–92, esp. 290. See further Richard North, "Image and Ascendancy in Úlfr's *Húsdrápa*," forthcoming.

[64] *Íslendingabók*, ed. Jakob Benediktsson, 5 (chap. 1); Strömbäck, *The Conversion of Iceland*, 61–67.

[65] *Edda II*, ed. Dronke, 8, 35–37, 116–17. My translation, adapted from Dronke. Dronke regards st. 5/5–8 [*recte* 5/5–0] as "an unskilled interpolation, drawn from a variant version of primordial times and attracted into the poem as a supplement to the repeated negations of stanza 3" (36). But of course the same poet could have composed the negations of st. 5 to do just that, to connect the stars' bewilderment with that of the audience at words of st. 3: "iǫrð fannz æva né upphiminn" ("earth was not to be found nor above it heaven"). At this moment in the poem the Norse cosmos is unfinished, because it is unnamed.

["From the south the sun, moon's companion, cast her right hand over the rim of the sky. Sun did not know where she had mansions, stars did not know where they had stations, Moon did not know what might he had."]

That is to say, there is as yet no calendar, whether solar, heliacal-stellar, or lunar. On this *tabula rasa* the primeval gods inscribe a series of names with the legal aplomb of the Icelandic parliament. In *Vǫluspá* 6, following on, they form the calendar by giving names to the sky's quarters, splitting day from night and dividing the day into four. Where the sun's "right hand" is concerned, "right" for "south" is known to be an Irish usage which is not found in Germanic dialects.[66] This likely provenance for the image of the sun's *hendi inni hægri* in *Vǫluspá* makes it plausible that the poet Christianized his mythology on the basis of contact with Irish Christians in his own country. A similar heathen-Christian contact is visible in the bottom of the west face of the Gosforth Cross, which was carved by Anglo-Scandinavians in Cumbria in the first half of the tenth century. This carving is a relief of Loki's punishment after Baldr, one of three reliefs associated with Ragnarǫk, within the larger pattern of Christ's Crucifixion.[67] Some of the poet's apocalyptic details could therefore have entered Icelandic paganism long before the composition of *Vǫluspá*: the poet may not have seen them as new.

That the poet of *Vǫluspá* was a heathen by upbringing, whatever the nature of his Christian experience, is clear in his rich mythology. No Christian-Judaic apocalyptic scheme could have sanctioned the objectivity of the divine theme in *Vǫluspá* in combination with the horror with which the human condition is here revealed. In this way the poet of *Vǫluspá* sought to blend his own traditions with those of apocalyptic Christianity. He treats the Norse gods with a certain care, detaching their errors from moral causes, presenting these as the unlucky but anticipated steps to Ragnarǫk: "a gradual disaster, like the physical frailties of age."[68] In *Vǫluspá* 35–44, in contrast, it is left to mankind to reflect divine failures as a moral downfall. Men live in another dimension, which the poet seems to have integrated with his heathen mythology out of deference to the Christian faith; again, like the author of Revelation, the poet of *Vǫluspá* seems to know that human history can

---

[66] Ruggerini, "St Michael and the Dragon," 28. See also *Asser's Life of Alfred: De Rebus Gestis Ælfredi*, ed. W. H. Stevenson, with supplementary article by Dorothy Whitelock (Oxford, 1959), 27 (chap. 35.10), 64 (chap. 79.4: Asser's use of *dextralis* for Welsh *dehou*, "south"), and 234: "there are no traces of [this usage] in the Germanic dialects."

[67] *Cumberland, Westmorland and Lancashire North-of-the-Sands*, ed. Rosemary Cramp and Richard N. Bailey, Corpus of Anglo-Saxon Stone Sculpture 2 (Oxford, 1988), 100–9, esp. 100–2 (ills. 288–308). For a summary of the evidence, see McKinnell, "Eddic Poetry in Anglo-Scandinavian Northern England," 328–29.

[68] Dronke, "*Vǫluspá* and Sibylline Traditions," 15.

be expressed surreally through the battles of heathen gods and giants. It is impossible to know, however, how far he gave symbolic rather than literal meanings to these creatures. The less real the gods were for this poet, the more likely it is that he believed himself to be Christian. It has been argued that the poet had been (no more than) a catechumen, a partaker in the Easter Liturgy.[69]

In short, *Vǫluspá*'s heathen-Christian blend seems sure enough of itself to predate the duels and showdowns of the late 990s. What envoy of Tryggvason's in Iceland could have suffered the embodiment of heathen gods into the good side of the Apocalypse? The Christianized character of *Vǫluspá* seems to belong to a more tolerant time. Adso, in his *De ortu* of ca. 950, makes use of part of *Expositio in Thessalonicenses II*, a commentary on 2 Thess. 2 which was originally written before 853 by a former pupil of Alcuin, Bishop Haymo of Halberstadt in Saxony:

> Qui aduersatur, id est contrarius est Christo Deo omnibusque membris eius, et extollitur, id est, in superbiam erigitur super omne quod dicitur Deus, id est, supra omnes deos gentium, Herculem uidelicet, Apollinem, Iouem, Mercurium, quos pagani deos esse estimant. Super omnes istos deos extolletur Antichristus, quia maiorem et fortiorem se iis omnibus faciet: et non solum supra hos, sed etiam supra omne quod colitur, id est, supra sanctam Trinitatem, que solummodo colenda et adoranda est ab omni creatura.[70]

> ["'He who rebels': that is, he who opposes Christ God in all his members; 'and is raised up': that is, he who is exalted in pride 'over all that is said to be god': that is, above all gods of the nations, for example Hercules, Apollo, Jupiter, Mercury, whom the pagans believe to be gods. Antichrist will be raised above all these gods, for he will make himself bigger and stronger than all of them: and not only over these, but also above everything that is worshipped, that is, above the Holy Trinity, that which alone must be worshipped and adored by each and every one of its created things."]

Although the *De ortu* is a work of millennial anxiety that may have inspired the confrontational behavior of Þangbrandr and others, this older text that it embodies could be taken to realign the northern Olympians, Þórr, Týr, and Óðinn, on the side of the Lamb. This is the style in *Vǫluspá*, whose heathen gods are otherwise hard to explain. Adso's text could have arrived in Iceland through an Ottonian missionary, such as Friðrekr in the early 980s.

To return to Friðrekr, the thirteenth-century *Þorvalds þáttr* says that he preached in the home territory of his minder Þorvaldr Koðránsson, in north-

---

[69] McKinnell, "*Vǫluspá* and the Feast of Easter," 372.
[70] *De Ortu et Tempore Antichristi*, ed. Verhelst, 26–27; cf. *PL* 117.550, 779; 118.761.

western Iceland, until Þórvaldr killed a couple of lampoonists who called him and the bishop *ragir* ("queers").[71] After more trouble, their enforced departure from Iceland and Þórvaldr's settling of an old score in Norway, Friðrekr is said to have returned to *Saxland* (Saxony) on his own. Clearly it was his style to reject violence, and in this matter he and Þangbrandr are far apart. On the other hand, Friðrekr could be regarded as Þangbrandr's Ottonian harbinger in that he probably had something to do with the spread of millennarial fears in Icelandic society in the early 980s. There was a fear of End Time spreading across France and Germany, and of course England, at least a generation before then. Abbo of Fleury, in his *Apologeticus* of ca. 995, says that when he was a young man, presumably in the 960s, he heard a sermon about the End of the World in the cathedral in Paris, *quod statim finito mille annorum numero Antichristus adveniret, et non longa post tempore universale judicium succederet* ["according to which, as soon as the number of a thousand years was complete, the Antichrist would come and the Last Judgment would follow in a brief time"].[72] As we have seen in its rarity with Archbishop Wulfstan in ca. 1002, the chiliastic view ran counter to orthodoxy; but in the same passage, Abbo says that his old abbot asked him at this time to take issue with a panic spreading in Lotharingia, that the End would occur when Good Friday coincided with the Annunciation on 25 March (as in 2005). This text is evidence of a chiliastic subculture across western Europe. It is hard to see how particularly the "thousand years" were unknown to Bishop Friðrekr, through whom a knowledge of it could have passed on to his minder Þórvaldr and any other open-minded heathens. Nor is it easy to see how a belief in the thousand years did not spread to Iceland when Friðrekr made his first attempt to align the *goðar* ("chieftains") with the Christian calendar.

There is a verse attributed to Þórvaldr, made when he helped Friðrekr to preach in his home in the northwest fjords of Iceland. In it he appears to call the new religion "judgment," as if this were the perception of Christianity in Iceland at the time:

Fórk með dóm enn dýra;   drengr hlýddi mér engi;
gátum háð at hreyti   hlautteins, goða sveini,
en við enga svinnu   aldin rýgr við skaldi
(þá kreppi goð gyðju)   gall af heiðnum stalla.[73]

---

[71] *Kristni Saga*, ed. Kahle, 11.

[72] *Apologeticus*, PL 139. 461–472, esp. 471–472.

[73] *Den norsk-islandske Skjaldedigtning*, ed. Finnur Jónsson, 4 vols. [A, I, II; B, I, II] (Copenhagen and Christiania [Oslo], 1912–1915), B, I, 105. See also *Kristni Saga*, ed. Kahle, 8–11, esp. 9 (chap. 2).

["I went there with the precious Judgment; no man heeded me; we got scorn from the sprinkler of the lot-twig, the gods' servant, and with no wisdom did an aged lady (may God cripple the priestess) chant at the poet from the heathen altar."]

It is tempting to identify this lady, whom the saga calls Friðgerðr, as a *vǫlva*, such as those that are used as heathen props in other Icelandic sagas.[74] The versifier, probably a forger in the twelfth or thirteenth century, contrasts Þorvaldr's *dómr* with a lack of wisdom (*við enga svinnu*) in this priestess, as if to show that God will punish heathen obdurates in hell. It thus seems clear that Icelanders in the eleventh century or later saw their conversion in terms of ideological confrontation. Yet even through this tarnish of re-interpretation the word *dómr* rings true as a term of high currency from before the millennium: *Godes dom* ("God's Judgment") is naturally Wulfstan's theme in *Secundum Marcum* and elsewhere.[75] *Godes dom* is also the idea of the unique *regindómr* ("court of Judgment") to which, according to *Hauksbók* stanza 62, the Almighty descends at the close of *Vǫluspá*. So some light is thrown on the circumstances of *Vǫluspá* by the fear of Doomsday. We might even say of its poet, misusing Patrick Wormald's words on Wulfstan, that his priority was to fortify a heathen society "to meet first its arch-enemy, Antichrist, and then its Maker, Christ himself in clouds descending."[76] At any rate, it is probably the poet's debt to Revelation, a book that was taken to date the End at A.D. 1000, which gives *Vǫluspá* its *terminus ad quem* in the same year.

To sum up, two conversion techniques may be seen as having given rise to *Vǫluspá* towards the end of the tenth century. First, through its allusions to Revelation, *Vǫluspá* conveys something of the language of millennarial missionaries. Second, however, it seems that this apocalyptic in *Vǫluspá* is imposed on an older Christianizing world-view that seeks to integrate and embody. At its heart, *Vǫluspá* suggests the older effects of a conversion from within, an eirenic, probably Irish, attempt to inculturate Christianity in Iceland within the language of paganism. Thus the poet of *Vǫluspá* not only celebrates and mourns the Norse gods but also launches their progeny without embarrassment into the new world order of sts. 57–62. With H 62 so apposite to the context of Judgment in these stanzas, he appears to be at ease with the subordination of all his gods to *inn ríki*

---

[74] On these, see John McKinnell, "Encounters with Völur," in *Old Norse Myths, Literature and Society: Proceedings of the 11th International Saga Conference, 2-7 July 2000*, ed. Geraldine Barnes and Margaret Clunies Ross (Sydney, 2000), 239–51, esp. 243–48.

[75] *The Homilies of Wulfstan*, ed. Bethurum, 129 (homily IV.31: *De temporibus Antichristi*), 141 (homily V.114: *Secundum Marcum*), 155 (homily VI.208: *Incipiunt sermones Lupi episcopi*), 161 (VII.106: *De fide catholica*), 167 (VIIa.32–4: *To eallum folke*).

[76] Wormald, "Archbishop Wulfstan: Eleventh-Century State-Builder," 17.

("the Mighty One"), *sá er ǫllu ræðr* ("Who rules all"). His is a recruitment of Æsir to the Christian cause. Behind him there may be a preacher working with a text of Adso's *De Ortu et Tempore Antichristi*. By the end of the tenth century, however, it seems that the last traces of inculturation were overwhelmed by Ottonian activists such as Stefnir, Hjalti, and Þangbrandr who sought to confront and destroy. Even if the poet of *Vǫluspá* was taught of the imminence of A.D. 1000, as some ten parallels with Revelation suggest, it is reasonable to suppose that he hated the new evangelism, indeed composed *Vǫluspá* in reaction to its exclusion of good heathens from heaven. In this way it was probably an idea of End Time that drove him to meet the new millennium with a masterpiece. And it may also be fair to say that *Vǫluspá* was born of a conflict, not between two religions, but between two opposed models of conversion.

INDEX

A

Aaron, brother of Moses, 71, 207 n102
Aaron, martyr, 6
Abbesses, 158–59, 161, 162, 165, 191 n.59
Abbo of Fleury, *Apologeticus*, 234
Abbots, 161, 162, 165
   lists of, 109, 114, 130, 192
Abingdon, 184, 185 n42
Abraham, 204
Acta Andreae apud anthropophagus, 72
Acta Quiriaci, 12
Acta Sanctorum, 139
Adam, 114, 127, 129
Adamnán of Iona, 83, 86, 93
   De locis sanctis, 93
Adelard, *Vita S. Dunstani*, 179
Ado of Vienne, 135
Adrian and Ritheus, 207 n102
Adso, of Montier-en-Der, 229–30, 233, 236
Advent, 176, 182, 188, 190, 207, 210
Advent Lyrics, 169–211
Ælfric, 74, 78, 79, 81, 88, 175 n13, 225
   De Natale S. Pauli, 79
   De temporibus, 111, 112, 113 n15
   Grammar, 74
   Letter to the Monks of Eynsham, 153, 184 n38
   Letter to Wulfsige, 160
   Homily for Christmas, 197
   Homily for Palm Sunday, 166
   Homily for the Second Sunday after Easter, 196
   Homily for the Second Sunday after Pentecost, 79–80, 196
   Homily on the Discovery of the Cross, 138, 139, 147
   Life of St. Basil, 74

Life of St. Maurus, 186
Lives of Saints, 180, 181
Prayer of Moses, 180
Ælfweard, abbot of Glastonbury, 114
Ælfweard, bishop of London, 81
Æsir, 220, 222, 224, 236
Æthelbehrt, king of Kent, 28
Æthelflæd, lady of the Mercians, 136
Æthelred, king of England, 114, 127
Æthelstan, king of the English, 136, 143, 207 n100
Æthelthryth, saint, 60
Æthelwold, bishop of Winchester, 154, 169, 170, 172 n9, 177, 182, 184, 185, 191, 194, 196, 207 n100, 208
   "King Edgar's Establishment of the Monasteries," 176, 186, 190, 191 n59
   See also manuscripts, London, BL, Additional 49598
Æthelwulf, 140
Africa, 86, 87, 90
Aidan, saint and bishop of Lindisfarne, 4, 6
Aire, river, 38
Akerman, John Yonge, 38
Alban, saint, 6
Albinus, abbot of Canterbury, 10, 27, 28
Alcuin, 20, 215, 233
Aldhelm, 5, 12, 13
   De Virginitate, 138
   Enigmata, 73
Alexander the Great, 63, 90, 91, 94
Alexander's Letter to Aristotle, 94
Alfred, king, 77–78, 83–108, 136
   Boethius, 88, 91, 97, 101, 104–05, 106
   Pastoral Care, 92, 95–96, 101, 102–04